The Golden Age of
the Classics in America

THE GOLDEN AGE OF THE CLASSICS IN AMERICA

Greece, Rome, and the

Antebellum United States

CARL J. RICHARD

HARVARD UNIVERSITY PRESS
Cambridge, Massachusetts
London, England
2009

Copyright © 2009 by the President and Fellows of Harvard College
All rights reserved
Printed in the United States of America

Library of Congress Cataloging-in-Publication Data
Richard, Carl J.
The golden age of the classics in America : Greece,
Rome, and the antebellum United States / Carl J. Richard.
p.   cm.
ISBN 978-0-674-03264-4 (alk. paper)
1. United States—Civilization—Classical influences.   2. United States—Civilization—
1783–1865.   3. United States—Intellectual life—1783–1865.   4. Civilization,
Classical—Study and teaching—United States—History—19th century.   5. Classical
literature—Study and teaching—United States—History—19th century.   6. Greece—Study
and teaching—United States—History—19th century.   7. Rome—Study and teaching—
United States—History—19th century.   8. Political culture—United States—History—
19th century.   9. Education—United States—History—19th century.   10. United
States—Social conditions—To 1865.   I. Title.
E165.R513   2009
973.3—dc22   2008032970

*For my Greek teachers, Richard Cusimano,
Thomas McGinn, and Susan Wiltshire*

ζητῶ γάρ τήν ἀλήθειαν, ὑφ᾽ ἧς οὐδείς πώποτε ἐβλάβη

For I seek the truth, by which no one was ever harmed.

MARCUS AURELIUS

Contents

	Preface	ix
1	Classical Conditioning: School, Home, and Society	1
2	Democracy	41
3	Pastoralism and Utilitarianism	83
4	Nationalism	105
5	Romanticism	120
6	Christianity	152
7	Slavery	181
	Epilogue	204
	Notes	213
	Index	250

Preface

THIS IS THE FIRST book-length study of the influence of the Greek and Roman classics in antebellum America. While several scholarly books have explored the impact of the classics on the founders of the United States, the study of the influence of Greece and Rome on the subsequent generation of Americans has suffered comparative neglect.[1]

The fullest discussions of this topic are contained in Meyer Reinhold's *Classica Americana: The Greek and Roman Heritage in the United States* (1984) and Caroline Winterer's *The Culture of Classicism: Ancient Greece and Rome in American Intellectual Life, 1780–1910* (2002), but neither of these broad works focuses exclusively on the antebellum period. Furthermore, Winterer's superb but brief book concentrates largely on the nineteenth-century educational system, a crucial topic but one that only marginally addresses such equally important issues as the interaction between the classics and democracy, the Industrial Revolution, nationalism, romanticism, the Second Great Awakening, and slavery. Her more recent book, *The Mirror of Antiquity: American Women and the Classical Tradition, 1750–1900* (2007), likewise excellent but brief, contains about fifty pages concerning antebellum women.[2]

More troubling, Reinhold's pioneering work hypothesized a decline in classical influence during the early national and antebellum periods. Indeed, Reinhold went so far as to term the Revolutionary and Constitutional eras "the golden age" of the classics in America, in contrast to "the silver age" of the early national and antebellum periods, a use of metals to symbolize degeneration that began with the Greek poet Hesiod and that scholars later applied to Roman literature. (Reinhold does not follow Hesiod in positing even worse bronze and iron ages of classical influence.) Oddly, much of Reinhold's own research contradicted his conclusion. Reinhold's judgment probably had more to do with his (and most other Americans') contrasting valuations of the founding and antebellum generations than with the degree of classical influence on each. The founding generation is idolized as the cohort that defeated the greatest power on earth, established the nation's independence, and drafted the most durable written constitution in world history. Its failings, such as the continuation of slavery, are largely glossed over. By contrast, the antebellum generation is most famous for its failure to avoid a calamitous civil war that killed more Americans than any other war in American history.[3]

The truth is that antebellum Americans of all sections of the country continued to use the classics in the same way that the founding generation had used them, as a favored source of symbols, knowledge, and ideas. Like their parents, antebellum Americans used classical symbols to communicate, to impress, and to persuade. They continued to derive from the classics both models and antimodels of personal behavior, social practice, and government form. They persisted in viewing the study of the classics as an indispensable training in virtue and in considering their favorite ancient authors wise old friends. They continued to display the classical obsession with alleged conspiracies against liberty. Like their parents, they derived from the classics a sense of identity and purpose that bound them together with one another and with their ancestors in a common struggle. They continued to draw from the ancient poets and political theorists a pastoralism that glorified the rural, agricultural lifestyle. They persisted in valuing the simplicity, ethics, and love of nature exhibited by classical authors and artists. In short, the classics continued to provide Americans with one of their principal sets of ideological tools. Even the utilitarian, nationalist, moral, and religious arguments of the critics of the classics remained the same, as did their failure to defeat the classics' virtual monopoly on the American educational system.

In fact, it is more apt to reverse Reinhold's terminology and to speak of the antebellum period as the golden age of the classics and the founding era as the silver age. After all, it was during the antebellum period that the classics expanded far beyond the narrow confines of the eastern aristocratic elite, affecting new economic classes and geographical regions. As the number of schools, both public and private, increased exponentially, the middle class was introduced to the classics on a large scale for the first time, and the classics were carried to the very frontiers of American civilization. New towns were given classical names and filled with Greek buildings, as the trickle of neoclassical architecture became a raging flood. "Athenaeums" were built to house classical books and art. With the establishment of female academies and colleges, numerous women were trained in the classics for the first time. Although some Americans continued to admire Cornelia and other Roman matrons for their virtue and devotion to children, others began to admire them for their intelligence and erudition. In a few northern cities schools taught the classics to African Americans for the first time. While advances in printing made possible a plethora of cheap grammar texts and of journals that dissected every aspect of the classics and classical civilization, and manufacturers churned out inexpensive reproductions of classical and neoclassical statues, paintings, and knickknacks to decorate even modest homes, railroads carried lyceum lecturers, popular works on Greek mythology and history, and historical novels to small towns to further popularize antiquity. More Americans than ever before traveled to Italy (and, to a lesser extent, Greece) to see the ruins of classical civilization; nearly all of them were profoundly affected by the experience. Even cemeteries were established on a Greek model and filled with Grecian urns. In short, for the first time in history, the classics were, to a great extent, democratized. No longer the exclusive preserve of aristocratic, eastern males, they became the possession of a much larger segment of society than ever before.

Furthermore, a new pedagogy greatly increased students' appreciation of the classics. The unimaginative techniques of rote memorization that had prevailed for centuries, techniques that emphasized fine technical points over the beauty and meaning of classical works, were gradually displaced by a lecture format designed to explain to students the historical context in which the works had appeared and to inspire students with the "classical spirit." The masterpieces of Greek and Roman literature, once presented as little more than a series of pegs on which to hang grammatical rules, now came alive in the minds and hearts of many students. As democracy spread and the reputation of the Greek republics improved, the Greek language finally stepped out of the shadows of Latin and became more than its neglected stepsister. For the first time, Greek drama became a staple of education. The expansion of classical interest beyond ancient political history and theory, the great preoccupations of the founders' age, to include classical mythology, as found in Greek drama and Roman poetry, gave the politically disfranchised and others focused on self-improvement a greater connection to the classics than had previously been possible.

The new pedagogy helped produce the first national literature. While the Transcendentalists discussed classical mythology at length in their essays, letters, and conversations, romantic fiction writers used it to provide their narratives with structure and meaning. As a romantic literature emerged, the emotional elements of classical civilization, as epitomized by Greek drama and mythology, were increasingly valued and allowed to augment, without displacing, the more rationalist elements that had previously monopolized Americans' time. While ancient political history and theory were still studied and revered, and the Transcendentalists embraced Platonism and certain elements of Stoicism more deeply than had the founders, Americans were now exposed more fully than ever before to the passionate, mystical side of the classical world. Just as the Renaissance had not really constituted a "rebirth" of classical learning, which had never died, but a broadening of the works studied and a new spirit of interpretation, so antebellum American classicism broadened and deepened that of the Enlightenment.

But there was a dark side to classical influence. Antebellum southerners appealed to the classical heritage in support of slavery. Not only had the ancient Greeks and Romans owned slaves, but Aristotle, one of the most revered of Greek philosophers, had issued a highly influential defense of the institution. Antebellum southerners relied on Aristotle's defense of slavery and on the argument that the institution had served as the foundation of classical civilization to convince both themselves and others that slavery was not just a necessary evil but a positive good.

Yet the abolitionists did not lack classical resources of their own. They drew upon histories written by the ancients themselves to argue that slavery had been the greatest flaw of classical civilization. In addition, they used the classical theory of natural law, the belief in a universal moral code discoverable by humans, to contend for the natural right of freedom for all humans. In the process they interpreted natural law in a different fashion than most of the ancients, to delegitimize slavery. In so doing they demonstrated the flexibility of the theory. Just as the U.S. Constitution has proved flexible enough to withstand the profound social changes of over two centuries, so the classics have proved flexible enough to withstand the even more profound social changes of over two millennia.

Antebellum Americans' conflicting interpretations of the Greco-Roman classics, when joined with their conflicting interpretations of the Bible, helped produce a tragic civil war. When that war was over, the South lay in ruins, and the classics began a gradual decline due to social, economic, and intellectual forces. But by then the classics had played a leading role in shaping the nation's values during its formative years.

If one measures the success of the classics according to the number of specialized scholarly monographs produced, the antebellum period was definitely not their golden age. Later eras, including our own, witnessed more impressive scholarship. But if one measures the success of the classics according to the proportion of the American public that consider them relevant to their daily lives, the antebellum period was clearly the golden age of the classics in America.

Despite the relative democratization of the classics in the antebellum period, historians would call most of the sources cited in this study "elite sources." It is unfortunate that the historical evidence for the classical interests of the antebellum middle class, like so much historical evidence in general, often comes to us secondhand from aristocrats, but it is unavoidable. Affluent Americans possessed greater leisure to write, and their papers were more likely to be collected in archives and published because of their greater prominence in politics and other fields traditionally considered important. Even so, the blanket application of the term "elite sources" to the papers of all prominent families is misleading; the Adams family, for instance, despite producing two presidents, was, for a long time, a middle-class family. Others influenced by the classics also rose from humble beginnings to a prominence great enough to encourage the publication of their papers. In a land of relatively high literacy and social mobility, such stories are not uncommon. Indeed, one of the great ironies of the early American republic was that the "aristocratic classics" provided a means of social mobility for the middle class, allowing ingenious men of limited means like John Adams to rise to prominence, at least in part, by rivaling and even surpassing the more affluent in their acquisition and elucidation of classical knowledge. At a minimum, historians should avoid the tautology of labeling anyone who was interested in the classics an aristocrat and then insisting that only aristocrats were interested in the classics.

I WOULD LIKE TO extend special thanks to Paul K. Conkin, Dolores Egger Labbe, Michael O'Brien, and Caroline Winterer, all of whom reviewed the manuscript and offered sage advice. I would also like to thank Charles N. Eberline for contributing his considerable editorial skills to the book's improvement. As always, I also wish to thank my precious wife, Debbie, for her love, prayers, and support.

CHAPTER ONE

Classical Conditioning: School, Home, and Society

LIKE THEIR FOREBEARS, many antebellum Americans were socially conditioned in the schools, at home, and in society at large to venerate the classics. Most antebellum Americans who were familiar with the classics first encountered them in grammar schools and academies, the number of which steadily increased as the population grew and the United States expanded westward. Instruction at these schools, which focused on the study of the Greek and Latin languages, differed remarkably little from the training that colonial students had received two centuries earlier. Colleges increased classical knowledge further among the growing number of Americans who attended them. For the first time, many women and African Americans were formally trained in the classics. Greek, once the neglected stepsister of Latin, began to approach equality with it as Greek drama was added to the classical curriculum. Parents often took care to reinforce this classical conditioning in the home. Most American leaders continued to insist that the classics were essential to the production of a virtuous and republican citizenry. As a result, school curricula continued to emphasize Greek and Latin until the late nineteenth century. By then the classics had left a lasting imprint on American society, shaping the new nation's rhetoric, art, architecture, books, plays, journals, and law.

The Golden Age of the Classics in America — 2

Grammar Schools and Academies

The origins of the American educational system lie in medieval Europe. Even after the Reformation, Catholics and Protestants shared a common emphasis on the study of classical literature, especially the works of Homer, Cicero, Virgil, Horace, and Ovid. This system of education was transplanted to the English colonies of North America and transmitted by each generation to the next. The "grammar" in colonial grammar schools referred to Greek and Latin grammar, not English; not until after the American Revolution did students begin to study their mother tongue in grammar schools, and even then some educators continued to consider it unworthy of academic attention.[1]

Colonial Americans would have felt quite comfortable with the curriculum at the Round Hill School at Northampton, Massachusetts, an antebellum academy that emphasized the classical languages and attracted students from across the United States. Indeed, in seeking to introduce high German standards, the academy surpassed most colonial grammar schools in rigor. The academy's directors, Joseph Cogswell and George Bancroft, boasted that their students' training in Greek and Latin, which included the reading of the works of Aeschylus, Sophocles, and Juvenal, easily exceeded college entrance requirements. The school sent 291 graduates to college between 1823 and 1831, 50 of them to Harvard.[2]

Though exceptional, Round Hill was not unique. Boston Latin School was even more famous for its classical education. Its curriculum included Phaedrus, Cornelius Nepos, Caesar, Sallust, Ovid's *Metamorphoses*, Cicero's orations, Tacitus' *Agricola* and *Germania*, Horace's *Odes* and *Epodes*, the Greek Gospels, and Homer's *Iliad*. Charles Francis Adams, the son and grandson of U.S. presidents and the U.S. minister to Great Britain during the Civil War, recalled his favorite teacher at the school, Francis Jenks, with great fondness. While a student at Harvard, Adams wrote in his diary regarding Jenks: "He implanted or strengthened in me an early taste for reading by a simple method which I should always recommend to a good schoolmaster. After having got my lesson, he used to permit me to read a Plutarch which he kept on purpose in the school and gave it to me as a mark of distinction and scholarship, in this way exciting me by every motive which can act upon a boy to gain instruction. I believe it is to this I owe my clear ideas on the subject of history."[3]

Nor was the South deprived of such schools. At his various boarding schools in Georgia and South Carolina, which were said to have resounded with the echoes of Homer, Virgil, and Horace, the Reverend Moses Waddel taught such luminaries as William H. Crawford, a future secretary of the

Treasury, and his own brother-in-law John C. Calhoun. After two years of study under Waddel, during which he read Latin and studied the New Testament in the original Greek, Calhoun was prepared to enter Yale as a junior. Calhoun's biographer Charles M. Wiltse noted: "The training of the day was almost exclusively classical, and Moses Waddel, with his ministerial background, was even more strictly a classicist than most. So great was the emphasis on the works of the ancient world that to construe a mere 150 lines of Virgil or Horace as a day's assignment was considered [the] next thing to failing altogether." The record at one of Waddel's schools was set at 1,212 lines of Virgil in a single day. While president of Franklin College, which became the University of Georgia, Waddel later taught Alexander Stephens, who went on to serve as a congressional representative from Georgia and as vice president of the Confederacy. The historian Joseph Berrigan attributed Stephens's mental acuity and linguistic precision to his early training in the classics.[4]

The United States was unique among Western nations in offering girls classical instruction on a large scale. Hundreds of new female academies instructed their students in the classical languages. Between 1810 and 1870 more than half the catalogs of female academies advertised the teaching of Greek, Latin, or both. This statistic is all the more remarkable in view of the fact that girls' schools were not as concerned with meeting college entrance requirements in the classics as boys', since far fewer colleges admitted women than men. In Pendleton, South Carolina, a group of thirteen- and fourteen-year-old girls outperformed a group of boys in an examination in Greek and Latin. Although boys continued to receive more classical training than girls—for instance, between 1790 and 1840, 91 percent of boys' schools in Virginia and North Carolina advertised Greek, Latin, or both—girls received far more instruction in Greek and Latin than they ever had before. One female academy in North Carolina was even named the Sparta Academy, although it is doubtful that its students were allowed to run around half-naked like Spartan girls.[5]

Founded largely by middle-class women and appealing to middle-class as well as elite girls, female academies validated reading as a woman's pursuit and offered young girls educated role models. Students often established literary societies at these academies and then went on to organize adult versions among the women of their communities, both urban and rural. Furthermore, the friendships that girls formed in the academies became the foundation for networks that made women key players in crucial antebellum reform movements.[6]

Generally considered appropriate reading for girls, ancient history found its way into their private studies as well as their formal academic training.

In 1841 young Harriott Horry Rutledge wrote: "Dear Mamma I am reading the Roman History. I followed Greece to where it became a Roman province. Aunt H says I am fonder of those grim old warriors than of my pretty smiling doll, she says it is because I have not to make them clothes, but it is not, it is because it has life and spirit in it."[7]

By the 1850s a few schools in large northern cities like Philadelphia were offering a classical education to African American students, female and male. The coeducational Institute for Colored Youth advertised a classical curriculum that included Virgil's *Aeneid*, Horace's *Odes*, Cicero's *Orations*, Xenophon's *Anabasis*, and the Greek New Testament. Baltimore's William Watkins Academy for Negro Youth also emphasized Greek and Latin. As with white girls, classical education led to African American reading societies, such as the Philadelphia Colored Reading Society, which contended that from classical literature "a fund of ideas is acquired on a variety of subjects; the taste is greatly improved by conversing with the best models; the imagination is enriched by the fine scenery with which the classics abound; and an acquaintance is formed with human nature, together with the history, customs, and manners of antiquity." Black women established the Female Minervian Association in 1832, declaring that "the cultivation of the mind [is] all important, and far more so than the adornment of the body." The following year African Americans in Washington, D.C., raised money to emancipate a slave by hosting a program of orations that included "Plato and the Immortality of the Soul," "Brutus," and "Epilogue to Addison's 'Cato.'"[8]

Even the famous McGuffey readers, which were designed to teach young schoolchildren the glories of the English language, as well as morality and patriotism, featured classical themes. Included was Lord Byron's "Song of the Bard," which begins:

> The isles of Greece! the isles of Greece!
> Where burning Sappho loved and sung,
> Where grew the arts of war and peace,—
> Where Delos rose, and Phoebus sprung!
> Eternal summer gilds them yet,
> But all, except their sun, is set.

McGuffey also included Byron's "Rome" and scenes from Shakespeare's *Julius Caesar*, such as the quarrel between Brutus and Cassius and Antony's speech over Caesar's body. In "A View of the Colosseum" Orville Dewey exults: "I went to see the Colosseum by moonlight. It is the monarch, the majesty of ruins; there is nothing like it." In "The Last Days of Herculaneum" Edwin Atherstone tells the story of a wrongly imprisoned Roman soldier who dies with his son following the eruption of Mount Vesuvius. Other passages include an anonymous essay on Alexander the Great and Washington Irving's "Description of Pompey's Pillar." The inclusion of material concerning the classical world in an English reader is not so surprising when one considers that the editor of the series, William H. McGuffey, was a professor of ancient languages. One hundred twenty million McGuffey readers were sold between 1836 and 1920.[9]

Colleges and Universities

Entrance requirements at antebellum American colleges and universities differed little from the requirements of colonial colleges. When John Winthrop's nephew, George Downing, applied to Harvard in the mid-seventeenth century, he was required to "understand Tully [Cicero], Virgil, or any such classical authors, and readily to speak or write true Latin in prose and have skill in making Latin verse, and be completely grounded in the Greek language." In 1816, when Horace Mann applied for entrance to Brown University, he faced remarkably similar requirements: the ability "to read accurately, construe, and parse Tully and the Greek Testament and Virgil . . . to write true Latin in prose, and [to know] the rules of Prosody." Colleges were interested in a candidate's ability to read Latin and Greek and little else.[10]

These entrance requirements were not restricted to the prestigious universities of what is now the Ivy League. From the colonial period to the Civil War, the number of American colleges increased from 9 to 182, and nearly all the new colleges required entering students to demonstrate proficiency in the classical languages. Davidson College in North Carolina required a mastery of Latin and Greek grammar and of ancient geography for entrance into the college. Entering students were expected to demonstrate a close familiarity with Caesar, Sallust, Cicero's orations against Catiline, Virgil's *Bucolics*, *Georgics*, and *Aeneid*, and Xenophon's *Anabasis*. Emory and Henry College in Virginia demanded knowledge of ancient history, Virgil, Cicero, and the Greek language. Sharon College in Mississippi insisted on knowledge of Latin, including the works of Caesar, Ovid, Virgil, and Sallust. The University of Alabama required "the ability to commence the reading [of] the higher Latin and Greek authors." The University of North Carolina demanded proficiency in Greek and Latin, including Virgil's *Aeneid* and the works of Caesar and Sallust. South Carolina College (later the University of South Carolina) required translations from Cornelius Nepos, Sallust, Caesar, Virgil, and the Greek New Testament.[11]

College and university curricula were designed to increase the classical knowledge of entering students. During the antebellum period Yale required Greek and Latin each of the four years. Freshmen at Dickinson College in Pennsylvania read Sallust, Horace, and Xenophon, sophomores Cicero, Horace, Xenophon, and Euripides, juniors Sophocles, Euripides, Cicero, Juvenal, and Perseus, and seniors Aeschylus, Tacitus, and Terence. Though adding new courses in chemistry, geography, English grammar, surveying, navigation, and modern languages as electives, Harvard, Yale, Dartmouth, Wesleyan, and most other universities did not require these new courses, in sharp contrast to the persistent requirement of the classical languages. Even when universities like Columbia offered alternative courses of study, such as programs in science or modern literature, they generally refused to award a bachelor of arts degree to those who completed the new curricula, substituting lesser certificates. Jeremiah Day, the president of Yale, typified the low regard for nonclassical subjects when, in response to Yale's decision to offer a noncredit course in the ancient Anglo-Saxon language, he sighed: "It might soon be necessary to appoint an instructor in whittling."[12]

Even at the new colleges on the northwestern frontier the classics were king. During the antebellum period a plethora of colleges were established there to serve as symbols of civic pride, as magnets to attract settlers, and as bastions of civilization against the feared barbarism of the frontier. The classics suited each of these goals perfectly. Therefore, Allegheny College embedded some mortar from Virgil's tomb, along with a piece of Plymouth Rock, in its cornerstone and introduced the customary Latin orations at its first commencement. Ohio University emphasized the Greek New Testament, Xenophon, Herodotus, Homer, Greek tragedies and orations, Sallust, Livy, Horace, Cicero, Virgil, Tacitus, and Juvenal. The University of Michigan and the University of Wisconsin also focused on classical instruction. In 1852 the University of Michigan boasted that its courses emphasized "a constant comparison between the ancient and modern world." Whenever nonclassical courses were offered, they were often accompanied by an apology, as in the Hanover College catalog of 1852: "The scientific curriculum was set up for those who have not time or (financial) opportunity to pursue the Classical course." Students who pursued these nonclassical options were generally regarded as lacking in intellectual ability or ambition. A study of thirty northwestern colleges reveals that 87 percent of students rated the value of the classics as outstanding in 1860 (compared with only 17 percent in 1920). In the 1870s John G. Coulter, a dean at Purdue University, recalled that the antebellum classical curriculum was "a scholastic regime whose efficiency for the development of intellectual power was never challenged." James Garfield, the future president, began his career as a Latin teacher at the Eclectic Institute (later Hiram College) in Ohio in 1858. As the historian Walter Agard claimed: "The classics served to bring intellectual and aesthetic values to the brutally pragmatic Frontier and . . . helped keep vital the traditions of Western Europe, supplementing the ones forged by the challenging new environment." Agard noted that even Frederick Jackson Turner, the originator of the thesis that the frontier was the prime determinant of American culture, was himself classically trained and began his teaching career as an assistant to a Latin scholar.[13]

The classics dominated the college and university curricula of the antebellum South as well, both in the older colleges of the Southeast and in the newer ones of the Southwest. As in the Northwest, the Southwest witnessed an explosion in new colleges. In 1824 there was no college within 200 miles of Nashville; by 1848 there were thirty, nine of them within 50 miles. These colleges preserved the traditional classical curriculum. Blount College in eastern Tennessee examined its students on Virgil and Horace. Students at South Carolina College and at Wake Forest College studied the classical languages all four years. At the former institution Robert Henry added a large dose of instruction in Aristotelian logic. Freshmen at the University of North Carolina studied Livy, Virgil, and Cicero, sophomores the *Iliad*, Horace, Juvenal, and Demosthenes, juniors Tacitus and Greek tragedy, and seniors more Greek tragedy and Horace's *Art of Poetry*. In fact, in 1851–1852 the university's freshmen spent 83 percent of their time on Greek and Latin, its sophomores about 60 percent, its juniors more than half, and its seniors about one-third. (The corresponding figures for the French language were 0, 18, 47, and 18 percent, respectively.) At Davidson College students studied Cicero, Livy, Horace's *Odes* and *Epodes*, Homer, Herodotus, and Thucydides their freshman year, Horace's *Satires* and *Epistles*, Demosthenes, Xenophon's *Memorabilia of Socrates*, and Plato their sophomore year, Horace's *Art of Poetry*, Tacitus, Cicero, and Euripides' *Medea* their junior year, and Juvenal and Aristotle their senior year. At Sharon College students studied Horace, Cicero's orations, Livy, and Tacitus their freshman year, the Greek New Testament, Xenophon, Herodotus, Thucydides, Isocrates, Demosthenes, Plato, and Aristotle their sophomore year, and the *Iliad*, Euclid, and ancient geography their junior year. At Hampden-Sydney College in Virginia, freshmen studied Cicero, Sallust, and Xenophon, sophomores Homer, Longinus, Euclid, and Livy, and juniors Horace. Washington College (later Washington and Lee) devoted the whole freshman year to the classics. Even at the University of Virginia, which became notorious for its elective system, students could not graduate without demonstrating proficiency in Latin, so all of the university's students continued to take courses in it. In 1857, years after the university had adopted the elective system, its Latin school continued to have a larger enrollment than any other branch of the university. The following year the Texas legislature not only set aside land for the establishment of a University of Texas but also listed "Ancient and Modern Languages" first among the branches of learning to be taught there.[14]

Even military colleges emphasized classical learning. When Robert E. Lee applied to West Point in 1824, he asked his instructor, W. B. Leary, to write a letter of recommendation to Secretary of War John C. Calhoun. Aware that military cadets were expected to exhibit classical knowledge, Leary wrote regarding Lee: "With me he has read all the minor classics in addition to Homer & Longinus, Tacitus & Cicero. He is well versed in arithmetic, Algebra, and Euclid. In regard to what he has read with me I am certain that when examined he will neither disappoint me or his friends." When Lee became president of Washington College after the Civil War, he personally examined students in Greek. When James H. Rion sought an appointment to West Point in 1843, Rion, not yet sixteen, made a point of noting that he had read Euclid, Caesar, Virgil, Sallust, and Cicero. Latin was studied at the Virginia Military Institute as well. An 1860 editorial in the *Louisiana Democrat* reassured the parents of prospective students at the new Military Academy of Louisiana (later Louisiana State University) that their sons would receive as rigorous a training "in Latin and Greek as can be enjoyed in any American College." Under the regulations prepared by William T. Sherman, the first president of the new academy and future Union general, Latin and Greek were among the subjects given the greatest weight in ranking cadets.[15]

Some of the new female colleges established during the antebellum period provided classical training as well. In 1824 a newspaper advertisement for Catharine and Mary Beecher's Hartford Female Seminary touted its offerings in Latin grammar, Greek and Roman history, Euclid, and Virgil. Their sister Harriet Beecher Stowe later recalled with pride her translation of Ovid, which was recited at the school's final exhibition one year. Emma Willard, the founder of Troy Female Seminary, which enrolled 12,000 students in its first fifty years (1821–1871), sought to offer a classical education comparable to that received by college men. Her vice-principal Almira Phelps scoffed at admonitions against "females pursuing what are called masculine studies" and urged her students to study the classical languages. By the mid-1830s a number of schools modeled on the "Troy plan" had been established in Maryland, Ohio, South Carolina, and other areas. Some of the most outspoken feminists of the nineteenth century, such as Elizabeth Cady Stanton, fondly recalled "the profound self-respect" inculcated by the education they received at Troy. Cincinnati Female College taught women Greek and Latin and awarded medals for proficiency in these subjects at its commencement exercises. Mary Atkins, a graduate of Oberlin, undertook the arduous journey westward to California via the Isthmus of Panama and became principal of Benicia Seminary for Young Ladies, which later became Mills College. Benicia prided itself on turning out Protestant girls who could read Latin. Northern middle-class women used their classical education at female colleges as an entry point into the teaching profession, now open to women for the first time.[16]

Female colleges were even more prevalent in the South than in the rest of the country. By 1859, thirty-two of the nation's thirty-nine female colleges were located in the South; every southern state except Florida possessed at least one. The president of Mississippi Female College, the Reverend William Carey Crane, himself a professor of ancient languages, hired Caroline Way to instruct the students in Latin. Students at Spartanburg Female College in South Carolina studied Latin for three of the four years. South Carolina Female Collegiate Institute required Latin three of the students' four years and offered an advanced course on Cicero's *Immortality of the Soul* and other Latin readings, as well as a course in ancient history from the Persian Wars to the reign of Augustus. Sharon Female College in Mississippi included a preparatory department that taught Greek and Latin and a course of study that began with ancient and modern languages. Judson College (Alabama), Wesleyan Female College (Georgia), Goldsboro Female Academy (North Carolina), Greensboro Female College (Tennessee), and numerous others taught ancient history, Greek, and Latin. At Mansfield Female College in Louisiana pupils studied Virgil in the freshman year, Cicero in the sophomore year, Horace and Juvenal in the junior year, and Livy in the senior year, as well as four years of Greek. Even the so-called English curriculum that was offered as the sole alternative to the classical curriculum at these colleges generally also featured a choice of Latin or French. Latin was the favorite subject of Susan Dimock, who became North Carolina's first female physician after the Civil War. By the 1850s many schools shared the view of the Richmond Female Institute that "the fairer sex ought to enjoy advantages for liberal culture equal in grade to that afforded the other." Such was the demand for classical instruction for girls that an 1853 satirical piece in *Godey's Lady Book* has a mother who is enrolling her daughter in college declare:

> I'd have her taught Spanish and Latin,
> Including the language of France;
> Never mind her bad English,
> Teach her that when you find a good chance.[17]

Some American women received the admiration of men for their considerable knowledge of the classics. Horace Mann called Elizabeth Peabody, his sister-in-law and the leader of the kindergarten movement, "Miss Thesaura," from the Greek word for treasure, because of her treasury of knowledge about ancient history. Her nephew Julian Hawthorne recalled: "She was probably the most learned person in the world, certainly the most learned woman, in an era of female pundits.... Greek, Latin, Sanskrit and Hebrew were household tongues with Aunt Lizzie. And not content with knowing things, she wanted everybody else to know them, and had invented ingenious ways of instructing them." She translated Plato's *Phaedo* and *Crito* into English and discussed them with William Ellery Channing.[18]

Increasingly, American educators could turn to classical grammar books, anthologies, and dictionaries produced in the United States, rather than having to import them from Europe. Edward Everett and George Bancroft published English-language editions of University of Berlin professor Phillipp Buttman's *Greek Grammar*, which was so superior to the grammatical texts it replaced that it became a mainstay of freshman and sophomore classes until the middle of the century. In 1823 Everett also published the first English-language edition of Friedrich Jacobs's *Greek Reader*. This anthology of extracts from Greek classics soon replaced the *Graeca Majora* (1789) as the favored Greek anthology. (Despised by many students, the *Graeca Majora* was a disjointed collection of excerpts, completely devoid of grammatical aids and even of contextual information, except for some Latin notes positioned at the end of the bulky, two-volume set.) Jacobs's reader went through fifty-five editions over the next fifty years, and mastery of it became a requirement for admission to colleges across the country. Charles Anthon, professor of Greek and Latin at Columbia University after 1820, published almost fifty editions of classical texts that also drew heavily on German scholarship. John Pickering's *Comprehensive Lexicon of the Greek Language* (1826) was the best Greek-English dictionary of the time. Such works were godsends to the average teacher, who was no longer compelled to spend valuable time correcting the multiple errors of previous texts.[19]

As in earlier times, student societies served as an additional conduit of classical learning. Colleges within a college, these societies formulated and taught their own curricula, awarded their own diplomas, operated their own libraries (which were sometimes larger than the college's), established and enforced their own codes of conduct, and set the ideological tone for the student body. Members expanded the classical curriculum by reading unassigned works from the libraries. For instance, the American Whig Society expanded classical instruction at Princeton to include Ovid, Tacitus, Terence, and Herodotus. Initiates were often assigned the name of a classical historical figure. The American Whig Society's seal featured Minerva (Athena), the goddess of wisdom, guiding a youth up a mountain to the Temple of Virtue, an image based on Xenophon's story of Heracles' choice of virtue over vice.[20]

Commencement ceremonies provided ideal opportunities for college graduates to display their classical knowledge. Most such ceremonies featured a Latin oration by a leading student; many included Greek orations or dialogues. They were sometimes a rite of passage by which future social and political leaders were introduced to the current leadership. For instance, after 1835 the president of South Carolina College led each graduate to the front row of the audience, where he shook the hands of the state's leading politicians, ministers, merchants, planters, and academics.[21]

The New Hellenism

As democracy expanded and the Western world became enthralled by the Greek quest for independence from the Ottoman Empire, American educators placed a new emphasis on the ancient Greek language and culture, studies that had traditionally taken a back seat to Latin in the schools. In 1815, at the age of twenty-one, Edward Everett received the Eliot Professorship of Greek Literature at Harvard. After four years traveling in Europe, during which he viewed the Elgin Marbles and toured Greece with the aid of a letter introduction from Lord Byron, Everett returned to the university, where he became one of the leaders of the American Hellenist movement. Everett captivated Ralph Waldo Emerson and numerous other students with his remarkably wide-ranging and detailed lectures on Greek literature and culture in a course required of seniors. Emerson recalled: "The rudest undergraduate found a new morning opened to him in the lecture room of Harvard Hall.... It was not original thought but the manner of presentation [that created] a new perception of Grecian beauty.... There was an influence on the young people from Everett's genius which was almost comparable to that of Pericles of Athens." Emerson recorded Everett's line of reasoning: "The Phoenicians gave the Greeks their Alphabet, yet not a line of all which they wrote has come down, while their pupils have built themselves an imperishable monument of fame. The Greeks have left us a literature the most complete in all its parts the world has ever known.... The moderns' best efforts have only imitated them & the mod[erns] composed theirs with them for models but they theirs without." According to Charles Francis Adams's notes, Everett declared that Rome, like the rest of the Western world, was indebted to Greece for all of its literature: "To Greece we owe our finest models in the drama, in poetry, history, and all the organization of modern letters. . . . Their decisions in taste are not contravened to this day, our ways of writing being similar. . . . The study of letters in the Greek language has indeed an intrinsic value and while there is sympathy between mind and mind, the catalogue of distinguished men must excite the admiration and respect of every age." In the poems of Homer, which had "never since been equaled," "Man's genius had reached its acme in its first flight."[22]

Everett passed the Hellenic torch to his successor Cornelius Conway Felton, who had received a Ph.D. at the University of Tübingen and who later became president of Harvard. In an 1824 article Felton praised Homer and Herodotus as favorable to "virtue and liberty." Homer's epics presented "as a mirror the purest qualities of our nature." Six years later Felton related his feelings on reading the orations of Demosthenes: "I become loftier, and am no longer the man I was. I seem to myself to be Demosthenes, standing upon the tribunal, pronouncing that same oration, exhorting the assembled Athenians to imitate the valor and win the glory of their ancestors." Felton praised Alcestis, the title character of Euripides' play, who agrees to die in place of her husband, as "a noble-minded woman . . . a being in whom all thought of self is merged in an absorbing love of those to whom she is bound by conjugal and maternal ties." By contrast with Latin, Greek now benefited from its reputation as the language of a more egalitarian, individualistic, and intellectual people.[23]

Everett and Felton successfully implanted the belief in Greek superiority over Rome in the minds of their students. After claiming that many of the Roman republic's "best institutions were borrowed from Greece," Charles Francis Adams wrote in his diary concerning the Greeks: "This was a wonderful people, and the world is more indebted to them than to any mere men it ever produced. They shone through the powers of the mind. While the Romans always shared this superiority more equally with that which came from the body." As late as 1855 Emerson wrote, "History says the Romans conquered the Greeks, but I analyze the Roman language, I read the Roman books, I behold the Roman buildings, I dig up marbles in the Roman Gardens, and I find Greeks everywhere still paramount, in art, in thought—and in my history, the Greeks conquered Rome."[24]

The new Hellenism flourished south of the Mason-Dixon Line as well. In 1828 Hugh Swinton Legaré, the future editor of the influential *Southern Review*, wrote, "If Americans are to study any foreign literature at all, it ought undoubtedly to be the Classical, and especially the Greek." Legaré contended that "Roman genius . . . did but dimly reflect the glories of the Attic muse." Legaré noted regarding the Romans, "It was five whole centuries after the building of the city before that nation of sages and warriors could boast of a single author." He called Thucydides the greatest of historians. He considered "the masterpieces" of Demosthenes "the true and only models of popular eloquence . . . made like the Apollo or the Parthenon for all times and all nations, and worthy of study and imitation wherever genius shall be called to move masses of men by the power of the living word." Legaré added, "His natural impulses were all as high as his sensibility was deep and exquisite." In Demosthenes' simple but "sublime" speeches, "You see absolutely nothing of the artist; nay, you forget the speaker altogether: it is the statesman, or the man only that is before you." Legaré claimed that Demosthenes "was of that peculiar race—that chosen people—to whom the image of ideal beauty was first revealed, and who cherished it ever as the highest and holiest and divinest of things, with a devotion in which it is hard to tell whether deep love or just and exquisite discernment predominated." Legaré wrote, "The thoughts of all men with curiosity and wonder [are fixed] upon the barren little peninsula between Mount Cithaeron and Cape Sunium and the islands and shores around it, as they stand out in lonely brightness and dazzling relief, amidst the barbarian of the west on the one hand, and the dark and silent and lifeless wastes of oriental despotism on the other." The Greek language was "equally adapted to every variety of style and subject—to the most shadowy subtlety of distinction and the utmost exaction of definition, as well as to the energy and the pathos of popular eloquence—to the majesty, the elevation, and the variety of the epic, and the boldest license of the dithyrambic, no less than to the sweetness of the elegy, the simplicity of the pastoral, or the heedless gaiety and delicate characterization of comedy." Legaré admired a culture in which "the verses of Euripides softened even the bitterness of hatred and hostility and saved from butchery, in a war of extermination, all who were fortunate enough to be able to repeat them." Legaré endured a long, cholera-ridden ocean voyage by reading through the plays of Athens' great tragedians.[25]

George Fitzhugh had an equally passionate love of Greece. He called Roman civilization "an imitation but a falling off from that of Greece." In a different work he claimed, "Rome imitated and fell short of Greece in all the departments of moral philosophy, in pure metaphysics, in poetry, in architecture, in sculpture, in oratory, in the drama, and in painting." Fitzhugh contended that Americans should imitate the Greeks' cultivation of different dialects: "The little States of Greece each had its dialect, and cultivated it, and took pride in it. Now, dialects are [considered] vulgar and provincial. We shall have no men like the Greeks till the manners, dress, and dialect[s] of gentlemen betray, like the wines of Europe, the very neighborhood whence they come."[26]

Greek drama rose to prominence in college curricula for the first time during the antebellum period. After 1820 American scholars published a number of German editions of the plays of Aeschylus, Sophocles, Euripides, and Aristophanes for classroom use. Daniel Fletcher Webster, son of the famous statesman, wrote to his father from Harvard on Christmas Eve in 1830: "We have read *Oedipus* and *Medea* in Greek, and Trigonometry in Mathematics. These are the principal subjects about which I have been employed this term." South Carolina College made Sophocles' *Oedipus Tyrannus* a part of its curriculum in 1837 (and added Greek lyric poetry in the 1840s). Even Henry Adams, who was highly critical of the education he received at Harvard in the 1850s, made the exception of "two or three Greek plays." Colleges often produced and performed Greek plays for the general public, as well as for the student body. Euripides' *Medea* was staged in New York City fourteen times between 1845 and 1881. Popular journals like the *Southern Literary Messenger* began publishing scholarly discussions of the Greek dramatists, such as the lengthy series written by Charles Minnigerode, a professor at the College of William and Mary. As Meyer Reinhold put it: "The recognition of the Greek tragedians as among the greatest authors of all time is largely a phenomenon of the nineteenth century." The founders had certainly not studied Greek plays in college.[27]

The new Hellenism affected college curricula in other ways as well. In 1856 William J. Rivers was appointed to a newly created chair in Greek literature at South Carolina College. Rivers wrote, "The study of Greek is not confined in its results exclusively to the distant past, but is linked with the present, and possesses an extraordinary utility." He urged the study of the Athenian constitution. The same year the University of Virginia divided the chair of ancient languages, raising Greek to the dignity of a separate professorship. The new professorship was not an empty gesture by the university; it was first assigned to George Frederick Holmes, an expert on classical literature and one of the intellectual leaders of the antebellum South, before being taken over by Basil Lanneau Gildersleeve, perhaps the greatest American classicist of the nineteenth century. In 1843 Holmes had asked, "What nation subsequent to the Greeks has aided in the civilization and advancement of humanity, which does not refer to them as the fountain whence their own refinement flowed?" While the movement to make the Greek language a higher priority than Latin ultimately failed, it succeeded in raising the profile of Greek authors.[28]

The increased influence of ancient Greece in antebellum America was partly the product of German Hellenism. Everett had spent four and a half years studying abroad, mostly at the University of Göttingen, the greatest university in Europe for classical studies. Upon his return Everett substituted the German lecture format for the traditional recitation method, which involved drilling students in the memorization of fine grammatical points. Everett subsequently translated into English several seminal German texts on the classics. George Bancroft, one of the first historians of the United States, also studied at the University of Göttingen, as did Gildersleeve. In 1835 the trustees of South Carolina College hired a completely new faculty that began to teach the classics on the German model. The following year Francis Lieber, a German who had gone to Greece to help fight the Turks and had been forced out of Prussia for his liberal views, became a professor of history and political economy at the college. In 1840 Lieber edited a college text called *Great Events Described by Distinguished Historians, Chroniclers, and Other Writers* that included Herodotus' account of the Battle of Thermopylae and Plato's account of the death of Socrates. Busts of Demosthenes and Cicero stared down at Lieber's students. It was even said that some German immigrants who worked on the railroads and in the shops read Homer in the original Greek.[29]

The New Pedagogy

The revolution in pedagogy went well beyond a greater emphasis on the Greek language. As epitomized by Everett, Felton, and Gildersleeve, it also involved the thorough study of Greco-Roman culture in order to place the students' classical reading into its proper historical context, to motivate them to greater diligence in their linguistic study, and, most important, to infuse them with the very "spirit of Greece and Rome." Felton decried the overemphasis on rote memorization of grammatical rules. In 1830 he wrote: "A course of lectures should contain an account of the physical character, the scenery, the climate and the productions of Greece, with the early and later mythology, and the fabulous traditions of the heroic age. . . . Private life in all its forms, opinions in all their shades, the intellectual character and physical conformation of the people, should be fully illustrated." Felton added: "The student who would enter fully into the merits of a classical author must take himself out of the influences immediately around him; must transport himself back to a remote age, must lay aside the associations most familiar to him; must forget his country, his prejudices, his superior light, and place himself upon a level with the intellect whose labors he essays to comprehend." One of Gildersleeve's students, William M. Thornton, who later became dean of engineering at the University of Virginia, commented on Gildersleeve's similar approach. While other professors of ancient languages at the university, like the competent but unimaginative

Gessner Harrison, considered grammatical training more important than the reading, comprehension, and study of literature, the brash but enthusiastic Gildersleeve had opened "windows on Hellas." Thornton recalled: "We saw a living Hellas with that busy, curious race of adventurous spirits which in olden times revealed to the world the very pinnacles of beauty and wisdom and laid for the world the ultimate foundations of truth and science." Gildersleeve went on to help establish the American Philological Association (1869) and the *American Journal of Philology* (1880), serving as the president of the former in 1878 and the editor of the latter from 1880 to 1919.[30]

Hugh Swinton Legaré not only typified the new appreciation for this type of education but also ascribed it to the Greeks themselves. He wrote: "In this republic we may revive the habits of the 'old schools of Greece'—educate man, not as a technical or artificial being known only by one part of his divine nature . . . but educate him with a view to all the relations and duties of an intellectually social & active being. . . . For I am far from being of those idolaters who blaspheme the name of learning by imputing it to the pedants who feed upon the false quantities of old Greek Epigrams & admire Homer for the language he wrote in, instead of admiring the language because it contains the writings of Homer."[31]

Some Latin professors not only employed the new pedagogy but also established museums in order to implant students in the Roman world. Having been appointed a classics professor at the University of Michigan in 1854, Henry Frieze received permission to journey to Italy to procure "specimens of Ancient art illustrative of the classics," with the aim of "laying the foundation for a classical museum in the University." Frieze gathered books, engravings, plaster casts, maps, and photographs for the museum. The museum enabled Frieze to teach in a new way—to place classical authors in their proper context by giving students visual evidence of the society that produced them. James Angell, a student of Frieze who later served as president of the university, recalled concerning his teacher: "Upon no point was he accustomed to dwell in these later years with so much fervor as upon the transcendent importance of teaching Latin literature not merely as a collection of works of gifted men, but as the expression of the life of the great Roman nation, uttering itself in history, philosophy, and poetry. . . . According to his conception, it was not Latin we should study so much as Roman, the achievements, the spirit, the vital power of the Roman race."[32]

The study of history first entered American schools as an attempt to provide students with the historical background necessary to comprehend and appreciate the classical works that formed the core of their education.

Oliver Goldsmith's texts on Greek and Roman history, first published in the 1770s, were gradually replaced by the new texts of Charles Anthon, Samuel Griswold Goodrich, William Cooke Taylor, and Samuel Whelpley. Even after historical instruction was expanded to include American and world history, more courses were taught in ancient history than in any other field, and classical history played a large role even in world history courses. Twenty-six percent of the space in the 113 world history texts used in the United States in 1860 was devoted to Greek and Roman history. Only the period of world history from 1400 to 1800 received slightly more attention in these texts.[33]

Unfortunately, the "pedagogical revolution" was more of an evolution, slow and uneven. For years Harvard students complained of the old-fashioned, unimaginative technique of rote memorization employed by John Popkin. James Freeman, a Unitarian minister who had studied under Popkin in the late 1820s, recalled: "No attempt was made to interest us in our studies. We were expected to wade through Homer as though the *Iliad* were a bog, and it was our duty to get along at such a rate per diem. Nothing was said of the glory and grandeur, the tenderness and charm of this immortal epic. As only a few of the class recited well enough for us to learn anything from what they said, those hours were not only wasted, but put us in a condition of mental torpor." Another student of Popkin remembered, "In all points of grammar he was rigid and punctilious; and the drift of his teaching was rather to make exact verbal critics than enthusiastic lovers of scholarship." In this Popkin was similar to Thomas Park at South Carolina College and to numerous other professors throughout the nation. In fact, two students from South Carolina College who were caught discharging their guns in town were punished by being forced to recite fifty lines from the *Aeneid* before the faculty in 1824, thereby indicating that even the college's administration perceived a relationship between rote memorization of the classics and punishment. Hugh Swinton Legaré bemoaned the "stupid, unaspiring ignorance" of many teachers, the "wretched, vulgar, and worthless smattering of classical literature" they taught, and their mode of instruction. But he added that the German philologists offered "the dawn of a brighter hope."[34]

The Continuing Appeal of Rome

While Greek became a more equal partner with Latin in the classical curriculum during the antebellum period, Latin was not displaced, and Americans retained a deep interest in Roman history and culture. Although Daniel

Webster had begun the study of Virgil and Cicero at fifteen, a relatively late age, he recalled: "I conceived pleasure in the study of them, especially the latter, which rendered application no longer a task. With what vehemence did I denounce Cataline! With what earnestness did I struggle for Milo!" As a young lawyer, he remembered: "My principal occupation with books, when not law books, was with the Latin Classics. . . . I made myself familiar with most of Tully's orations, committed to memory large passages of some of them, read Sallust & Caesar & Horace. Some of Horace's odes I translated into poor English rhymes." During one of his brother's vacations, the Websters read Juvenal together. Webster's speech on the bicentennial of the Pilgrim landings attained the approval of the aging founder John Adams for its classical learning. An avid classicist himself, Adams wrote, "The observations on the Greeks and Romans . . . were sagacious, profound, and affecting in a high degree." Webster must have been pleased when his son wrote from Harvard to say that he had completed the first five books of Tacitus' *Annals*.[35]

As in the days of the founders, Cicero was the most revered of the Romans. Theophilus Parsons, chief justice of the Massachusetts Supreme Court, recommended Conyers Middleton's famous biography of Cicero as particularly suitable reading for all young lawyers. Upon the death of one of his children, Joseph Story, a justice of the United States Supreme Court, was comforted by Cicero's philosophical writings. Story saw the classics as "refining the taste" and "warming the heart with elevated sentiments." He asked, "What should we say of the jurist who never aspired to learn the maxims of law and equity which adorn the Roman codes?" U.S. senator Rufus Choate instructed those who studied law with him: "Soak your mind with Cicero." Choate explained that Cicero's writings "form the sentiments and . . . enlarge the mind of a young man aspiring to be a lawyer and statesman." In 1844 he translated Cicero's orations against Catiline during a respite from his senatorial duties. Choate kept busts of Cicero and Demosthenes in his library. Hugh Swinton Legaré wrote, "In a word, if one were called to name the man, in all history, who had made the most of great natural gifts . . . he could scarcely fail to ascribe that enviable distinction to Cicero." Legaré declared, "The learning that I would aim at is that of Cicero—a learning that can be instrumental in promoting the purposes of active life, in elevating the man of business into the sage & the mere statement of wholesome truths into sublime and touching eloquence." Concerning the Roman statesman, Legaré enthused:

> Wonderful that he should have combined in the oratory of the Forum and the Senate the vehemence and force of Demosthenes (which he sometimes equalled) with the sweetness of Isocrates and the majesty and copiousness of Plato—that his dialogues on ethical and metaphysical subjects . . . should be

inferior to nothing that Athens produced . . . and that even his familiar epistles, thrown off, generally, without the least premeditation, often in haste, in sickness, in sorrow, under some of the severest trials and vexations that man ever encountered, should afford the most perfect model imaginable of that engaging species of composition! Still more wonderful that he reconciled the highest excellences of the speculative character with the greatest ability and success in active life.[36]

Americans loved Virgil and Tacitus as well. Legaré marveled at the combination of elegance and instruction in Virgil's *Georgics:* "The wonder is how the poet was able to reconcile his genius to his subject—how he could describe a plough, for instance, without ever sinking down into prose or elevating his style so far above the matter, and how he has contrived to throw a sort of Epic dignity and animation without any air of burlesque, into his pictures of the Beehive. . . . The perfection of the *Georgics* is unapproachable in Didactic poetry, and were it not that we have that work and Lucretius' *De Rerum Natura* before our eyes, we should even doubt whether the very phrase 'Didactic poetry' were not somewhat of a contradiction in terms." Legaré admired the literature of Augustan Rome because in it the Romans allowed their traditional practicality to be moderated by Greek elegance. Jefferson Davis was also devoted to Virgil. When the future president James K. Polk read David Ramsay's *History of the American Revolution* (1789) while a student at the University of North Carolina, Polk called Ramsay "the Tacitus of this western hemisphere to transmit to posterity in the unpolished language of the truth, the spirit of liberty which actuated the first founders of our republic."[37]

Although Greece remained dangerous to visit, more Americans than ever before included Italy in their European tours. Among the many American visitors to Rome and to the ruins of Pompeii and Herculaneum were Henry Adams, Nathaniel Hawthorne, George Bancroft, James Fenimore Cooper, Herman Melville, and Charles Sumner. Adams recalled that "Rome before 1870 was seductive beyond resistance" and that "an American parent, curiously enough while bitterly hostile to Paris, seemed rather disposed to accept Rome as legitimate education." After immersing himself in classical art in the museums of Rome, Hawthorne wrote, "I am partly sensible that some unwritten rules of taste are making their way into my mind; that all of this Greek beauty has done something toward refining me, who still am, however, a very sturdy Goth." After seeing the *Laocoön*, the famous Hellenistic sculpture of the Trojan priest and his sons in the throes of an agonizing death from a giant serpent, at the Vatican Museum, Hawthorne wrote: "There was such a type of human beings struggling with an inextricable trouble and entangled in complication which they can never free themselves from by their own efforts, and out of which Heaven will not help them. It was a most powerful mind, and one capable of reducing a complex idea to unity, that imagined this groupe." In Florence he fell in love with the *Venus de Medici,* a variation of Praxiteles' *Venus:* "Surely, it makes one ready to believe in the high destinies of the human race to think that this beautiful form is but Nature's plan for all womankind and that the nearer the actual woman approaches to it, the more natural she is." At Lake Trasimene, the site of Hannibal's thrashing of the Roman army, Hawthorne wrote: "I doubt whether I should feel so much on the field of Saratoga or Monmouth, but these old classic battle-fields belong to the whole world, and each man feels as if his own forefathers fought there." Melville's similar voyage inspired him to deliver a lecture to audiences throughout the northern and western United States entitled "Statues in Rome" in 1857–1858. In that lecture Melville said of the *Apollo Belvedere:* "Its very presence is overawing. Few speak, or even whisper, when they enter the cabinet where it stands. It is not a mere work of art that one gazes on; for there is a kind of divinity in it that lifts the imagination of the beholder above 'things rank and gross in nature' and makes ordinary criticism impossible.... How well in the *Apollo* is expressed the idea of the perfect man. Who could better it? Can art, not life, make the ideal?" Bancroft wrote to a friend from Naples concerning Pompeii, "When you see it, you will declare it interesting enough to employ the thoughts for days altogether." He added, "The ruins around Rome are more grand and sublime, but those near Naples are more singular." Cooper, who ascended Mount Vesuvius, wrote that there was "a sublimity in the catastrophe of Herculaneum, a grandeur in desolation, that has no parallel." He called the Temple of Neptune at Paestum "the most impressive, and I had almost said the most imposing, edifice I know." He reflected, "What a speck does the history of America become in this long vista of events."[38]

Not all Americans were impressed by their Roman sojourns, of course. In 1836 Ralph Izzard Middleton of South Carolina was largely unmoved by the city's antiquities. Concluding that the Colosseum alone was worth seeing, he declared: "The triumphal arches and old tottering columns, the dilapidated statues and smoked frescoes, all these are fudge." The *Belvedere Hercules* in the Vatican Museum was but "a weather beaten piece of stone somewhat in the shape of a man's body, curtailed of head, arms, and legs." Middleton perceived no inkling of "the godlike majesty" attributed to the torso by his guidebook. Maybe artists should look at it, he wrote, but for people "who could not model a dog out of a piece of wax (among which I enroll myself) to go and spend hours together in the middle of winter in the Vatican constantly exclaiming how beautiful, how beautiful, when they are all the while thinking how cold, how cold, this I think utterly absurd." But the fact that so many other American tourists felt compelled to lavish such praise on a stone torso speaks volumes about the reverence commanded by all things classical.[39]

Roman civil law continued to play an important role in the nation's legal system. Many of the founders, including Thomas Jefferson, Alexander Hamilton, John Adams, George Wythe, James Wilson, and Samuel Chase, had urged a larger role for Roman civil law, which they considered more rational and more truly based on natural law than the English common law. Criticism of the chaotic nature of the common law and, hence, its vulnerability to abuse by judges increased as democracy spread and as animosity toward England grew. In addition, because land was abundant and labor scarce in America—the precise opposite of the context in which the common law had evolved in feudal England—some considered the common law less suited to the New World than the civil law.[40]

By the antebellum period Joseph Story was leading the effort to use Roman legal concepts to reform the common law and to provide guidance in those areas in which the common law was silent. Story's *Commentaries* (1832–1845), a series of legal texts, were especially influential in promoting the use of Roman law. Story was joined in his effort by Hugh Swinton Legaré, who served as attorney general under John Tyler, Francis Lieber (*Legal and Political Hermeneutics*, 1839), and James Murdoch Walker, a South Carolina legislator who wrote *An Inquiry into the Use and Authority of Roman Jurisprudence in the Law Concerning Real Estate* (1850) and *The Theory of Common Law* (1852), which discussed the relationship between common and civil law. Legaré's library consisted of 143 Latin works and 77 Greek works, compared with only 36 in English; most of his French and other modern European works were civil-law texts. His article for the *New York Review*, "The Origin, History, and Influence of Roman Legislation," was a tour de force of contemporary learning on the civil law, ranging from a discussion of early Roman history to the latest German scholarship. He wrote that because of its systematic and rational nature, "the largest portion" of Roman law was "suitable not only to other countries, but to all other countries." He added, "It is as applicable at Boston as at Paris and has served equally to guide the legislation of Napoleon and to enlighten the judgment of Story." Roman and civil jurists drew their materials from a longer and more diversified experience than that which had formed the common law. For instance, the problem of apportioning rights of use between two states separated by a river, a problem unknown to an island under a single government like Britain, had long been settled by Roman law; therefore, American jurists faced with such a problem and unable to find a solution in the common law should consult the rational principles of Roman law rather than attempting to fashion new solutions from within the insular common-law tradition. In eulogizing Legaré, Story praised his devotion to "the enlarged and liberal principles and just morality of the Roman jurisprudence."[41]

Interest in the civil law was enhanced by the purchase or annexation of Louisiana, Florida, Texas, and the Mexican Cession, territories previously administered by France and Spain according to civil law. Indeed, Louisiana was allowed to retain a version of it. Roman civil law greatly influenced water and commercial law elsewhere in the United States and provided the foundation for international law. The desire to use civil-law concepts to systematize common law was especially popular among law-school professors, who sought to displace legal apprenticeship with a more academic form of training that would draw added prestige from the use of Latin terms. Such was the interest in Roman law that the Confederate general Albert Pike devoted his spare time during the Civil War to translating the whole *Corpus Juris Civilis* as a means of relaxation.[42]

Americans also wrote popular plays about Rome. John Howard Payne, most famous for the poem *Home, Sweet Home,* also penned *Brutus, or The Fall of Tarquin* (1818). Other notable plays include David Paul Brown's *Sertorius* (1830), Charles Jared Ingersoll's *Julian* (1831), Jonas B. Phillips's *Camillus* (1833), Nathaniel H. Bannister's *Gaulantus* (1837), and Louisa McCord's *Caius Gracchus* (1851). Robert Montgomery Bird's *The Gladiator* (1831), about Spartacus, was staged more than 1,000 times.[43]

Adams Family Values: A Case Study in Classical Transmission

The antebellum educational system's emphasis on the classics reflected the will of most parents, who reinforced this conditioning in the home. The family of John Adams provides a striking illustration of the fact that love and reverence for the classics were transmitted from each generation to the next not only through the schools but via families themselves. When John Adams's father forced his reluctant son to return to his Latin lexicon by substituting ditch-digging for it, the lesson was not lost on the future president: knowledge of the classics produced a glorious life of upward mobility, its neglect a wretched life of manual labor. Adams later wrote, "If I have gained any distinction, it has been owing to the two days' labor in that abominable ditch." Adams was so successful in his own campaign to steep his eldest son in the classics that by 1785, when John Quincy entered Harvard, his father could boast of him: "It is rare to find a youth possessed of so much knowledge. He has translated Virgil's *Aeneid*, Suetonius, the whole of Sallust, and Tacitus' *Agricola*, his *Germany*, and several books of his *Annals*, a great part of Horace, some of Ovid, some of Caesar's commentaries, in writing, besides a number of Tully's orations. . . . In Greek his progress has not been equal; yet he has studied morsels in Aristotle's *Poetics*, in Plutarch's *Lives*, and Lucian's *Dialogues*, the choice of Hercules in Xenophon, and lately he has gone through several books in Homer's *Iliad*." By the 1790s John Quincy enjoyed reading classical poetry not only in the original languages but in various modern European translations as well. While in Europe, he debated the merits of both the original works and the various translations with European diplomats. The energetic John Quincy held the chair of rhetoric at Harvard while serving as a U.S. senator in 1806, though his father feared for his health. John Adams noted anxiously: "Aristotle, Dionysius Halicarnassensis, Longinus, Quintilian, Demosthenes, and Cicero, with twenty others, are not easily read and studied by a man of the world and a senator of the United States."[44]

John Quincy's devotion to the classics only increased with time. On becoming his nation's first minister to Russia in 1809, he carried Plutarch's *Lives* with him, rereading the biographies of Lycurgus and Solon on the ship en route to St. Petersburg. He continued to discuss the merits of various German, English, and Spanish translations of the classics with European diplomats. He read the Platonic dialogues in 1811 and compared them with Cicero's. He believed that the *Crito* expressed a "sublime morality" and wrote concerning the *Apology of Socrates*, "The mildness of his tone and manner, the firmness of his adherence to his principles, the sportive playfulness of his satire, and the exalted purity of his doctrines, are all but divine." Even while serving energetically as secretary of state in 1819, John Quincy ordered copies of the works of Cicero and Tacitus. He confessed in his diary: "I cannot indulge myself in the luxury of giving two hours a day to these writers; but to live without having a Cicero and a Tacitus at hand seems to me as if it was a privation of one of my limbs." John Quincy called Virgil's *Georgics* "the most perfect composition that ever issued from the mind of man." Praising its "transcendent excellence," he noted that some passages had been "the special delight of twenty centuries" and would "enchant the ear of harmony and transport the soul of fancy as long as sentiment shall last among mankind."[45]

John Quincy frequently referred to the classics during his presidency. In 1825 he copied Horace's admonition, which he himself translated from the Latin: "Rule thy soul, which *must* obey, or *will* control. Curb thy proud soul with bit and rein. And bind him fast with iron chain." The following year he thought of one of Horace's odes while sailing. In 1827 he compared the original works of Tacitus with two translations, concluding, "It is impossible to convey the meaning of Tacitus without circumlocution and paraphrase, and that must necessarily lose his sententious brevity." He noted that Tacitus "always instructs and charms." The following year, while seeking reelection, the president noted in his diary: "Mr. [Nicholas] Biddle, the president of the U. S. Bank, called with his brother Richard, from Pittsburgh. There had been a question between them whether the quotation 'Video meliora proboque, deteriora sequor' was from Horace or Ovid. I had pronounced it from Horace, so had the President of the bank, and Mr. [Edward] Everett. They had now ascertained that it is the *Metamorphoses*, Book VII, Lines 20 and 21—a speech of Medea." When his son Charles Francis criticized the moral principles inherent in Cicero's letter to Lentulus, a defense of the Roman's actions during the time of the First Triumvirate, John Quincy immediately read the "long and deeply interesting letter" and compared it with two different translations. He concluded regarding Cicero's actions, "I perceive little in them that can be blamed," and noted, "These researches absorbed again more than all the leisure of the day." The six bronze busts that adorned the mantelpiece of John Quincy's study at the Executive Mansion depicted Cicero, Demosthenes, Homer, Plato, Socrates, and Virgil.[46]

Whether or not John Quincy's classical reading impeded his reelection campaign, it is certain that his defeat allowed him to spend even more time studying the classics. Believing that Andrew Jackson's election presaged the decline of the American republic, John Quincy immediately began reading Cicero's *Philippics* against Mark Antony, as well as Plutarch's lives of Cicero, Antony, and Brutus, all chronicles of the fall of the Roman republic. He claimed that among the "fine sentiments" in the eleventh Philippic was: "It is the duty of a wise man to premeditate everything that can happen to him; to bear it with fortitude. There is more of wisdom in providing against the event, but not less of spirit to bear it bravely if it happens." He wrote, "It is lamentable to see the liberties of a republic sustained by such eloquence as that of Cicero bought and sold by a boy like Octavius and a profligate like Antony." Although the former president found "too much sameness" in the *Philippics*, "both of form and subject," he believed that "the noble sentiments contained in them will preserve them forever." He even read Cicero's much-ridiculed poetry, thereby completing "the perusal of everything written by him now known to be extant." He noted, "It has occupied an average of two hours a day for ten months and has left me with a desire to spend at least as much or more time in studying him more profoundly." He lamented that he had not studied Cicero more thoroughly earlier in life: "Had I forty years ago . . . perseveringly devoted the leisure of one year without interruption to the study of Cicero in his own language, my time would have been better occupied than it was, and perhaps my life might have been more useful to my country and my fellow-creatures than it has been." He considered Cicero "the noblest spirit that ever lived in the Tide of Times." John Quincy's wife, Louisa, noted ruefully that Cicero was his "passion."[47]

It was in such trying times that the classics were most important to John Quincy, serving as a powerful source of solace. He had emphasized this use of the classics in his *Lectures on Rhetoric and Oratory* two decades earlier: "At no hour of your life will the love of letters ever oppress you as a burden or fail you as a resource. . . . In social converse with the mighty dead of ancient days, you will never smart under the galling sense of dependence upon the mighty living in the present age, and in your struggles with the world, should a crisis ever occur, when even friendship may deem it prudent to desert you; when even your country may seem ready to abandon herself & you; when priest & levite shall come & look on you & pass on by the other side, seek refuge, my unfailing friends, and be assured you will find it, in the friendship of Laelius & Scipio & in the patriotism of Cicero, Demosthenes, & Burke." Evidently needing some solace of his own, Ralph Waldo Emerson copied this passage into his journal during the first year of the Civil War.[48]

While in retirement, John Quincy also devoted countless hours to Latin poetry. When riding or walking, he composed verse translations of Horace's odes, though he lamented, "It is impossible to concentrate thought into single words in English as it is in the Latin." His life was "happier than I have ever enjoyed." After studying Horace in comparison with Pindar, Anacreon, and other great poets, including the psalmist, John Quincy wrote: "What are the essential characteristics of Horace's Odes? 1. Unity—a seminal idea pervading the whole. 2. Rich imagery. 3. Picturesque descriptions of nature. 4. Sublime and lofty sentiment. 5. Maxims of wisdom sententiously expressed. 6. Harmonious versification." Regarding Horace's ode to Lollius, John Quincy exulted: "What a magnificent panegyric upon his friend! What consciousness of his own transcendent powers! What a sublime conception of the gifts of poetical inspiration! But, then, what a sad falling off, that all his praise was bestowed upon a worthless man!" After praising Ovid's description of a stag hunt in the *Metamorphoses*, John Quincy wrote: "A translator (it was [Joseph] Addison) who sunk under the difficulty of rendering this into English verse ought not to have ventured to encounter the *Metamorphoses* of Ovid."[49]

John Quincy continued to love and to use Plutarch as well. In 1838 he attended a convention of the Plymouth County (Massachusetts) Association for the Improvement of Common Schools, held in an Episcopal church, in which he heard state secretary of education Horace Mann advocate the creation of a teacher-training institute. When Adams was asked to speak without warning, his mind faltered until he remembered Plutarch's story of the traditional Spartan festival in which a choir of old men sang, "We were once valiant young men," a choir of young men sang, "But we are the valiant ones now; put us to the test if you wish," and a choir of boys sang, "But we shall be far mightier." After relating the anecdote, John Quincy told the crowd that well might a representative of the elders present state, "We have been in days of old wise and generous, brave and bold," a representative of the young men declare, "That which in days of yore ye were, we at the present moment are," and one of the boys might say, "Hereafter, at our country's call, we promise to surpass you all." John Quincy recorded in his diary: "A shout of laughter and a thundering clap of hands followed, and I returned to the pew where I had been sitting at the side of Mr. [Daniel] Webster, who said, 'Well, you have turned Plutarch to good account.'" The next year John Quincy reread Plutarch's essay "On the Delay of Divine Justice," recording: "This dissertation interested me so much that the sun went down and I had done nothing." Regarding his eclectic classical studies, he concluded, "I can compare myself to nothing but the humming-bird which visits my althea-trees in August, when they are in full bloom, buzzing upon the wing from cup to cup without alighting anywhere, and sipping liquid honey with a long needle beak from the bottom of each cup."[50]

When John Quincy returned to politics as the congressional representative from Plymouth, a post some considered degrading for a former president, he quoted Cicero, "I will not desert in my old age the Republic I defended in my youth." A manufacturer in Meriden, Connecticut, proud of John Quincy's defense of antislavery petitions to Congress and of his courtroom defense of the fugitive slaves aboard the *Amistad*, sent him a yard-long ivory cane, tipped with silver and steel and topped by a golden eagle and a ring that bore an inscription from Horace, which John Quincy translated as "A man just and tenacious in purpose." Appreciating the sentiment but determined to exhibit Ciceronian integrity, John Quincy replied that he could not, as a matter of policy, accept such gifts. Ironically, Cicero himself, like nearly all Roman lawyers, who were technically unpaid, had possessed few qualms about accepting gifts, including large bequests in wills.[51]

Like his father before him, John Quincy trained his sons in the classics. In 1812 he started badgering his eldest son, the eleven-year-old George Washington Adams, in a style eerily similar to that employed by his own father before him, to study Greek and Latin "until you can write them correctly and read Homer, Demosthenes, and Thucydides, Lucretius, Horace, Livy, Tacitus, and *all* Cicero with *almost* as much ease and readiness as if they were written in English" (emphases in original). John Quincy added that George should study these geniuses not for "vain glory" but for "wisdom." John Quincy hoped to hear from his son that he was a good Latin scholar "and that you will before long be a good Greek one." In 1824, while seeking the presidency, John Quincy paraphrased these lines from the "Golden Verses of Pythagoras" for his three sons:

> Let not thine eyelids close at parting day
> Till, with thyself communing, thou shalt say,
> "What deed of good or evil have I done
> Since Morning last restored the radiant Sun?"
> In strict review the day before thee pass,
> And see thyself in Truth's unerring glass.
> If scorning self delusion's fraudful ways,
> Her solemn voice, reproving conscience raise,
> With keen contrition, and divine aid implore
> Each error to redeem and wrong no more.
> Or should that faithful guardian witness bear
> That all thy actions have been just and fair,
> Rejoice, and Heaven intreat with soul sincere,
> In virtue's perfect path to persevere.

When George was elected to the Massachusetts legislature, John Quincy advised him to read Plutarch and to employ "all the Stoic virtues—Prudence, Temperance, Fortitude, Justice." While president, he urged his son Charles Francis to peruse great epistles like those of Pliny the Younger and to read Cicero, beginning with *On Duties,* examining it as a system of ethics, as well as a literary composition and an autobiographical work. In fact, John Quincy may have believed that his own letters of advice to Charles Francis followed in the tradition of *On Duties,* which was addressed by Cicero to his son Marcus. To supplement his son's formal education, John Quincy filled several letters with short essays on Cicero's orations. He also willed Charles Francis his favorite art, the paintings and busts of classical figures that Charles Francis had kept safe for him for a time after he had left the presidency. In 1832 John Quincy wrote to Charles Francis: "Of all my Prints, that which you have of Cicero at his Villa has the deepest and strongest hold upon my affections, and next to that, my six little bronze Busts, the two Philosophers, the two Orators, and the two Poets, come closest to my heart. I would not speak it profanely, but to me they are as household Gods. I have missed them from my mantel piece the last four years, but hope to have them replaced there at Quincy next Spring, and that in due time they will pass from mine to yours."[52]

In the effort to steep his sons in the classics John Quincy had at least two capable accomplices. In 1813 John Adams gave a copy of Philippe Brunck's *Ethike Poiesis,* a collection of Greek maxims, to his grandson George, then preparing for Harvard. Three years later, at the age of eighty-one, John excerpted approximately 140 passages from Terence's six extant plays for his grandchildren. Better yet, John Quincy had the help of an intelligent and uncommonly educated wife. In 1819 John Quincy recorded in his diary: "My wife has made a translation of the first and second Alcibiades of Plato.... She made it for the benefit of her sons, and I this morning finished the revisal of it, in which I have made very little alteration. I read the first Alcibiades at Auteuil, in the year 1784, at the age of seventeen." He recalled that he had learned from the work the importance of preparation for government service and the soul's greater significance than the body and that he had been struck by "the pure and glorious moral sentiments inculcated in his discourse." He added, "I wish my sons to read, and to be penetrated as deeply as I have been with, the lessons of the first Alicbiades."[53]

John Quincy and his accomplices successfully transmitted the love of the classics to Charles Francis. As early as 1820 Charles Francis was reading Cicero's orations against Catiline, as well as the works of Virgil and Xenophon. Three years later Thomas Kirkland, the president of Harvard, characterized Charles Francis as "a good student in Latin." In 1824 he studied Homer, Sappho, and Tacitus. Regarding Tacitus, he wrote, "I had selected the life of Agricola as an exercise [for translation] for next Vacation, being very much pleased when I lately read it." Between sessions of his Harvard drinking and card-playing group called the Lyceum Club, Charles Francis began translating the *Agricola* for pleasure. He recorded in his diary: "In looking over a copy which was in my g[rand]father's library I came to a mark of my father's in which he put down his progress forty years ago. I determined to pursue the same course and for today I translated three sections." He then read William Mitford's *History of Greece,* which led him to consult several of Plutarch's lives. In the autumn of 1825 Charles Francis read Horace almost daily, in the spring of 1827 Tacitus. The following year, in reply to his father's pleas that he read Cicero, Charles Francis replied that the Roman had lacked "firmness of character" and that he preferred Cato the Younger, thus giving his father the satisfaction of knowing that his son had learned enough of the classics to debate the merits of classical figures with him. Nevertheless, Charles Francis then began reading Cicero's orations, in addition to Conyers Middleton's *Life of Marcus Tullius Cicero* and various Platonic dialogues. He concluded that Cicero's *Oration for Roscius* "is one of the boldest specimens of forcible eloquence I have read." John Quincy wrote to his son: "Your letters are becoming a necessary of life to me. I have not in seven years read so much of classical literature as since I began these Letters to you. And I might add I have not in seven years engaged in so much luxurious entertainment."[54]

Thereafter, for decades Charles Francis made it a part of his daily routine to read (and often reread) a wide variety of classics, both in the original languages and in translation. These included the works of Aeschines, Aeschylus, Aristophanes, Aristotle, Demosthenes, Euripides, Herodotus, Homer, Horace, Livy, Lucan, Lucretius, Martial, Plato, Pliny the Younger, Plutarch, Quintilian, Seneca, Sophocles, Suetonius, Tacitus, Thucydides, and Virgil. In 1836 Charles Francis wrote, "There is no part of my daily life which gives me so much pleasure as the short period spent in reading the Classics." The following year he wrote: "I enjoy particularly the Greek, in which I incline to make myself more proficient. . . . It is refreshing to get into a quiet, retired place and dwell in antiquity and beautiful pictures. I enjoy it as a relief from anxieties both public and private." In 1839 he wrote: "Classical study is like drinking wine. A stimulating pleasure." The remarkably detailed and insightful journal entries he penned concerning a dazzling variety of classics reveal that he read each carefully and pondered each deeply.[55]

In the 1850s Charles Francis demonstrated that he had mastered the art of classical analogy, an art now essential to the success of statesmen. In his edition of his grandfather's papers he laid both John Adams and Thomas Jefferson to rest with a classical analogy both men would have relished. After noting that the two colossi of the American Revolution had died on the same day, July 4, 1826, the fiftieth anniversary of the Declaration of Independence, Charles Francis related the story, from Herodotus' *Histories* (1.30–31), of Solon's voyage to the wealthy kingdom of Lydia in Asia Minor. Having shown Solon his vast treasury, Croesus, the Lydian monarch, asked the wise Athenian, "Who, of all men that you have seen, do you deem the most fortunate?" The king expected, of course, that Solon would answer, "Croesus." But Solon "named two brothers, Cleobis and Biton, who once put themselves to the wagon and drew their mother to Juno's temple, and then, after sacrificing and feasting, went to rest and died together at the height of their reputation of filial piety." Charles Francis concluded regarding Adams and Jefferson: "How much more deserving to be called blessed is the life of these two, who drew their nursing-mother, against strong resistance, to the temple of liberty and who, after a long period of labors and services devoted to her welfare, went to the same rest under auspices a thousand-fold more sublime."[56]

Other Families

While the Adamses were unusually accomplished, their devotion to the classics was not uncommon. Convinced, like their fathers before them, that the classics were essential to both moral and political education, antebellum leaders of all political parties and sections of the United States urged the youth to apply themselves diligently to their classical studies. In 1836 John C. Calhoun advised Thomas J. Johnson regarding a young friend who wished to study law: "As to history, he will of course study the ancient classicks; to be followed by Gibbon's decline and fall of the Roman empire." In 1847 Calhoun was relieved to report to one grandson, James Edward, that another, William, had overcome his initial struggles with Latin and was now demonstrating prowess in the subject. Calhoun explained, "I go over his lesson every evening with him." After noting the utility of the exercise in brushing up his own Latin, Calhoun urged James Edward: "You must write to him and encourage him. It will have a good effect." To his daughter Anna, Calhoun wrote that he was "gratified" by William's progress. In yet another letter to James Edward the following year, he noted of William, with a palpable sense of relief, "His aversion to Latin and Greek seems to have disappeared entirely." Calhoun added the reminder, "I hope you will write to him occasionally in a manner to encourage him." Similarly, Francis Leak, a planter in Mississippi, urged his son John, a student at the University of North Carolina, "Get acquainted with the histories of the United States, England, Greece & Rome, a proper knowledge for every American."[57]

Ralph Waldo Emerson made certain that his sons, daughter, and nephew received the benefit of a classical education, as he had. In 1836 he wrote in his journal regarding one son: "Waldo & I read, as we have opportunity, in the *Electra*. It is very charming to me, the severe taste of these Greeks. I am never offended & there is an aristocratic pleasure in these lofty & removed studies. It is as if you left the noisy, fuming world of mortal men.... Waldo and I finished the *Electra* & he is quite enamored of the severe beauty of the Greek tragic muse. Do you not think it sets the action before you with a more real presence than even Shakespeare drama?" He sent his nephew William Jr. a volume of Euripides. He encouraged his daughter Ellen to read a Latin grammar, Virgil, and Plutarch. While in St. Louis to deliver a lecture, he wrote to his wife, "Tell the dear children that Papa thinks he will never go away again & that Edward must be the best Latin scholar that he can be."[58]

Even those who lacked a classical education, or who lost their facility with Greek and Latin, often urged others to pursue a classical education.

Classical Conditioning: School, Home, and Society

Henry Clay never learned the classical languages but fell under the classical influence while serving as George Wythe's secretary from the age of sixteen to twenty-one. A member of Virginia's High Court of Chancery, Wythe had been a signer of the Declaration of Independence and the chief mentor of Thomas Jefferson, John Marshall, and James Monroe. One of the greatest experts on the classics in the country, Wythe often salted his correspondence with Greek and Latin quotations and classical references. As the historian Bernard Mayo noted: "Often the venerable judge would have the tow-headed youth rest from his copying while he explained some literary reference, pointed out the merits and defects of a particular work, or held him enthralled by reading Homer in sonorous Greek. He would discuss for Henry's edification the classical orators, compare the historians Thucydides and Herodotus [and] the dramatists Sophocles and Euripides. . . . Always he found amusement in classical analogies to the tribulations of Virginia litigants." Wythe urged Clay to make use of his vast library and to read the books there, including translations of Homer and of Plutarch's *Lives*, carefully, not skimming them. Remembering Wythe's instruction, Clay wrote to his own son and namesake, "I think you would do well to refresh your recollection of the dead languages. I never enjoyed the advantage of knowing them, but I have remarked that those who do find a resource in them throughout life, and sometimes at a late period of it."[59]

The Classics in American Society

American society both reflected and reinforced this classical conditioning. The conditioning in reverence for the classics that an increasing number of Americans experienced in their homes and schools could not help but filter down into the rest of American society, which, in turn, reinforced the conditioning.

The urge to re-create classical civilization in the United States found expression in the naming of numerous towns, cities, ships, and even people in every state of the Union. While the most popular names of towns and cities were Athens, Sparta, Rome, Troy, Carthage, and Arcadia, others included Corinth, Ithaca, Utica, Corfu, Laconia, Marcellus, Ovid, Pandora, Homer, Euclid, Seneca, Virgil, Aurora, Minerva, Neptune, Atlas, Orion, Antiquity, Elysian Fields, Eureka, Mirabile, Philippi, and the River Styx. The last of these was a town in Ohio, a state that topped the Northwest with thirty-five classically named towns. Syracuse was selected as the name of a town in New York specifically because the town, like the ancient Greek colony in Sicily, was established near a swamp and underground springs. Even those cities that lacked classical names often made up for this by adopting such titles as the "Athens of America" (Boston and Charleston) or the "Athens of the West" (Lexington, Kentucky). By contrast, a humble North Carolinian was content to have his state called "the Thebes of America." (In this, if nothing else, he agreed with the South Carolinian who sniffed that North Carolina was a "modern Boeotia." Boeotia was an area north of Athens, led by Thebes, that was commonly ridiculed by Athenian comic playwrights for its alleged rusticity and ignorance.) The docks of coastal cities were often filled with ships bearing names like the *Hector,* the *Horace,* the *Venus,* the *Leonidas,* and the *Spartan.* Parents named their children Claudia, Cornelia, Hannibal, Homer, Horace, Lucius, Virgil, and, as the Confederacy later learned, Ulysses. Masters continued to give their slaves classical names, though none named them Spartacus. Even Native Americans were sometimes swept up in the classical mania; a leader of the Penobscot tribe called himself Neptune, and a Cherokee leader went by the name Roman Nose.[60]

Cities often boasted a library or learned club called an Athenaeum that was filled with classical busts and paintings, as well as books. In 1822 a young Ralph Waldo Emerson relished the statues of the new Boston Athenaeum that "attract the eye in every corner from the tedious joys of writing and reading." He added, "The beholder instantly feels the spirit of the connoisseur stealing over him & ere he can exorcise it, rubs up his Latin & Italian lore, & among the gazers you may see the scholar, at pains to show his acquaintance with the lordly strangers & his disdain of the 'ignobile vulgus' who stare and stare and are never the wiser." Three decades later, when his daughter Ellen saw Harriet Hosmer's bust of Medusa at the Athenaeum, she gushed: "I'll go wild with delight. I can't think how Hatty Hosmer survived the joy of finishing that Medusa, of realizing such a beautiful, beautiful idea. Such a face, such a position of the head, so fine an expression."[61]

Even small frontier towns belonged to the National American Lyceum, founded by Josiah Holbrook in the 1830s, or to some other lyceum. Named after Aristotle's famous school in Athens, these lecture circuits featured a wide variety of political, intellectual, and artistic leaders. Lyceum lectures generally attracted large crowds seeking both knowledge and entertainment. Lecturers frequently spoke about classical topics and alluded to the classics even when discussing modern issues.[62]

The lectures sometimes led to the formation of reading clubs. Among the best sellers in the antebellum United States were Edward Bulwer-Lytton's historical novel *The Last Days of Pompeii* (1834), Charles Anthon's erudite *A Manual of Greek and Roman Antiquities* (2 volumes; 1851–1852),

Samuel Eliot's heavily classical *History of Liberty* (4 volumes; 1853), and Thomas Bulfinch's *The Age of Fable* (1855).[63]

The last of these works was a compendium of Greco-Roman myths, drawn largely from Ovid, Homer, Virgil, and Sophocles. A bank clerk who wrote in his spare time, Bulfinch penned this dedication of his book: "To Henry Wadsworth Longfellow, the poet alike of the many and of the few, this attempt to popularize mythology and extend the enjoyment of elegant literature, is respectfully inscribed." In his preface Bulfinch wrote:

> Our book is not for the learned, not for the theologian, nor for the philosopher, but for the reader of English literature, of either sex, who wishes to comprehend the allusions so frequently made by public speakers, lecturers, essayists, and poets, and those which occur in polite conversation. We trust our young readers will find it a source of entertainment; those more advanced a useful companion in their reading; those who travel and visit museums and galleries of art an interpreter of paintings and sculptures; those who mingle in cultivated society a key to allusions which are occasionally made; and last of all, those in advanced life pleasure in retracing a path of literature which leads them back to the days of their childhood, and revives at every step the associations of the morning of life.

Indeed, not content merely to relate a tale from Greek mythology, Bulfinch generally quoted famous references of modern European and American poets to the characters in the myth, or referred to modern works of art that were based on the tale. A competent Latinist who had taught briefly at Boston Latin School, Bulfinch was thoroughly familiar with Ovid and succeeded in capturing his sprightliness and charm. Popularly known as "Bulfinch's Mythology," the volume became one of the most popular books ever published in the United States and the standard work on classical mythology for nearly a century, until Edith Hamilton's *Greek Mythology* was published in 1942.[64]

Neoclassical structures graced most American towns. Antebellum architects built upon the neoclassical foundation laid by Thomas Jefferson, Benjamin Latrobe, and other eighteenth- and early nineteenth-century architects. In an 1825 address to the Virginia General Assembly, the future president John Tyler expressed a common sentiment when he declared that the "beautiful buildings" of Jefferson's University of Virginia had "introduced architecture as in the pleasing dress which she wore the best days of Greece and Italy." But, unlike Jefferson, antebellum architects preferred Greek to Roman models. Robert Mills, the first native-born professional architect, wrote concerning the Greek Revival: "It was fortunate that this style was so early introduced into our country, both on the ground of economy and of correct taste, and it exactly suited the character of our political institutions, and pecuniary means. Mr. Jefferson was a Roman in his views of architecture. . . . It required all the talents and good taste of such a man as Mr. Latrobe to correct it by introducing a better. The national good taste and the unprejudiced eye of our citizens required only a few examples of the Greek style for public structures, and its simplicity recommended its introduction into our private dwellings." Mills's U.S. Treasury Building possessed slender Ionic columns based on those found in the Erechtheum on the Athenian Acropolis, and his original design for the Washington Monument featured a row of Doric columns in a circular plan around the base of the obelisk. By 1860, tens of thousands of Greek columns lined the piazzas of his native Charleston. The first Doric temple in the city, based on the Hephaesteum in Athens, was the synagogue of the Beth Elohim congregation, constructed in 1839. A character in James Fenimore Cooper's *Home as Found* (1838) notes: "Public sentiment just now runs almost exclusively and popularly in the Grecian school. We build little besides temples for our churches, our banks, our taverns, our courthouses, and our dwellings"—and for our breweries too, he added. Even Abraham Lincoln, who was not much of a classicist, made additions to his house in the Greek Revival style, a style widely considered simple, chaste, dignified, and democratic. Common in the Northwest, these homes were often built by local contractors using manuals published in New England by Asher Benjamin. Sometimes the carving was done in the East and the columns were shipped from Buffalo through the Great Lakes on cargo boats.[65]

Convinced that "the two great truths in the world are the Bible and Greek architecture," Nicholas Biddle was one of the leading advocates of Greek Revival architecture. Having become enamored of Greece while studying at Princeton, Biddle had become one of the first Americans to travel there in 1806. As the director of the Second Bank of the United States, he saw to it that the bank reflected his preference for the Doric style when it was constructed in Philadelphia in 1819. The architect, William Strickland, placed eight columns in the front portico, the same uncommon number as that found in the same part of the Parthenon. Banks throughout the nation followed suit, though cold weather often necessitated the inclusion of a chimney projecting from the flat Greek roof. Biddle also commissioned Thomas U. Walter to add a Greek portico to his own home in 1833–1834, as well as a library to house his collection of classical sculptures and his substantial bookcases topped by Greek pediments. In the 1850s Walter went on to design the current wings and dome of the U.S. Capitol, which he expanded from their previous neoclassical design.[66]

Throughout the nation, from the Canadian border to the Gulf of Mexico, from the Atlantic to the Pacific oceans, state capitols, governors' mansions, courthouses, customs houses, colleges, banks, hotels, private homes, and even churches, synagogues, and jails were constructed in the neoclassical form. Even small villages generally possessed a courthouse fashioned in the Greek Revival style, prominently positioned in the town square as an object of civic pride. States and counties considered it a source of profound embarrassment if they did not possess a classical structure to rival that of their neighbors. Nor was this mere window dressing: popular journals contained numerous articles that offered detailed critical analyses of the architectural details of various neoclassical structures. When Edward Brickell White's Second Baptist Church of Charleston was completed in 1842, a critic writing under the pseudonym "Calvin" complained that the building departed from its model, the Hephaesteum, in that the side doors under the portico were located behind the columns rather than between them—prompting White to answer immediately that the position of the doors had been determined by the building committee, not the architect. As the architectural historian Talbot Hamlin has noted, "It was as though Greek culture and Roman culture had suddenly become symbols of all that was free, refined, thoughtful, and—especially—beautiful in human life."[67]

Even the private homes of middle-class Americans were often adorned with classical objects, such as small statues, busts, and urns, as badges of taste and culture. Tables, mantels, teapots, pitchers, ewers, urns, candelabra, and even stoves were richly ornamented with caryatids, cupids, griffins, scrolls, columns, cornucopias, garlands, satyr masks, lyres, grapevines, and other classical motifs. Ironically, these mass-produced objects were intended, at least in part, to symbolize the repudiation of modern commercial values for classical simplicity, frugality, and virtue. Greek decorative motifs, employed on a large scale for the façades of buildings, were also used on a small scale for windows, cornices, and fireplaces, adhering to a very high standard of craftsmanship. As the historian Richard L. Bushman has written: "The culture of the educated elite in the eighteenth century had become by 1840 the primary stylistic vocabulary of the entire nation."[68]

Despite the mania for buildings in the Greek Revival style, Americans still maintained an enthusiasm for Roman structural forms as well. Numerous triumphal arches were erected to celebrate the Marquis de Lafayette's tour of the United States in 1824–1825. In Philadelphia alone, William Strickland designed thirteen such arches, including one at Independence Hall modeled on the Arch of Severus in the Roman Forum. Forty-five feet high and thirty-five feet wide, the arch was crowned by figures of Justice and Wisdom in classical dress.[69]

Paintings and sculptures with classical themes were as much in demand as neoclassical structures. In 1834 William Dunlap opened his summary of the arts in America with the observations that the human form was the most perfect of all forms and that "the sculptors of ancient Greece alone attained the knowledge of this form in its perfection, and the power to represent it." He added, "We have no standard of beauty but that which is derived from the country of Homer and Phidias." The Boston Athenaeum exhibited Thomas Crawford's elegant bas-relief *Anacreon Ode LXXII*, which depicted the poet seated, playing the lyre beneath a grapevine. The Athenaeum also exhibited various copies of the *Venus de Medici*, the *Capitoline Venus*, the *Capitoline Antinous*, the *Gladiator Borghese*, the *Discobolus*, the *Laocoön*, and other Greek statues, as well as neoclassical sculptures by Antonio Canova, including his exquisite *Venus*. The ancient Venuses, de Medici and de Milo, became central to the corset debates of the 1820s and 1830s. Anticorseting tracts contrasted the Venuses, depicted as natural, healthy, straight-spined women, with modern, sickly, corseted women whose spines had been bent by tight stays. The University of Virginia was proud of its copy of Raphael's *School of Athens*. Neoclassical sculptures by American artists included Horatio Greenough's *Love Captive* (1835) and *Venus Victrix* (1841), Thomas Crawford's *Orpheus* (1839) and *Ganymede with Hebe* (1842), William Wetmore Story's *Arcadian Shepherd Boy* (1853) and *Libyan Sibyl* (1861), Harriet Hosmer's *Daphne* (1854), and Hiram Powers's *Proserpine* (1844), the best-selling bust of the century, reproduced over 100 times.[70]

Edward Everett urged a friend to purchase Henry Barker's and John and Robert Buford's *Panorama of Athens* in London and donate it to Harvard. Lit by a skylight, the painting was designed to be hung on the interior wall of a circular hall. The top and bottom of the canvas were hidden so that the painting appeared frameless, giving viewers the illusion of being surrounded by a real landscape. The *Panorama* represented ancient Athens from the Parthenon and Erechtheum on the left to the Temple of Theseus on the right. An accompanying key provided information on each important site. Viewers would believe themselves to be looking at Athens from a nearby hill. In Everett's words, the *Panorama* was to be "exhibited for the gratification and instruction of the students of the University and the liberal public." Everett advertised the arrival of the painting with a series of lectures on ancient Athens in Boston. Harvard then loaned the giant painting to John Vanderlyn, who showed it in his classically inspired Rotunda in New York City and in a few other cities. Vanderlyn, himself famous for his own widely exhibited paintings of *Ariadne Asleep on the Island of Naxos* (1814) and *Caius Marius and the Ruins of Carthage* (1832), claimed concerning the *Panorama*, "On such a scene no citizen of a free and enlightened Nation ought to look with indifference." Rather, since Athens was the birthplace of democracy, literature, and art, the *Panorama* should elicit "the warmest sensations of gratitude and admiration." The painting enjoyed numerous public exhibits between 1820 and 1845. Though damaged by travel, it was finally put on permanent display at a fire-engine house on the Harvard campus, only to burn in a fire that engulfed the house in 1845. Other widely exhibited paintings, such as Washington Allston's *Italian Landscape* and Joshua Shaw's *Dido and Aeneas Going to the Hunt*, combined primitive landscapes with classical structures or themes.[71]

In one of his most famous works, the series entitled *The Course of Empire* (1836), the painter Thomas Cole not only embodied the classical, cyclical theory of history but portrayed it in a classical style. In *The Arcadian or Pastoral State* nature dominates, but a classical structure occupies the center of the painting, and an old man draws Pythagorean symbols on the ground, demonstrating the existence of some civilization and culture. A shepherd leads his flock, and a lightly garlanded couple dance to the music of a flute player. In the central panel, *The Consummation*, which depicts the zenith of empire in Roman terms, a triumphant general arrives via a port from which Roman monumental architecture has eliminated all natural contours. A gesticulating horde thrills to the blare of trumpets and raises laurel wreaths to the imperial hero. In *Desolation*, the last of the series, a large, solitary Roman pillar stands in the foreground, the ruins of an aqueduct on the left. The scene is devoid of human figures, leaving the viewer to meditate on the cycle of history. The series was inspired by the "melancholy desolation" of the Italian countryside Cole witnessed while sitting on a ruined column at sunset after a long walk. Other American artists painted the Roman Forum and Pompey's tomb.[72]

Even American national heroes were not safe from artistic depiction as latter-day Greeks and Romans. The most famous example of this practice was Horatio Greenough's twelve-ton statue of George Washington in classical dress, which was delivered to the U.S. Capitol in 1841. But the statue, based on Phidias' *Zeus*, was hardly unique. After all, Antonio Canova's statue of Washington depicted him in Roman military garb, and Giuseppe Ceracchi's bust portrayed the Virginian with classical curls. Both John Trumbull and Charles Willson Peale painted Washington as Cincinnatus. John Quincy Adams, Andrew Jackson, Daniel Webster, John C. Calhoun, and many lesser figures were depicted in classical dress as well. Hiram Powers sculpted a statue of Calhoun in Roman garb for the City Council of Charleston. A depiction of Daniel Webster in modern dress came under sharp criticism, as though Webster had been slighted. After all, affluent women often had the honor of being painted and sculpted in classical dress, with a corresponding hairstyle, and some young children the horror of being painted as Cupid. But if Webster missed classical representation on this occasion, he achieved the next best thing: though Chester Harding's painting of Webster, commissioned by the Boston Athenaeum, depicted him in modern clothing in the foreground, in the background stood a statue of Washington in classical drapery—thereby linking Webster with both classical and modern heroes.[73]

Greek art and architecture not only symbolized Greek democracy, as well as classical simplicity, rationality, and elegance, but were considered even more democratic than classical literature because they could be appreciated without specialized linguistic knowledge. After noting that the classical languages were difficult to learn, Edward Everett wrote, "But a beautiful temple, or a column of a temple, or ancient statue, or relievo, is an object on which we can gaze with all the freshness of both sense and emotion, that belonged to the age of its production."[74]

Even in death Americans could not escape classical art. In 1831 Edward Everett participated in the creation of Mount Auburn, the Cambridge, Massachusetts, cemetery based on ancient Athens' Kerameikos. At the new cemetery's dedication Joseph Story remarked: "The Greeks exhausted the resources of their exquisite art in adorning the habitations of the dead. They discouraged interments within the limits of cities and consigned their reliques [relics] to shady groves in the neighborhood of murmuring streams and merry fountains, close by the favorite resorts of those who were engaged in the study of philosophy and nature, and called them, with the eloquent expressiveness of their own beautiful language, cemeteries or 'places of repose.'" Mount Auburn represented the beginning of a rural cemetery movement that moved graves away from urban churchyards and vaults to more natural settings. Grecian urns frequently dotted the gravesites at both urban and rural cemeteries.[75]

Writers of political essays and pamphlets continued to use classical pseudonyms to bolster their causes. One such author signed a pamphlet called *Freedom's Defence,* which attacked southern efforts to suppress abolitionist literature sent by mail, with the venerable name "Cincinnatus." By contrast, a South Carolinian used "Gracchus" as a pseudonym for a pro-nullification pamphlet, and a Virginian used the same name for a series of essays attacking calls for the recolonization of slaves in Africa. Others used "Aristides," "Cimon," "Lycurgus," "Sallust," "Agricola," and "Phocion" as pseudonyms. The women of New Harmony, Indiana, formed the Minerva Club, named after the Roman goddess of wisdom, to promote education. An Irish street gang in New York City dubbed itself "The Spartan Club."[76]

The essays that dominated the numerous new periodicals of the antebellum period not only were filled with classical allusions but frequently made classical history their central focus. One of the most prolific contributors to southern periodicals, George Frederick Holmes, had spent every morning before nine o'clock studying classical works as an attorney, before becoming a classics professor. In the 1840s and 1850s Holmes wrote a series of articles on Greece and Rome for the *Southern Quarterly Review*. In one essay he compared the Native American tribes to those of ancient Italy. Hugh Swinton Legaré wrote similar essays on a wide variety of classical topics. Some magazines even adopted classical names, such as the *Minerva*, the *Portico*, or the *Parthenon*, and numerous magazine covers featured classical icons or depictions. These and other magazines presented extracts from various classics and stories about Greek mythology or ruins. In 1835 Francis Glass even wrote *A Life of George Washington in Latin Prose*. The many rural folk and townsmen who submitted their own poems to newspapers had to be careful not to plagiarize ancient authors, for, even in frontier Alabama, editors and printers recognized the classical poets in disguise.[77]

Others, like William Munford, devoted the precious leisure time of their busy lives to translating Greek and Latin classics into English. A prominent legislator who also served as the official reporter of the decisions of the Virginia Supreme Court of Appeals, Munford spent thirty years translating Homer's *Iliad* into blank verse in his spare time. Munford chose the *Iliad* for translation because of the "unparalleled beauty and solemnity of the original." The translation, which was not published until 1846, twenty-one years after Munford's death, earned the praise of George Frederick Holmes, Charles Felton, and other reviewers, who applauded its simple dignity and lack of affectation. Munford's translation of Hector's farewell to his son Astyanax in the sixth book of the *Iliad* displayed deeper feeling than Alexander Pope's famous translation and greater clarity than William Cowper's.[78]

Innovations in printing rendered English translations of the classics like Munford's cheap and abundant. Beginning in 1817, Harper's, a newly-established press in New York, published thirty-seven translations of various Greek and Roman classics at affordable prices. By the late 1820s the success of this collection made Harper's the largest book printer in the United States. In 1831 the *Workingman's Advocate* endorsed Harper's "Classical Library," exulting, "It will be one means of breaking down the monopoly of knowledge which has so long enabled the few to rule and oppress the many." Meanwhile, in this age before copyright enforcement, backwoods editors continued to reprint standard translations of the classics without permission.[79]

It should be no surprise then that when the distinguished English scholars George Long and Thomas Hewett Key became members of the first faculty at the University of Virginia in 1825, they were amazed at the classical knowledge of local amateurs like Thomas Mann Randolph and Francis Walker Gilmer. A son-in-law of Thomas Jefferson who contributed greatly to the theory and practice of contour plowing, Randolph often devoted an hour or so each day to reading classical authors under a tree. Gilmer wrote *Sketches of American Orators* (1816), in which he analyzed contemporary American speakers using Cicero's criteria. The classics were the province of all educated Americans, not merely of specialized scholars.[80]

The classics not only maintained their dominance over the American educational system throughout the antebellum period but also spread their profound influence beyond previous confines to new regions and economic classes, as well as to women and African Americans. Although other subjects, such as modern languages, modern history, science, and economics, were added to college curricula, Greek and Latin were still regarded as the core of a sound education in grammar schools, academies, and colleges. Perhaps more important, the sights and sounds of even small frontier towns—the names, the buildings, the art, and the speeches—all served to reinforce the popular notion that the United States was the chief heir to the ideals of Greece and Rome, a classical republic reborn.

CHAPTER TWO

Democracy

IN THE SAME YEARS that a plethora of new grammar schools, academies, and colleges were introducing the classics to the western frontier, to a rising middle class, to girls and women, and to African Americans, states were expanding the voting population to include all free adult males. While the spread of manhood suffrage led to a more democratic style of politics, the expansion of classical education ensured that the orations that resounded in the courtrooms and legislative halls of the United States, as well as numerous newspaper essays and private letters, continued to bristle with classical allusions. Although some of the stump speeches that became essential to election lacked such references, most political leaders took advantage of every opportunity to showcase their classical learning, not only to their peers but also to any broader audience they had reason to hope might respect, if not fully comprehend, these allusions. Classically trained in the schools, most American political leaders lived a double rhetorical life, attempting by studied plainness to assure common voters of their ability to empathize with their concerns while simultaneously attempting through classical allusions to convince one another, and even some of their less educated constituents, of their wisdom and virtue. Fifth-century B.C. Athens, the first major democracy in history, provided a crucial bridge: American statesmen learned that they could make classical references before even the least educated audiences without seeming aristocratic, if those allusions concerned the glories of Athenian democracy.

Classical Oratory in a Democratic Age

Daniel Webster loved the classics and peppered his addresses to august bodies, like Congress and the Supreme Court, with classical references, but exhibited an occasional reticence about using them in speeches geared to less educated audiences. In arguing a famous case for Dartmouth College before the Supreme Court, Webster closed with a melodramatic, Ciceronian flourish: "Sir, I know not how others may feel (glancing at the opponents of the College before him), but, for myself, when I see my alma mater surrounded, like Caesar in the senate house, by those who are reiterating stab after stab, I would not, for this right hand, have her turn to me, and say, 'Et tu quoque mi fili!' 'And thou too, my son!' " (Webster was not deterred by the irony involved in wrapping the words of Julius Caesar in a Ciceronian cloak, nor by the irony of the fact, later noted in his autobiography, that Dartmouth had given him only "a very scanty" classical training that he himself had been forced to augment.) In 1845, according to Ralph Waldo Emerson, Webster was a major contributor to the situation that prevailed at Edward Everett's inauguration as president of Harvard: "Latin allusions flew all day." In 1851, the year before his death, while watching his beloved Union beginning to crumble before his eyes, Webster closed his last Fourth of July speech with a Latin line that meant: "I wish these things: one, that in dying I may leave a free people; nothing greater than this can be given me by the immortal gods; the second, that each man may prove worthy of the republic." The following year Webster declared in his final speech: "Classical history is the epic of real life. It places the actions of men in an attractive and interesting light. Rejecting what is improper and superfluous, it fills its picture with real, just, and well drawn images.... Classical history is not a memoir. It is not a crude collection of acts, occurrences, and dates. It adopts nothing that is not true; but it does not embrace all minor truths and all minor transactions. It is a composition, a production, which has unity of design, like a work of statuary or of painting, and keeps constantly in view one great end or result." Yet Webster had avoided using Latin phrases in his appeals to juries and, in 1841, had persuaded William Henry Harrison, an avid reader of Cicero and of Charles Rollin's *Ancient History*, to delete obscure classical references from his inaugural address. Webster joked that he had killed "seventeen Roman pro-consuls as dead as smelts." Delivered in the freezing rain, the address was still too long, contributing to Harrison's death a month later.[1]

It is true that, in the western states particularly, the "Age of Egalitarianism" opened political offices to a number of men like Abraham Lincoln, Sam Houston, and Andrew Jackson who possessed little formal education.

The son of nearly illiterate parents, Lincoln was raised in a rugged frontier environment in which study was regarded as laziness, an environment that, in Lincoln's own words, possessed "nothing to excite ambition for education." The backwoods schools Lincoln attended sporadically were conducted by teachers with meager qualifications. Lincoln joked, "If a straggler supposed to understand latin happened to sojourn in the neighborhood, he was looked upon as a wizard." Though an avid reader who struggled tenaciously with words, passages, and ideas he did not understand, young Lincoln did not have access to a wide variety of books. His reading consisted of the Bible, *Aesop's Fables* (his sole classical reading as a child), *The Pilgrim's Progress, Robinson Crusoe,* and a few writings of Benjamin Franklin and George Washington. As a busy attorney, he read little more than newspapers and law books, the tools of his trade. Lincoln's law partner, William Herndon, remarked that Lincoln "read less and thought more than any man in his sphere in America."[2]

But the lack of a classical education did not necessarily make a man an enemy of the classics or prevent him from acquiring classical knowledge indirectly, through English translations or contemporary speeches and essays. Lincoln was proud of his command of Euclid's *Elements*, a level of mastery that awed Herndon and others. Herndon recalled that Lincoln often studied Euclid by candlelight until two in the morning, while the other attorneys riding circuit with him snored loudly. Lincoln frequently spoke of "the theorems and axioms of democracy," comparing them with Euclid's propositions.[3]

More important, as Garry Wills has demonstrated, the similarities between Lincoln's Gettysburg Address (1863) and Pericles' Funeral Oration (429 B.C.) are so striking as to suggest at least some indirect influence on the part of the latter, especially since Pericles' famous speech, as recounted by Thucydides, was widely copied, praised, and cited in antebellum America. Just as the purpose of Pericles' oration had been to honor the Athenian dead of the Peloponnesian War, so Lincoln's intent was to memorialize the Union war dead. Yet both statesmen emphasized that the dead had won such honor through their own heroic sacrifice that mere words could hardly gain them any additional glory. Both stressed that the only way for the survivors to venerate the dead was to finish their crucial work of saving the democratic experiment from its enemies. Both appealed to revered ancestors—in Pericles' case the heroes of the Persian Wars, in Lincoln's the patriots of the Revolutionary War—thereby yoking the past to the present. Both employed such dichotomies as word versus deed, mortality versus immortality, the past versus the present, and democracy versus tyranny. Both speeches were extraordinarily concise, devoted to general principles rather than to particulars. Lincoln followed Edward Everett's two-hour oration, a speech filled with references to Periclean Athens, with a two-minute speech stripped of all such allusions, yet following Pericles' line of argument closely. In short, while Everett referred to Pericles, Lincoln embodied him. Nor was Roman influence completely absent from Lincoln's speech. He borrowed the phrase "a new birth of freedom" from the historian Livy, who had coined it in reference to the Roman law that ended enslavement for debt (*History of Rome* 8.28).[4]

Another westerner who lacked formal training in the classics, Sam Houston, the Tennessee legislator and Texas governor, memorized all 500 pages of Alexander Pope's translation of the *Iliad* as a sixteen-year-old in 1809. When Houston demanded that his teacher at a local academy in eastern Tennessee teach the ancient languages and the teacher refused, Houston declared that he would never recite another lesson again and stormed out of the school. When Houston's brothers then found him living with the Cherokees, he told them that he "liked the wild liberty of Red men better than the tyranny of his own brothers, and if he could not study Latin in the Academy he could, at least, read a translation from the Greek in the woods, and read it in peace." The translation to which he referred was Pope's *Iliad*, which he recited to Cherokee girls from memory on long walks in order to impress them. Houston's biographer M. K. Wisehart attributes his flamboyance, heroic self-image, and oratorical and literary style to Pope's *Iliad*. While visiting Nashville in 1831, Houston commissioned a painting of himself as the Roman consul Marius. In a speech before Congress regarding the Compromise of 1850 Houston likened Henry Clay to Ajax in the thick of battle. On another occasion he compared his fallen comrades at the Alamo to the Spartans who died at Thermopylae.[5]

Even Andrew Jackson, who was once praised for his lack of classical learning, could still show his respect for the classics in symbolic ways. Andrew Stevenson of Virginia suggested that Jackson had benefited from his ignorance of Greek and Latin, writing: "Regular and classical education has been thought by some distinguished men to be unfavorable to great vigour and originality of the understanding; and that, like civilization, whilst it made society more interesting and agreeable, yet, at the same time, it levelled the distinctions of nature." Yet as president, Jackson appointed the famous neoclassical architect Robert Mills as the official architect of his administration. In fact, when Jackson's own estate, the Hermitage, burned in 1835, Jackson appears to have sought Mills's advice in reconstructing it. The capitals of the new Corinthian columns that fronted the house were modeled on those of the Temple of the Winds in Athens. Jackson probably also sought Mills's advice concerning his domed tomb. (Mills, like Nicholas

Biddle's favorite architect, William Strickland, had been a student of Benjamin Latrobe. Ardent foes in the political and economic arenas, Jackson and Biddle shared the same architectural preferences.) Jackson also selected an expensive wallpaper designed by the Frenchman Joseph Dufour, a panoramic series of panels that included Minerva tossing Telemachus off the cliffs of the island of Calypso in order to break the spell of the nymph Eucharis, a story told by François de Salignac de La Mothe-Fénelon in *Les Aventures de Télémaque* (1699). Imitating Jackson in architecture as in other matters, Jackson's political ally and fellow Tennesseans James K. Polk, who liked to converse with a former classmate in Greek, also built a home in the Greek Revival style in the early 1840s. On the grounds sat a Doric tomb, built to house Polk's remains soon after his death in 1849. As the historian Wendy Cooper has noted, "Just as Americans aped Europeans, so the fashions of the wealthy on this side of the Atlantic were copied by others aspiring to similar heights of refinement and fashion." This was true even of those who presented themselves as champions of the masses.[6]

It is true that some of the poorly educated new voters considered the classics useless vestiges of aristocracy and that politicians sometimes sought to capitalize on their anti-intellectualism by denigrating the classical languages. In 1859 Senator John Hale of New Hampshire reflected the anticlassicism of some uneducated Americans when he remarked: "Whenever I hear a judge in court give an opinion in Latin, I generally conclude that he is about to announce some infernal doctrine that he is ashamed to speak in English."[7]

But most politicians acted differently when speaking to one another and, increasingly, when addressing any audience they thought might be even mildly learned or respectful of learning. In fact, when speaking to one another, they sometimes carried their classicism to absurd lengths. In 1841 John G. Palfrey complained that Virginia legislators were likely to flaunt their classical erudition "even on a question of renewing the upholstery of the Representatives' Chamber, or paying the Sergeant-at-Arms." When John Quincy Adams sneered at John Randolph's numerous quotations of Latin poets in Congress, calling them mere "scraps of Latin from the Dictionary of Quotations," the genuinely learned Randolph retorted that he had never met "a Yankee who knew anything about the classics." Both men understood the importance of maintaining their respective reputations for classical knowledge. Yet they at least avoided the extreme sensitivity of Judge John Rowan, who killed Dr. James Chambers in a duel over which man possessed the more thorough knowledge of Greek and Latin. Rowan went on to serve in the House of Representatives and the U.S. Senate, where he was presumably safe from any imputations against his classical prowess.[8]

The Rehabilitation of Athenian Democracy

Antebellum politicians learned quickly that one way to appear erudite without seeming aristocratic was to praise Athenian democracy. Whereas the founders had regarded the Roman republic as the greatest political model of antiquity and had feared the instability of democratic Athens, the antebellum generation embraced Athenian democracy.

This phenomenon was not confined to the United States. In response to the standard histories that had criticized Athens, the British historian Thomas Macaulay retorted that "freedom produced excellence" there. He claimed, "We suspect that the average Athenian citizen was, in political intelligence, above the average English Member of Parliament." Macaulay rebuked some historians for neglecting literature and the arts so completely in favor of war and politics as to slight what democracy had accomplished in Athens. He added, "Wherever literature consoles sorrow or assuages pain, wherever it brings gladness to eyes which fail with wakefulness and tears, and ache for the dark house and the long sleep, there is exhibited, in its noblest form, the immortal influence of Athens." Responding to the desire of Macaulay and others for historical revision, George Grote published his twelve-volume *History of Greece*, a work profoundly influenced by German Hellenism, in 1846–1856. Grote contended, "It is to democracy alone . . . that we owe that unparalleled brilliancy and diversity of individual talent which constitutes the charm and glory of Grecian history." Grote attributed Athens' failures not to democracy but to mental habits, such as religious superstition, that predated the establishment of democracy there. John Stuart Mill, an associate with Grote in the effort to expand the franchise in Britain, argued that the Battle of Marathon was more important to the world, and even more important to Britain itself, than the Battle of Hastings. Mill believed that Athens was "far nobler as well as greater and wiser" than Sparta, Rome's partner in the pantheon of those who preferred mixed government to pure democracy.[9]

The connection between the love of Athens and the love of democracy was clear in all countries. George Bancroft, who translated Arnold H. Heeren's pro-Athenian *Ancient Greece* from the original German into English, became a leading Jacksonian Democrat. He contrasted the sycophantic Roman literature of the Augustan age with the more manly and democratic writing of Athens. Bancroft wrote: "In Roman literature we have sometimes cause to be disgusted with servile adulation. We could wish that Horace had not employed his genius in celebrating the victories of Augustus, and should cherish Virgil the more if something of the rustic republicanism of the elder days were discoverable in his verse." By contrast, it could be said of the Greeks, and especially of the Athenians, that "though they sometimes flattered kings, [they] never eulogised the regal form of government." Walter Savage Landor dedicated the second volume of his *Pericles and Aspasia* (1836) to President Jackson. The *Methodist Quarterly Review* claimed that the Periclean age in Athens showed how "the power of the democracy . . . created and sustained the widely-diffused and magnificent public spirit . . . of every imaginative and cultivated Athenian." Thomas Dew, president of the College of William and Mary, wrote, "Such a government produces exuberance of energy, genius, and real greatness." Dew contended that the "short but crowded and energetic life" of Athenian democracy was preferable to the "age of noiseless slavery" that constituted the history of Asian monarchies. Dew added: "Athens was the instructress of Greece, and every citizen seemed capable of dedicating his faculties to the most multifarious objects with dexterity and grace. . . . Foreigners were more mildly treated there than elsewhere. Slaves were better treated there than in any other city of Greece, and there was less cruelty in the execution of her laws and her repentance of her misdeeds was often candid and cordial." Ralph Waldo Emerson thought that he saw in the American masses "the same energy [as] in [the] Greek Demos." Of Greek history he wrote, "The valuable part is the age of Pericles and the next generation"—in other words, the democratic age. He added, "The sincere Greek history of the period must be drawn from Demosthenes, especially from the business orations, and from the comic poets," not from aristocratic historians, past and present.[10]

Many Americans, following in the path of Thomas Jefferson, began to consider the speeches of the Athenian Demosthenes against the Macedonian king Philip II superior as rhetorical models to those of Cicero because their directness and concision better suited a democratic age. As J. C. Gray wrote concerning Demosthenes' rhetoric, "We perceive in it nothing vague or extravagant, nothing florid or redundant." Though faulting Demosthenes for his lack of imagination and humor, John Quincy Adams declared: "His eloquence is characteristic of democracy, as that of Cicero is of aristocracy. It is the Doric to the Corinthian pillar." Thomas Dew agreed, adding that while Cicero's flashiness might have won more applause from his audiences, Demosthenes' simplicity was more persuasive: "When Cicero spoke, the man was admired, the oration was praised. When Demosthenes had spoken, the crowd went away denouncing Philip." Dew added, "The history of ancient republics has most conclusively proven that no audience is so favorable to the production of close, concise, and powerful oratory as the popular assembly." Following the profusion of stump speeches delivered throughout the United States as part of the presidential campaign of 1840, the *Southern*

Literary Messenger declared: "Our country seems fast approaching to that peculiar state which called forth the unrivalled efforts of Grecian oratory. We seem destined to enact Greece, if I may so say, on a gigantic scale.... All history has shown that genuine eloquence can only flourish under institutions of republican character. Under arbitrary governments ... persuasion is of no avail.... The oratorical campaign of 1840 has, in truth, furnished the true key to the secret of Grecian eloquence; henceforth, the American student will find no difficulty in understanding the real character of Demosthenes." The author included the usual statement of preference for Demosthenes over Cicero, noting concerning the former's speeches: "They are always to the point; there are no digressions—no common-places—nothing for mere ornament ... whereas Cicero often amplifies and deals in philosophical reflections, some of which are mere common-places."[11]

Others, like Edward Everett, used Ciceronian rhetoric to glorify Periclean Athens. At his speech at Gettysburg, Everett connected Athens to American democracy in one of the longest sentences in human history:

> Shall I, fellow citizens, who, after an interval of twenty-three centuries, a youthful pilgrim from the world unknown to ancient Greece, have wandered over that illustrious plain, ready to put off shoes from my feet, as one that stands on holy ground—who have gazed with respectful emotion on the mound which still protects the dust of those who rolled back the tide of Persian invasion, and rescued the land of popular liberty, of letters, and of arts, from the ruthless foe—stand unmoved over the graves of dear brethren who so lately, on three of the all-important days which decide a nation's history—days on whose issue it depended whether this august republican Union, founded by some of the wisest statesmen that ever lived, cemented with the blood of some of the purest patriots that ever died, should perish or endure—rolled back the tide of invasion, not less unprovoked, not less ruthless, than that which came to plant the dark banner of Asiatic despotism and slavery on the free soil of Greece? Heaven forbid!

Everett concluded his speech: "'The whole earth,' said Pericles as he stood over the remains of his fellow citizens, who had fallen in the first year of the Peloponnesian War, 'the whole earth is the sepulchre of illustrious men.' All time, he might have added, is the millennium of their glory.... Wheresoever throughout the civilized world the accounts of this great warfare are read, and down to the latest period of recorded time, in the glorious annals of our common country, there will be no brighter page than that which relates to The Battles of Gettysburg."[12]

Such speeches, whether of the simple Demosthenian or of the more ornate Ciceronian variety, were highly valued. As the historian Daniel Walker Howe has written: "By stressing the arts of rhetoric, classical studies helped direct political argumentation toward the declamatory style of Webster and Calhoun. The political speeches of the time, like the lyceum lectures, sermons, ceremonial discourses, and lawyers' arguments, constituted a popular body of oral literature. Paradoxically, the written culture of the classics underwrote and legitimated this oral culture." Perhaps this was because classical culture had been an oral one too; since written manuscripts were rare and expensive in antiquity, nearly all classical authors intended their works to be read aloud and, therefore, focused considerable attention on perfecting their aural qualities.[13]

Most southern supporters of state rights praised Greece not only for its democracy but also for its decentralized government. In opposing Andrew Jackson's threat of force against South Carolina during the Nullification Crisis of 1832–1833, John C. Calhoun noted that each member of the Achaean League, a famous confederacy of Greek democracies in the Peloponnesus, had possessed its own assembly, magistrates, and judges and had united only for a few common purposes, like national defense. He suggested that the United States should hold to such a model. During the 1850 discussions concerning secession, William Boyce made the same recommendation, offering as "an illustrious and suggestive precedent" the Achaean League, "the union of the *southern* states of Greece . . . caused by the pressure of the Macedonian power" (emphasis in original). Thomas Dew wrote, "In casting a glance over the nations of antiquity, our attention is arrested by none so forcibly as by the little Democracies of Greece." After noting the achievements of Greece in warding off "the countless hosts of Persia" and in perfecting philosophy, art, rhetoric, and historical writing, Dew asked, "What then . . . could have generated so much greatness of mind, so much energy and loftiness of character in this apparently secluded corner of Europe, scarcely visible on the world map?" He answered: "It was this system of small independent state governments which so completely identified each citizen of Greece with that little body politic with which his destiny was connected—which breathed into his soul that ardent patriotism which can sacrifice self upon the altar of our country's happiness. . . . These little democratic cauldrons were always boiling, and true genius and energy of soul were sure, sooner or later, to rise to the top." While it was true that the Greek democracies had fallen because of their inability to unite into a stronger federation, there was an equal danger in too great a centralization of power, and even the Greek failure was far nobler than any success acquired at the cost of liberty. From the aftermath of the Macedonian conquest of Greece, Dew hoped that the student of its history "will learn above all things to dread the evil of consolidation, which extinguishes individual energy and greatness of soul, by grinding down all to the same ignominious level." Dew concluded, "Should the evil hour ever arrive (which may Heaven avert!) when this great union shall be sundered, and our confederation separated into its original elements, the history of Greece will shed a twilight over the dark scene—inspire some consolation amid the general gloom; by showing that, bad as is the system of small, divided, and hostile states, it yet produces a compensating energy which generates more of what constitutes the true glory of man than can ever be found in the greatest empires of the world." Similarly, Senator Robert M. T. Hunter of Virginia wrote, "It was the competition among the free States of ancient Greece which gave even to that ill-fated confederacy its surpassing excellency in arts of literature."[14]

Even Charles Francis Adams, who remained as skeptical as his grandfather concerning the wisdom and prospects of democracy, changed his opinion of Athens under the onslaught of pro-Athenian rhetoric. In 1824 Charles Francis not only read and admired William Mitford's aristocratic history of Greece (1784–1810) but pronounced it fair "to all parties." While conceding that, in the democratic age of Pericles, "Athens was in its greatest glory, the most powerful, the richest, the most elegant and literate commonwealth of Greece, which was the first in arts in the world," Adams ascribed this success not to democracy, but to Themistocles' wise encouragement of maritime commerce, a policy similar to that of the English in modern times. Adams wrote, "The Athenians, hitherto unknown, by embracing this course, became powerful and rich and by these means gave that encouragement to literature and elegance which has continued them to this day." Democracy had actually been an impediment to Athenian greatness. Adams concluded concerning Athens: "The people of this city were unfortunate, but the nature of their government must have prevented their success, for the people had become unmanageable. It is a question not yet decided whether a people are able to govern themselves, and it is exceedingly doubtful whether even our experiment will succeed." Thus wrote Lincoln's future minister to Britain in words remarkably like those of the Gettysburg Address, but with a far more pessimistic turn. Under the influence of Mitford, Adams admired the Spartan system of government more than the Athenian, which had at times been nothing more than the "unbridled licentiousness of a mob" that was "made a tool by the designing even against their greatest benefactors." Although Adams disliked the Spartans' neglect of knowledge, he concluded that Sparta had possessed a "government which never has since and probably never will again see its equal." Adams considered Mitford's largely favorable account of oligarchic Sparta "an astonishing record of the most persevering and successful victories over the weaknesses and passions of nature."[15]

Just five years later, Adams's opinion of Mitford and Sparta had been transformed and his opinion of Athenian democracy had improved, though he was still plagued by doubts about the viability of democracy. In 1829 Adams wrote that, upon reexamining Mitford's history, he had been "infinitely provoked with his impudent perversion of History." He added: "I think his Book ought to be thrown into the Fire. How much mischief History philosophically written, to use a fashionable word of the present day, by a prejudiced man, will occasion." The following year Adams recorded in his journal: "Read Mitford and felt as usual. It is a sin for a man to sit down to write a history if he feels in his bosom one iota of inclination to a prejudice against particular systems, for if he does, his work will surely taste of it." He called Mitford's antidemocratic and anti-Athenian conclusions "the most prejudiced and unfair statements I ever read in History." Adams was equally provoked by the British translator Thomas Mitchell's statement about the demagogue Agoracritus in Aristophanes' *Knights*: "The picture itself is such as a republic only could furnish, and something like a parallel to it might, I believe, be still found in the free states of America." Adams replied in his diary, "The Comments upon republican usages are altogether unjust . . . [and Mitchell is] manifestly ignorant to a great degree of our Institutions." Regarding Sparta, Adams now wrote:

> The Republic of Lycurgus is always cited as an authority for the most hypothetical projects, and, moreover, as an example. Now to me nothing appears more unnatural and more undesirable than those very Institutions. Was Man made to fight his Neighbours, or to employ Slaves to keep him in suitable idleness for the purpose? Where is the so much vaunted equality of man? Where is the Law of the Creator that he shall live by the sweat of his brow? Where are all the qualities that adorn and sweeten life? The gentle affections, the social bonds formed by nature, and only severed by the caprices and art of Man? Let us hear no more of the Republic of Lycurgus as an example. An abominable perversion of all natural principles.

Adams's conversion was all the more remarkable in light of the fact that he still possessed doubts about democracy. Regarding the Peloponnesian War, he wrote: "It was a contest between two principles of government, neither of which are capable of well ordering mankind. It would seem, however, as if the world was on a larger scale destined to exhibit the same scenes. May they not close as before in a military despotism."[16]

This is not to deny that Americans continued to admire certain Spartan traits, such as courage, frugality, self-discipline, and patriotism. It is probable that the defenders of the Alamo remembered Thermopylae, the battle in which 300 Spartan volunteers under King Leonidas laid down their lives to cover the retreat of the Greek army against a massive Persian force.

Certainly, many Americans connected the Alamo with Thermopylae. A mere twenty days after the garrison at the Alamo was overwhelmed, the citizens of Nacogdoches, Texas, issued a resolution praising the defenders. The resolution declared: "They died martyrs to liberty; and on the altar of their sacrifice will be made many a vow that shall break the shackles of tyranny. Thermopylae is no longer without a parallel, and when time shall consecrate the dead of the Alamo, [Colonel William] Travis and his companions will be named in rivalry with Leonidas and his Spartan band."[17]

While the Greek struggle for independence against the Ottoman Empire in the 1820s reinforced antebellum Hellenism by providing an ideal opportunity for speeches on the glories of ancient Greece, antebellum Hellenism, in turn, influenced American sentiment regarding the independence struggle. Even in the very Monroe Doctrine Speech (1823) in which President James Monroe pledged that the United States would stay out of European affairs, the president expressed sympathy for Greece. Daniel Webster delivered one of his earliest congressional speeches on behalf of a resolution to provide funds for a federal commissioner to Greece. Webster obtained the information for his speech from a series of articles in the *North American Review* by his friend Edward Everett. In the speech Webster shrewdly declared that political discussion of modern Greece must avoid sentimentality about ancient Greece—just before violating his own dictum and brandishing his trademark sentimentality. Of his sentiments Webster declared:

> I shall endeavor properly to repress them, although it is impossible that they should be altogether extinguished. We must, indeed, fly beyond the civilized world; we must pass the dominion of law and the boundaries of knowledge; we must, more especially, withdraw ourselves from this place, and the scenes and objects which here surround us—if we would separate ourselves entirely from the influence of those memorials of herself which ancient Greece has transmitted for the admiration and the benefit of mankind. This free form of government, this popular assembly, the common council held for the common good—where have we contemplated its earliest models? This practice of free debate and public discussion, the contest of mind with mind, and that popular eloquence which, if it were now here, on a subject like this, would move the stones of the Capitol—whose was the language in which all these were first exhibited? Even the edifice itself in which we assemble, these proportioned columns, this ornamented architecture, all remind us that Greece has existed and that we, like the rest of mankind, are greatly her debtors.

Privately, Webster complained to Everett about the Monroe Doctrine's complete identification of the United States with the Western Hemisphere. The proud owner of a statue of Demosthenes, Webster declared, "We have as much Community with the Greeks as with the inhabitants of the Andes."

Webster added that John C. Calhoun "desires me to say that he is as friendly to the Greeks as yourself." Sam Houston spoke in support of Webster's resolution; Henry Clay not only supported it but, in the words of Charles Francis Adams, who was seated in the House gallery, issued "a sweeping challenge of the whole House, daring them to go back to their constituents and to show a vote on this question against the resolution."[18]

Recognizing the strong passion of Americans in support of Greek independence based on the love of ancient Greece, Secretary of State John Quincy Adams wrote to a Greek agent in London wishing the Greek rebels success and published the correspondence, even as he quietly opposed Webster's bill and attempted to negotiate a commercial treaty with the Ottomans. Hoping to secure the presidency that year (1824), Adams walked a tightrope between respect for the American public's passion for the Greeks and his commitment to the principles of the Monroe Doctrine, a doctrine he had played a key role in formulating.[19]

This balancing act was all the more difficult for Adams since he shared fully the American passion for ancient Greek democracy. In 1811 he had written in his diary:

> The Athenians were not altogether blameless in their proceedings towards Philip [of Macedon]. But their faults were all of petty extent, and in the nature of defence. Philip's wrong was enormous; it was the design of subjugating to himself all Greece. He winds his web around them like a spider round a fly. When I read those noble sentiments of Demosthenes in which he compares the fortune of Athenians with that of Philip and prefers it upon the principle that truth and justice must be favored by Heaven; when he contends that success and prosperity founded on fraud and treachery must be short-lived, I cannot avoid a feeling of sorrow that these maxims were not sanctioned by the event—that the triumph of fraud and treachery was complete, and that liberty sunk under the genius and industry of the tyrant.

But after attending a cabinet meeting in which "Calhoun descanted upon his great enthusiasm for the cause of the Greeks," the secretary of state concluded regarding such advocates: "Their enthusiasm for the Greeks is all sentiment, and the standard of this is the prevailing popular feeling. . . . I have not much esteem for the enthusiasm which evaporates in words; and I told the President I thought not quite so lightly of a war with Turkey." Adams reasoned that since the United States could do nothing practical for Greece, to offer mere words of encouragement would be to antagonize the Turks without benefiting the Greeks. Nevertheless, as president, Adams concluded "that the prejudice in favor of the Greeks in this country is so warm that even the attempt to negotiate with the Turks would meet with censure."[20]

The Continuing Appeal of Rome

Even as Greece advanced in the esteem of most Americans, Rome never lost its luster. On the contrary, men like George Frederick Holmes emphasized that the Roman reverence for law constituted a crucial check on the Greek love of liberty. As much as Hugh Swinton Legaré loved Greek literature and art, he found it incredible that it originated in "the wildest democracy that ever existed—a tumultuary and excitable mob, wayward, fitful and refractory, alternately slave and tyrant—now a passive instrument of the demagogue, then 'like a dev'lish engine back recoiling upon the rash hand that aspired to direct it.'" Conversely, the history of the Roman republic was "one bright record of virtues and achievements almost too heroic for the infirmities of human nature." When advocating public education, Charles Fenton Mercer cited Cincinnatus as an example of the principle that poverty need not breed vice. After all, George Washington, "the American Cincinnatus" with "a Roman face," had, like the original Cincinnatus, engaged in hard labor. The poor could learn as well as the rich, since everyone learned from someone else: "Egypt and Asia instructed Greece; Greece taught her Roman masters; Rome and Greece all modern Europe." In a speech to the Phi Beta Kappa Society at Harvard, Edward Everett alluded to the powerful emotions engendered by his recent visit to the Roman Forum: "As I have wandered over the spots, once the scene of their labors, and mused among the prostrate columns of their Senate Houses and Forums, I have seemed almost to hear a voice . . . from the sepulchre of the nations. . . . They exhort us, they adjure us, to be faithful to our trust. . . . By the wrecks of time, by the eloquent ruins of nations, they conjure us not to quench the light which is rising in the world."[21]

Naturally, the Romans were admired for their military prowess, as well as for their republican government. While serving as the United States' first minister to Russia in 1812, John Quincy Adams wrote to his mother from St. Petersburg, ascribing both the Russian victory over Napoleon that year and the American victory in the Revolutionary War to guerilla tactics that had originated with the Roman general Fabius, tactics that had depleted Hannibal's force. The same year William Henry Harrison, already the hero of Tippecanoe, offered to place his troops under the command of Governor Isaac Shelby of Kentucky, noting, "Scipio, the conqueror of Carthage, did not disdain to act as a Lieutenant of his younger and less experienced brother Lucius." Both during and after the War of 1812, Harrison urged conscription based on Greek and Roman models. In 1813 he delivered this toast: "The Militia of the United States. They possess the Roman spirit and when our Government shall think proper to give them that organization and discipline of which they are susceptible, they will perform deeds that will emulate those of legions led by Marcellus and Scipio." As a congressman in 1817, he proposed universal military training, claiming that the same ancient republics whose example had proved useful in founding the nation's political institutions could also furnish "a most perfect model for our system of national defense." He added: "The whole secret of ancient military glory—the foundation of that wonderful combination of military skill and exalted valor which enabled the Republic of Athens to resist the mighty torrent of Persian invasion, which formed the walls of Sparta, and conducted the Roman legions . . . to the conquest of the world will be found in the military education of youth." In 1836 he relished the toast given him in Brookville, Indiana: "General Harrison—Like Cato, his countrymen are about to call him from the usual pursuits which have occupied his attention in latter years to preside as Chief Magistrate." That prophecy was premature, but only by four years.[22]

The admirers of John C. Calhoun praised him by comparing him to various Roman heroes. The *Charleston Mercury* called him "as pure a patriot as ever bore a Grecian or Roman name." Stephen H. Branch compared him to Cicero and Demosthenes. In 1844 James Henry Hammond compared Calhoun to Cato and Cicero, "whose glory it was that they wished to have saved their country, and only failed to do so because their country rejected their services." P. J. Sullivan compared the South Carolinian to Cincinnatus "for patriotism, morality, and unrivaled talents." Fitzwilliam Byrdsall compared him to Horatius: "Like the beautiful allegory of the Roman patriot who plunged into the gulph to save his Country, You alone—sacrificing personal considerations of popularity—cast yourself into the midst of the engulfing tumult of the 'whole of Oregon or none,' until others, encouraged by your example, followed, and at length peace, the real and proper policy of our government, is reestablished." In *Carolina Tribute to Calhoun*, a collection of eulogies published in 1857, Hammond wrote, "The fame of Mr. Calhoun will rest chiefly on his character as a Statesman"—a character "of the Roman stamp." Even Calhoun's rival Daniel Webster considered him like "a Senator of Rome, while Rome survived," a phrase borrowed from Joseph Addison's *Cato*. Webster also called Calhoun "Scipio Africanus South Caroliniensis." Senator Lewis Cass of Michigan referred to him as "Ultimus Romanorum—the last of the Romans."[23]

Like the founders, antebellum Americans invoked Carthage, Rome's nemesis, far less frequently than Greece or Rome. However, one famous instance occurred in 1850 when the normally moderate Senator Robert Toombs of Georgia, the future Confederate secretary of state, became agitated over northern talk of excluding slavery from the new territories acquired in the Mexican War. Toombs declared on the Senate floor: "Deprive us of this right and appropriate the common property to yourselves, it is then your government, not mine. Then I am its enemy, and I will then, if I can, bring my children and my constituents to the altar of liberty, and like Hamilcar, I would swear them to eternal hostility to your foul domination." This was a reference to the Greek historian Polybius' account (*Histories* 3.11) of the occasion when Hamilcar Barca, Carthage's greatest general in the First Punic War, made his nine-year-old son Hannibal swear on an altar to Baal that he would oppose Rome his whole life. Hannibal, Carthage's greatest general of the Second Punic War, was true to his vow.[24]

The Role of Women in a Democratic Society

Most American democrats no more envisioned political equality for women than had Athenian democrats or Roman republicans. Like the founders, most antebellum Americans considered Cornelia, the mother of Tiberius and Gaius Gracchus, the model of republican motherhood because of her virtue and her single-minded devotion to her children. Cornelia, the widowed daughter of the great general Scipio Africanus, had even rejected the marriage proposals of kings so that she might focus her energy completely on raising virtuous sons. According to Plutarch, when a frivolous lady asked to see Cornelia's jewels, she presented her sons. So Senator Robert Y. Hayne of South Carolina once declared, "Virginia, like the mother of the Gracchi, when asked for her jewels, points to her sons." In 1819 *Ladies' Magazine,* published in Savannah, declared that the story of Cornelia and her jewels was an object lesson for women "in a Republic like this," teaching frugality as well as motherhood. It was necessary for *Ladies' Magazine* to highlight the tale's lesson in frugality since images of the story, often emblazoned on silk embroideries and other luxury items, had ironically become a popular commercial vehicle. In his address at the opening of the Female High and Normal School in Charleston in 1859, C. G. Memminger contended: "It is, therefore, obvious that the real destinies of the child are chiefly in the hands of the mother, and that its future usefulness and virtue are, under God, mainly dependent upon her training. The history of the world has demonstrated this great truth. From the record of Cornelia, the mother of the Gracchi, down to the mother of our own Washington, the evidence is uniform and convincing." A writer for the *New York Herald* claimed concerning John C. Calhoun's wife Floride: "She governs her household in a style that no Roman matron, in the old times, ever surpassed. Cornelia, the daughter at home, is a most affectionate companion for the mother." Through his sly reference to Cornelia, Floride's daughter, the author suggested to the reader that there were two Cornelias in the Calhoun household, one who modeled herself upon the Roman matron and another who was named after her.²⁵

Louisa McCord, the South's foremost proponent of the doctrine that women were inherently suited to the domestic life, wrote a play called *Caius Gracchus* (1851) based on Plutarch's biographies of Tiberius and Gaius Gracchus that was as much about Cornelia and republican motherhood as about Gaius. In McCord's play, which she dedicated to her son, Cornelia is the orator of the home, Gaius of the Forum. Cornelia speaks in accord with McCord's essays concerning the natural role of women in society, and her pleas to her son recall the exhortations to restraint and reason in McCord's essay on political and economy theory. Cornelia advises her son:

> Be cool! Be cool! and heed that you do not,
> In blaming one extreme, to the other rush.

To her daughter-in-law Licinia, Cornelia declares:

> Nay, stay within doors, daughter; 'tis the place
> Most meet and fitting woman. . . .
> A quiet comeliness there is, becomes
> A woman's greeting; and believe me, dear,
> However daring bold himself may be,
> Man never loves, within a woman's eye,
> To see the mimic of his conduct glassed.
> 'Tis meek endurance, quiet fortitude,
> That make her life and beauty. We may rear
> Heroes, whose dauntless acts will shall shake the world,
> Or like a moral Atlas, bear its burden,
> A universe of care, upon their shoulders.
> But in our bosoms, if too fierce the flame
> That feeds such spirit-struggles, we must check,
> Or drive it back, at least, to seeming quiet.
> If hard the effort, it is woman's task.
> Her passions, if not smothered, must be hid,
> Till in their faintly-beating pulse, herself
> Will scarcely know her blood the same which bounds
> Through manlier veins unchecked.

Licinia confesses:

> I would I were a man, with a man's soul
> And not the coward nature modelled me.

Cornelia briefly flouts her own admonition against Licinia's going out and finds Gaius taking refuge from assassins in the Temple of Diana. Cornelia urges courage and action. He replies:

> Mother, I go.
> May heaven so bless you, as your son shall strive
> To prove the honor and the love he bears you,
> By working out the noble thoughts you teach.

Thus the weeping Cornelia performs the role of a chorus, supplying the moral context for action but not the action itself. The role of the republican mother was to exhort her sons to patriotic activity, but not to partake in such "manly" action herself.[26]

McCord's play received rave reviews. Ironically, *De Bow's Review* ascribed her success to the same masculine qualities she disdained in women. The reviewer exulted: "She is wholly unlike any of her sisters of the lyre and writes with a terseness, vigor, earnestness, and masculine energy, which shows her altogether of a different order. . . . Her acquaintance with the poets of Greece and Rome in their own language has enabled her to impart to [her tragedy] a purely classical tone which no unlearned writer could have given." Nevertheless, McCord's admirers were willing to forgive her "masculine qualities," as well as to overlook the irony inherent in her public exhortations to women to remain domestic. Hiram Powers sculpted a bust of McCord in the clothing of a Roman matron, and James Woods Davidson, who served as tutor to her children, claimed: "Her mind is Roman in its cast and heroic in its mould. She was Roman, always Roman." Her son, whom she had exhorted to heroic action, died in battle for the Confederacy.[27]

As the critic for *De Bow's Review* guessed, McCord's classical education went beyond even that offered at most of the new female academies. As a child, she had possessed such a passion for learning that she hid behind a door and took notes while a tutor taught her brothers. When she was caught, her father, Langdon Cheves, said that anyone so desirous of learning should have it, and she was given a thorough training in classics and mathematics.[28]

McCord's opposition to a direct political role for women was particularly striking, given her advocacy of such a role for lower-class white males. Her father, who served as president of the national bank, attorney general of

South Carolina, and Speaker of the U.S. House of Representatives, was a self-made man and a powerful orator whose thundering speeches reminded Washington Irving of Cicero and Demosthenes. In her play Gaius declares:

> Oh! Learn ye that there is no higher place
> Than that from which the self-ennobled, turns
> A helping hand to lend to those who would rise
> Like him from abjectness.

Just as Gaius expresses an unfashionable pride in his father's plebeian background, McCord expressed pride in her father's rise from lowly origins. Her Gaius refers to the "reflected deity in man" and declares:

> Reason wakes
> To know man's rights, and forward progress points.

Jacksonian democracy, like Gaius' supposedly radical brand of republicanism, extended to poor white males but not to women.[29]

McCord was far from alone in her belief that women should exhort their sons to virtuous public activity while themselves eschewing such action. Published between 1785 and 1835, Noah Webster's popular and influential English primers, the first of their kind in America and the forerunners to the McGuffey readers, praised Joseph Addison's *Cato* (1713) for its depiction of Cato's daughter Marcia. In particular, Webster valued Marcia's "modesty," writing, "I would have all ladies who have a mind to be thought well bred, to think seriously on this virtue, which he so beautifully calls the sanctity of manners." George Frederick Holmes lamented that Greek women of the classical period had been treated as little more than slaves, not because he believed that they were entitled to political rights, but because their lowly status had deprived them of the ability to provide a strong moral influence in the home. Timothy Dwight Woolsey, the editor of the first American edition of Sophocles' *Antigone,* assured readers that while the title character's public action in defying King Creon's edict against burying her brother might superficially appear to make her "masculine," her valuation of family, morality, and religion above all else made her "exquisitely tender and feminine." Like many other antebellum Americans, George Fitzhugh believed that even poetry and art were public actions, unsuited to women. He wrote: "Poetry and painting require boldness, originality, and inventiveness. The ladies are too modest to practice these qualities, and only become coarse when they attempt to be bold. Sappho is an exception, but Sappho, we suspect, was a Myth or a man."[30]

By contrast, Sarah Grimké chose to emphasize Cornelia's uncommon intelligence and erudition rather than her domesticity. In *Letters on the Equality of the Sexes* (1838) Grimké wrote: "In spite, however, of the obstacles which impede the progress of women towards that state of high mental cultivation for which her Creator prepared her . . . a few have surmounted every hindrance and proved beyond dispute that they have talents equal to their brethren. Cornelia, the daughter of Scipio Africanus, was distinguished for virtue, learning, and good sense. She wrote and spoke with uncommon elegance and purity. Cicero and Quintilian bestow high praise upon her letters, and the eloquence of her children was attributed to her careful superintendence." Indeed, Grimké claimed: "In the history of Rome we find a little spot of sunshine in the valley where woman has been destined to live, unable from her lowly situation to take an expansive view of that field of moral and mental improvement. . . . In the earliest and best days of Rome . . . there reigned union and concord and industry, supported by mutual affections. The most beautiful woman depended for distinction on her economy and endeavors to assist in crowning her husband's diligence with prosperity. All was in common between them; nothing was thought to belong more to one than another." She quoted Brutus regarding his wife, "I must not answer Portia in the words of Hector, 'Mind your wheel, and to your maids give law,' for in courage, activity, and concern for her country's freedom, she is inferior to none of us." The patriotism of Roman women displayed itself both in acts of service during the Punic Wars and in a successful public protest against taxes later used to fund a civil war, a protest led by the talented Hortensia. Grimké seemed oblivious to the irony in her attribution of the relatively high status of Roman women to Roman male gratitude, early in the republic's history, for the willing submission of the Sabine women whom they kidnapped and married.[31]

Grimké found strong women among the ancient Greeks and Germans as well. While noting with disapproval the statement of Pericles in the funeral oration recounted by Thucydides, "She is the best woman of whom the least is said, either of good or of harm," Grimké also wrote, "In Greece women were admitted to the priesthood, enjoyed its highest dignities and were regarded with great veneration." This practice stood in obvious contrast to the refusal of Christian churches to ordain women. She also quoted Tacitus: "The Germans suppose some divine and prophetic quality in their women, and are careful neither to disregard their admonitions nor neglect their answers."[32]

The contrast between McCord's and Grimké's conceptions of the proper role of women in a republican society is especially interesting given the fact that both had been compelled to plead for a classical education as children.

Grimké recalled regarding her childhood request for a tutor: "The only answer to my earnest pleadings was 'You are a girl—what do you want with Latin and Greek etc.? You can never use them,' accompanied by a smile, sometimes a sneer." Yet Grimké's persistence was rewarded as well as McCord's; she was eventually allowed to sit in on the lessons in the classical languages given to her brother Thomas.[33]

Like Grimké, Margaret Bayard Smith emphasized the intellectual attributes of Roman women. In a series of short stories for *Ladies' Magazine* in the early 1830s Smith made an implicit analogy between Roman matrons and the classically educated women of her day. She noted: "The social circles of Rome, at least those of the higher classes, were always composed of both sexes. Virtuous and learned women mingled with statesmen and philosophers and imparted to society that refinement which they alone can impart.... They had ceased to be the slaves and had become the friends and companions of men." Considering "the epithet of Roman matron a title of honor," Smith applauded the superior selflessness of matrons, who had sacrificed for their country without the hope of glory that animated their male counterparts. She wrote concerning the men: "Allowing however the devotedness and fortitude of these heroes to be greater than that of the Roman matron—were not their supports greater? Were they not more than rewarded for temporary pain by immortal glory?"[34]

Greek women had generally been so secluded and so poorly educated that even fairly conservative American men found them less appealing than their Roman counterparts. Thomas Dew wrote, "Montesquieu asserts that Grecian women were conspicuous for virtue. If so, it was because [the] system of education made them too uninteresting to be objects of desire, or seclusion deprived them of the temptation.... Seclusion is but a sorry substitute for intelligence and liberty. Lock and key are but poor guarantees of the chastity of woman—virtuous principle, fortified by mental culture, is [the] best guardian of connubial fidelity, when woman, the equal of man, enjoys his entire confidence and love, in possession of a full liberty, which but the more attaches her to her family and fireside, where she feels that she is the true divinity." It was the uneducated nature of Greek women that had caused Greek men to seek foreign mistresses, a practice that "must ever be regarded as a melancholy memorial of that corruption which must ever result from that injustice to woman which would systematically degrade her by neglecting her mental culture." Yet Dew's ideal of womanhood continued to be that of a cheerleader for men: "Woman's praise has inspired a large proportion of the noble achievements which have been accomplished in this world. Hence the great moral beauty of those matrimonial connections where the woman can comprehend the whole character of her husband and sympathize with him in all the vicissitudes of his fortunes."[35]

But even the conservative South could not always resist strong heroines. The best-selling novel of the Confederacy was Augusta Jane Evans's *Macaria, or Altars of Sacrifice* (1864), which drew parallels between a southern woman who sacrificed herself for the Confederate cause and a self-sacrificing woman in classical Greece.[36]

The Lingering Specter of Caesar

Americans plumbed classical political history for villains as well as for heroes and heroines. Like the founders, antebellum Americans' greatest villain was Julius Caesar, since they held him most responsible for the fall of the revered Roman republic. Just as Jefferson and Hamilton had accused each other of being a Caesar, so antebellum political leaders accused one another of similar conspiracies against the republic. When New England Federalists spoke of secession before the War of 1812, John Quincy Adams categorized them as mini-Caesars, writing: "To rise upon a division system is, unfortunately, one of the most obvious and apparently easy courses which plays before the eyes of individual ambition in every section of the Union. It is the natural resource of all the small statesmen who, feeling like Caesar, and finding that Rome is too large an object for their grasp, would strike off a village where they might aspire to the first station without exposing themselves to derision." Later, during his own administration, it was probably also Adams who wrote a series of essays under the pseudonym "Patrick Henry" suggesting that John C. Calhoun was another Caesar. "Patrick Henry" wrote: "An affected moderation is often the clearest *indicium* of aspiring designs. Julius Caesar thrice refused the kingly crown; both Octavius and Tiberius assumed it with violent reluctance; and Oliver Cromwell 'struggled hard with the Lord' before he could be persuaded to subvert the liberties of England." James Monroe invoked the specter of Caesar at the Virginia Constitutional Convention in 1830 in an effort to prevent the popular election of the state's governor. Monroe declared:

> If we look to history on this subject, we see the demonstration that the more you connect the people with the Executive, and the greater you make his power, the greater is the danger to Republican Government. What overthrew the ancient Republics? Go to Rome, and what do you find there? Was it not their own Consuls, whom they themselves had chosen, that overthrew the liberties of the State? Marius and Sylla, Pompey and Caesar, till Caesar made himself a despot? It was the people who elected him, and they stuck to him

and their own destruction. The Republic was broken up into parties: their contentions were pushed to extremes, and ruin was the consequence.... Self-government depends for its success on keeping the people in a state of calmness. The less you give them to do in exercising their executive privilege, the safer they will be.[37]

The American most frequently compared to Caesar was Andrew Jackson. Jackson's numerous political opponents frequently made the comparison, both publicly and privately, noting that both Caesar and Jackson were generals who were extremely popular with the masses. As early as 1818, while Speaker of the House, Henry Clay recommended Jackson's censure for the general's unauthorized invasion of Florida. At that time Clay declared: "Remember that Greece had her Alexander, Rome had her Caesar, England her Cromwell, France her Bonaparte, and that if we would escape the rock on which they split, we must avoid their errors.... In the provinces were laid the abuses and seeds of the ambitious projects which overturned the liberties of Rome." After losing the election of 1828 to Jackson, John Quincy Adams immersed himself in Cicero's *Philippics* against Mark Antony, noting in his diary its "melancholy interest" as a record of "the expiring agonies of Roman liberty." Adams then spent more than two hours per day for the next ten months studying Cicero's letters and works, in the process seeing parallels between Jackson and Caesar and himself and Cicero, with whom he even shared the grief of losing a child. Adams wrote concerning Cicero's letters: "I see him approach me like the image of a Fantasmagoria—he seems opening his lips to speak to me and passes off, but his words as if they had fallen upon my ears are left deeply stamped upon the memory. I watch with his sleepless nights. I hear his solitary sighs. I feel the agitation of his pulse.... There is something so much in it of painful reality that I close the book. No tragedy was ever half so pathetic. My morning always ends with a hearty execration of Caesar, and with what is perhaps not so right, a sensation of relief at the 23 stabs of the Ides of March, and the fall at the feet of Pompey's statue."[38]

The Whigs complained that the Jacksonian Democrats, like the factions of the late Roman republic, gave their allegiance to a man rather than to a set of principles. Samuel Southard of New Jersey urged, "Let us not bear upon our foreheads the names we follow and be the advocates of Pompey or the satellites of Caesar, and thus wear the livery of slaves." Representative John A. Collier of New York declared that, like Cassius, he was "not among those who think 'the world was made for Caesar.'" Clay was gratified in 1832 when his friend and fellow Whig R. S. Browning made a pilgrimage to Cicero's tomb and sent him a cane fashioned from a branch that shaded Cicero's grave. Brooding over Cicero's honorable but futile resistance to

Caesar, Browning wrote to Clay that he wished the American people would "prove to the world they are not deluded by the success of a military chieftain" by electing Clay over Jackson in the presidential election that year. Browning did not get his wish, partly because Jackson was able to take advantage of popular distrust of the national bank to make it the central issue of the election.[39]

Interpreting his reelection as a popular mandate to destroy the bank, Jackson took extralegal action to ruin it, thereby spurring the Whigs to even more heated denunciations of the new Caesar. When Secretary of the Treasury William J. Duane refused to follow Jackson's order to remove vital funds from the bank, Jackson fired Duane. On the Senate floor Henry Clay compared Jackson's action to that of Caesar in entering the Roman treasury, sword in hand, to confiscate public funds in order to prosecute his civil war against Pompey. Clay read from Plutarch's life of Caesar, interjecting his own comments: "As Metellus, the tribune, opposed his taking the money out of the public treasury, and cited some laws against it (such, sir, I suppose, as I have endeavored to cite on this occasion), Caesar said, 'If you are not pleased with what I am about, you have only to withdraw (Leave the office, Mr. Duane!)'. . . . Having said this, he approached the doors of the treasury, and as the keys were not produced, he sent for workmen to break them open. Metellus again opposed him, and gained credit with some for his firmness; but Caesar . . . threatened to put him to death, if he gave any further trouble. . . . Metellus, terrified by the measure, retired." Calhoun, by then a fellow enemy of Jackson, seized upon the analogy, declaring:

> The Senator from Kentucky, in connexion with this part of his argument, read a striking passage from one of the most pleasing and instructive writers in any language (Plutarch), giving the description of Caesar forcing himself, sword in hand, into the treasury of the Roman Commonwealth. We are at the same stage of our political revolution, and the analogy between the two cases is complete, varied only by the character of the actors and the circumstances of the times. That was a case of an intrepid and bold warrior as an open plunderer, seizing forcibly the treasury of the country, which, in that Republic, as well as ours, was confided to the custody of the legislative department of the Government. The actors in our case are of a different character—artful, cunning, and corrupt politicians, not fearless warriors. They have entered the treasury, not sword in hand, as public plunderers, but with the false keys of sophistry, as pilferers, under the silence of midnight. The motive and object are the same. . . . "With money I will get men, and with men money" was the maxim of the Roman plunderer. With money we will get partizans, with partizans votes, and with votes money, is the maxim of our public pilferers. With men and money Caesar struck down Roman liberty at the fatal battle of

Phillippi [actually, Pharsalus], never to rise again; from which disastrous hour, all the powers of the Roman republic were consolidated in the person of Caesar, and perpetuated in his line. With money and corrupt partizans, a great effort is now making to choke and stifle the voice of American liberty, through all its natural organs.[40]

Calhoun's speech portraying Jackson as an American Caesar was so compelling that the *Washington Globe* blamed it for the first presidential assassination attempt in American history, Richard Lawrence's unsuccessful effort to shoot Jackson. Regarding Lawrence, an anonymous writer for the *Globe* insinuated, "Whether he has become infatuated with the chimeras which have troubled the brains of the disappointed orators who have depicted the President as a Caesar who ought to have a Brutus—as a Cromwell—a Nero—a Tiberius, we know not." The author, who singled out Calhoun for blame, was wrong about Lawrence, a delusional house painter who had probably sniffed too much lead paint. Nevertheless, it was probably no accident that the first successful presidential assassin, John Wilkes Booth—the son and brother of men named Junius Brutus Booth, after the ancestor of Caesar's assassin who drove Tarquin, the corrupt king, from Rome—allegedly shouted, "Sic semper tyrannis" (Thus be it ever for tyrants) after killing Abraham Lincoln. The state motto of Virginia both reflected and reinforced the republican fear of tyrants. Booth and two of his brothers had appeared in a stage production of William Shakespeare's *Julius Caesar* in New York City less than five months before Lincoln's assassination.[41]

Ironically, the only time Jackson ever quoted Caesar was in an incident involving Calhoun, then his vice president, in 1830. After discovering that it had been Calhoun who had spoken against him at a cabinet meeting over a decade earlier, Jackson had written to Calhoun, "I had a right to believe that you were my sincere friend and, until now, never expected to have occasion to say of you, in the language of Caesar, *et tu Brute*."[42]

Even some relatively calm observers accepted the validity of the Jackson-Caesar analogy. Supreme Court justice Joseph Story wrote, "I seem almost . . . to be in a dream and to be called back to the last days of the Roman Republic, when the people shouted for Caesar, and liberty itself expired with the dark but prophetic words of Cicero." Representative Francis W. Pickens of South Carolina declared, "It is the reign of Caesar, and we are cowards, dastards, slaves, if we submit to this state of things." Representative Dutie J. Pierce of Rhode Island noted that since Caesar, like Jackson, had been popular with the masses, "the popularity of the head of an administration" was not "the conclusive evidence of the correctness of that administration." Senator Peleg Sprague of Maine declared that the United

States was like the late Roman republic, when "two tremendous powers, the Executive and the people," joined together to crush liberty.[43]

Even after Jackson left office peaceably, thereby ruining the Caesar analogy, Jackson's foes refused to abandon it. When Jackson's destruction of the national bank led to the Panic of 1837, an economic recession that fell hard on his successor Martin Van Buren, Representative Henry A. Wise of Virginia remarked, "Truly, truly, it may be said, sir, that the evil which General Jackson did lives after him," a clear reference to Shakespeare's version of Mark Antony's speech concerning Caesar. Regarding Van Buren's reluctant repudiation of Jackson's state banking system in favor of the independent treasury plan, Wise added: "This meant that Old Hickory was not, as it was thought, a god! He was but a poor, weak mortal; his wisdom was fallible! This our Caesar did feed on meat as other men."[44]

Jackson's opponents compared him to other Roman despots as well. Representative Thomas Corwin of Ohio claimed that Jackson's spoils system was based on Sulla's maxim: "Gratitude for friends and revenge for foes." Calhoun compared it to the patronage distributed by the Roman emperors. Calhoun also complained that Jackson's Force Bill, in which Congress granted the president authorization to use force against South Carolina during the Nullification Crisis, resembled "the bloody edicts of Nero and Caligula." Senator Benjamin Watkins Leigh of Virginia claimed that Jackson's protest against Clay's censure resolution was couched "in the imperial style of the Caesars to the degraded Senate of Rome." Calhoun denounced the Jacksonians' attempt to expunge remarks critical of Jackson from the Senate journal, in the process comparing Jackson to Caligula. An observer noted concerning Calhoun: "He thought they had the same right to express disapprobation of as to flatter the Executive. When they had arrived at such a period as either they must flatter or be silent, they should be equal to the most degenerate days of the Roman Republic [sic], when the horse of the emperor was declared consul." Two years later, in 1837, when the Jacksonians moved to expunge the Senate's censure of Jackson, Calhoun declared: "This act originates in pure, unmixed, personal idolatry. It is the melancholy evidence of a broken spirit, ready to bow at the feet of power. The former act [Jackson's removal of deposits from the national bank] was such a one as might have been perpetrated in the days of Pompey and Caesar; but an act like this could never have been consummated by a Roman Senate until the times of Caligula and Nero." The Whigs often compared Jackson to Tiberius and Van Buren to Sejanus, the head of Tiberius' Praetorian Guard, perhaps hoping that the two men would eventually turn against each another like Tiberius and Sejanus. One congressman wrote of Jackson's efforts to elect Van Buren, "He has shown the young Caesar to the Praetorian guards at the seat of Government, and last fall made the tour of the North with him, to show him the distant legions." Indeed, after Van Buren was elected, some claimed that Jackson was running the country from the Hermitage, like Tiberius from Capri. In the wake of the Panic of 1837, John Pendleton Kennedy claimed that Jackson, "reversing the boast of the Roman emperor [Augustus], might have exclaimed at his departure from the capital, 'I have found Rome marble, and I have left it brick.' " To Clay, Jackson's apathy regarding the economic distress caused by his destruction of the national bank "resembled the conduct of Nero," the worst of the Roman emperors, "who contemplated with indifference the conflagration of the mistress of the world." Even decades later, in a eulogy of Calhoun, Robert Hunter of Virginia continued to insist that, by Jackson's second term, "the Government had become the same with that of the Romans under Octavius [Augustus]: the forms of freedom were speciously observed . . . but in reality the empire had found a master."[45]

The Whigs' denunciation of party politics, even as they themselves practiced it, stemmed from the classical equation of virtue with independence of thought and action and vice with "factionalism." Roman historians had despised the *factio* as the favored instrument of demagogues, thereby contributing greatly to the antiparty sentiment that dominated the early history of the United States. According to the classical doctrine, political partisanship inevitably involved defending the indefensible vices of one's allies and attempting to dominate one's fellow citizens in order to satisfy a narrow self-interest. Both Federalists and Democratic-Republicans had decried "party spirit," considering their own parties temporary aberrations, necessary only to block the antirepublican ambitions of their opponents, and had looked forward to the day when they could be safely eliminated. George Washington had devoted most of his Farewell Address to an attack on political parties, which he feared might produce civil war. Many Americans had breathed a sigh of relief when American politics reverted to a partyless condition following the death of the Federalist Party in 1816. The "Era of Good Feelings" seemed a return to the mythical days of patriot unanimity during the American Revolution. John Quincy Adams inherited his father's determination to resist party favoritism. As president, he refused to remove hundreds of political opponents from federal office. Members of the Whig Party, still tied to classical theory, continued to perceive parties as an evil. They dubbed Andrew Jackson "King Andrew," claiming that his wholesale replacement of opponents resembled the corrupt patronage of both George III and Caesar.[46]

Jacksonian Democrats considered the Caesar-Jackson analogy preposterous, of course. As early as Jackson's invasion of Florida, his defenders argued that far from being a Caesar, Jackson was analogous to those ancients whose heroic deeds had been rewarded with the ingratitude of the very people they served. He had crossed no Rubicon against his own government but had added territory to the American empire in imitation of the greatest generals of the Roman republic. Representative George Poindexter made the same point by spoofing Patrick Henry's famous Stamp Act Speech against George III, a favorite of antebellum Whigs, who liked to apply it to Jackson. Whereas Henry had declared, "Caesar had his Brutus, Charles the First his Cromwell, and George III [cries of 'Treason!'] may profit by their example," Poindexter declared, "Greece had her Miltiades, Rome her Bellisarius [sic], Carthage her Hannibal, and may we . . . profit by the example!" Future president James Buchanan cited many military commanders who had shown "a capacity for civil command" in a republic, including Pericles, Cincinnatus, and George Washington. (Henry Clay retorted that Jackson was no Washington, who had possessed wisdom, sound judgment, and control of his passions, all qualities Jackson lacked.) Representative Balie Peyton of Tennessee compared Jackson to Cincinnatus: "They talk to us of Caesar and of Rome. When Caesar won his battles, he crossed the Rubicon and marched at the head of his Gallic legions to a throne. When Andrew Jackson had won for himself imperishable renown [at the Battle of New Orleans] . . . he disbanded his soldiers and retired to his farm. . . . [Later] he was taken from his farm by the call of his fellow-citizens; placed by the spontaneous suffrages of a free people in the most exalted station on the earth; and, unlike Caesar, when he marched to Rome, he spread no dismay, dispersed no Senate; but the plain old man was hailed everywhere as a friend to his country." Peyton also compared Jackson to Cato the Younger, the friend of the republic, and Clay, Calhoun, and Nicholas Biddle to the First Triumvirate of Caesar, Pompey, and Crassus, who had undermined the republic.[47]

Other Jackson supporters joined in likening him to the heroes of the Roman republic. In his first speech before Congress, Jackson's fellow Tennesseean Sam Houston compared him to Cincinnatus. Similarly, Senator Thomas Hart Benton of Missouri equated Jackson with Cicero, declaring: "Cicero extinguished the Catilinean conspiracy, and saved Rome; President Jackson defeated the conspiracy of the bank, and saved our America." Jackson's frequent use of the veto "was nothing but a qualified copy of the famous . . . power vested in the tribunes of the people among the Romans, and intended to suspend the passage of a law until the people themselves should have time to consider it."[48]

Jacksonian Democrats attributed the fall of the Roman republic to the same type of aristocratic corruption and oppression of the people practiced by the Whigs and thwarted by Jackson. Indeed, Jackson himself responded to the Caesar analogy in a letter to his son: "It was a corrupt and venal senate that overturned the liberty of Rome before Caesar reached her gates." If the American republic should be corrupted, it would be by the aristocratic Whig Senate, not by himself.[49]

By bringing to prominence a new set of generals like Zachary Taylor and Winfield Scott (ironically, both Whigs), the Mexican War again spurred fears of an American Caesar. Henry Clay, who had strong presidential ambitions of his own, still worried that "military chieftain will succeed military chieftain until at last one will reach the Presidency who, more unscrupulous than his predecessors, will . . . establish a throne of despotism." Franklin Smith wrote to John C. Calhoun: "The Presidency could confer on you no honor. The Caesars are forgotten but Cato lives in imperishable renown. A party is springing up in our country that is enamoured with the spoils of war and eager for plunder. A party is forming that expects to live by war and to fill the national exchequer by the same means, a proconsular party destined, if not checked, to run the same career as they did in old Rome. . . . It is now admitted that the general who first conquers Mexico must be president." Smith added, "Unless this war is stopped our epitaph is written. It is recorded in the history of Rome." James Gadsden was equally distressed, writing: "Like the Romans, all our American Generals are for War and American Provinces. Each probably claims a state as their share of the spoils." On the verge of Taylor's victory in the election of 1848, Sylvester Graham of Massachusetts asked Calhoun, "Do you not tremble at the popular madness which selects a briefly and narrowly successful military chieftain for the supreme Magistrate of this great nation, and chains to the wheels of his triumphal car the most learned civilians and ablest Statesmen in the land?" In a similar vein George Frederick Holmes, after referring to Santa Anna as "this modern Jugurtha," identified Taylor as the modern Marius and Scott as the modern Metellus. Jugurtha was the Numidian king whose rebellion against Rome had almost given Marius the opportunity to seize power by force of arms; Metellus was Marius' colleague during the campaign against Jugurtha. Holmes wrote ruefully: "The intellectual lights of the day are deemed but of use in the subordinate offices: the Calhouns, the Legarés, and Clays veritably do make most excellent secretaries and attorneys! But in this . . . our day is true to her mother, antiquity: for what, but spokesmen, were Cicero and Demosthenes? The mere equerries that held the stirrups of ambition." A democratic age preferred generals to statesmen.[50]

But, as in the days of Washington, Americans still desired military chieftains in the guise of Cincinnatus, not Caesar. For this reason, when Nathaniel Hawthorne wrote to his friend Franklin Pierce about his campaign biography in 1852, Hawthorne advised that while Pierce's Mexican War experience should be included, it "ought not to be so much as to overshadow you as a man of peaceful pursuits. 'Cedant arma togae.' A statesman in your proper life—a gallant soldier in the hour of your country's need—such, in the circumstances, is the best mode of presenting you." The Latin phrase, Cicero's famous declaration of the importance of civilian rule in republican government (*On Duties* 1.22.77), which translates, "Let arms yield to the toga," was widely quoted in antebellum America. American liberty survived the brief administration of Taylor, as it had the even briefer term of Harrison and the longer terms of Washington, Jackson, and Pierce, the nation's other military presidents before the Civil War.[51]

The Debate over Federal Power

In addition to dreading military despotism, some southerners also feared that the expansion of federal power would culminate in a new Roman Empire that would be similarly tyrannical toward the "provinces." Even as early as 1816, when John C. Calhoun still favored federal funding for internal improvements, he emphasized, "Let us make great permanent roads, not like the Romans, with views of subjecting and ruling provinces, but for the honorable purposes of defence, and connecting more closely the interests of the various sections of the country." In 1832 Representative George McDuffie of South Carolina claimed that the massive federal tariff was "in no degree less oppressive and disastrous" than the "cruel exactions of the Roman Government" on vanquished nations. In opposition to the Wilmot Proviso, which would have banned slavery from the land taken by the United States in the Mexican War, Muscoe Russell Hunter Garnett of Virginia compared the southern states to the Roman provinces, "whose citizens were usually forbidden . . . to possess any portion of the soil in territories they had aided to conquer." In 1850 Representative Isaac E. Holmes of South Carolina wrote: "The North has become like unto Rome, and from the same causes. She has subjected provinces more productive than the Egyptian or African." In 1860, the year of secession, J. D. B. De Bow wrote, "The Roman empire, in its most debauched and basest times, never sunk half so low in venality, corruption, and vulgarity as our federal government has sunk." But the next year, after civil war had erupted, De Bow changed the analogy. The northern invaders now became Goths and Huns, the southern defenders Roman republicans. De Bow wrote, "Let the hordes of Alaric and Attila come, a degenerate race does not occupy the old Roman fields."[52]

Not everyone agreed that the federal government of the United States was analogous to the imperial government of Rome. In 1832 William Henry Harrison wrote to Calhoun that there was a crucial difference in the historical contexts: the Romans had not possessed a written constitution like the U.S. Constitution of 1787, which limited the power of the central government. Furthermore, Harrison contended: "In vain, however, in examining our system of government shall we discover any motive upon the part of the majority of the people, or their agents who administer the government, to usurp upon the reserved rights of the States, and 'degrade them into mere dependent corporations.' The people themselves would never think of such a thing." Harrison wrote regarding treachery, "If our government is to fall in that way, the powers reserved by the States will enjoy the privilege of Ulysses in the cave of Polyphemus, 'the last to be devoured.'" It would be far more effective for a traitor to destroy the Union by demolishing "the General Government." In fact, the best protection against the kind of corruption most likely to destroy the republic was a strong federal judiciary. Harrison concluded, "If the progress of luxury should effect a change in the manners and principles of the people, and corruption seize upon the other departments of the government, that, like the far-famed Athenian court [the Areopagus] (and under the influence of similar causes), whatever of virtue or talents which remain in the nation will be found on the bench of the Supreme Court of the United States."[53]

Antebellum Americans were as anxious to avoid the fatal mistakes of the Greek republics, which had been overthrown by Philip II of Macedon, as those of the Roman republic. All agreed that the loss of its independence had been a disaster for Greece in every sense, politically, socially, and artistically. As a boy, John Randolph cried "for indignation at the success of Philip's arts and arms over the liberties of Greece." Concerning the Athenians, Edward Everett wrote: "It was for this lawless, merciless, but free people that the most chaste and accomplished literature which the world has known was produced. With the decline of liberty in Greece began the decline of her letters and her arts." Thomas Dew concurred:

And when, at last, a great state arose in the north of Greece, and placed a monarch upon its throne, who substituted the obedient spirit of the mercenary soldier and crouching courtier for the independent genius of liberty and patriotism—who overawed Greece by his armies, and silenced the Council of Amphictyon by his presence—then it was found that the days of Grecian greatness had been numbered, and that the glory of the republics was destroyed forever; then was it seen that the Spartan lost his patriotism, and the Athenians that energy of mind almost creative, which could lead armies and navies to battle and to victory, adorn and enrich the stores of philosophy and literature, agitate the public assemblies from the *Bema*, or make the marble and its canvas breathe. The battle of Cheronea overthrew at the same time the state governments, the liberties, the prosperity, and, worst of all, the virtue and the towering intellect of Greece.

Dew added a sermon against the alarming growth of federal power in the United States: "And such will always be the destiny of states as soon as they are moulded into one consolidated empire, with a controlling despotism at the centre.... When a great consolidated central government shall have fixed its embrace on the Union—the sun of her glory will have set forever." George Fitzhugh agreed: "Almost the only secret of high civilization and national greatness consists in narrow and confined territorial limits.... History, ancient and modern, teaches but one lesson on this subject. Little Phoenicia and little Carthage, the hundred little states of Greece, and Rome whilst her dominion was confined to Italy, were truly great. When Alexander had conquered Egypt and Persia, and died for want of other worlds to conquer, Greece fell to rise no more, and in her fall involved the conquered in one common ruin. Rome conquered the world, and forthwith Cimmerian darkness began to cover her empire."[54]

But explanations for the fall of the Greek republics varied considerably. Charles Fenton Mercer attributed the Macedonian conquest of Athens to rampant materialism: "Athens contained sixty thousand citizens when, aided by the rest of Greece, she expelled the hosts of Xerxes. She had the same number when Demetrius sold them as slaves in the public market; when they had refused their wealth to defense, and reserved it for public festivals and shows." By contrast, when upset by intense Federalist opposition to the War of 1812, a young John C. Calhoun had attributed the destruction of Greece and of other republics to factionalism. Calhoun declared: "Admired and lamented republics of antiquity! Athens, Carthage, and Rome, you are the victims and witnesses of the fell spirit of factious opposition! Fatal fields of Zama and Chaeronea, you can attest the destructive cruelty! What is the history of Polybius, and that of the other historians of the free states of antiquity? What the political speeches of Cicero and the orations of Demosthenes, those models of eloquence and wisdom, but the volumes of evidence attesting that an opposition founded in faction, unrestrained by moderation and a regard to the general welfare, is the most dangerous of political evils?"[55]

Such analogies between the past and the present reflected a widespread belief in an unchanging human nature. At the Virginia Constitutional Convention of 1829–1830, Benjamin Watkins Leigh declared: "There has been no change in the natural feelings, passions, and appetites of men, any more than in their outward form, from the days of Solon to those of George

Washington. Like political or moral causes put in action have ever produced, and must ever produce, everywhere like effects—in Athens, in Rome, in France, and in America." Similarly, George Fitzhugh wrote: "So little has human nature changed that we find the men of to-day, with all their virtues and vices, passions and peculiarities, more exactly and faithfully portrayed in the Old Testament, and by the Greek and Latin poets, than by any English or American author of the present day." Thomas Hart Benton declared, "It is the same now . . . that it was when the People of Greece and Rome carried the glory and prosperity of those republics to the highest pitch of human greatness."[56]

Calhoun's Adaptation of Mixed Government Theory

Perhaps the most interesting use of classical political theory in the antebellum period was John C. Calhoun's desperate but failed effort to save the Union through a modern adaptation of mixed government theory. In the fourth century B.C. Plato had identified three simple forms of government: monarchy, aristocracy, and democracy—rule by the one, the few, and the many. Each of these forms, he claimed in the *Laws* (756e–757a) and in the *Politicus* (291d–303c), deteriorated over time: monarchy into tyranny, aristocracy into oligarchy, and democracy into ochlocracy (mob rule). Plato suggested that the best form of government would be a mixed government, one that balanced the power of the three orders of society. (This theory represented a marked departure from the one Plato had elaborated in the *Republic* more than a decade earlier, when he had advocated a simple aristocracy of guardians led by a philosopher-king.) Aristotle then immortalized mixed government theory, making it the centerpiece of his *Politics* (3.7), in which he cited numerous examples of mixed government in the ancient world. The Greek historian Polybius claimed that the Roman republic at the time of the Second Punic War (218–202 B.C.) was the most outstanding example of mixed government. In fact, Polybius (*Histories*, book 6) claimed that the balance of power between the consuls, the Senate, and the popular assemblies was the secret of Roman success, since it minimized internal strife, thereby allowing the Romans to conquer their external enemies. Cicero (*Republic* 2.23–30) then seized upon mixed government theory to thwart the increasing efforts of Romans to consolidate their own power at the republic's expense.

Mixed government theory survived the collapse of the Roman Empire. Such disparate theorists as Thomas Aquinas, John Calvin, Niccolò Machiavelli, and Francesco Guicciardini all advocated mixed government during the Middle Ages and the Renaissance. In the early modern era British Whigs like Algernon Sidney not only reasserted classical arguments against the simple systems of government but also added Great Britain to their list of successful mixed governments. The British king, the House of Lords, and the House of Commons joined the Spartan and Roman governments in the pantheon of mixed government theorists.[57]

Seventeenth-century British political theorist James Harrington contributed a concept central to any American adaptation of mixed government theory, the concept of "natural aristocracy." Even in a new country like Oceana (Harrington's fictional utopia), which lacked a titled aristocracy, certain men would possess greater talent than others. In any free society this natural difference in talent would produce unequal wealth. Unequal wealth would, in turn, produce class conflict. Mixed government, combined with a few laws limiting the size of landholdings, was the only means of preventing violent struggles between the classes and the tyranny that inevitably followed these civil wars. Hence Oceana's government consisted of a senate that represented the natural aristocracy, a huge assembly elected from the common people, and an executive to provide a balancing center of power. Like Polybius, Harrington believed that such a system would produce good laws, which would, in turn, produce good men.[58]

As heirs to this Western tradition of mixed government theory, the founders of the United States attributed the unprecedented parliamentary taxation of the 1760s and 1770s to a degeneration of the mixture of the British constitution and sought to establish mixed governments in their states through the new constitutions necessitated by the American Revolution. Patriot leaders charged that King George III had destroyed the delicate balance of the British constitution by using his patronage powers to buy the House of Commons and to pack the House of Lords. The chief dilemma of these patriots was how to create mixed systems in societies that no longer possessed a monarch and that had never possessed a titled aristocracy. The framers of the state constitutions decided that these essential roles should be played by an elected governor and by a senate consisting of Harrington's "natural aristocracy." They reasoned that since education and talent often accompanied wealth, and since wealth (unlike either talent or virtue) could be easily quantified, property was the most appropriate criterion for identifying the natural aristocracy that would provide their governments with the necessary senatorial stability. The state senates were generally smaller than the lower houses, the senators had to meet higher property qualifications, and they generally served longer, staggered terms to diminish their vulnerability to popular pressure.[59]

Most of the delegates to the U.S. Constitutional Convention of 1787 advocated a mixed government at the federal level as well. James Madison, often called the "Father of the Constitution" because of his leading role in its drafting and ratification, argued for a nine-year term for senators, declaring: "Landholders ought to have a share in the government to support these invaluable interests and to balance and check the other [the many]. They ought to be so constituted as to protect the minority of the opulent against the majority. The senate, therefore, ought to be this body; and to answer these purposes, they ought to have permanency and stability. Various have been the propositions; but my opinion is, the longer they continue in office, the better will these views be answered." It was useless to deny the existence of an American aristocracy, though there were no "hereditary distinctions" and though inequalities of wealth were minor by comparison with Europe. Madison continued: "There will be debtors and creditors, and an unequal possession of property, and hence arise different views and different objects in government. This, indeed, is the ground work of aristocracy; and we find it blended in every government, both ancient and modern." Madison concluded that even in his own day America could not be regarded as "one homogeneous mass" and that there were recent "symptoms of a leveling spirit" that he feared might lead to "agrarian acts" (land redistribution). Heeding Madison's advice, the convention approved a constitution that balanced the power of the one, the few, and the many: a powerful president selected by the Electoral College, a strong senate selected by the state legislatures for six-year terms, and a house of representatives directly elected by the people for two-year terms. In *Federalist* essays 47 and 63 Madison endorsed this new constitution as having established a mixed government. In the same year Madison warned Thomas Jefferson: "Wherever the real power in Government lies, there is the danger of oppression. In our Governments the real power lies in the majority of the Community, and the invasion of private rights is chiefly to be apprehended not from acts of Government contrary to the sense of its constituents, but from acts in which the Government is the mere instrument of the major number of the constituents." John Adams, Alexander Hamilton, John Dickinson, and numerous other Federalists also supported the Constitution on mixed government grounds, and numerous Anti-Federalists attacked it on the same terms.[60]

Yet in *Federalist* 10, an essay that was largely ignored at the time but became famous much later, Madison proposed a different solution to the problem of majority tyranny. He suggested that unlike the ancient republics, a modern commercial nation like the United States possessed more than two factions, "the few" and "the many." For instance, planters and merchants, though both wealthy, possessed different interests. Furthermore, Madison recognized that religious and ideological considerations would also create factions. Hence the number of factions in the United States would be so great that majorities must be weak coalitions incapable of prolonged tyranny. (Representation would enhance this effect by preventing majorities from acting on sudden impulse). As the years passed, Madison clung ever more fervently to this solution to the problem of majority tyranny, a solution that not only seemed more appropriate to the American context but also justified democratic reforms supported by his constituents. Undertaken by the states, these reforms included the elimination of property qualifications for voting and the linkage of the selection of presidential electors to a popular vote. Indeed, the rise of political parties so soon after the inauguration of the new government, parties that failed to follow class lines and that received support from members of each branch of government, proved that mixed government in its rigid Polybian form was unsuited to a modern commercial nation like the United States. Madison had been correct in noting that modern commercial nations were heterogeneous, possessing more than Polybius' two interests, the few and the many.[61]

Unfortunately, as the antebellum period progressed, it became clear that one of the nation's numerous divisions was increasingly overshadowing all the others, thereby threatening the Union. It was not the division feared by most of the founders, that between the rich and the poor, but the division between the free states of the North and the slave states of the South.

John C. Calhoun struggled for most of his career to preserve the Union by formulating and promoting various institutional arrangements through which the South might adequately defend its own interests and way of life, so that southern states would not be forced to leave the Union. This quest for institutional protections for the South was necessitated by the disproportionate growth of the northern population relative to the southern population throughout the antebellum period. As the northern majority grew ever larger, its power within the federal government increased proportionally. The northern majority attempted to use this power to enact tariffs that would protect northern industries from the competition of British and French manufacturers, thereby forcing southerners to purchase higher-priced northern goods and reducing the amount of capital the British and French could employ to purchase southern cotton. The northern majority also attempted to secure federal funding for railroads and canals in the North. (Because of the South's internal river systems, southerners felt little need for these "internal improvements.") Finally, the northern majority began to demand laws prohibiting slavery in the western territories. (This movement had less to do with moral outrage over slavery than with the northern fear that slave labor would drive out free labor.) Thus Calhoun struggled with the same dilemma that had obsessed Madison at the Constitutional Convention: how to protect minorities from "majority tyranny." While Madison had pondered how to protect the natural aristocracy from oppression by the masses, Calhoun now grappled with the question of how to protect the southern minority from the northern majority.[62]

Calhoun's solution to the problem of majority tyranny, the theory of concurrent majority, combined the insights of Aristotle and Madison—the theory of mixed government and the theory of the multiplicity of interests in a modern commercial nation. In 1849, shortly before his death, Calhoun expressed his theory in the *Disquisition on Government*. Calhoun argued that each "major interest" in society must possess a veto on legislation. To avoid tyranny, a nation's constitution must "give to each division or interest, through its appropriate organ, either a concurrent voice in making and executing the laws or a veto on their execution." Sounding much like Polybius (6.18), Calhoun explained that such a system would compel compromise, which would, in turn, produce harmony and unity. Since the rights of each major interest would be protected by its veto on the legislation of competing interests, there would be no dissatisfaction and, hence, no need for rebellion or secession.[63]

By contrast, democracy, in its pure form, was tyrannical, granting the majority the power to trample on the rights of minorities. Calhoun complained that Americans too often confused "the numerical majority" with "the people," of which it was but a part. (Sixteen years earlier, Calhoun had written in a similar vein: "The Government of the absolute majority, instead of the Government of the people, is but the Government of the strongest interests; and when not effectually checked, is the most tyrannical and oppressive that can be devised.") Again following Polybius, Calhoun added that not only was absolute government by the majority unjust, it also led inevitably to "absolute government of some other form," usually monarchy. Calhoun contended that one of the advantages of the system he proposed was that under it universal suffrage could be safely enacted, whereas under a strict system of majority rule, universal suffrage placed the government "under the control of the more ignorant and dependent portions of the community." Calhoun added concerning one of his favorite examples of government by concurrent majority, the American jury system: "If the necessity of unanimity were dispensed with and the finding of a jury made to depend on a bare majority, jury trial, instead of being one of the greatest improvements in the judicial department of government, would be one of the greatest evils that could be inflicted on the community. It would be, in such a case, the conduit through which all the factious feelings of the day would enter and contaminate justice at its source." Calhoun considered constitutional protections of minority rights, such as those contained in the U.S. Bill of Rights, inadequate, since officials chosen by the majority possessed the power to interpret the Constitution so loosely as to invalidate such protections. Likewise, the separation of powers between the legislative, executive, and judicial branches merely divided power among the agents of the majority and contributed nothing to the protection of minorities.[64]

Aware that he was proposing a modern version of classical mixed government theory, Calhoun joined Polybius in citing the early Roman republic as "the most distinguished" example of "a constitutional" or mixed system. Drawing from Cicero (*Republic* 2.33–34) and Livy (*History of Rome* 2.32–35), Calhoun praised the compromise between the patricians and the plebeians that had prevented the secession of the plebeians, thereby implying a historical parallel with the threatened southern secession. The compromise in question (ca. 494 B.C.) was the popular election of two (later ten) tribunes, officials who had possessed a veto power over senate legislation. This innovation, Calhoun claimed, converted Rome "from an aristocracy into a republic," thereby laying "the solid foundation of Roman liberty and greatness." The granting of a veto power to the plebeians blessed Rome with "concord and harmony," "unequaled strength," and a life of "great length and immortal glory." Calhoun concluded, "It moderated the conflicts between the orders, harmonized their interests, and blended them into one, substituted devotion to country in place of devotion to particular orders, called forth the united strength and energy of the whole in the hour of danger, raised to power the wise and patriotic, elevated the Roman name above all others, extended her authority and dominion over the greatest part of the then known world and transmitted the influence of her laws and institutions to the present day."[65]

Calhoun's theory was plagued with difficulties. First, he failed to specify the criteria by which his system would distinguish between a "major interest," worthy of the veto power, and a minor one. Nor did he make clear how the system could be updated to account for the rise and decline of various interests over time. Indeed, Calhoun conceded that since all "constitutional governments" (mixed systems) were much more difficult to construct than any "absolute government," most had evolved slowly through trial and error. Yet in the *Disquisition* Calhoun neglected to provide even a hint of how his proposed system of government could be put into actual operation. True, he provided partial answers in two other documents. In the famous *South Carolina Exposition and Protest* (1828) Calhoun had seized upon the Virginia and Kentucky Resolutions (1798) of Jefferson and Madison to assert the authority of states to nullify federal laws they considered unconstitutional. Such a veto power over federal legislation by each state would certainly have protected many, if not all, major interests from oppression. But, grateful to President Jackson for his aid in removing Native American tribes to lands west of the Mississippi River, the other southern states had sided with Jackson against the nullification doctrine, thereby forcing South Carolina to back down in the face of Jackson's threats and to accept Congress's olive branch in the form of a reduction in the offending tariffs. The death of the nullification doctrine ended one possible avenue of government by concurrent majority. Later, in 1849, in a last desperate effort to forestall secession and civil war, Calhoun proposed the drafting of a constitutional amendment to establish a dual executive consisting of one northern and one southern president. Calhoun noted: "The two most distinguished constitutional governments of antiquity, both in respect to permanence and power, had a dual executive. I refer to those of Sparta and Rome. The former had two hereditary, and the latter two elective, chief magistrates." But Calhoun's proposal attracted little support, and even if such an amendment had been ratified and had succeeded in defusing the immediate crisis, a mere two presidents could hardly have served as effective representatives of all the major interests of the United States.[66]

The second difficulty with Calhoun's theory was the danger that his proposed system would lead to governmental paralysis. Although Calhoun began his *Disquisition* with a discourse on innate human selfishness—a discourse essential to his premise that all absolute governments were tyrannical—he seems to have forgotten his own theory of human nature when writing about the remarkable harmony his proposed system would create. Paralleling Polybius (6.18), Calhoun wrote: "The prevailing desire would be to promote the common interests of the whole; and hence the competition would be, not which should yield the least to promote the common good, but which should yield the most. It is thus that concession would cease to be considered a sacrifice—would become a free-will offering on the altar of the country and lose the name of compromise." The reader's surprise at finding so naïve a statement in a work written by a realist like Calhoun is reduced only by recalling a similar passage written by John Adams, another advocate of mixed government theory. In his passion for mixed government Adams had concluded that it was possible for a constitution to last forever if only it possessed a proper balance between the orders. Adams explained: "The best republics will be virtuous and have been so; but we may hazard a conjecture, that the virtues have been the effect of the well-ordered constitution, rather than the cause: and perhaps it would be impossible to prove that a republic cannot exist even among highwaymen, by setting one rogue to watch another; and the knaves themselves may, in time, be made honest men by the struggle." According to Adams and Calhoun, mixed government compelled a habit of compromise that eventuated in virtue, the desire to place the common good above one's own immediate interests. But a consistent realist—as opposed to one who views human nature pessimistically when analyzing absolute governments but optimistically when hypothesizing concerning mixed government—might reject the latter half of the equation entirely and question the universality of the first half. There is little evidence that compromise produces virtue, and while mixed government sometimes leads to compromise, it sometimes leads to paralysis. In glorifying the Roman tribunes Calhoun neglected to note what most educated Americans knew: that later tribunes were corrupted from their early role as defenders of the masses. It was, after all, a tribune who, under aristocratic influence, vetoed the land-redistribution law of Tiberius Gracchus. The greater the number of persons exercising a veto power, the greater the danger of paralysis. Thus if some modern Americans complain of "gridlock" due to the constitutional requirement that four separate entities (the president, the Senate, the House of Representatives, and the Supreme Court) concur on all federal legislation, how much greater would the threat of paralysis be if the consent of each of the fifty states—or some comparable number of major interests—were required to enact every federal law?[67]

Finally, Calhoun's expressions of disgust for "majority tyranny," along with his corresponding calls for the protection of "minority rights," inevitably ring hollow to modern ears when emanating from one of the leading defenders of slavery. The majority tyranny that southern whites exercised over African American slaves was incomparably greater than anything the northern majority ever inflicted on the southern white minority. Aware of the inconsistency, Calhoun had little choice but to follow Aristotle beyond mixed government and also embrace his equally famous doctrine of the natural slave (*Politics* 2), the theory that some men were born to lead and others to follow. When Calhoun advised a young man to "read the best elementary treatises on Government, including Aristotle's, which I regard as among the best," he was endorsing not only Aristotle's mixed government theory but also his defense of slavery. By equating African Americans with Aristotle's natural slaves, Calhoun was able to deny them the right of resistance to majority tyranny that southern whites possessed.[68]

The Civil War was, in large part, a product of the failure of American mixed government. When the South became too small a minority to retain its senatorial and presidential veto powers, and the northern majority refused to obey the Supreme Court's Dred Scott decision, many southern whites feared that they had lost the ability to defend themselves against all manner of northern legislation. They believed that their only remaining choice was between submission to majority tyranny and secession from the Union. They chose secession. Yet, though constituting only a minority of the American public, the southern white population was large enough to prosecute a war that inflicted more American casualties than any other war in the nation's history.[69]

It was Calhoun's tragedy that he foresaw the approaching calamity but could not avert it. Shortly before he died, while the nation was embroiled in a passionate debate over the Compromise of 1850, Calhoun prophesied to James M. Mason that the Union would be dissolved: "I fix its probable occurrence within twelve years or three presidential terms. You and others of your age will probably live to see it; I shall not. The mode by which it will be done is not so clear; it may be brought about in a manner that no one now foresees. But the probability is, it will explode in a presidential election." One month after Abraham Lincoln's election in 1860, a campaign in which Lincoln won a majority of the nation's electoral votes without even appearing on most southern ballots, South Carolina seceded from the Union, followed soon after by ten other southern states.[70]

The secession and bloody civil war that Calhoun had labored to prevent might have been averted had any of his proposed modifications to American mixed government been adopted. The lives of over 600,000 Americans might have been saved. The destruction that impoverished the postbellum South, along with the intense bitterness that poisoned sectional relations for decades, might have been forestalled. On the other hand, American government might have been paralyzed by Calhoun's innovations, and, absent the Civil War, slavery would certainly have continued for several decades at least, if not indefinitely. Only one thing is certain: the South that Calhoun knew and loved was destroyed by the war he struggled in vain to avert.[71]

Calhoun's failure was the product not of a decline in American classicism but of its transformation. The founders' classicism, as reflected in the federal and state constitutions they drafted and ratified, looked upon Athenian democracy with horror, as a disgusting form of mob rule, and viewed the alleged mixed government of Rome with reverence. But the succeeding generation quickly reinterpreted these constitutions—and their framers—as democratic and set about revising the former to make them so in reality. Performing the neat trick of venerating the founders while attempting to refashion their handiwork, most antebellum Americans regarded all obstacles to complete majority rule as heretical. While still regarding individual Roman aristocrats with reverence, antebellum Americans tossed aside the mixed government of Rome for the dynamic, artistic democracy of Athens. In one sense, then, Calhoun really was among "the last of the Romans."

CHAPTER THREE

Pastoralism and Utilitarianism

T HE GROWTH of democracy in antebellum America was accompanied by the spread of a type of utilitarianism that held that only those practices contributing to immediate economic progress should be adopted. In a nation in which status was determined by wealth rather than birth, it was only natural that Americans should be preoccupied with acquiring wealth. The Industrial Revolution, which began in Britain in the late eighteenth century and spread to the United States in the early nineteenth century, encouraged this utilitarianism by providing new opportunities for wealth. But the effects of the Industrial Revolution on American society were felt much more profoundly in the late nineteenth century than during the antebellum period. The vast majority of Americans were still farmers in the years before the Civil War, and though their agriculture was increasingly commercial, the pace and structure of farm life differed little from those of previous generations. Furthermore, as in nearly all past periods of commercial prosperity, the very surge in wealth created an anticommercial backlash that relied heavily on the classics. John T. Kirkland, the president of Harvard, was not alone in 1818 when he expressed the wish that America might "produce fruit of the mind," not just an "unsanctified, Carthaginian, perishable prosperity." Finally, the Industrial Revolution produced a new middle class eager to acquire some of the refinement of the upper classes through the acquisition of classical knowledge and of classical items with which to adorn their homes. Ironically, the very factories that challenged classical pastoralism also, for the first time, filled the private homes of ordinary people with items that represented the classical heritage, while steam-powered presses churned out inexpensive classical texts. Ralph Waldo Emerson asked: "How can the age be a bad one which gives me Plato and Paul and Plutarch . . . besides its own riches? Our presses groan every year with new editions of all the select pieces of the first of mankind." As the historian Richard L. Bushman put it: "Never before had a high-end style reached so far into society and culture; never had fashion been democratized as profoundly as was the classical taste." The breadth of the American reverence for the classics, as much as its depth, explains why the utilitarians failed to displace them from the schools even in a democratic age that must have seemed ideal for their project.[1]

Classical Pastoralism

Antebellum America was not the first prosperous society to experience a romantic backlash against excessive commercialism. Indeed, many of the classical pastoral writers to whom early Americans appealed were themselves denizens of commercial societies. Too often modern historians interpret the pastoral ideal of the classical authors as a description of classical society rather than as a protest against the money-grubbing commerce that frequently pervaded it. Aside from Hesiod (who was hardly romantic about agriculture, emphasizing the hard work required to eke out a living on the rather barren soil of most of Greece), the most famous classical pastoralists were all protestors against the urban, commercial societies in which they lived, societies whose commercial prosperity ironically financed their romantic, nostalgic poetry about the rural life. Theocritus and the Alexandrian poets who first established pastoral poetry as a genre of Greek literature lived in the greatest commercial city of the Hellenistic Age. Among the Romans the leading pastoralists were Virgil and Horace, who owned farms but who spent a good deal of time in Rome, the imperial center and seat of commerce for the whole Western world, and who received financial support from the emperor Augustus through his adviser Maecenas. Horace's statement, which Emerson loved to quote in the original Latin, "The whole chorus of poets loves the grove and flees the town," was as dubious in Horace's age as it was in Emerson's—as dubious as Cato the Elder's statement, "The Countryman has the fewest evil thoughts."[2]

Among these city dwellers, no theme was more ubiquitous than that of the superiority of the rural, agricultural existence, a lifestyle that rested comfortably between the extremes of "savage" and "sophisticated." Convinced that farmers were the backbone of Rome, Virgil exhorted his fellow Romans to regenerate the community after a century of civil war by returning to the plow (*Georgics* 2.458–474):

> How lucky the farmers are—wish they knew!
> The Earth herself, most just, pours forth for them
> An easy living from the soil, far off
> From clashing weapons. Though the farmer has
> No mansion with proud portals which spits out
> A monster wave of morning visitors
> From every room, nor do his callers gasp
> At inlaid columns, bright with tortoiseshell,
> Or gold-embroidered clothes or bronzes from
> Ephyre, nor in his house is plain white wool
> Dyed with Assyrian poison, nor does he
> Corrupt his olive oil with foreign spice,
> He has untroubled sleep and honest life.
> Rich in all sorts of riches, with a vast
> Estate, he has all the leisure to enjoy
> A cave, a natural pond, a valley where
> The air is cool—the mooing of the cows
> Is ever present, and to sleep beneath
> A tree is sweet. Wild animals abound
> For hunting, and young people grow up strong,
> Hardworking, satisfied with poverty:
> Their gods are holy; parents are revered.
> Surely, when Justice left the earth she stayed
> Last with these folks, and left some tokens here.

The farmer's lifestyle was the source of republican virtue.[3]

The pastoral theme was as much a staple of classical political theory and history as of Greek and Roman poetry. Aristotle argued that the best republics were predominantly agricultural. Polybius, Sallust, Livy, and Plutarch considered Sparta and early republican Rome models not merely because they had possessed mixed governments but also because they had been agricultural societies. These historians credited the triumph of Sparta and Rome over their vice-ridden, commercial adversaries, Athens and Carthage, as much to their pastoral virtues as to their government forms. Both produced virtue, the agricultural life by fostering frugality, temperance, and independence, the balanced constitution by encouraging moderation, cooperation, and compromise. The plow was both the symbol and the cause of Cincinnatus' "Roman virtue." Furthermore, classical historians attributed the fall of the Roman republic to the "Punic Curse," the commercialization of Rome that had resulted from the republic's conquest of the Carthaginian Empire.

The curse of commercial wealth had transformed Rome from a modest village into an imperial city. Whether by choice or necessity, farmers had abandoned the soil for the iniquitous life of the city. Deprived of the dignity that an independent means of subsistence affords the farmer, these former bastions of republicanism had become the clients of dictators, prepared to sell the once-glorious republic for the paltry price of bread and circuses. Disgruntled by their forced subservience to emperors, the aristocratic poets and historians who painted this compelling portrait idealized an epoch their class had dominated, though their own lifestyles would hardly have suited them to the rustic existence their works immortalized. Like most worshipers of agriculture who succeeded them, the Roman pastoralists lived a life distant from the manual labor they extolled. Far less romantic about their lot, many of the farmers the pastoralists glorified preferred the freedom from "noble toil" that life in the city afforded—hence Virgil's need to tell the farmers how lucky they were.[4]

Thus it is not surprising that pastoralism was especially popular in Britain and the United States in the mid- to late eighteenth century, precisely the time when both nations were undergoing commercial revolutions. An enthusiastic supporter of agriculture, King George III was fond of his nickname "Farmer George." Both Farmer Georges, the king and the rebel Washington, corresponded with Arthur Young, one of the high priests of the eighteenth-century pastoral movement. Young declared, "Perhaps we might, without any great impropriety, call farming the reigning taste of the present times." Ironically, pastoralism also inspired many of the early classical economists, whose ideas proved the eventual ruin of classical republicanism. The French Physiocrats, the economists who first coined the term "laissez-faire," fondly cited Socrates on the greater morality, as well as the greater prosperity, produced by agriculture. It is no accident that Adam Smith began his career as a moral philosopher and that his brand of laissez-faire economics favored agriculture over industry, in sharp contrast to the later theories of David Ricardo. Early economists of all varieties were motivated as much by moral as by economic concerns. While laissez-faire economics was indeed something very new, it was developed, at least in part, to protect something very old—the agricultural lifestyle, which was threatened by mercantilist tariffs designed to aid new industries against foreign competition. For this reason, Thomas Jefferson, James Madison, and the Democratic-Republicans supported free trade against Alexander Hamilton's neomercantilist program, often issuing encomiums to agriculture that sounded much like Virgil's. Jefferson purchased Louisiana, even though he believed that the purchase was unconstitutional, in order to extend the nation's agricultural base and, hence, its virtue and longevity. He often compared his nemesis Great Britain to corrupt Carthage, implying an analogy between the United States and the frugal Roman republic.[5]

Such analogies continued in the antebellum period. Since the vast majority of Americans were farmers, pastoralism seemed to accord well with antebellum democracy. Like most western congressmen, Senator Thomas Hart Benton of Missouri advocated setting the price of public land in the West as low as possible, a trend that would culminate in the Homestead Act of 1862, in order to maintain a society of Virgilian farmers such as had existed in the early Roman republic and whose loss had led to the fall of that republic. In 1826 Benton wrote: "Tenantry is unfavorable to freedom. It lays the foundation for separate orders in society, annihilates the love of country, and weakens the spirit of independence. . . . The freeholder, on the contrary, is the natural supporter of a free government." Two years later he wrote concerning the Roman republic, "It was this interest in the soil of the country which made the love of that country so strong a passion in the breast of the Roman citizen." He invoked the Gracchi, who had sought unsuccessfully to revive the yeoman class and restore the republic. In 1838 he wrote that small farmers were "the best of citizens . . . brave, hospitable, patriotic, and industrious, living upon their own labor, and that labor the primeval occupation of man and the first command of God." Similarly, an 1840 article in the periodical the *Rough-Hewer* compared Americans to Romans. The author wrote, "The ancient Romans venerated the plough, and at the earliest, purest time of the Republic, the greatest praise which could be given to an illustrious character was [that he was] a judicious and industrious husbandman." In a play about the Battle of New Orleans an American dramatist placed these words in General John Coffee's mouth: "Our western wilds preserve the ancient glory." Thomas Buchanan Read, who had lived in Rome for many years, wrote *The New Pastoral* and *Sylvia, or The Last Shepherd: An Eclogue*, neoclassical poems set in Read's native Pennsylvania ("Penn's Woods" in Latin). In Read's imagination "shy nymphs" from the caves of the Susquehanna sang in praise of "that middle life, betwixt the hut and the palace." Likewise, Thomas Cole's painting *Dream of Arcadia* (1838) depicted a pristine Greek temple overlooking a pastoral vale in which figures lounged, danced, waded, and worshipped—but did not work.[6]

A similar romanticism pervaded the pastoralism of Henry David Thoreau. In 1838 he wrote, "In imagination I hie me to Greece as to enchanted ground." In his idealized image of ancient Greece, "No storms vex her coasts, no clouds encircle her Helicon or Olympus, no tempests sweep the peaceful Tempe or ruffle the bosom of the placid Aegean; but always the beams of the summer's sun gleam along the entablature of the Acropolis, or are reflected through the mellow atmosphere from a thousand consecrated groves and fountains; always her sea-girt isles are dallying with their zephyr guests, and the low of kine is heard along the meads, and the landscape sleeps—valley and hill and woodland—a dreamy sleep. Each of her sons created a new heaven and a new earth for Greece."[7]

While Thoreau sometimes immersed himself in the earthy practical advice contained in Roman agricultural treatises, the mystical pastoral ideal was never far from his thoughts. In 1851, after dining with Bronson Alcott, he took home his host's copy of a collection of extracts from the manuals of Cato the Elder, Varro, Columella, and Palladius. Considering farming the noblest of occupations, Thoreau noted the similarities between Roman and modern agriculture: "The more we know about the ancients the more we find they were like the moderns. When I read Marcus Cato's *De Re Rustica*, a small treatise or Farmer's Manual of those days, fresh from the field of Roman life, all reeking with and redolent of the life of those days . . . here is a simple, direct, pertinent word addressed to the Romans. . . . The farmer's was pretty much the same routine then as now." He quoted Cato in Latin on the preparation and application of dung, adding, "Just such directions as you find in the Farmer's Almanac to-day." He concluded: "How much the Roman must have been indebted to his agriculture, dealing with the earth, its clods and stubble, its dust and mire. Their farmer consuls were their glory, and they well knew the farm to be the nursery of soldiers. Read Cato to see what kind of legs the Romans stood on." He wrote: "In reading Columella I am frequently reminded, not only by the general tone, but even by the particular warnings and directions, of our agricultural journals and reports of farmers' clubs. Often what is last and most insisted on among us was most insisted on by the Romans. As when he says it is better to cultivate a little land well than a great deal ill." Thoreau added: "The Romans introduced husbandry into England, where but little was practiced, and the English have introduced it into America. So we may well read the Roman authors for a list of this art as practiced by us." He quoted the first book of Virgil's *Georgics* at length on the joys of winter. Thoreau composed his own Virgilian pastorals and Catonian essays, imitations that indicated a thorough familiarity with the originals.[8]

The Utilitarian Assault on the Classical Languages Requirement

As the Industrial Revolution advanced in the antebellum United States, utilitarian arguments against the requirement of Greek and Latin in the schools increased, though the arguments themselves were no different from those that had been put forward by Benjamin Franklin, Benjamin Rush, and Thomas Paine (and by others even before these), and the antebellum utilitarians suffered almost as complete a defeat as their predecessors had. Indeed, their defeat was caused, at least in part, by the romantic backlash against excessive commercialism that the Industrial Revolution itself unleashed.[9]

In 1811 Jonathan Maxcy, president of South Carolina College, caused a firestorm by proposing a reduction in the amount of time college students spent on ancient texts. Maxcy urged the replacement of the classics with math and science courses during the students' junior and senior years. Under Maxcy's proposal, knowledge of Greek and Latin would still be required for admission to the college, and students would still receive instruction in the classical languages during their freshman year.[10]

Though Maxcy's proposal was defeated, the issue was not settled. In 1823 George Ticknor, Harvard's modern language professor, advocated a program of elective choice for students willing to forgo a bachelor of arts degree. Ticknor's proposal was modest but nonetheless remarkable, considering that he had been awe-stricken by the antiquities of Rome as a tourist six years earlier, using worn copies of Pliny, Livy, Horace, and Virgil as his guidebooks, had studied ancient sculptures and ruins with an archaeologist there, had raised money for American neoclassical artists, and had quoted Johann Winckelmann's dictum, "The only way in which we can become great . . . is by imitating the ancients." In 1825 Philip Lindsley, the new president of the University of Nashville, proposed a similar system of electives, as did James Marsh, the new president of the University of Vermont, the following year. Lindsley favored courses on government, manufacturing, and commerce. In 1827 the faculty members at Amherst College issued two reports stating that the traditional curriculum provided no advantages "in an age of universal improvements, and in a young, free, and prosperous country like ours, it is absurd to cling so tenaciously to the prescriptive forces of other countries." The authors of the reports claimed that the public was dissatisfied with the current educational system because "it is not sufficiently modern and comprehensive to meet the exigencies of the age." They proposed a parallel course to the classics that would emphasize English literature, modern languages and history, civil and political law, physics, and chemistry. The following year an essayist named "A Modern" published "The Study of the Classics" in both the *South Carolina State Gazette* and the *Columbia Advertiser*. "A Modern" wrote:

> The stores of knowledge are not now, as formerly, locked up in the hidden Languages of past Ages, but spread before us in our Mother tongue. All that is

profound in Science; in Poetry, sublime and beautiful—all that is useful, as necessary to our existence, or agreeable, as a relaxation from severer duties of life [is] . . . now to us [as] familiar as household words. . . . Instead, therefore, of wasting those years, when the mind is most pliable, in the fruitless study of a Language which is acquired but to be thrown aside; how much more commendable, as well as useful, to employ that time in the critical study of their own tongue. . . . For it is no uncommon thing to meet with young men who have gone through a Collegiate course not only most vilely deficient in the very rudiments of English, but incapable to spell or pronounce words of the most common occurrence in the language. . . . In a land like ours, where our youth are called into the business of life at an early age, it behooves us to engage their minds in that way which is most likely to fit them for their pursuits.[11]

In 1830 Henry Vethake, who taught mathematics and philosophy at Princeton, contended that the traditional requirement of Greek and Latin must give way to an elective system better suited to the needs of modern society. Vethake claimed that while it had been necessary "some two or three centuries ago" to study Latin for scientific information, most scientists now wrote in their own vernacular language, and "everything which antiquity has left us worth the perusal" had been translated into English. Vethake continued:

> The progress of knowledge, more especially of mathematical and physical science, has been such as to render the older authors of no value, except insofar as the gratification of the curiosity of those who are interested in tracing the gradual advances made by the human mind gives them one. . . . In the United States, the number of individuals desirous of gaining useful information vastly exceeds that of those who have the time and money to enable them to go through the whole course of education prescribed by our colleges. . . . I see no reason why . . . young men should be told that unless they learn Latin and Greek, they shall not be permitted to learn anything else. Whilst I would have ample provision made in our colleges for instruction, and able instruction, in these languages, as well as in every branch of literature and science, I would leave the supply of instruction in all to be regulated by the proportional demand of the public for each.

In an age of scientific and economic specialization, the broad classical education offered by most colleges was inadequate: "The most educated men are, in general, acquainted, to a certain extent, with all things under the sun, rather than with any one branch of knowledge thoroughly so as to be able to be of much practical service to their fellow men, or to contribute in any striking degree to the progress of invention or discovery. And it will be well, perhaps, for the interests of education, if our literary institutions were to administer some check to this prevalent evil, instead of encouraging it by teaching, as some of them do, a mere smattering of many things."[12]

The same year Albert Gallatin, the former U.S. secretary of the Treasury and a member of the council that established New York University, sought to persuade his colleagues to make the study of the classics optional at the university. He wrote: "If before the Reformation the way to the word of God and to his worship was obstructed by the improper use of the Latin language, we now find the same impediment arresting a more general diffusion of human knowledge." The rigid application of the classical languages requirement was as detrimental to the prosperity of the United States as the Catholic Church's insistence on the Latin Vulgate Bible, itself a translation, over the vernacular translations had been to true religion.[13]

Also in 1830 Jacob Bigelow, Harvard's first professor of applied science, suggested an elective system. He wrote to his president, Josiah Quincy: "Is it not useful that education in our seminaries should have reference to the conditions and future pursuits of the young men who compose them? A great majority of graduates at our college are dispersed through the interior of the country where their lives are spent in contact with the middling and operative classes of the community, whose pursuits they must in some measure assimilate to their own. . . . A professional man may pass his whole life without a single call for his knowledge of astronomy, of metaphysics, of Greek or of German. But it is not so with the practical and useful applications of science."[14]

In 1842 the *Southern Literary Messenger,* which often published articles regarding classical subjects, published a satiric attack on the classics. The author chose not to divulge his identity, probably a wise decision considering the sharpness of his humor. He wrote:

> Of Latin and Greek: two ancient and barbarous tongues—the vernacular of savages now extinct—a fossil Chocktaw, the study of which was introduced to the West through the influence of monks and others belonging to the antirecuperative sect, who attempt to stifle the energies of mind. Use: said to be the reading of a blind beggar-man's songs—and some miserable apologies for plays, where certain chorusses supply the place of the present stage-trick and pantomime. . . . The real use: to make a show in speeches by quoting these tongues—a capital trick when you balk or are posed by an antagonist's argument. Rule: lay up a store of short, pithy sentences, not exceeding a dozen words—get them out of unused books, such as Lucretius, Terence & c., so that they may have an air of research; and if you should thereby awaken the attention of some cobwebbed bookworm, and he begins to hold communion with you about the classics, assume the virtue of modesty, though you have it not; and if he bore you, as such rude persons are apt to do, you may walk away without fear. Such individuals are seldom courageous enough to resent an insult, or of sufficient consequence for you to care about their friendship. . . . Always smile patronizingly when you hear a quotation; and if the person, as

is usual with young men, translate it, thank him in a cold, contemptuous manner for it—by which he will become persuaded to envy you for your attainments, a consummation devoutly to be prayed for, inasmuch as it produces the impression of power from you. The very best circumstance under which to exhibit your scholarship is before guests at your own table—picked by you with some aim. Never be afraid of the people called professors of languages, or of the humanities; they are usually needy and mean specimens of humanity. With a certain amount of the Godlike virtue Assurance, you will create a sensation in this department, and it is of consequence you should, for people esteem it a test of a liberal education—it is the passport of a gentleman.[15]

In 1849 James D. B. De Bow published an article in his own journal, entitled "The Commercial Age," in which he criticized colleges for emphasizing the classics over what he regarded as more practical subjects such as engineering, economics, agriculture, chemistry, and commerce. He wrote: "Theory and fact are the poles of ancient and modern philosophy. Bacon has risen up against Aristotle and vindicated *fact* in the face of all nations and men." If the South were to prosper, it must place commerce on the pedestal it was "destined to occupy." Against the pastoralists who favored Rome, De Bow touted Carthage as a resourceful state, and other contributors to his journal preferred the city's commercial spirit to Roman militarism.[16]

In 1850 Francis Wayland, the president of Brown University, proposed a system of electives that would include modern languages, science, political economy, agriculture, and pedagogy. Wayland took the unusual approach of attempting to advance this utilitarian project with religious language. He declared, "God intended us for progress, and we counteract his design when we deify antiquity and bow down and worship an opinion, not because it is either wise or true, but simply because it is ancient."[17]

The utilitarian onslaught on the classics continued in the 1850s. In 1853 another president of South Carolina College, James H. Thornwell, wrote to the state's governor complaining of the dominance of classical studies at the university. Thornwell asserted that some students "do not want Latin, Greek, and philosophy, and it is hard that they cannot be permitted to get a little chemistry, a little engineering, or a little natural philosophy, without going through Homer and Virgil, Aristotle and Locke." He claimed that many graduates lost their classical knowledge within a few years, retaining only a smug sense of superiority over common citizens. The following year Henry Harrisse, an instructor of French at the University of North Carolina, proposed the replacement of the university's rigorous classical languages requirement with courses in ancient and modern history, as well as other subjects. Harrisse denied that the study of Greek and Latin disciplined the mind "in a higher degree than other studies which, besides possessing this quality, may also impart a great deal of useful and necessary knowledge." In 1856 a state senator in Texas even opposed the establishment of a public university on the grounds that the classics tended to dominate universities. The senator declared: "The diffusion of useful knowledge among the people generally should be our first care—discarding all the useless reading of the age. Of what avail is it that the youth can tell you of lost languages or obsolete sciences?" Even Anna Calhoun Clemson urged her father, in a letter written in Brussels, to moderate his insistence on the classical training of his grandsons: "In this travelling age of the world, the knowledge of one or more modern languages is much more essential than the ancient, and I entreat you to cause James and Willy to take every opportunity of perfecting themselves in French, at least."[18]

Although he never proposed the elimination of the Greek and Latin requirement, often made classical references himself, and placed a quintessentially classical emphasis on the role of education in fostering civic virtue, even the famed educational reformer Horace Mann implied that the scientific and technological revolutions of the immediate past had diminished the relevance of the ancients. Mann claimed: "In no respect is the contrast or disparity between the ancient and modern times more remarkable than in their ignorance of, and our acquaintance with, the natural sciences. . . . Following Pythagoras were Socrates, Plato, and Aristotle among the Greeks, and Quintilian among the Romans—great men, indeed, but with not enough great men around them to correct their errors; and hence it may be questioned whether the authority of their names has not propagated, through succeeding times, more of error than of truth." If not for the modern Scientific Revolution, "we should be teaching Aristotle's Physics to-day—that the planets move around the earth in circles, because the circle is the perfect form of motion, and Nature's abhorrence of a vacuum—the very doctrine that made the human mind the vacuum it denied." (Mann's blanket dismissal of Greek science based on Aristotle's error was more than a bit harsh. After all, the modern Scientific Revolution began when Copernicus rediscovered the heliocentric theory of Aristarchus, and the ancient Greeks not only anticipated some of the key theories of modern science but also developed the very scientific method that modern scientists used to surpass them.) Furthermore, Mann asked concerning the ancients: "Why was it that they built the Parthenon and the Colosseum before they knew how to construct a comfortable, healthful dwelling-house? Why did they construct the Roman aqueducts before they constructed a saw-mill? Or why did they achieve the noblest models in eloquence, poetry, and in the drama before they invented movable type?" His answer was that "the aristocratic or patrician orders not only disdained labor for themselves and their children, which was one fatal mistake, but they supposed that knowledge was of no use to a laborer, which was a mistake still more fatal." The failure of the ancients to educate the masses through the type of public education Mann sought for America was the root cause of their inability to produce the technology that the Industrial Revolution was now using to improve lives.[19]

California journalist John S. Hittel spoke for many when he claimed, "The superiority of our time over antiquity is due . . . to the possession of machinery." Hittel was so romantic about materialism that he declared, "If I were a poet and felt myself capable of maintaining the epic flight, I think I would find in the great Californian gold discovery and its results a subject more congenial to the taste of this age, richer in impressive suggestions, in strange and romantic incidents, and generally in material for a great poem than the conquest of Troy or Jerusalem, the adventures of Ulysses or Aeneas."[20]

The Classical Counterattack

Responding with fury to nearly every utilitarian assault, the defenders of the classics achieved a victory that could hardly have been more complete. In 1827, two years after the Connecticut legislature, under the leadership of state senator Noyes Darling, requested that Yale abolish its Greek and Latin entrance requirement in favor of modern languages, languages the legislature considered more useful to a modern economy, the university authorized a committee to study the possibility of curriculum change. When the committee asked the faculty's opinion in 1828, Yale president Jeremiah Day responded by coauthoring the famous "Yale Report" with classics professor James Luce Kingsley. In his section of the report Day, who was also a professor of mathematics and natural philosophy, asked, "Is a man to have no other object than to obtain a living by professional pursuits? Has he not duties to perform to his fellow citizens, to his country, duties which require various and extensive intellectual furniture?" While the classics were vital to the moral and political education of the citizenry and could be taught only in schools, the mercantile, mechanical, and agricultural trades could be taught well only at the sites where they were practiced. Day wrote: "As in our primary schools, reading, writing, and arithmetic are taught to all, however different their prospects, so in a college, all should be instructed in those branches of knowledge of which no one destined to the higher walks of life ought to be ignorant. . . . Merchants, manufacturers, and farmers, as well as professional gentlemen, take their place in our public councils. A thorough education ought therefore to be extended to all these classes."[21]

A classical education was required to keep men from becoming too narrow and materialistic. Day continued concerning businessmen:

> Is it not desirable that they should be men of superior education, of large and liberal views, of those solid and elegant attainments, which will raise them to a higher distinction than the mere possession of property, which will not allow them to hoard their treasures, or waste them in senseless extravagance, which will enable them to adorn society by their learning, to move in the more intelligent circles with dignity, and to make such an application of their wealth, as will be most honorable to themselves, and most beneficial to their country? The active, enterprising character of our population renders it highly important that this bustle and energy should be directed by sound intelligence, the result of deep thought and early discipline. The greater the impulse to action, the greater is the need of wise and skillful guidance. . . . Where a free government gives full liberty to human intellect to expand and operate, education should be proportionally liberal and ample.

The classics were ideally suited to provide such an education. Day concluded:

> The learned world long ago settled this matter and subsequent events and experience have confirmed their decision. We are the people, the genius of whose government and institutions more especially and imperiously than any other, demands that the field of classical learning be industriously and thoroughly explored and cultivated. . . . The models of ancient literature, which are put into the hands of the young student, can hardly fail to imbue his mind with the principles of liberty, to inspire the liveliest patriotism, and to excite [him] to noble and generous action, and are therefore peculiarly adapted to the American youth.[22]

Professor Kingsley concurred with President Day. He noted: "The proper question is,—what course of discipline affords the best mental culture, leads to the most thorough knowledge of our own literature, and lays the best foundation for professional study? The ancient languages here have a decided advantage. . . . Those who have excelled in classical literature and have likewise acquired a competent knowledge of some one modern European language besides the English have found themselves the best qualified to make a full use of their new advantages. . . . Ancient literature is too deeply inwrought into the whole system of modern literature to be so easily laid aside." Doing so would only foster public distrust in the quality of a Yale education.[23]

Persuaded by the arguments of Day and Kingsley, the university committee confirmed their position as the committee's own. Indeed, the committee's chairman, Gideon Tomlinson, paraphrased Day, writing, "The models of ancient literature which are put into the hands of the young student can hardly fail to imbue his mind with the principles of liberty, to inspire the liveliest patriotism, and to excite to noble and generous action." The committee had come to the conclusion, therefore, "that it is inexpedient so to alter the regular course of instruction at this college as to leave out . . . the study of the ancient languages." The committee even added that "the terms of admission may very properly be gradually raised so as ultimately to render necessary, as a condition of admission, much greater requirements, especially in the classics, than the laws of the college at present prescribe."[24]

Meyer Reinhold has called the Yale Report "the most influential document in American higher education in the first half of the nineteenth century" because it "assured the entrenchment of the classics, not only at Yale, but throughout the country, until after the Civil War." Yale's status as the largest and most diverse college of the time, boasting students from a greater number of states than any other college, contributed to this effect. Benjamin Silliman, Yale's professor of chemistry and mineralogy, quickly published the report in the *American Journal of Science and Arts*. College speakers throughout the 1830s paraphrased the report, and Yale was applauded throughout the nation for defending the classics. Lindsley was unsuccessful in securing acceptance of his elective system at the University of Nashville. Amherst quickly dropped its parallel course of study in 1831, only four years after launching it, because the majority of the faculty acknowledged that both students and the general public did not believe that the new degree possessed the same prestige as the old. The same thing occurred at Brown, where students protested that the parallel program had ruined Brown's reputation, thereby casting a pall over even the standard degree. Wayland's successor lamented, "We are now literally receiving the refuse of other colleges." Albert Gallatin felt compelled to resign from the New York University council when he failed to persuade his colleagues to make the study of the classics optional. Even Yale's chief rival, Harvard, demonstrated its agreement by dramatically increasing its classical admissions requirements in the 1830s and 1840s; by 1850 the Harvard qualifying examination lasted eight hours. Harvard president Josiah Quincy believed that the classics provided "the sure and solid foundation on which you may, in after life, build whatsoever intellectual frame you will." He responded to an appeal by William Ellery Channing to make Harvard more "popular" by declaring, "Let there be at least one institution in the country the criterion of whose worth and merit shall be measured by something other than the number of its polls." Western Reserve and Illinois College both proclaimed themselves the "Yale of the West." The first catalog of Beloit College on the Wisconsin frontier proudly announced a classical curriculum "drawn up exactly on the Yale plan." As a trustee of the College of

California, Day's son Sherman later succeeded in removing the college's Spanish language requirement and reducing its French requirement on behalf of the classical languages. Yale became the northern school of choice for southerners, and its graduates played a leading role in establishing schools and colleges on the frontier. Thirty-six of the nation's seventy-five college presidents in 1840 were Yale alumni. In the antebellum period Yale helped found sixteen colleges in various sections of the country.[25]

But the Yale Report was neither the first nor the last influential defense of the classics. In 1820 the *Western Review* of Cincinnati had declared, "Should the time ever come when Latin and Greek should be banished from our Universities, and the study of Cicero and Demosthenes, of Homer and Virgil, should be considered as unnecessary for the formation of a scholar, we should regard mankind as fast sinking into absolute barbarism and the gloom of mental darkness as likely to increase until it should become universal." In a lecture to the American Institute of Instructors in 1830 Cornelius Felton argued that utilitarians missed the point. Felton conceded that knowledge of Greece and Rome "may not lead to the invention of a single new mechanical agent; it may not be the direct means of increasing our fortunes a single dollar." He added: "But it will give us an enlarged view of our nature . . . it will teach us to judge charitably of others' minds and hearts; it will teach us that intellect and sensibility, and genius, have existed beyond the narrow circle in which we have moved—beyond the limits of our country—centuries before our age. Such lessons are needed in the every day concerns of life." Meanwhile, Joseph Story, who had supported Ticknor's modest reforms initially but had then changed his mind, wrote, "The importance of classical learning to professional education is so obvious that the surprise is that it could ever have become a matter of disputation." He emphasized that classical training was crucial to doctors, lawyers, and ministers. He wrote to Josiah Quincy: "It is a comfort to me in these days of reform and wild speculation that there are those among us who stick to the good old doctrines of other times and to the studies by which learning and taste and genius have been achieved in other days. . . . I shall be very glad if you can revive the desire of classical attainments less superficial and more thorough than we had." Story saw Harvard as a counterweight to the growing materialism of American society. The provost at Columbia University declared that sound learning depended on Greek and Latin: "It is now too late for ignorance, indolence, eccentricity, or infidelity to dispute what has been ratified by the seal of the ages."[26]

Hugh Swinton Legaré responded passionately to utilitarian attacks on the classics. Legaré noted slyly that his chief opponent in the dispute, Thomas Grimké, could not have attacked the classics so forcefully had not

Grimké's adversary, the classics, trained him for battle and supplied him with rhetorical arms. Legaré rejected the assertion that the ancients were masters of style but not of substance. In fact, one could not separate the two, any more than one could separate art from practical endeavor. Legaré noted, "Sophocles held the rank of General along with Thucydides and Pericles—a matchless combination!" Against utilitarian arguments, Legaré responded, "The capital object of education [should be] to form the moral character, not by teaching what to think but persuading to act well; not by loading the memory with cold and barren precepts, but forming the sensibility by the habitual, fervid, and rapturous contemplation of high and heroic models of excellence; not by definitions of virtue and speculations about the principle of obligation, but making us love the one and feel the sacredness of the other." A classical education could accomplish this goal; a utilitarian trade school could not. A utilitarian education was not likely to be useful if it neglected the necessity of firing the imagination. Greece was a "lonely brightness" that exemplified harmony of thought and action, style and substance, a civilization possessed of an extraordinary language as near to perfection as humans had contrived. The English language was so formed by Latin that it could not be properly understood and appreciated without recourse to its ancestor. Legaré concluded, "Above all, our American youth will learn [from the classics] that liberty—which is sweet to all men, but which is the passion of proud minds that cannot stoop to less—has been the nurse of all that is sublime in character and genius."[27]

Legaré conceded that some had idolized the ancients too much in the past but felt that modern utilitarians erred in the opposite direction. He wrote: "It was quite fashionable about 200 years ago to compare the moderns in their intellectual relation to the ancients to a dwarf mounted upon the back of a giant—seeing further, indeed, from the advantage of position, but no more to be compared with the mighty being under him than any other dependent with him on whose bounty he subsists. In these times the picture is exactly reversed. The giant is mounted upon the dwarf and is to go on, it seems, increasing in dimensions until his stature shall reach the skies. The superstition of Europe believed too much of the past—the enthusiasm of America expects too much from the future." While Legaré conceded that Plato and Aristotle had been wrong to suggest that "the exercise of any mechanic art . . . [was] altogether inconsistent with the character of a freeman and a good citizen," a conclusion that could only be regarded as ludicrous in the land of Benjamin Franklin, it was equally fallacious to elevate industry and commerce above all other concerns. Legaré viewed utilitarianism as a "grievous malady . . . rapidly becoming epidemical." While his defense of classical learning was hailed throughout the South, Grimké's own eulogist was apologetic about his anticlassical tirades.²⁸

In an 1832 address to his fellow members of the Literary and Philosophical Society of Charleston, the Catholic bishop John English lauded classical education. He stressed the value of ancient history as an antidote to the dangerous cult of progress, derided the demand for a more "practical" system of education, and recommended Homer, Demosthenes, Virgil, Caesar, Horace, and Cicero as stylistic models. Indeed, English went on to publish an essay on Virgil ("The Descent of Aeneas to the Shades") in the *Southern Literary Journal* a few years later.²⁹

The South Carolina artist Charles Fraser protested the deadening effect of utilitarianism in the *American Monthly Magazine* in 1835. Seeing the attack on the classics as a masked assault on all humanizing culture, including art itself, he wrote regarding utilitarianism, "What have we not to fear from this bold but insidious enemy of the elegant arts, when we see it aiming its attacks at classical learning—fortified as that is by the veneration of the ages, and binding together every enlightened nation by common associations and a common fountain of intelligence and taste?" He continued facetiously: "Yes; let modern reformers cut off the streams of intellectual refreshment by drying up the source—let them substitute arithmetical numbers for those breathed by the spirit of classic poetry—let them change the language of a Cicero for the dry commercial phrase of the desk and the counting-house—and let them expunge from their codes of education all that has embellished and enriched those minds which we revere for their attainments." Fraser contended that nations won lasting glory from their intellectual and artistic achievements, not from their wealth. If wealth was "to be considered as the end of all enterprize and exertion, and not as a means of still further improvement in shedding over the whole the charm that the mind, and mind alone, bestows, our lot will not be that of national greatness, and Nature will in vain have lavished upon us the means of attaining it." Greece had few resources but the great minds of its citizens: "The nations of antiquity were not the most favored in their physical resources whose fame we most delight to cherish. What of Greece do we remember with more delight than its philosophy, its sculpture, its painting, and its literature?" It was the land "of Pericles, of Plato, and Xenophon—the land of the *Apollo*, the *Laocoön*, and the Parthenon."³⁰

In 1845 Henry David Thoreau defended the classics against their detractors in *Walden*. He declared:

> They only talk of forgetting them who never knew them. It will be soon enough to forget them when we have the learning and the genius which will

enable us to attend to and appreciate them.... It is not in vain that the farmer remembers and repeats the few Latin words which he has heard. Men sometimes speak as if the study of the classics would at length make way for more modern and practical studies; but the adventurous student will always study the classics, in whatever language they may be written and however ancient they may be.... We might as well omit to study Nature because she is old.... These works of art have such an immortality as the works of nature and are modern at the same time that they are ancient, like the sun and stars, and occupy by right no small share of the present.... Two thousand summers have imparted to the monuments of Greek literature, as to her marbles, only a maturer golden and autumnal tint.

It was good that the reader had to exert himself to take from the page what the Greek or Roman poet placed there. Thoreau, who always calculated the value of a thing by the amount of life one had to spend in exchange for it, wrote, "It is worth the expense of youthful days and costly hours if you learn only some words of an ancient language, which are raised out of the trivialness of the street, to be perpetual suggestions and provocations."[31]

Ralph Waldo Emerson agreed with Thoreau. He stated his educational philosophy: "It is better to teach the child arithmetic and Latin grammar than geography or rhetoric or moral philosophy, because these first require an exactitude of performance in the pupil.... He can very easily learn anything which is important to him now that the power to learn is secured.... Out of this valid stock choose the validest boy & in the flower of this strength open to him the whole Dorian & Attic beauty and the proceeding ripeness of the same in Italy. Give him the very best of this Classic beverage. He shall travel to Florence & Rome in his early manhood." Emerson might well have been referring to his own education.[32]

While a professor at the University of Mississippi in 1849, George Frederick Holmes argued that the study of the classical languages was necessary for the acquisition of ancient wisdom. He contended, "We must learn to think in their own language as the Greeks thought before we can truly inhale the glorious and inspiring atmosphere of Athenian wisdom—and we must learn to feel as the Romans felt before we can become participants in the profound and practical sagacity of ancient Rome."[33]

Basil Manly, president of the University of Alabama, agreed. In 1852 Manly noted, in a letter to the trustees of the university, that "the severest assault has been made" on the classics by those who considered them a waste of time. Manly continued:

> To this it is replied that these languages are the most finished and refined ever spoken or written; that they are fountains of eloquence never surpassed, seldom equalled; that, if it be one of the highest attainments of a man of action

and thought to reason, instruct, convince, and persuade, the knowledge of such an instrument as these can afford cannot be dispensed with but gives him a double advantage—that of the mastery of language and of sharpening his own powers by intercourse with the master-minds of the world. These languages have been deemed indispensable to a thorough education for the last thousand years, in every clime, under all governments, and by every fraternity of learned men. If we should agree to call men learned without them, would the rest of the world think so?

The classics not only trained men in eloquence, an art essential in a democracy, but also held the key to knowledge of the English language. Manly wrote, "So large a part of our own language, especially in the terminology of the learned professions and of the sciences, is derived from the ancient classics that we cannot be masters of our own languages without them." He concluded: "The study of language and mathematics affords an equable culture of various powers—attention, memory, comparison, abstraction, association, analysis, and the methods of reasoning by induction and analogy. For this purpose, no substitute has ever been found for them."[34]

Most of Manly's professors concurred fervently. A committee of the faculty urged the university trustees to reject all proposals to adopt an elective system like that of the University of Virginia. Indeed, the committee responded to the prospect of such a system with alarm and indignation:

> The perpetual recurrence of this idea [of an elective system] in all the writing of the modern advocates of new systems of collegiate instruction is truly disheartening. . . . Is it possible, then, that the Trustees of the University will deliberately resolve to award the honor of graduation, to confer the diploma which, from the earliest history of colleges, has been recognized only as the certificate of genuine scholarship, upon men who willfully neglect that which has always been, and inevitably must be, the first essential to the scholar? Is it possible they will do this ruinous thing . . . in view of the fact that the proposition for a change, published everywhere throughout the State, has awakened only an occasional and feeble response, while it has at the same time elicited from the scattered friends of sound education so numerous and elaborate and able vindications of the existing order of things, as to prove beyond all question that the sound sense of the people is satisfied with what we have, and asks for nothing better?

The committee added that the findings of the Yale Report, written over a quarter century earlier by "some of the most distinguished and experienced instructors whom this country has produced," were still endorsed by the current president of Yale.[35]

The editors of the *Southern Quarterly Review* also defended the classics against the utilitarians in 1852. They claimed: "The great end of education seems to be forgotten. The object of collegiate instruction is not to turn out professional men, but to prepare young men to pursue with advantage any profession. Men are taught to think, to reason; to learn general principles—the practical application of which is to be made, either by themselves unaided, or developed at more specialized schools. In all the colleges of Europe the principle of instruction is based upon the cultivation of the taste, the memory, and the judgment—by means of the study of rhetoric and the classics, which are emphatically distinguished by the name of humanity."[36]

Even the novelist Herman Melville, who had little interest in educational theory, defended classical art against the utilitarians. In "Statues in Rome" (1857–1858) he argued that modern man was wrong to undervalue art on materialist grounds. Melville claimed, "Science is beneath art, just as the instinct is beneath reason." He asked regarding the classical treasures of Rome's art museums, "Do all our modern triumphs equal those of the heroes and divinities that stand there silent, the incarnation of grandeur and beauty?" Melville contended that just as the nation's "best architecture" rested on Roman arches, and American law rested, to some extent, on the Code of Justinian, so Americans, like the Greeks and Romans, should make art the repository of their visions.[37]

To these arguments against modern utilitarians' narrow definition of utility, some defenders of the classics added an assault on modern commercialism itself. George Fitzhugh contended that modern commercial society was devastating to the family, noting: "Homer, too, especially in his *Odyssey,* charms and enchains us with his beautiful descriptions of family felicity and family purity. As conquest and commerce introduced wealth and corrupted morals and manners, the family was corrupted and disrupted, as it is now, at the most commercial points in the North." Fitzhugh feared now "to see a railroad profaning the field of Marathon, or a cotton factory built upon the site of the Parthenon."[38]

Fitzhugh denied that modern science and industry had secured real progress for humanity. He declared: "It is idle to talk of progress when we look two thousand years back for models of perfection. So vast was Grecian superiority in art above ours that it is a common theory that they possessed an ideal to guide them which has been lost, and which loss is irreparable. The ancients understood the art, practice, and science of government better than we. There was more intelligence, more energy, more learning, more happiness, more people, and more wealth around the Levant, and in its islands, in the days of Herodotus than are now to be found in all Europe." Though the last part of Fitzhugh's statement was highly dubious, he continued regarding the ancients: "In the moral sciences they were our equals, in the fine arts vastly our superiors. Their poetry, their painting, their sculpture, their drama, their elocution, and their architecture are models which we imitate but never equal. In the science of government and of morals, in pure metaphysics, and in all the walks of intellectual philosophy, we have been beating the air with our wings or revolving in circles, but we have not advanced an inch. Kant is not ahead of Aristotle." The principal result of the invention of the printing press had been the publication of much rubbish (Fitzhugh presumably exempted his own books and essays from this judgment), in stark contrast to the admirable selectivity of the ancients, whose literature justly excited admiration. (This alleged selectivity is largely an illusion. The ancients wrote a great deal of rubbish too; the difference is that much of it failed to survive because few were willing to spend the hours necessary to make copies of it, a form of literary natural selection in which only the fittest survived.)[39]

Fitzhugh would not even concede the reality of progress in agriculture. He alleged, "The farmers of Judea, Egypt, Greece, and Rome, two and four thousand years ago, were better than ours." Fitzhugh contended that this agricultural decline was a result of excessive rationalism, of the kind now prevalent in modern commercial societies: "Farming rapidly declined in Rome, as soon as Cato and others attempted to make it a science. The most potent qualities of soils and atmospheres evade all analysis. . . . The great secrets of animal and vegetable life, and of their health, growth, and decay, are in a great measure hidden from human search. Philosophy makes no advances in this direction. Galen and Hippocrates were as good physicians as the latest graduate of Edinburgh, and Cato as good a farmer as [the modern agriculturalist] Mr. [John] Newton."[40]

Indeed, in an 1846 pamphlet James Henry Hammond began his discussion of the use of marl as fertilizer by referring back to Varro and Pliny. He noted, "Marling . . . is certainly no novelty—no untried experiment that can for a moment be classed among modern humbugs." Hammond regaled his neighbors in the ABC Farmers Club of Beech Island with Cato's views on manure. Though Hammond agreed with Aristotle that intellectual endeavors constituted "a more virtuous energy" than commercial enterprises, he was not opposed to the latter and maintained that the classics could be practical as well as elevating.[41]

Even the nation's manufacturers could not escape classical influence. In 1816 a committee of businessmen presented an address to the American Society for the Encouragement of Domestic Manufactures. The committee declared: "The fictions and fables of antiquity are realized in the short annals of our country. Like the young Heracles, it strangled in its cradle the destroying serpents and would prove equal to every labour. But foreign manufactures, like the garment poisoned by the Hydra's blood, threaten our dissolution; our funeral pile is lighted; but the mighty hand will interpose and rescue us from death to immortality. And if it be asked who has that power? We say it is The People!" If a subject as prosaic as protective tariffs could call forth a barrage of classical references and imagery from sober businessmen, where could the truly anticlassical turn for refuge?[42]

Antebellum critics of the classical languages requirement in the schools presented the same utilitarian arguments that would-be reformers had presented in the days of the founders, received the same rebukes for their heresy, and suffered the same defeat. From the beginning, Americans had been a pragmatic and commercial people, but one who had simultaneously harbored a reverence for tradition, both Christian and classical, and who had seen in these theistic and humanistic traditions a crucial means of moderating their own penchant for utilitarianism and materialism. Like nearly all the founders, most antebellum Americans assumed that they should study only what was "useful" but defined usefulness broadly.

CHAPTER FOUR

Nationalism

NATIONALIST CRITICISMS of Greco-Roman civilization were as old as the utilitarian assaults on the classical languages requirement in the schools. It is true that the nationalism that had first trickled through the cracks of Enlightenment cosmopolitanism during the American Revolution gushed forth during the antebellum period. But although classical heroes surrendered the chief place of honor in the American pantheon to George Washington, Thomas Jefferson, and other national heroes, the Greek and Roman republicans retained significant positions thereafter. They were not dashed from their pedestals. Just as the Greeks and Romans had differentiated between primary and secondary gods, antebellum Americans distinguished between the nearly divine founders and their slightly more flawed classical heroes. Indeed, classical conceptions of heroism so enthralled the antebellum generation that the new mythology they constructed around the founders was itself imbued with classical themes. During this age of Manifest Destiny, Americans saw their expanding nation as a new empire that would exceed the past empires of Athens and Rome, both in size and in fidelity to democratic principles. But their boastfulness about American superiority continued to display the same defensiveness it had always exhibited.

The Claim of American Superiority

As early as 1776, in an effort to improve patriot morale by appealing to national pride, Thomas Paine had urged Americans to get over their inferiority complex concerning the ancient Greeks and Romans in order to surpass them. Paine declared: "The wisdom, civil government, and sense of honor of the states of Greece and Rome are frequently held up as objects of excellence and imitation. But why do we need to go back two or three thousand years for lessons and examples? Clear away the mists of antiquity!" He added: "The Grecians and Romans were strongly possessed of the spirit of liberty, but not the principle, for at the time that they were determined not to be slaves themselves, they employed their power to enslave the rest of mankind. But this distinguished era is blotted by no one misanthropical vice." He contended: "A good opinion of ourselves is exceedingly necessary in private life, but absolutely necessary in public life, and of the utmost importance in supporting national character. I have no intention of yielding the palm of the United States to any Grecians or Romans that were ever born. We have equalled the bravest in times of danger, and excelled the wisest in the construction of civil governments. . . . Could the mists of antiquity be cleared away, and men and things be viewed as they really were, it is more than probable that they would admire us, rather than we them." In another essay Paine contrasted the glorious establishment of the United States with the ignoble founding of Rome by "a band of ruffians."[1]

James Wilson, a signer of both the Declaration of Independence and the U.S. Constitution, issued similar nationalist appeals. In a Fourth of July speech that also celebrated the ratification of the Constitution in 1788, Wilson contrasted ancient republican institutions, imposed by the fiat of temporary dictators like Numa, Lycurgus, and Solon, with the U.S. Constitution, drafted and ratified by conventions specifically elected for that purpose. He concluded that although the ancients had introduced the theory of popular sovereignty, only the United States had put it into practice. Two years later Wilson took issue with those Americans who considered their country inferior to the Greek and Roman republics. Though great, the Greeks were overrated because "their virtues [have been] transmitted to posterity by writers who excelled those of every other country in abilities and elegance." Wilson declared, "But in real worth and excellence, I boldly venture to compare them [the United States] with the most illustrious commonwealths which adorn the records of time. When some future Xenophon or Thucydides shall arise to do justice to their virtues and their actions, the glory of America will rival—it will outshine the glory of Greece."[2]

Antebellum Americans were even better equipped to proclaim American superiority to the Greeks and Romans because the founders had left them something they themselves had lacked: a set of national heroes. In Edward Everett's 1825 speech on the Battle of Concord he asked, "Are we to be eternally ringing the changes upon Marathon and Thermopylae and going back to find in obscure texts of Greek and Latin the great exemplars of patriotic virtue?" He answered his own rhetorical question: "We feel a glow of admiration at the heroism displayed at Marathon, by the ten thousand champions of invaded Greece; but we cannot forget that the tenth part of the number were slaves, unchained from the workshops and doorposts of their masters, to go and fight the battles of freedom. I do not mean that these examples are to destroy the interest with which we read the history of ancient times; they possibly increase that interest, by the singular contrast they exhibit. But they do warn us, if we need the warning, to seek our great political lessons of patriotism at home, out of the exploits and sacrifices of which our own country is the theatre, out of the character of our own fathers." Similarly, George Fitzhugh wrote, "Study the past, but be careful not to copy it, and never travel abroad until age has matured your love and respect for your native land." Senator Bedford Brown of North Carolina declared: "History gives to Cincinnatus high civic virtues, to Aristides the quality of justice, and to Fabius Maximus consummate prudence and courage in war, but the honor and glory of their being united in the person of a single individual was reserved for exemplification in the character of George Washington."³

Some Americans proclaimed their confidence that the future glory of the United States would far exceed that of the classical republics. A young Ralph Waldo Emerson wrote in his journal in 1822 that an American "points to his native land as the only one where freedom has not degenerated into licentiousness . . . in whose well ordered districts education & intelligence dwell with good morals; whose rich estates peacefully descend from sire to son without the shadow of an interference from private violence or public tyranny; whose offices of trust and seats of science are filled by minds of republican strength and elegant accomplishments." He added, "Xenophon and Thucydides would have thought it a theme better worthy of their powers than Persia or Greece, and . . . [the American] Revolution would furnish Plutarch with a list of heroes." In the same vein he concluded: "When the glory of Plato, of Cicero & of Shakespeare shall have died, who are they that are to write their names where all time shall read them & their words be the oracle of millions? Let those who would pluck the lot of Immortality from Fate's Urn look well to the future prospects of America." The following year Emerson imagined Cicero saying to George Washington: "I esteem myself happy to stand in the company of one to whom heaven seems to have united me by a certain similarity of fortune & the common glory of saving a state. But the fates have given you an advantage, O most illustrious man, above my lot, in granting you an honorable decline & death amid the regrets of your country, while I fell by the vengeance of the flagitious Antony." In 1824 Emerson wrote a letter to Plato in which he claimed, "I live in a land which you alone & your contemporaries prophesied where is founded a political system more wise & successful than Utopia or the Atlantis."[4]

Emerson was far from alone in expressing a belief in American superiority to the ancients. In 1839 the *United States Magazine and Democratic Review* editorialized: "We have no interest in the scenes of antiquity, only as lessons of avoidance of nearly all their examples. The expansive future is our arena.... We are entering on its untrodden space, with the truth of God in our minds, beneficent objects in our hearts, and with a clear conscience unsullied by the past. We are the nation of human progress, and who will, what can, set limits to our onward march?" Three years later Charles Carter Lee wrote, "If we may judge of the ultimate consequences from those which have already followed our Revolution, it appears certain that a deeper interest must hereafter attach to its history than now belongs to that of . . . the Commonwealth of Rome." The sculptor Thomas Crawford declared, "We have surpassed already the republics of Greece in our political institutions, and I see no reason why we should not approach their excellence in the Fine Arts, which, as much as anything else, has secured undying fame to Grecian genius."[5]

Frederick Porcher of Charleston assaulted neoclassical art from a nationalist perspective. In his essay "Modern Art" (1852) Porcher wrote: "George Washington was a great American. Would he have been a great Frenchman, a great Roman, a great Grecian? We believe not, and we feel disposed to glory in this belief, because we fancy that greatness like his, so far superior to anything in the conception of the Gallic, Grecian, or Roman mind, adds a new lustre to the great Northern race to which he belonged, and which he honored and adorned." Porcher continued: "When Houdon was executing the statue of Washington, he consulted that illustrious man on the subject of his dress, and he, acting on the principles of common sense which so greatly distinguished him . . . chose the costume of his day. And Houdon's *Washington* remains the statue of the father of his country." (Indeed, Washington had written, "A little deviation in favour of the modern costume would be more expedient than a servile adherence to the garb of antiquity.") Porcher considered Hiram Powers's statue of John C. Calhoun in a toga as ridiculous as Horatio Greenough's "half-naked" statue of Washington in similar dress. Of Powers's statue Porcher wrote: "The first glance of curiosity satisfied, the statue stands unheeded, in the City Hall, and there it will stand, a monument of the public spirit of the citizens and of their disappointment. We asked for our statesman and have received a Roman Senator." By contrast, Calhoun himself "was a man who will probably live with posterity because he lived with and for his contemporaries."⁶

Porcher bemoaned the slavishness of contemporary artists. He complained: "No sculptor of our times dares hope to become anything but a humble imitator of Phidias. The amateur . . . cannot distinguish between the works of Phidias and those of Canova; and Canova and his host of admirers proclaim this is the greatest triumph of which he is capable." Porcher claimed concerning the imitator of the classics: "He imitates merely that which is obvious, but has no conception of the thought which the model was designed to express. Hence his productions have no vitality. Like the daguerreotype impressions of the face of a corpse they present an accurate likeness of the features, but they are images of death." Porcher declared: "It would be a desirable accomplishment to be able to write Latin in such a manner that scholars might compare one with Cicero; but how infinitely more desirable is the ability to speak English with the eloquence of a Henry or a Chatham."⁷

Porcher was not alone in his opinion. Even the neoclassical architect Robert Mills agreed with Porcher on the artistic portrayal of moderns in ancient dress. He claimed: "The colossal statue of Washington within the eastern enclosure of the Capitol at Washington—a splendid work—has failed to meet public approval, not only from the costume used but the sitting attitude of the figure . . . but let the American visit the capitol at Richmond and view the statue of Washington [by Houdon], and all other statues fall into the shade before this beautiful and correct representation of the father of his country. . . . Study your country's taste and requirements, and make classic ground here for your art. Go not to the old world for your examples. We have tasted a new era in the history of the world; it is our destiny to lead, not to be led." Davy Crockett declared regarding Sir Francis Chantrey's semiclassical statue of Washington (1826): "I do not like the statue of Washington in the State House [in Boston]. They have a Roman gown on him and he was an American; this ain't right. They did a better thing in Richmond, in Virginia, where they have him in the old blue and buff [the colors of the Continental army]. He belonged to his country—heart, soul, and body, and I don't want any other country to have any part of him—not even his clothes."⁸

But none of these men rejected the classics; on the contrary, nearly all were fervent classicists. Almost all of Mills's buildings were classical in inspiration—from the Treasury Building in Washington to the Insane

Asylum in Columbia, South Carolina. Emerson filled his journals with discussions of classical texts. Everett's and Fitzhugh's protests against the alleged popular preference for classical over American heroes reveal that they considered it a potential problem. They are similar to the complaints of Hugh Blair Grigsby and Henry A. Washington, as late as the 1840s, that Virginians knew the history of Greece and Rome better than that of their own state. Far from testifying to the decline of the classics, they attest to its continued vitality.[9]

Indeed, the antebellum generation was so influenced by classical conceptions of heroism that the new mythology they constructed around the founders was itself imbued with classical themes. The qualities ascribed to George Washington and the other founders were the very qualities that Americans, including the founders themselves, had learned to appreciate from reading classical works: courage, patriotism, frugality, self-discipline, prudence, and justice. In his famous biography of Washington, Parson Weems stated the popular image of Washington aptly: "Washington was as pious as Numa, just as Aristides, temperate as Epictetus, and patriotic as Regulus. In giving public trusts, impartial as Severus; in victory, modest as Scipio—prudent as Fabius, rapid as Marcellus, undaunted as Hannibal, as Cincinnatus disinterested, to liberty firm as Cato, and respectful of the laws as Socrates." Lest any philologist consider this cavalcade of classical analogies insufficient, Weems added regarded Washington's father, "Never did the wise Ulysses take more pains with his beloved Telemachus than did Mr. Washington with George."[10]

Nationalist claims of American superiority to the classical republics were not manifestations of an antipathy toward the classics but evidence of almost universal reverence for them. Nearly all antebellum orators lingered on the greatness of the classical world before defensively asserting the superiority of American achievement. The greatest master of this rhetorical trope was Daniel Webster. In an oration to mark the bicentennial of the Pilgrim landing at Plymouth, in 1820, Webster joined the arrival of the Pilgrims with the Battle of Marathon. This peculiar coupling of seemingly disparate historical events seemed perfectly rational in Webster's mind because both had advanced the cause of freedom and civilization. Webster intoned:

> When the traveller pauses on the plain of Marathon, what are the emotions which most strongly agitate his breast? What is that glorious recollection which thrills his frame, and suffuses his eyes? Not, I imagine, that Grecian skill and Grecian valor were here most signally displayed, but that Greece herself was saved. It is because to this spot, and to the event which has rendered it immortal, he refers all the succeeding glories of the republic. It is because, if that day

had gone otherwise, Greece had perished. It is because he perceives that her philosophers and orators, her sculptors and architects, her governments and free institutions, point backward to Marathon, and that their future existence seems to have been suspended on the contingency, whether the Persian or the Grecian banner should wave victorious in the beams of that day's setting sun. And, as his imagination kindles at the retrospect, he is transported back to the interesting moment; he counts the fearful odds of the contending hosts; his interest for the result overwhelms him; he trembles, as if it were still uncertain, and seems to doubt whether he may consider Socrates and Plato, Demosthenes, Sophocles and Phidias as secure, yet, to himself and to the world.

"If we conquer," said the Athenian commander on the approach of that decisive day, "if we conquer, we shall make Athens the greatest city of Greece." A prophecy how well fulfilled! "If God prosper us," might have been the more appropriate language of our fathers when they landed upon this Rock, "if God prosper us, we shall here begin a work which shall last for ages; we shall plant here a new society, in the principles of the fullest liberty and the purest religion; we shall subdue this wilderness which is before us; we shall fill this region of the continent, which stretches almost from pole to pole, with civilization and Christianity."[11]

Twelve years later, when delivering a Washington Day speech in the midst of the Nullification Crisis in South Carolina, Webster again united American democracy with classical republicanism while claiming superiority for the former. Webster declared concerning the danger of disunion:

Who shall reconstruct the fabric of the demolished government? Who shall rear again the well-proportioned columns of constitutional liberty? Who shall frame together the skilful architecture which unites national sovereignty with State rights, individual liberty and public prosperity? No, if these columns fall, they will not be raised again. Like the Coliseum and the Parthenon, they will be destined to a mournful, melancholy immortality. Bitterer tears, however, will flow over them than were ever shed over the monuments of Roman or Grecian art; for they will be the remnants of a more glorious edifice than Greece or Rome ever saw, the edifice of constitutional American liberty.[12]

In a Fourth of July speech commemorating the laying of a cornerstone to an addition to the U.S. Capitol in 1851, Webster, again sensing the threat of disunion, made similar remarks:

Fellow-citizens, this inheritance which we enjoy to-day is not only an inheritance of liberty, but of our own peculiar American liberty. Liberty has existed in other times, in other countries, and in other forms. There has been a Grecian liberty, bold and powerful, full of spirit, eloquence, and fire; a liberty which produced multitudes of great men, and has transmitted one immortal name, Demosthenes, to posterity. But still it was a liberty of disconnected states, sometimes united, indeed, by temporary leagues and confederacies, but often involved in wars between themselves. . . . Let the truth sink deep into all American minds, that it was WANT OF UNION among her several states which finally gave the mastery of Greece to Philip of Macedon.

And there has also been a Roman liberty, a proud, ambitious domineering spirit, professing free and popular principles in Rome itself, but even in the best days of the republic, ready to carry slavery and chains into her provinces, and through every country over which her eagles could be borne.

True to his theme until the very end, in his final speech in 1852 Webster declared that the United States exceeded "all praise as much as it exceeds all former examples of political associations," even the revered Greek and Roman republics.[13]

It became so common to begin Independence Day speeches with praise for the ancients, followed by a declaration of American superiority to them, that some orators found the task tedious. Even as early as 1822 Hugh Swinton Legaré began his Independence Day speech in Charleston in the expected manner: "What were the victories of Pompey [compared] to the united achievements of our Washingtons and Montgomerys and Greens—our Franklins and Jeffersons and Adams[es] and Laurens[es]—of the Senate of Sages, whose wisdom conducted—of the band of warriors whose valour accomplished—of the noble army of martyrs whose blood sealed and consecrated—the Revolution of '76?" But Legaré's heart was not in it. He then admitted that such panegyrics, "however interesting in themselves, and eminently well fitted for the purposes of popular declamation, are become so trite that it would be difficult, by any art of composition, to bestow upon them the graces of novelty." The habit of claiming American superiority to the ancients had become so ingrained, and was so transparent a rhetorical device, that it was beginning to embarrass intellectuals.[14]

Rare was the American who refused to declare American superiority to the classical civilizations. In his *Sketches of American Orators* Francis Gilmer praised Patrick Henry and Henry Clay but was bold enough to conclude that the former lacked the education that might have made him the equal of Cicero and Demosthenes and that the latter lacked the taste of Virgil and Cicero.[15]

Rome as a Model of Expansionist Nationalism

Some Americans considered Rome a model of expansionist nationalism, a form of patriotism that exalted a particular lifestyle, connected it with a specific citizenry, and promoted the territorial expansion of this society as a universal good. Thomas Dew asked: "And what, let me ask, was the great idea which animated every Roman writer? It was the idea of Rome herself—of Rome so wonderful in her ancient manners and laws—so great even in her errors and crimes. It was this idea which was breathed from the lips of her orators and embalmed in her literature, it was this idea which stamps the character of independent dignity and grandeur on the page of her philosophy, her history, and her poetry." American authors should receive as much inspiration from the greatness of their country as the Roman writers had found in the grandeur of their own.[16]

As a young "War Hawk" in 1814, John C. Calhoun shared this vision of Rome as a model of nationalism. Calhoun contrasted the patriotism of the Romans with the Anglophilia of the Federalist opponents of the War of 1812, of whom he wrote: "In their zeal they often presume that we are wrong and our enemy right. . . . How contrary this to the maxims of Roman wisdom! That wise and virtuous people, so far from presuming their country to be wrong, considered it a crime in a citizen to doubt the justice of the public cause. In a state of war how worthy our imitation! It was the root of Roman greatness. Without it a free state will ever lose much of its peculiar and native strength." Even in later years, when southerners temporarily traded in their American nationalism for southern nationalism, they loved to quote Horace: "It is sweet and fitting to die for one's country."[17]

This consciousness of Rome as a model of expansionist nationalism can also be found in the influential readers of Noah Webster, which were published in seventy-seven editions between 1785 and 1835. In his third edition Webster included most of act 4, scene 4, of Joseph Addison's *Cato*, in which Juba, the king of Numidia, holds forth on the Roman duty to extend the blessings of civilization to primitive peoples:

> A Roman soul is bent on higher views;
> To civilize the rude unpolished world,
> And lay it under the restraint of laws;
> To make man mild, and sociable to man;
> To cultivate the wild licentious savage
> With wisdom, discipline, and lib'ral arts;
> Th'embellishments of life.

Ironically, Addison's paean to Roman imperialism had justified a British imperialism of which the American colonies had recently been a victim. But here Webster, the compiler of the first great dictionary of American English, clearly tied the Roman sense of mission to spread civilization to Manifest Destiny, the equally divine mission of the United States to expand the blessings of civilization and democracy across the North American continent.[18]

Even the few Americans who rejected both Roman and American expansionist nationalism noted the connection between them. In his Fourth of July address of 1845, entitled "The True Grandeur of Nations," delivered during the buildup to the Mexican War, Senator Charles Sumner of Massachusetts declared:

> There is still another influence stimulating War and interfering with the natural attractions of Peace: I refer to a selfish and exaggerated prejudice of country, leading to physical aggrandizement and political exaltation at the expense of other countries, and in disregard of justice. Nursed by the literature of antiquity, we imbibe the sentiment of heathen patriotism. Exclusive love for the land of birth belonged to the religion of Greece and Rome. . . . The schoolboy does not forget the victim of Verres, with the memorable cry which was to stay the descending fasces of the lictor, "I am a Roman citizen"—nor those other words echoing through the dark Past, "How sweet it is to die for country!" Of little avail the nobler cry, "I am a man," or the Christian ejaculation, swelling the soul, "How sweet and becoming to die for duty!" The beautiful genius of Cicero, instinct at times with truth almost divine, did not ascend to that heaven where it is taught that all mankind are neighbors and kindred. To the love of universal man may be applied those words by which the great Roman elevated his selfish patriotism to virtue, when he said that country alone embraced all the charities of all. Attach this admired phrase to the single idea of country and you see how contracted are its charities compared with that world-wide circle where our neighbor is the suffering man, though at the farthest pole.[19]

Margaret Fuller and William Ware agreed with Sumner's critique of expansionist nationalism. Although Fuller believed that Rome had "brought some things to perfection that the world will probably never see again" and that America had "scarce achieved a Roman nobleness, a Roman liberty," she was sufficiently concerned about the American emulation of Roman imperialism to write that she hoped that the American eagle would not imitate its Roman ancestor ("the fierce Roman bird") with regard to Mexico. For her, the question was whether the American eagle was "to soar toward the sky or to stoop for helpless prey." In his popular historical novel *Zenobia*, Ware launched a similar attack against the Roman model of imperialism fueled by overbearing nationalism. In the novel a Roman character declares: "Men . . . have not inquired, is the cause of my country just, but merely what it is. That has ever been the cry of Rome. 'Our country! our country!—right or wrong—our country!' . . . I am no Roman in this sense." The phrase "Our country, right or wrong" was a clear reference to Stephen Decatur's "My country, right or wrong!" spoken with regard to the United States.[20]

American Nationalism and the Greek Revival

The interaction between American nationalism and classicism can be seen in the Greek Revival architecture of the antebellum period. To a large extent, the adoption of neoclassical architecture was a declaration of independence from Great Britain and its influence, as manifested in the "Colonial style." As the architectural historian William H. Pierson Jr. has noted: "The anti-British sentiment released both by the Revolution and by the War of 1812 fostered, even demanded, a rejection of established English tradition in favor of new forms more expressive of the ideals of American democracy. Indeed, it was at this point that the full impact of the Neoclassical movement was felt in the United States and the Greek Revival played its major and highly nationalistic role." American neoclassical architects did not merely substitute one form of enslavement to the past for another. Although they built a profusion of neoclassical structures for the burgeoning country, none of their buildings was a copy of any ancient structure. What the neoclassical architects received from the Greeks were not models to be copied (columnar proportions and relationships were routinely altered), but a style that was simple, grand, dignified, and rational.[21]

American architects adapted this style to local and national concerns in a variety of original ways. Ironically, it was a Frenchman, Major Pierre L'Enfant, who, in the Federal Hall (New York, 1789), first attempted to create an American order—a modified Doric column, with the American stars decorating the necking of the capitals and the triglyphs of the frieze. On Thomas Jefferson's suggestion, Benjamin Latrobe created another American order: in the entrance to the Senate, Latrobe's capitals featured ears and leaves of American corn in place of the usual acanthus leaves of the Corinthian order; his capitals in the Senate Rotunda featured tobacco leaves. Thomas Crawford's design for the classical pediment over the Senate wing (1850) consisted of ordinary Americans in the process of conquering the West. Other neoclassical buildings possessed lanterns, windows, cast-iron balconies, and other features absent from ancient structures. To take advantage of an irregularly shaped lot at a street corner in Philadelphia, William Strickland established the Mercantile Exchange (1836) as a large rectangle fronted by a circular colonnade topped by a delicate lantern. Nothing like it could be found in the ancient world. Other architects used rosettes and volutes in ways the Greeks never imagined. Many substituted a raked blocking course for the Greek pediment.[22]

American neoclassical architects consciously chose simplicity over the more ornate French classical style and even over the practices of the Greeks themselves, sometimes going so far as to omit flutes from their Doric columns. As the architectural historian Talbot Hamlin has noted, "The Greek forms were not divine revelations to be copied unthinkingly; they were, rather, a new alphabet of grace, restraint, and beauty with which a new and vital language could be formed." It was precisely because so much that was new and original might be done with the Greek forms that Greek Revival architecture became the first truly national architecture—a genre that represented the grace, dignity, simplicity, and majesty Americans of all regions wanted their new nation to appropriate from the ancient world, yet one that could be adapted to local needs.[23]

No one was clearer about the need to adopt the spirit, not copy the precise forms, of classical architecture than the neoclassical architects themselves. In 1841 American architect Robert Cary Long wrote: "It is as much out of the rule of rationality to think it possible to reinvigorate architecture by forcing it into an antique mold as to expect that, if disgusted with manhood, we can bring back simplicity and innocence by putting on the garments of youth. Architecture must grow naturally. . . . Let us all try and see which of us will first produce something in art peculiar—characteristic—suited to the age—national." Americans should adopt the free spirit of the Greeks, not become enslaved to them. Wherever appropriate, the beautiful forms of the Greeks could be employed, but only in new and innovative ways. Similarly, Thomas U. Walter said in a lecture, "The popular idea that to design a building in Grecian style is nothing more than to copy a Grecian building is altogether erroneous; even the Greeks themselves never made two buildings alike." What was needed, Walter added, was for American architects to think as the Greeks thought, not to do as they did. If American architects thought as the Greeks, then "our columnar architecture would possess a higher degree of originality and its character and expression would conform to the local circumstances of the country and the republican spirit of its institutions."[24]

Nationalism in Neoclassical Sculpture

American sculptors were equally shrewd in their adaptation of classical art to the American context. While generally draping their subjects in modern American dress, they copied the gestures of ancient figures, just as nineteenth-century American orators imitated the oratorical gestures recommended by Cicero and Quintilian when speaking on contemporary topics. Henry Kirke Brown's *DeWitt Clinton* (1850–1852) possesses the same stance and fold pattern in the cloak as the *Dresden Zeus*. Thomas

Ball's *Daniel Webster* (1853) features the same spacing and direction of the feet, attitude of the head, and right hand in the coat/cloak as an ancient statue of the emperor Hadrian. Thomas Crawford's *Dying Chief* (1856), though wearing a Native American headdress, possesses the same flexing muscles as the *Torso Belvedere* by Apollonius of Athens. In Emma Stebbins's *Commerce* and *Industry* her two subjects wear the attire of an antebellum American sailor and miner, but their stances are based on those of Praxiteles' *Satyr* and Polyclitus' *Doryphorus*, respectively. The shrewd tactic of combining classical postures with American dress later reached its apex in Daniel Chester French's *Seated Lincoln* (1916), which still graces the Greek temple known as the Lincoln Memorial. French's masterpiece was based almost as solidly on Phidias' *Zeus* as Horatio Greenough's *Washington*. Both copied Zeus' seated posture, his throne, and his footstool. But French had the good sense to allow Lincoln to keep his modern American clothes. French's graceful adaptation of classical art to the American context was as universally praised as Greenough's slavish copying of it had been vilified.[25]

America as the Unique Heir of Classical Civilization

Classicism could go hand in hand with nationalism in the United States because Americans assumed that the nation's chief sources of pride, its democracy and the cultural traits that issued from it and reinforced it, moved them closer to the ancients than any other nation in the modern world. A young Ralph Waldo Emerson, the day before Independence Day in 1822, took comfort in the possible failure of the American democratic experiment by likening it to the noble but failed experiments of the Greek and Roman republics: "Will it not be dreadful to discover that this experiment made by America, to ascertain if men can govern themselves, does not succeed? That too much knowledge & too much liberty makes them mad? Still we ourselves shall have the melancholy consolation of that magnanimous proverb—'The world will last our day' & also in that prophetic glory familiar to our countrymen, we will seek to believe that its corruption & decay shall be splendid with literature & the arts, to the latest time—splendid as the late day of Athens & Rome." In 1840 he wrote: "The discovery & planting of America & the American revolution & mechanic arts are Greek, Attic, or Antique . . . as much as the Parthenon or the 'Prometheus Chained.' I can easily see in our periodical Literature, for example, a diffused & weakened Athens."[26]

Others saw America as the unique heir of classical civilization as well. In 1851 Henry David Thoreau wrote in his journal: "The story of Romulus and Remus being suckled by a wolf is not a mere fable; the founders of every state which has risen to eminence have drawn their nourishment and vigor from a similar source. It is because the children of the empire were not suckled by wolves that they were conquered and displaced by the children of the northern forests who were. America is the she wolf to-day, and the children of exhausted Europe exposed on her uninhabited and savage shores are the Romulus and Remus who, having derived new life and vigor from her breast, have founded a new Rome in the West." While Thoreau identified the United States as a "new Rome," Walt Whitman asserted America's claim as the legitimate heir of the Greeks, even as he added the obligatory reference to American superiority:

> Come Muse migrate from Greece and Ionia,
> Cross out please those immensely overpaid accounts,
> That matter of Troy and Achilles' wrath, and Aeneas',
>   Odysseus' wanderings.
> Placard "Removed" and "To Let" on the rocks of your
>   snowy Parnassus....
> For know a better, fresher, busier sphere, a wide,
>   untried domain awaits, demands you.

Similarly, Thomas Dew wrote, "We are enacting Greece, if I may use the expression, on a grander scale.... We shall have millions of freemen where the Athenians had thousands."[27]

Popular appeals to Americans to study Greek and Roman history were often predicated on the belief in a close similarity between classical and American institutions. In 1851 the *Christian Review* contended: "To the American citizen, above all others, is it important that he become familiar with the history of Athens.... The similarity of their institutions to our own, the intense love of the individual and national freedom which pervaded all ranks of society, render the study of Athenian life of more than ordinary interest to the American citizen." The author urged Americans not merely to read Athens' "laws and her political history" but also to "become conversant with her poets, her historians, her philosophers, and her orators" in order to understand the "character of her leading men." The following year Thomas Dew wrote, "The history of Greece is particularly important to the American student. He can there learn the true value of the democratic principle and acknowledge its energizing influence, whilst he sees its corrupting tendency when not restrained." Similarly, the *Southern Literary Messenger* urged its readers to acquire "mental citizenship of Athens" in order to see the similarities between Athenian and American democracy.[28]

Even a scholar and professional classicist like Basil Gildersleeve could boast, in his 1878 Presidential Address to the American Philological Association, "It would not be saying too much to maintain that many of the aspects of American life enable us to understand the ancients better than some of our European contemporaries do." Gildersleeve alleged that while Americans were similar to the ancients in their audacity and inventiveness, the Germans were too "pedantic," the English too "sceptical," and the French too "erratic."[29]

What the historian Edwin A. Miles has written of colonial Americans applies equally to the founders' generation and to antebellum Americans: "One must not be misled by the constant claims of American superiority to the Greeks and Romans; the fact that such comparisons were deemed necessary is of weightier significance." Like the founders, antebellum Americans were in the position of the son who idolizes his father, though striving to surpass him. However great the son's success, his measuring stick remains the achievements of the father, his boastful claims reassuring himself that he has proven a worthy successor.[30]

CHAPTER FIVE

Romanticism

IN THE ANTEBELLUM period nationalism and democracy merged with romanticism to form the United States' first national literature. Although American romanticism emphasized enjoyment of the present over preoccupation with the past and nature over scholarship as the true source of enlightenment, emphases that might have caused the romantics to repudiate the classics, these very emphases were largely based on the Platonic valuation of intuition over reason and experience. While the romantics, like the founders before them, inveighed against the slavish, uncritical acceptance of all things classical, they revered the ancients, even suggesting that the ancients' position closer to the dawn of time had given them a clearer understanding of truth. The Transcendentalists liked the ancients' moralism and love of nature and viewed individual classical figures like Socrates as the greatest models of nonconformity—men whose courage had enabled them to heed their own inner voices in contradiction to the dogmas of their societies. From the Stoics the Transcendentalists learned pantheism, fatalism, the need for intellectual detachment, and the concept of natural law, a theory that led Henry David Thoreau to his highly influential essay "On Civil Disobedience." While the Transcendentalists exulted in the richness and vibrancy of classical mythology, the romantic fiction writers drew upon it extensively to provide their narratives with structure and meaning. Beloved by all, the biographer Plutarch helped inspire the "great-man theory" that prevailed among antebellum historians.

A National Literature for a Democratic, Romantic Age

Because the nation's first literary movement arose during a democratic and romantic era, an age that glorified majority rule and sought to temper the rationalism of the Enlightenment, it was inevitable that the literature it produced should be both democratic and romantic. American writers felt the need to refute, both explicitly and through the high quality of their works, the judgment of some Europeans that democracies were too utilitarian to finance and produce great literature, which flourished only under monarchies.

Thomas Dew attacked the European dogma, based on the glorious literature of Augustan Rome, that works of literary genius required royal patronage. Dew argued that democratic societies like Athens had generated literature devoid of the slavish flattery that so often marred the writings produced by monarchical societies. Furthermore, Dew noted that not all monarchs supported literature: "Even supposing that the progress of literature depends directly upon the amount of pecuniary patronage which it can command, it by no means follows that it will flourish most under a monarchical government. For granting that this kind of government may have the ability to patronise, it is by no means certain that it will always possess the will to do so. Augustus and Maecenas may lavish today the imperial treasures upon literature, but Tiberius and Sejanus may starve and proscribe it tomorrow." Even those monarchs who wished to encourage the production of great literature were not always successful: "Constantine the Great, seated on the throne of the Eastern Empire, with all the resources of the Roman world at his command, could not awaken the slumbering genius of a degenerate race, nor revive the decaying arts of the ancient empire. The literature of his reign, with all the patronage he could bestow upon it, did but too nearly resemble those gorgeous piles which his pride and vanity caused to be erected in his own imperial city, composed of the ruins of so many of the splendid monuments of antiquity."[1]

Dew could not decide whether to denigrate Augustan literature or to characterize it as the last remnants of the Roman republic, so he did both. He contended:

> Under the patronage of the first of the Roman Emperors we find, it is true, the arts and light literature rising to a pitch which perhaps they had not reached under the republic. After the death of Brutus the world of letters experienced a revolution almost as great as that of the political world. The literature of the Augustan age is distinguished by the tone and spirit which mark the downfall of liberty, and the consequent thraldom of the mind. The bold and manly

voice of eloquence was hushed. The high and lofty spirit of the republic was tamed down to a sickly and disgusting servility. The age of poetry came when that of eloquence and philosophy was past; and Virgil and Horace and Propertius, flattered, courted and enriched by an artful prince and an elegant courtier, could consent to sing the sycophantic praises of the monarch who had signed the proscriptions of the triumvirate and riveted a despotism on his country.

Following this harsh indictment of Augustan literature, Dew then took a new tack, ascribing its better qualities to the lingering effects of republicanism: "But the men who most adorned the various departments of learning during the long reign of Augustus were born in the last days of the republic. They saw what the glory of the commonwealth had been—they beheld with their own eyes the greatness of their country, and they had inhaled in their youth the breath of freedom. No Roman writer, for example, excels the Lyric Bard [Horace] in true feeling and sympathy for heroic greatness. We ever behold through the medium of his writings—even the gayest—a deep rooted sorrow locked up in his bosom for the subversion of the liberties of the commonwealth." Ovid, who was born too late to appreciate the republic, was an inferior poet, "too fanciful and effeminate." Dew added: "Even History itself, in which the Romans so far excelled, yielded to the corrupting influence of the Caesars.... Whilst Tiberius surrenders himself to the keeping of so vile a being as Sejanus—whilst Nero is fiddling and dancing, and Commodus [is] in the arena with the gladiators—all that is noble and great in the empire must retire into the shade and seek for safety in solitude and obscurity." Paradoxically, Dew praised Tacitus, without whom he would not have learned the antics of Tiberius and Nero. Evidently, there were some periods of the Roman Empire (such as the reign of Trajan) during which one could write honest history.[2]

After lauding the astonishing literature produced by the Greek democracies, works of genius that the European monarchists glossed over, Dew expressed his confidence in the future greatness of American letters. He predicted, "We shall then have an empire, formed by mere internal development, as populous as that of Rome and much more wealthy, speaking all the same language, and living under the same or similar institutions." Such a democratic empire, blessed by modern commercial prosperity, would provide a vast market for literature, a form of "patronage beyond what kings and princes can furnish." Better yet, the nation's writers would find in America an even greater heroine for their epics than Roman literary geniuses had found in Rome.[3]

The Repudiation of Slavishness

The romantics eschewed the antiquarianism and abject slavishness of some antebellum classicists, qualities that conflicted with the Transcendentalist emphases on living in the present and on nonconformity. Walt Whitman, the least classical of all the romantics, wrote concerning the classics:

> Regarding it all intently a long while, then dismissing it,
> I stand in my place with my own day here.

Whitman criticized the British poet John Keats for his slavishness: "Keats' poetry is ornamental, elaborated, rich in wrought imagery; it is imbued with the sentiment of the gods and goddesses of twenty-five hundred years ago. Its feeling is the feeling of a gentlemanly person, lately at college, accepting what was commanded him there, who moves and would only move in elegant society, reading classical books in libraries. Of life in the nineteenth century it has none, any more than the statues have. It does not come home at all to the direct wants of the bodies and souls of the century." Similarly, Edgar Allan Poe criticized the playwrights of his day for copying the Greeks: "The dramatist of today is prone to step too closely in the footprints of the dramatist of yesterday. In a word, there is less originality—less independence—less thought . . . in the drama than in any other single thing in existence which aspires to the dignity of Art. The spirit of imitation, developed in adherence to old, and therefore to uncouth models, has not caused drama to 'decline,' but has overthrown it by not permitting it to soar. While every other art has kept pace with the thinking and improving spirit of the age, it alone has remained stationary, prating about Aeschylus and the Chorus."[4]

Other romantics shared this distaste for the slavish imitation of classical works. While at the British Museum one day, Nathaniel Hawthorne could wish that "the Elgin marbles and the friezes of the Parthenon were all burnt into lime." He explained, "We have not time, in our earthly existence, to appreciate what is warm with life, and immediately around us; yet we heap up all these old shells, out of which human life has long emerged." (On a later visit Hawthorne not only repented of his desire to pulverize the Elgin Marbles but even doubted whether such an act could achieve its purpose, since "the grace and nobility seemed so deep in them as the very heart of the stone.") In his famous essay "Self-Reliance" Ralph Waldo Emerson repudiated the worship of the ancients and of other past heroes. He wrote: "The roses under my window make no reference to former roses or to better ones;

they are what they are; they exist with God today. . . . That which each can do best, none but his Maker can teach him. . . . Shakespeare will never be made by the study of Shakespeare." For Emerson, the key to genius was to listen to one's own inner voice, which constituted one's connection with God, rather than modeling oneself on anyone else, however esteemed. Emerson claimed, "The idiot, the Indian, the child, and unschooled farmer's boy stand nearer to the light by which nature is to be read than the dissector or the antiquary." He urged: "Reverence man & not Plato and Caesar. Wherever there is sense, reflexion, courage, admit it to the same honour—embrace it—quote it from a truckman as quick as from [Daniel] Webster." Henry David Thoreau wrote: "Perchance the time will come when we shall not be content to go back & forth upon a raft to some huge Homeric or Shakespearean Indiaman that lies upon the reef, but to build a bark out of that wreck and others that are buried in the sands of this desolate island, and such new timbers as may be required, in which to sail away to whole new worlds of light & life where our friends are."[5]

In their condemnation of slavishness the romantics were hardly alone. Even John Adams had paused in the midst of lecturing John Quincy on the importance of studying the classics to warn his eldest son: "These great Masters of Antiquity you must sooner or later be able to judge critically. But you must never imitate them. Study nature, and write accordingly, and you will resemble them. But it is nature, not the Ancients, that you are to imitate and copy." Likewise, even as thorough an opponent of romanticism and as fervent a supporter of the classics as George Fitzhugh thought that the eighteenth-century obsession with the so-called classical laws of literature had been taken too far. Fitzhugh noted: "French art is a mere rehash of Roman art, and very inferior to the original. . . . Nothing shows so strongly the want of originality and want of independence of taste and thought among these Latin nations as their contempt for Shakespeare. He violates all the rules of Greek and Roman art, and erects a higher art of his own; but Frenchmen, Italians, and Spaniards have no tastes and no ideas differing from, or in advance of, the ancients, and can neither understand nor appreciate the genius of Shakespeare." He added that the greatest classical artists had not created according to established rules: "The rules of art destroy art. Homer never could have produced the *Iliad* had he learned grammar and rhetoric and criticism. 'Tis well for the world he lived before Longinus [the rhetorician]. Euripides, Sophocles, and Aristophanes, and the Greek Masters in Sculpture and Painting knew nothing of the rules of art and canons of criticism. Without the modern helps to art, Grecian art so far excelled ours that it is a popular theory that they possessed an Ideal that has been lost. Early in the days of the Roman Empire, the rhetoricians, by attempting to teach eloquence by rule, so corrupted it that the Emperors found it necessary to banish them from Rome." Fitzhugh added: "We are no doubt indebted to the ignorance of the ancients for the invention of Gothic architecture. No one taught to reverence Greek architecture would have violated its rules by imitating the Gothic.... Study the past, but be careful not to copy it."[6]

Like Fitzhugh, who used classical examples to argue against "classical laws," Emerson quoted ancient authorities in support of his emphasis on the enjoyment of the present. As early as 1820 he quoted Horace, a poet who enjoyed the present as much as anyone: "Nor in thy youth neglect sweet love nor dances, while life is still in its bloom and crabbed age is far away!" The past was not to be studied for its own sake but for the benefit of the present. Emerson wrote: "The use of literature is to afford us a platform whence we may command a view of our present life, a purchase by which we may move it. We fill ourselves with ancient learning, install ourselves the best we can in Greek, in Punic, in Roman houses only that we may wiselier see French, English & American houses & modes of living." He saw no irony in quoting a line from Ovid in the original Latin that translates as "Let the ancient times delight other folk: I congratulate myself that I was not born till now."[7]

Embracing the "Classical Spirit"

While the romantics rejected a rigid adherence to classical laws, they embraced the "classical spirit," as manifested in the Greeks' and Romans' alleged closeness to nature and nonconformity. In 1839 Emerson wrote in his journal: "These lines of Greek and Latin which pass now current in all literatures as proverbs of wise old men are expressions of the very facts which the sky, the sea, the plant, the ox, the man, the picture said daily unto me.... And thou, good ancient brother, who to ancient nations, to earlier modes of life & politics & religion didst utter this my perception of today, I greet thee with reverence." The following year he wrote: "Whenever I read Plutarch or look at a Greek vase, I am inclined to accept the common opinion of the learned that the Greeks had cleverer wits than any other people in the universe. But there is anything but time in my idea of the Antique. A clear & natural expression by word or deed is that which we mean when we love & praise the Antique. In Society I do not find it; in modern books seldom, but the moment I get into the pastures I find Antiquity again." Nevertheless, the classics could be even more inspiring than nature at times: "We go musing into the vault of day and night; no constellation shines, no muse descends, the stars are white points, the roses brick-colored leaves, and frogs pipe, mice cheep, and wagons creak along the road. We return to the house and take up Plutarch or Augustine and read a few sentences or pages, and lo! the air swims with life, secrets of magnanimity and grandeur invite us in every hand, and life is made up of them. Such is our debt to a book." He quoted Georg Moller: "True art again is not imitation of the Greeks. Be Greek yourself."[8]

The romantics' principal point regarding the ancient Greeks was that Americans should not copy them but should emulate their simplicity and independence of mind, the true sources of their greatness. Emerson wrote:

> The highest merit we ascribe to Homer is that he forsook books & traditions & wrote not what men but what Homer thought. . . . You must exercise your genius in some form that has essential life now; do something which is proper to the hour & cannot but be done. But what is once well done lasts forever. As "the gladiator", the Apollo, the Parthenon, the *Iliad* . . . Phocion, Socrates, Anaxagoras, Diogenes present us the lively image of great men. But they leave no churches. He who is really of their church will be wholly his own man. The improvements of our time are merely mechanical. We have no greater men than Epaminondas & Agesilaus. . . . A great man is always a contradiction to his age & to foregoing history. If Plato had not been, you would say no Plato could be. . . . Our admiration of the Antique is not admiration of the Old but of the Natural. We admire the Greek in an American plough boy often. The Greeks as a nation were not reflective, but perfect in their senses, perfect in their health. The adults acted with the simplicity & grace of boys. They made vases & tragedies & statues such as healthy senses should, that is, in good taste. Such things have continued to be made in all ages & now wherever a healthy physiology exists, but owing to their decided superiority of the eye, they have done better as a class than any others & their local forms have usurped the conventional reverence. . . . Hold all conventions of society light in your reverence for simple instinct, so shall you revive the age of the Greeks.

In dubiously proclaiming the Greeks unreflective, Emerson (himself a Neoplatonist, no less) dismissed what the founders had regarded as the Greeks' best trait, their rationality, in favor of pure, childlike emotion. An admirer of the Greeks' alleged simplicity and nonconformity, Emerson claimed, "A person of childlike genius and inborn energy is still a Greek, and revives our love of the Muse of Hellas." The god Prometheus, who had defied Zeus by giving humans fire, was the ultimate nonconformist. Emerson called Prometheus "the Jesus of the old mythology," explaining, "He is the friend of man, stands between the unjust 'justice' of the Eternal Father and the race of mortals and readily suffers all things on their account." But Emerson also noted regarding the myth of Prometheus, "It departs from the Calvinistic Christianity and depicts him as the defier of Jove." Whereas

Jesus' sacrifice carried out God's will, Prometheus' defied Zeus. Emerson cited Plutarch on a Greek statesman's nonconformity: "Phocion, when the people applauded, turned to his friends & said, 'What have I said amiss?'" Emerson also quoted a Latin line from Horace that translates as "I would bend the world to myself, not myself to the world."[9]

Other romantics agreed with Emerson. Whitman argued that the greatness of Homer, like that of Shakespeare and all other great artists, lay in his capturing of his own time, not in his imitation of previous poets: "Homer and Shakespeare deserve all the reward that has been bestowed upon them. They did what was to be done, and did the work divinely. Homer poetized great wars, persons, events, throwing together in perfect proportion—a perfect poem, noisy, muscular, manly, amative, an amusement and excitement—a sustenance and health. . . . Shall there not be a poet of America doing no less than they but different from them? Stamping *this* age, and so all ages, in his poems?" Poe agreed that most of the ancient poets did not adhere to any "laws": "The Prosodies of the schools are mere collections of vague laws, with their more vague exceptions, based upon no principles whatever, but extorted in the most speculative manner from the usages of the ancients, who had no laws beyond those of their ears and fingers." The very genius of Greek poetry, like that of Greek sculpture, was its unpretentious simplicity, resulting in a faithful portrayal of nature. Emotional abandon, not a rigid adherence to laws, was "the essence of all antique song," "the soul of Homer," "the spirit of Anacreon," and "the genius of Aeschylus." Meanwhile, Thoreau seemed determined to convert his favorite dramatist Aeschylus, the most popular playwright of Athens during his own lifetime, into a nonconformist like himself: "The social condition of genius is the same in all ages. Aeschylus was undoubtedly alone and without sympathy in his simple reverence for the mystery of the universe." The Transcendentalists seemed not to note the paradox in their claim that the Greeks had been a race of nonconformists.[10]

The Transcendentalists' Neoplatonism and Stoicism

Paradoxically, the Transcendentalists derived their emphasis on intuition over reason from the formal philosophies of Platonism and Stoicism. Influenced by the Neoplatonist Plotinus, as well as by German idealists equally indebted to Plato, Emerson claimed that every person was a follower of either Plato or Aristotle—that is, a believer in either intuition (innate knowledge) or reason (logic acting on information provided by the senses), in either spirit or matter. In other words, a Platonist believed that knowledge was acquired from the inside out, an Aristotelian from the outside in. The Transcendentalists stood firmly with the Platonists. Like their Puritan ancestors, who had merged Plato with Protestant Christianity, they could not accept Aristotle's dictum "There is nothing in the mind that was not first in the senses." Indeed, they called themselves Transcendentalists because they sought to transcend reason and experience, relying instead upon intuition. As Daniel Walker Howe has noted, in their rejection of empiricism the Transcendentalists "returned to an idealist monism closer to that of the ancient world, of Plotinus and Plato" than the Neoplatonism of their other forebears had been. The Cambridge Platonists of the seventeenth century, the classical Unitarians, the Scottish commonsense philosophers, and the more philosophically minded founders, had all mingled their idealism with a dose of empiricism (in the last case, a rather large one).[11]

As early as 1820, in his Bowdoin Prize–winning essay at Harvard, "The Character of Socrates," Emerson praised the Athenian philosopher, as found in the dialogues of Plato. Emerson asserted: "Regard this character [of Socrates] . . . & we shall be inclined to wonder that men without revelation, merely by the light of reason & nature, could set forth a model of moral perfection which the wise in any age would do well to imitate. . . . This patriotic philosopher extended his wisdom to the body of the people in the first city in the world & communicated to his disciples not a mysterious or hieroglyphical scripture to amuse the learned & awe the ignorant but practical rules of life adapted immediately to their condition & little infected with the dogmas of the age." Eight years later Emerson wrote: "There was a citizen of Athens, the wisest certainly of all pagans that preceded Christ—I mean Socrates—who taught his countrymen that he was always attended by an invisible Genius which governed his actions. . . . I suppose that by this Daemon, Socrates designed to describe by a lively image the same judgment which we term conscience. We are all attended by this daemon. We are acquainted with that signal which is as the voice of God." Socrates was the first of "the great men of the world . . . who did not take their opinions on trust, but explored themselves, and that is the way ethics & religion were got out." Emerson even suggested that if the Greek republics had adopted Socratic philosophy, they might never have fallen. Two decades later Emerson quoted Socrates: "Those are profane who think there is nothing else than that which they are able to grasp with their hands."[12]

Emerson was well aware that it was impossible to separate Socrates from Plato, his student and chronicler. Ralph L. Rusk, the editor of a collection of Emerson's letters, noted, "It was Plato, poet in spite of his banishment of poets from his ideal republic, whom he chose in times of need as the chief guide through the dark jungle of the human mind." As early as 1824 Emerson wrote a letter to Plato, in which he declared: "The voice of antiquity has proclaimed, most venerable Shade, that if the Father of the Gods should converse with men, he would speak in the language of Plato. In cloisters & colleges, lovers of philosophy are found to this day who repeat this praise." He referred to "Plato, Plotinus & such godlike worthies who . . . showed that none could be a true philosopher that was not abstracted in spirit from all the effects of the body." In 1831 he wrote: "If we find a person who esteems excellence that we have loved we love him. . . . [If a person] is fond of flowers or of books, of poems, of De Stael, of Platonism, then I find a tie nearer & nearer as his tastes approach or unite with mine." Plato long reigned as the favorite in Emerson's library, and for a while in 1840 Emerson read his works every day. Emerson wrote regarding the Athenian: "A great Common Sense is his warrant & qualification to be the world's philosopher. He has Reason, as all the philosophic & poetic class have, but he has also what they have not, the strong solving Sense to reconcile his poetry with the appearances of the world & build a bridge from the streets of cities to the New Atlantis." After reading Platonic dialogues at the beach the following year, he exulted: "What a great uniform gentleman is Plato! . . . Never obtuse or saturnine; but so accomplished, so good humored, so perceptive, so uniting wisdom & poetry, acuteness & humanity into such a golden average that one understands how he should enjoy his long augustan empire in literature." He also wrote, "With what security & common sense this Plato treads the cliffs & pinnacles of Parnassus, as if he walked in a street, & comes down again into the street, as if he lived there." Emerson also read the Pythagoreans, who influenced Plato, and the Neoplatonists who followed in the Athenian's footsteps. Although he liked the philosophy of the latter group, he considered them inferior to their master in rhetorical ability; they were deep but too metaphysical, lacking Plato's "air of facts & society." He applauded Plato's idea, expressed in the *Republic*, of "the fraternity of the best joined for the benefit of all," an idea Emerson thought reproduced in a variety of forms throughout history, from the Theban Band to the Underground Railroad.[13]

Emerson's admiration for Plato was unbounded. He exulted:

> Plato is philosophy and philosophy Plato. . . . Vain are the laurels of Rome, vain the pride of England in her Newton, Milton & Shakespeare, whilst neither Saxon nor Roman have availed to add any idea to the categories of Plato. . . . Every brisk young man who says fine things to each reluctant generation in succession . . . is some reader of Plato translating into the vernacular wittily his good things. . . . It destroys how many originalities, pretended

originals, to read Plato. Here is the mountain from which all these detached boulders were torn. Plato was the bible of the learned for 2200 years.... It is easy to read Plato, difficult to read his commentators.... Nothing but God can give invention; everything else one would say the study of Plato would give: a discipline, it seems, in logic, in arithmetic, in taste or symmetry, in poetry, in language, in rhetoric, in science or ontology & in morals or practical wisdom.... Let the scholar measure his valour by his power to cope with intellectual giants. Others can count votes & calculate stocks. Can he weigh Plato?... Eyes outrun the feet & go where the feet & hands can never follow. So Plato the practicalists.... Plato is no Athenian. An Englishman says how English! A German, how Teutonic! An Italian, how Roman & how Greek! It transcends sectional lines, the great humane Plato.... Plato seems to us an American genius.

Indeed, Emerson wrote regarding two of the Platonic dialogues: "*Gorgias* and *Protagoras* are up to their fame & the best thing in Boston is its love of these." Recalling Plato's doctrine that the world of the senses was but an imperfect copy of the ideal world of the forms, Emerson wrote, "Santa Croce and St. Peter's are lame copies after a divine model." Similarly, Emerson wrote of Michelangelo's sculptures: "When I see these fine objects, I think of Plato's doctrine of the original forms that are in the Divine mind. These things take a place that seems to have waited for them in our own minds. They are almost recognized, as Fontenelle said of new truth." Emerson asked his friend and fellow Platonist John Heath: "Does the high Platonic Beauty still hover for you in that eastern heaven? Or is it left behind for realities less fair but nearer and, as it is pretended, more fit for man? I hope & will believe it still holds its place and will hold it evermore, changing its names & becoming more distinctly visible, but by drawing man up to itself, not by any descent on its part."[14]

When Emerson presented a series of lectures that ultimately became the book entitled *Representative Men,* Plato was first on his list of seven intellectual giants. The first sentence of that book declared: "Among secular books, Plato only is entitled to Omar's fanatical compliment to the *Koran* when he said, 'Burn the libraries; for their value is in this book.'" Calling Plato "the Euclid of holiness," Emerson noted, "In him the freest abandonment is united with the precision of a geometer." He concluded:

> The writings of Plato have preoccupied every school of learning, every lover of thought, every church, every poet—making it impossible to think, on certain levels, except through him.... His sense deepens, his merits multiply, with study.... You find in him that which you have already found in Homer, now ripened to thought—the poet converted to philosopher, with loftier strains of musical wisdom than Homer reached.... Whenever any skeptic or bigot claims to be heard on the questions of intellect and morals, we ask if he

is familiar with the books of Plato, where all his pert objections have once for all been disposed. If not, he has no right to our time. Let him go and find himself answered there.... Who can overestimate the images with which Plato has enriched the minds of men and which pass like bullion in the currency of all nations?"[15]

Henry David Thoreau and Margaret Fuller, other leading Transcendentalists, shared Emerson's Platonic idealism. Thoreau wrote: "But there is only necessary a moment's sanity and sound sense to teach us that there is a nature beyond the ordinary.... We live on the outskirts of that region. Is not Nature, rightly read, that of which she is commonly taken to be the symbol merely? ... I am not without hope that we may, even here and now, obtain some accurate information concerning that OTHER WORLD which the instinct of mankind so long predicted." In Thoreau's imagination ancient Greece was the closest earthly approximation to Plato's ideal world of the forms. He found Aristotle too rationalist and materialist. After reading Plato's *Phaedrus*, Fuller felt as if "returning to my native mountain air." She taught at Bronson Alcott's experimental Temple School in Boston and favored his Neoplatonic goals, though not his rather abstract, ethereal way of realizing them. She relished the Platonic idea of friends as people who help one another to achieve their full potential. In contrast to the Seneca Falls Declaration, with its Lockean emphasis on rights, Fuller's feminism was rooted in the Platonic idea of self-actualization into the ideal form. She wrote: "It is ... the law of growth that speaks in us and demands the perfection of each being in its kind, apple as apple, woman as woman."[16]

Though hardly a complete Platonist, Edgar Allan Poe joined the Transcendentalists in the belief that there existed a higher world of perfect Ideas, of which this world was but an imperfect copy. The women of Poe's works were idealized, abstract, unattainable visions of Platonic Beauty. He claimed that there was no greater poet than Plato because, though the Athenian had never written poetry as such, he had possessed a clear vision of the world of pure forms. In his own works Poe sought to combine Platonic inspiration with Aristotelian unity.[17]

To their Platonic idealism the Transcendentalists added Stoic pantheism and the Stoic belief in the necessity of intellectual detachment from the world. Emerson's "universal mind," the divine entity from which all souls arose, to which all souls eventually returned, which was diffused throughout the universe, was essentially the Stoic World Soul. Emerson wrote: "That a man is not so much an individual as a manifestation of the Eternal and Universal One is no new or peculiar doctrine.... The pious men of the Stoic sect received this faith, saying that the wise man differed from God in nothing but duration. It was also a maxim of their school that mind was God in man." In order to hear the whispered truths of the universal mind, the individual must detach himself from the corrupt teachings of society. Emerson wrote: "Let the Stoic open the resources of men and tell them that they are not leaning willows, but can and must detach themselves." He quoted the Stoic philosopher Epictetus: "My body, thou art but a little bit of the universe; but my mind or reason is neither worse nor less than the gods'. Will you not place your good there where you are equal to the gods?" Emerson noted that pantheism, while often associated with the Stoics, predated them. He quoted Pythagoras: "The soul is an emanation of the Divinity, a part of the Soul of the world, a ray from the source of light." Emerson also noted, "Anaxagoras said one single soul ran thro' all being, ordering matter but intimately present to man." Emerson adhered to the Platonic and Stoic conception of immortality as that of the disembodied spirit rather than to the biblical conception of the bodily resurrection.[18]

The Stoics influenced Thoreau, Whitman, and Poe as well. In an 1838 journal entry Thoreau compared himself with Zeno, the founder of Stoicism, "a man bred a merchant," who read Xenophon's *Memorabilia of Socrates* one day and became a philosopher, a solitary seeker of truth. After reading and thoroughly marking his copy of Epictetus' works, Whitman wrote in his notebook these lines of admiration for the philosopher's detachment and self-sufficiency under the heading "Epictetus" and the subheading "Description of a Wise Man":

> He reproves nobody,
> Praises nobody,
> Blames nobody,
> Nor even speaks of himself.
> If anyone praises him, in his own mind he condemns
>   the flatterer.
> If anyone reproves him, he looks with care that it
>   does not irritate him.
> All his desires depend on things within his power.
> He transfers all his aversions to those things which
>   Nature commands us to avoid.
> His appetites are always moderate.
> He is indifferent whether he be thought foolish or wise.
> He observes himself with the nicety of an enemy or spy,
>   and looks on his own wishes as betrayers.

Even Poe, who was less ardent a proponent of classical philosophy than the Transcendentalists, penned a poem entitled "Eureka," in which he espoused a form of pantheism similar to that of the Stoics.[19]

The Transcendentalists also adopted the Stoic emphasis on natural law, a universal code of ethics inherent in nature and discoverable by humans. Emerson echoed both Cicero and the Stoics concerning natural law: "[Moral laws] are out of time, out of space, and not subject to circumstance.... Man, fallen into superstition, into sensuality, is never wholly without the visions of the moral sentiment.... It is an intuition. It cannot be received at second hand. Truly speaking, it is not instruction, but provocation, that I can receive from another soul. What he announces, I must find true in me." Emerson urged "an ethics commensurate with nature" (forgetting, like all proponents of natural law, that nature is built upon species devouring one another). The individual understood natural law intuitively, not through instruction or scripture. Indeed, Emerson wrote, "It may be a question... whether we have not lost... by a Christianity entrenched in establishments and forms, some vigor of wild virtue."[20]

Like many early American believers in natural law, Thoreau was influenced as much by Sophocles' *Antigone* as by the Stoics. In the play Antigone defies the king's edict against burying her brother, who must be buried if his soul is to find rest. In his highly influential *Letters from a Pennsylvania Farmer* (1767) the patriot John Dickinson had quoted Antigone's declaration of natural law in support of his own resistance to parliamentary taxes:

> I never could think
> A mortal's law of power or strength sufficient
> To abrogate the unwritten law divine,
> Immutable, eternal, not like those
> Of yesterday, but made ere time began.

Less than a century later, Thoreau, like Dickinson, learned from Antigone's discourse on natural law and her resultant resistance to injustice that he must give his own allegiance to natural law rather than to human statutes. While writing his essay "On Resistance to Civil Government," Thoreau returned to *Antigone*, which he had read as an undergraduate, and translated passages concerning the heroine's defiance of civil authority. Thoreau's more famous essay "On Civil Disobedience" advocated resistance to statutes that conflicted with natural law, as determined by the individual conscience. In turn, Thoreau's essay inspired Mohandas Gandhi, Martin Luther King Jr., and other modern advocates of civil disobedience.[21]

The Transcendentalists occasionally even embraced a Stoic fatalism similar to the predestination of their Calvinist ancestors. Sometimes they seemed to suggest, like the Stoics, that few were destined to follow the path of enlightenment, while at other times they were more optimistic. On the one hand, Emerson quoted a line from Sophocles in Greek that translates as "For the dice of God are always loaded," yet in his more euphoric moments he could even suggest that laws and coercive power might one day be unnecessary: "Society can be maintained without artificial restraints as well as the solar system.... The private citizen might be reasonable and a good neighbor without the hint of a jail or a confiscation."[22]

The Romantics and Classical Mythology

While the founders' generation revered the more rational elements of classical literature, such as its history and political theory, the Transcendentalists valued classical mythology for its passion and mysticism. Emerson contended that Greek mythology was superior in moral wisdom to the "Gothic fables" concerning King Arthur and other medieval heroes: "In the beautiful creations of the Grecian muse every fable, though related as religious truth and believed by the multitude as history, is, at the same time, a fine allegory conveying a wise and consistent sense.... Compare the various incidents which we collect out of different poets respecting one of the Grecian Gods or demigods with the unchosen and miscellaneous prodigies which are related of Merlin and Arthur." The former myths conveyed lessons lacking in the latter, whose "whole object was amusement by the incidents of the story itself." Though the medieval legends generally advanced moral lessons in spite of themselves, they did so in a less coherent fashion. Emerson quoted Plato: "Poets utter great and wise things which they do not themselves understand." The medieval fabulists accidentally stumbled upon principles the Greek poets consciously understood and skillfully employed: "In endeavoring to make his hero agreeable the writer insensibly makes him virtuous. And being virtuous it is agreeable to our constitution to believe him powerful and successful." Emerson concluded: "When I think of the robust Greek mythology & what a cosmic imagination . . . they had, a power I mean of expressing in graceful fable the laws of the world, so that the mythology is beautiful poetry on one side—at any moment convertible into severe science on the other, then the English verse looks poor & purposeless, as if written for hire & not obeying the grandeur of Ideas.... I think it wonderful, the beauty of the Greeks as contrasted with the unbeautiful English nursery-stories, which, though now & then rarely admitting in their fable a natural fact . . . yet in the main are childish & insignificant like Blue Beard or Jack Giantkiller, whilst every word of the Greek is at once beautiful and also science." Emerson listed Homer as the first of the five Greek authors whom "we cannot spare," the others being Herodotus, Aeschylus, Plato, and Plutarch. He wrote:

> That wit and joy might find a tongue,
> And earth grow civil, Homer sung.

Emerson found as much instruction in Homer's tale of Troy as in the French Revolution. From it he learned the need for divine assistance, the beauty of patriotism, and the lethality of sexual passion.[23]

Thoreau preferred Greek mythology to Eastern mysticism, which he considered too contemplative and amoral, and to Christianity, which he considered too dogmatic and otherworldly. He wrote, "The *Iliad* represents no creed or opinion, and we read it now with a rare sense of freedom and irresponsibility." Yet the poem reflected a certain spirituality: "These single strains, these melodious cadences, which plainly proceed out of a very deep meaning and sustained soul, are the interjections of God. They are perhaps the expression of the perfect knowledge which the righteous at length attain to." Thoreau claimed:

> The Hebrew fable will not bear to be compared with the Grecian. The latter is infinitely more sublime and divine. . . . The one god of the Hebrews is not so much of a gentleman, not so gracious and divine, not so flexible and catholic, does not exert so intimate an influence on nature as many a one of the Greeks. He is not less human, though more absolute and unapproachable. The Grecian were youthful and living gods, but still of godlike or divine race, and had the virtues of gods. . . . The wisdom of some of those Greek fables is remarkable. . . . The fable which is truly and naturally composed, so as to please the imagination of a child, harmonious though strange like a wild-flower, is to the wise man an apothegm and admits his wisest interpretation.

The careless destruction of the forests around Concord led Thoreau to wish that the superstition of Cato's time concerning the sacredness of groves was still in effect.[24]

Thoreau loved Homer and Virgil because he believed that their poetry captured both nature and human nature. Thoreau wrote: "There are few books which are fit to be remembered in our wisest hours, but the *Iliad* is brightest in the serenest days, and embodies still all the sunlight that fell on Asia Minor. No modern joy or ecstasy of ours can lower its height or dim its lustre, but there it lies in the east of literature, as it were the earliest and latest production of the human mind." Thoreau especially admired Homer's fidelity to nature, his complete unwillingness to supplement, omit, exaggerate, or minimize any of its multifarious aspects: "It is enough if Homer but say the sun sets. He is as serene as nature, and we can hardly detect the enthusiasm of the bard. It is as if nature spoke." The *Iliad* was so close to nature that the cricket's song was one with it: "It matters not whether these strains originate there in the grass or float thitherward like atoms of light from the minstrel days of Greece." Thoreau added: "Three thousand years and the world so little changed. The Iliad seems like a natural sound which has reverberated to our days." "Fire-eyed Agamemnon" reminded him of the declaimers at New England town meetings and elections, and Nestor "of the old school" reminded him of a woman who visited his mother. Homer's characters had human weaknesses but also possessed dignity and courage. Concerning Virgil, Thoreau wrote: "I would read Virgil if only that I might be reminded of the identity of human nature in all ages. . . . It was the same world, and the same men inhabited it." The lines Thoreau quoted from Virgil often concerned nature as well: the valleys echoing to the stars, the birds swelling on the branches, and the apples scattered beneath the trees.[25]

Thoreau believed that the simplicity of Homer and Virgil, which captured the most basic and universal principles of existence, derived from their having lived at the dawn of civilization. Just as children were closer to nature and God because they had not yet been corrupted by the artificiality and dogmas of society, so the ancient civilizations possessed the same divine vitality, simplicity, and sense of wonder by virtue of their relative youth in the chronology of humankind. Thoreau wrote regarding the ancients: "We have gained nothing by the few ages which we have the start of them. The universal wondering at those old men is as if a matured grown person should discover that the aspirations of his youth argued a diviner life than the contented wisdom of his manhood." Thoreau added: "How much more fertile a nature has Grecian mythology its root in than English Literature! The nature which inspired mythology still flourishes. Mythology is the crop which the Old World bore before its soil was exhausted. The West is preparing to add its fables to those of the East." Thoreau thought that most English poetry lacked "the rudeness and vigor of youth," but liked Geoffrey Chaucer, regarding him as "the Homer of the English poets" and the "youthfullest of them all." In his last years Thoreau read Herodotus and Strabo for insights into the early history of the human race. He studied philology for the same reason, seeking the origins of language.[26]

When Thoreau began his life at Walden Pond, he took with him his copy of the *Iliad* and resolved to lead a simple life indicative of the heroes contained within it (absent the warfare, of course). He wrote in his journal: "Here I can read Homer, if I would have books, as well as in Ionia. . . . In such a place as this he wrote or sang. . . . No wonder Alexander carried his Homer in a precious casket on his expeditions. A word which may be translated into every dialect and suggests a truth to every mind is the most perfect work of human art." Unfortunately, this was the only book stolen from his cabin. At Walden, Thoreau wrote regarding the classics:

> These works of art have such an immortality as the works of nature, and are modern at the same time that they are ancient, like the sun and the stars, and occupy by right no small share of the present. This palpable beauty is the treasured wealth of the world and the proper inheritance of each generation. Books, the oldest and the best, stand rightfully on the shelves of every cottage. They have not to plead their cause, but they enlighten their readers and it is gained. When the illiterate and scornful rustic earns his imagined leisure and wealth, he turns inevitably at last—he or his children—to these still higher and yet inaccessible circles; and even when his descendant has attained to move in the highest rank of the wise men of his own age and country, he will still be sensible only of the imperfection of his culture and the vanity and inefficiency of his intellectual wealth, if his genius will not permit him to listen with somewhat of the equanimity of an equal to the fames of godlike men which yet, as it were, form an invisible upper class in every society.

Thoreau later recalled of his stay at Walden, "Both place and time were changed, and I dwelt nearer to those parts of the universe and to those eras in history which had most attracted me." He enjoyed reckoning time by the sun and sitting down to a simple meal after a day of hard work. In his journal he wrote that his house had the aura of Mount Olympus, the atmosphere in which Greek art had been created. On the other hand, he sometimes imagined that Walden was his Ithaca and that he was "a fellow wanderer and survivor of Ulysses." The natural objects he saw around him reminded him of the patterns in Greek art. Like Sam Houston, who had enjoyed reading Pope's translation of the *Iliad* while living among the Cherokees, Thoreau equated Homer with the wilderness and both with freedom.[27]

Thoreau also loved the mythology he found in the plays of Aeschylus, Sophocles, and Euripides, the three great tragedians of fifth-century B.C. Athens. Thoreau translated Aeschylus' *Prometheus Bound* for the *Dial* in 1843 and later translated *Seven against Thebes*, Pindar's *Odes*, and the *Anacreontics*, a collection of poems commonly attributed to the sixth-century B.C. Greek poet Anacreon. Thoreau wrote concerning Aeschylus, "Let the seer bring down his broad eye to the most stale and trivial fact, and he will make you believe it a new planet in the sky." Aeschylus' concision was "the standing aside of words to make room for thoughts." Thoreau continued: "His sublimity is Greek sincerity and simpleness. . . . The man's speech wants nothing. Whatever the common eye sees at all and expresses as best it may, he sees uncommonly and describes with rare completeness."

Like Emerson, Thoreau compared Prometheus to Christ, admiring his courage, intelligence, benevolence, and fortitude.[28]

Classical mythology also enthralled Margaret Fuller. When she was only six, her father Timothy, a man of humble means who later became a U.S. representative and Speaker of the Massachusetts House, had given her "a great pile of books," including some written in Greek and Latin. Horace, Ovid, Virgil, Cicero, and Caesar were her daily companions, lessons from whose works she recited for her demanding father every evening. She then studied Greek at the coeducational Cambridgeport Private Grammar School. There she was renowned for her huge vocabulary in English and Greek and for her skill at recitation. In her memoirs (1840) Fuller recalled "the influence of the great Romans, whose thoughts and lives were my daily food during those plastic years." Ovid had taught her Greek mythology: "Ovid gave me not Rome, nor himself, but a view into the enchanted gardens of the Greek mythology. This path I followed, I have been following ever since.... I loved to get away from the hum of the forum, and the mailed clang of Roman speech, to these shifting shows of nature, these Gods and Nymphs born of the sunbeam, the wave, and the shadows on the hill.... With these books I passed my days."[29]

From 1839 to 1844 Fuller organized ten series of conversations at a bookstore with women who paid twenty dollars to hear her speak about many different subjects. Her observations on classical mythology were considered so interesting that she was asked to repeat them for men. In these conversations Fuller expressed the opinion that some of the gods were representations of human faculties and attributes. Apollo was an origination power, Mercury an executive power. Apollo was the light side of genius, Bacchus its warm side. The story of Psyche was like that of Adam and Eve, in which suffering led to purification and redemption. Minerva, a model for women, was wisdom, which sprang from the "Intelligent Creative Power," just as Minerva had sprung from the head of Jupiter. Rhea represented Productive Energy, which rescued Jupiter, who represented Indomitable Will, from Saturn, who represented Time. Juno, the female form of Indomitable Will, always lost when she opposed Jupiter, the superior, male form. Jupiter's defeat of the Titans represented the victory of the will over "the low and sensual passions." Though Vulcan, who represented Mechanic Art, was powerful, he was "not comparable to the Perfect Wisdom, or Minerva, which sprang ready armed from the masculine Will." Fuller concluded that while "the age of Greece was an age of poetry," the nineteenth century was an analytical age, a fair assessment considering her own reduction of Greek mythology to a set of universal abstractions. While the "childhood of the world" represented in Greek mythology could never be restored, Americans could "admire this simple plastic period and gather from it some notion of the Greek genius." Like the other Transcendentalists, Fuller preferred Greek religion to orthodox Christianity, as well as to the cold Unitarianism of their parents' generation.[30]

In *Woman in the Nineteenth Century* (1845) Fuller claimed that the ancients had represented the two aspects of women's nature "as Muse and Minerva." While Muse was the traditional stereotype of women, inspiring man to create while not herself creating, Minerva partook of traditionally masculine qualities, including rationality and independence. Fuller emphasized the benefits of the Minerva personality for the sake of "many incarcerated souls that might be freed, could the idea of religious self-independence be established in them, could the weakening habit of dependence on others be broken up." Fuller wrote: "Nature provides exceptions to every rule. She sends women to battle and sets Hercules spinning; she enables women to bear immense burdens, cold, and frost; she enables the man who feels maternal love to nourish his infant like a mother. . . . Man partakes of the feminine in the Apollo, Woman of the masculine in the Minerva." Fuller, a self-sufficient virgin at the time, preferred Minerva, Diana, and Vesta, the self-sufficient virgin goddesses, to the lusty Venus. Fuller wrote regarding nineteenth-century woman: "Grant her, then, for a while, the armor and the javelin [of Minerva]. Let her put from her the press of other minds and meditate in virgin loneliness." If she must marry, she must insist on the fidelity of her husband, who was certainly capable of it: "Man is not of Satyr descent." Regarding a collection of the busts of gods and goddesses arranged in pairs, she wrote: "Male and female heads are distinct in expression, but equal in beauty, strength, and calmness. Each male head is that of a brother and a king—each female of a sister and a queen. Could the thought thus expressed be lived out, there would be nothing more to be desired. There would be unison in variety, congeniality in difference."[31]

Fuller died a tragic death when her ship, returning from Rome, was sunk by a hurricane. Unfortunately, the history of the Roman republic she had just completed perished with her. Thomas Carlyle wrote to Emerson that her life was as "wild as the prophecy of a Sibyl," the Roman oracle. Her focus on mythology demonstrated how the expansion of classical interest beyond political history and theory, the great preoccupations of the founders' age, to encompass drama and poetry could give politically disfranchised women and others focused on self-improvement a greater connection to the classics than had been possible in the eighteenth century.[32]

While the Transcendentalists discussed classical mythology, the fiction writers used it to provide structure and meaning to their own narratives. Throughout his *Sketch Book* (1819) Washington Irving drew heavily on

Homer's *Odyssey*. For instance, both Rip Van Winkle and Odysseus are absent from their homes for twenty years. Each returns to a dog outside his home. But here Irving produces a vivid contrast. Even though Odysseus is disguised perfectly by Athena for his own protection, his aged dog, a mere puppy at the time the hero left Ithaca for Troy, recognizes Odysseus' voice and the tread of his feet and wags his tail in response (17.344–347, 360–363). By contrast, the canine Rip encounters turns out not to be his dog after all, but a descendant of that dog who snarls at him. Through this contrast Irving demonstrates that Rip is no Odyssean hero; he deserves no recognition, for he has spent his two decades of exile sleeping, while Odysseus expended his toiling in war and suffering at sea.[33]

Some romantics drew upon classical mythology even more directly. In *Wonder Book for Boys and Girls* (1852) Nathaniel Hawthorne summarized six selected Greek myths for young readers—the stories of the Medusa, Midas, Pandora, Hercules and Atlas, Philemon and Baucis, and Bellerophon and the Pegasus—though "substituting a tone in some degree Gothic or Romantic." He allowed an editor to change Bacchus into Mercury in the Midas story, joking to a friend, "I did not see any method of strongly identifying Bacchus—unless supposing that King Midas merely fancied himself possessed of the golden faculty under the influence of the grape." The *Wonder Book* was so popular that in the following year Hawthorne published another six myths—those of the Minotaur, Hercules and the Pygmies, Cadmus, Circe, Ceres and Proserpina, and Jason and the Golden Fleece—under the title *Tanglewood Tales*. Hawthorne called the Greek tragedies that had immortalized classical mythology "the sternest forms of grief that ever the world saw."[34]

The direct product of his tour of Italy in the late 1850s, Hawthorne's *The Marble Faun* (1860) was subtitled *The Transformation* in a clear reference to Ovid's *Metamorphoses*. The protagonist, Donatello, is treated half as a mythical being, half as a human, somehow descended from gods. The villain meets his end in an apt way, being hurled from the Tarpeian Rock like the Roman traitors of old. After Donatello commits this act, he is abandoned by all of his animal friends, except for the owl, Athena's companion, which symbolizes Donatello's newfound wisdom, gained through sin and suffering. The penitent Miriam, an accessory to the murder, kneels in the light shining through the circular opening in the Pantheon, the same opening through which Hawthorne had loved to witness the play of the clouds.[35]

Praxiteles' *Faun* served as a source of inspiration for the novel. When Hawthorne saw the famous sculpture at the Capitoline Museum, he "was sensible of a peculiar charm in it, a sylvan beauty and homeliness, friendly and wild at once." He wrote in his journal: "Only a sculptor of the finest imagination, most delicate taste, and sweetest feeling could have dreamed of representing a Faun in this guise.... Its lengthened but not preposterous ears and the little tail which we infer behind have an exquisite effect and make the spectator smile in his very heart. The race of fauns was the most delightful of all that antiquity imagined. It seems to me that a story, with all sorts of fun and pathos in it, might be contrived on the idea of their species having become intermingled with the human race." Fauns seemed to Hawthorne "strange, sweet, playful, rustic creatures," "a natural and delightful link betwixt human and brute life, and with something of a divine character intermingled." As the literary historian Hubert H. Hoeltje explained Hawthorne's intention: "Out of the atmosphere of Italy he might draw that spell of hoar antiquity and that subdued tinge of the wild and wonderful which he had sought since the days of his young manhood." It also gave him the opportunity to put into the mouths of his many artist characters the ruminations on art that had filled his mind while studying classical sculptures in Europe for several years.[36]

It is indicative of the hold of the classical world on antebellum Americans that *The Marble Faun*, not *The Scarlet Letter* or any of Hawthorne's other stories set in the American past, was the most commercially and critically successful of his books. For decades American visitors to Rome brought a copy of the novel with them, relishing its beautiful descriptions of the sights and sounds of the Eternal City. Hawthorne himself wrote in the preface to *The Marble Faun*: "In re-writing these volumes, the Author was somewhat surprised to see the extent to which he had introduced descriptions of various Italian objects, antique, pictorial, and statuesque. Yet these things fuel the mind, everywhere in Italy, and especially in Rome, and cannot easily be kept from flowing out upon the page when one writes freely and with self-enjoyment. And, again, while reproducing the book ... [with] the northern blast always howling in my ears, the complete change of scene made these Italian reminiscences shine out so vividly that I could not find it in my heart to cancel them."[37]

Seeking to augment his minimal classical education, in 1849 Herman Melville purchased *Harper's Classical Library*, the thirty-seven-volume set of various classics in English translation. He read these works intently, especially the plays of Aeschylus, Sophocles, and Euripides, and immediately began to make use of the mythology they contained in his own work. In *Mardi* (1849) Melville referred to "Virgil my minstrel" and the "Trojan Aeneas," who wandered westward to "the pleasant land of Latium." He cited the *Iliad* as an example of timeless art and referred to sirens and to Circe from the *Odyssey*. Melville used the Homeric phrases "the finny tribes" and "finny flock" to refer to fish. In a nod to the *Odyssey*'s repeated references to the "rosy-fingered dawn" Melville wrote: "When thus my Yillah did daily dawn, how she lit up my world, tinging more rosily the roseate clouds that in her summer cheek played to and fro, like clouds in Italian air." He compared the drunken Annatoo to a Fury fiercer than those who pursued Orestes. Yillah's tale of having once been a blossom that "fell into the opening valve of a shell" that "in good time was cast upon the beach of the Island of Amma" recalls Botticelli's *Birth of Venus*. Melville described a shark as swimming "sluggishly . . . and ever anon shaking his Medusa locks, writhing and curling with horrible life." He foreshadowed Annatoo's death by referring to his "Penthesilian qualities." Penthesilea was an Amazon killed at Troy by Achilles, who then praised her in a eulogy. Regarding the tent in which Aleena and his sons secluded Yillah, Melville wrote, "They pointed toward the tent as if it contained their Eleusinian mysteries," thereby noting the supernatural and unattainable nature of Yillah and the blasphemous nature of Taji's relentless pursuit of the maiden.[38]

But it was in *Moby-Dick* (1851), perhaps the greatest of all American novels, that Melville moved beyond the use of classical mythology for descriptive purposes to a reliance upon it for tragic elevation and structure. Meditating deeply on the masterpieces of the Athenian stage, as well as on Shakespearian dramas that his edition of Shakespeare compared to the Greek tragedies, Melville learned that tragedy was based on three elements: the greatness of the hero, the seriousness of his crime, and the torment of his suffering. Each of these elements Melville employed successfully in *Moby-Dick*. His Ahab was based partly on Prometheus. Just as Prometheus defies Zeus, so Ahab defies God in pursuit of the white whale. Ahab declares concerning the whale: "I see in him outrageous strength, with an inscrutable malice sinewing in it. That inscrutable thing is chiefly what I hate; and be the white whale agent, or be the white whale principal, I will wreak that hate upon him." Just as Prometheus unjustly imagines that Zeus is withholding fire from humanity in order to destroy it, though Aeschylus plainly suggests that the god's real motive is to halt the degeneration of humankind that has resulted from the excessive luxury of the Golden Age, so Ahab imagines the worst of a God that would allow suffering in the world, such as the loss of his own leg. As with Prometheus, Ahab's view of God as malevolent is more a reflection of his own inner depravity than of that of the divinity. Melville even highlights Ahab's propensity to project his own nature onto others by having Ahab refer to the ship's blacksmith as "Prometheus." Both Prometheus and Ahab are infected with an arrogance that causes them to believe that they cannot only comprehend but even thwart the allegedly evil design of the divinity.[39]

Romanticism — 143

This fatal pride causes them to engage in unholy acts. Starbuck refers to Ahab's quest to kill the whale, a quest for which Ahab is willing to sacrifice his entire crew, as "blasphemous" and a "heaven-insulting purpose." The whale is referred to as having a "god-like dignity in brow." Ahab himself admits that he is as "proud as a Greek god." Melville even has lightning strike Ahab's harpoon, which he then wields against his own crew to suppress mutiny—a stealing of fire from the heavens similar to Prometheus' theft. Both Prometheus and Ahab are justly accused of madness in seeking to overcome an awesome power that cannot be overcome. Each befriends a genuinely mad person because each perceives in the sufferings of the lunatic a dim reflection of his own madness, but both disregard the clear warning that complete madness is what awaits if they persist on their rebellious course. Both disregard other warnings concerning the immense power of the adversary as well: in Aeschylus' play Prometheus ignores Oceanus' and the chorus's warnings about the fate of past rebels against Zeus, and Ahab ignores the warnings of Starbuck and of other whalers concerning the end suffered by those who have tangled with the white whale. Ishmael plays the role of the chorus in providing information and sympathetic commentary, while Starbuck, who possesses the same fear, awe, and practicality as the chorus, takes on its role of warning the protagonist. While the chorus reminds Prometheus of his happier days with his wife, something in Starbuck's eyes reminds Ahab of his own wife and child. There is the suggestion that both men might return to such happiness if they would turn aside from their rash enterprise, but both refuse.[40]

The similarities do not end there. Both protagonists feel psychic and physical pain. Just as Prometheus' liver is eaten daily by an eagle in punishment for his crime, Ahab keeps breaking the replacements for his leg and still feels pain from the absent limb—physical representations of the self-perpetuating inner anguish of the protagonists. (Indeed, the Greeks considered the liver the seat of the passions.) At one point Ishmael actually declares, "God help thee, old man, thy thoughts have created a creature in thee; and he whose intense thinking thus makes him a Prometheus; a vulture feeds upon that heart forever; that vulture the very creature he creates." Starbuck says: "That chick that's in him pecks the shell. 'Twill soon be out." In the end, just as Prometheus is staked to the rock eternally, Ahab is bound by ropes to the whale, forms of physical bondage that are emblematic of the protagonists' emotional bondage to pride and rage. Though the protagonists themselves learn nothing, their survivors, Io and Ishmael, learn from the fates of Prometheus and Ahab what the two men themselves should have learned.[41]

Melville used classical mythology in *Moby-Dick* in other ways as well. He based Ahab not only on Prometheus but also on Oedipus. Ahab questions the head of a whale, which Melville specifically compares with the Sphinx, whose riddle Oedipus solved. Both Ahab and Oedipus are lame and blind, both internally and externally. Ahab is physically blinded twice, by fire and water. Both are intelligent but ignorant of themselves and their worlds, an ignorance stemming from rage and pride. Both disdain or willfully misinterpret prophetic warnings, including bird omens. Ahab's projection onto the whale of his own "inscrutable malice" is like Oedipus' projection onto Creon and the seer Tiresias of evil in the form of a plot to use prophecy to overthrow him. The difference is that Oedipus finally reaches a self-knowledge—the sight amid his physical blindness—that Ahab never does.[42]

Ahab was based on Narcissus as well. Melville explicitly refers to "Narcissus, who because he could not grasp the tormenting, mild image he saw in the fountain, plunged into it and was drowned." Melville adds: "But the same image we ourselves see in all rivers and oceans. It is the ungraspable phantom of life; and this is the key to it all." Ahab, like Narcissus, does not realize that his perception of the whale is a reflection of himself. While Narcissus projects a beautiful image that he loves, Ahab projects an ugly image that he loathes. Melville describes Ahab and the whale in similar terms: both are scarred or wounded and possess prominent, gnarled or wrinkled brows or foreheads. Both are described as isolated, enraged beings given to masking themselves. On the third day of the chase Ahab highlights the similarity by declaring, "Forehead to forehead I meet thee, this third time, Moby Dick!" Like Narcissus, Ahab drowns, forever united with his mysterious self-image.[43]

Melville based Ishmael partly on Ixion. Before Ishmael is saved, he revolves "like another Ixion" in the vortex created by the sinking *Pequod*. Just as Ixion was punished for the attempted rape of Hera, so Ishmael is punished for his complicity in Ahab's attempt to penetrate the whale with his harpoon. (Interestingly, one version of the Prometheus myth, popular during the Renaissance, claimed that Prometheus was punished for the attempted rape of Athena.) But Ishmael's punishment is not eternal like Ixion's, and he learns the folly of human attempts to penetrate the veil of nature and divinity.[44]

Melville based the protagonist of *Pierre* (1855) on Orestes. Early in the novel Melville details Pierre's family history, which is full of images of royalty and aristocracy, in order to erect an American counterpart to the house of Atreus. As with the house of Atreus, the house of Glendinning has degenerated morally over time. Both Orestes and Pierre fondly remember their dead fathers and seek to avenge them, Orestes by killing his mother Clytemnestra, the murderer of his father Agamemnon, Pierre through a pseudomarriage to his half sister Isabel, who had been abandoned by his father at the instigation of his mother long before, a marriage that causes the suicide of his mother. While Mrs. Glendinning did not physically murder her husband, unlike Clytemnestra, as the agent of his transformation from a sensitive to a coldhearted, ambitious man, who is guilty of his spiritual murder. Both mothers are hard and calculating and express the desire to murder their sons. Isabel is an orphan; Electra, Orestes' sister, considers herself one. Both Isabel and Electra possess royal blood but live in lowly situations they detest. Both yearn for their brother to save them from their condition. Melville even coyly suggests the connection between Isabel and Electra by referring to the "sparkling electricity" in which Isabel "seemed to swim" and the "flashes of . . . electricalness" that came from her. Just as Pierre knowingly hurts his mother by his pseudomarriage in response to a letter from Isabel and to the feeling of "divine commands upon him to befriend and champion Isabel," so Orestes is convinced by Electra, as well as by the god Apollo through the oracle of Delphi, to murder his mother. Pierre even has a vision of Isabel's face, hears her shriek, and remarks, "Such Delphic shriek could only come from such a source."[45]

The similarities do not end there. Isabel plays a magical guitar like Apollo's lyre and has mysterious, dancelike contortions while playing, similar to those of the oracle of Delphi. Both protagonists act in accord with divine laws of justice but against powerful social norms (against matricide and incest, respectively) and so are ostracized. Just as Orestes must flee the Furies, so Pierre must depart Saddle Meadows. Melville makes the connection explicit, stating that in Pierre's first night in the city he is "surrounded by a crowd of contending hackmen, all holding whips in their hands," and "this sudden tumultuous surrounding of him by whip-stalks and lashes seemed like the onset of the chastening fiends upon Orestes." Both begin to second-guess themselves and to question the divinity.[46]

But God does not save Pierre as Apollo does Orestes, perhaps because there is more uncertainty in the divinity of Pierre's command. (The subtitle of Melville's novel is *The Ambiguities*.) Pierre also reads a pamphlet by Plotinus Plinlimmon which counsels "a virtuous expediency." Plinlimmon's pamphlet ends with the Greek word *ei* ("if," a word suggesting the contingency of wisdom and morality), one of the words engraved over the gate at Apollo's temple at Delphi, and Plinlimmon is described as having an eye in which "the gay, immortal youth Apollo seemed enshrined." Thus Pierre has received two conflicting "Delphic" oracles, one from Isabel and the other from Plinlimmon. As in Euripides' *Electra*, the second, conflicting oracle is not brought in until after the protagonist has already taken decisive action. Tyndarus, Clytemnestra's father, does not appear at Orestes' trial to argue for social mores until after Orestes has murdered his mother, just as Plinlimmon's pamphlet does not appear until after Pierre has already "crossed the Rubicon." Thus both oracles only state what the hero should *not* have done. By the end Orestes is vengeful, violent, and bordering on insanity as he plots to kill Menelaus' wife and daughter, Electra, and himself. Likewise, by the end of *Pierre* it is clear that rage and self-destructive tendencies have made Pierre guilty of Glen Stanly's murder. Neither protagonist is a simple victim of societal condemnation; both are self-serving even in their obedience to divine commands. While it is true that Pierre and Isabel die by suicide, while Euripides uses Apollo to save Orestes and Electra from mass homicide and suicide, Euripides' ending is so jarring and false to the rest of the play as to constitute an authorial wink to the audience. In fact, Castor and Pollux make the extraordinary statement that Apollo's advice of vengeance was "not wise." Thus Euripides' questioning of both human motives and divine wisdom was quite similar to that of Melville in *Pierre*.[47]

In the late 1840s and 1850s Melville was fascinated by the Hellenistic sculpture group the *Laocoön* and by the myth behind it. In *Mardi* the travelers find on the island of Maramma a "gigantic palm-shaft, belted round by saplings, springing from its roots." Melville adds, "But Laocoön-like, sire and sons stood locked in the serpent folds of gnarled, distorted banians; and the banian-bark, eating into their vital wood, corrupted their veins of sap, till all those palm-nuts were poisoned chalices." In *Redburn* a gambling house contains "Laocoön-like chairs, in the antique taste, draped with heavy fringes of bullion and silk." In *Pierre*, after the protagonist has decided to act, Melville writes: "Ascending toward his mother's chamber, he heard a coming step, and met her on the great middle landing of the stairs, where in an ample niche, a marble group of the temple-polluting Laocoön and his two innocent children, caught in inextricable snarls of snakes, writhed in eternal torment." Melville was using the version of the myth in which Laocoön and his sons' sufferings stemmed from his having had intercourse before the statue of Apollo, so that the sculpture symbolizes the agonies of Pierre, caused by the home-polluting sexual transgressions of his father. In his lecture "Statues in Rome" Melville declared: "In a niche of the Vatican stands the *Laocoön*, the very semblance of a great and powerful man writhing with the inevitable destiny he cannot throw off. Throes and pangs and struggles are given with a meaning that is not withheld. The hideous monsters embrace him in their mighty folds, and torture him with agonizing embraces. The *Laocoön* is grand and impressive, gaining half its significance from its symbolism—the fable that it represents: otherwise, it would be no more than Paul Potter's 'Bear Hunt' at Amsterdam."[48]

Although Melville continued to include classical allusions in his writings after the Civil War, he no longer used classical mythology as he had in *Moby-Dick* and *Pierre* to provide structure and tragic elevation for his narratives. After the very real tragedy of the nation's bloodiest war, American literature passed from the era of romanticism to the age of realism, a genre that emphasized the meaninglessness of human suffering and the pointlessness of life in general. This was reflected in the greatly reduced stature of Melville's postbellum characters. Unlike Ahab, they did not war against God; they merely noted His absence. The antihero had arrived, a massive violation of the first rule of Greek (and Shakespearian) tragedy: the protagonist must have greatness. While Melville's postbellum works, like those of the realists, depicted sorrow, they were not tragedies in the Greek sense.[49]

Edgar Allan Poe frequently used classical mythology as well. In Poe's most famous poem, "The Raven" (1845), the narrator demands of the raven: "Tell me what thy lordly name is on the Night's Plutonian shore!" This was a paraphrase of a line from Horace (*Carmina* 1.4.16) in reference to Hades. The line "Respite—respite and nepenthe from thy memories of Lenore" refers to the draught Helen gave her guests in the *Odyssey* (4. 219–220) to help them lose all memory of their troubles. Poe's very use of the raven as his prophet of doom may have stemmed from references in Pliny the Elder's *Natural History* (10.15) and Ovid's *Metamorphoses* (2.654–776), works with which Poe was intimately familiar, to the raven's association with Apollo and prophecy. Pliny claimed that ravens were "the only birds that comprehend their [own] auspices." Ovid alleged that Apollo, the god of prophecy, had turned the raven black for bringing him the terrible news that his beloved nymph Coronis was unfaithful, the bird's dark color symbolizing its reputation for issuing dark prophecies. Poe may also have known that Cicero, one of his favorite authors, was said to have been forewarned of his own imminent death by the fluttering of ravens. The raven's eternal resting place on the bust of Pallas Athena, the goddess of wisdom, was no accident either, symbolizing the fact that the narrator's obsession with his grief obscures his view of the wisdom the bust represents. Poe's practice of continual repetition of key words mirrored that of Homer, Sappho, and Catullus. Poe's blank-verse tragedy *Politian* included his own translation of a large passage from the *Odyssey*. He took the name of the title character of his short story "Ligeia" (1839), a woman whose voice possessed "more than mortal melody" and whom he praised for her classical knowledge, from one of the sirens. The house of Usher (1839), with its past of familial murder, was based as much on the house of Atreus as Melville's Glendinnings. Finally, Poe penned some of the most famous and enduring lines concerning Greco-Roman civilization in his ode "To Helen" (1831):

> On desperate seas long wont to roam,
> Thy hyacinth hair, thy classic face,
> They Naiad airs have brought me home
> To the glory that was Greece
> And the grandeur that was Rome.

A model of classical restraint and controlled imagination, the poem influenced the neoclassical poetry of the French Parnassians.[50]

The Romantics and Plutarch

While the romantics embraced the more passionate elements of Greco-Roman culture, including the mythology contained in classical poetry and drama, they did not abandon the classical historical writings that had enthralled the founders' generation, especially Plutarch's *Parallel Lives*. The Greek biographer's genial humanity and remarkable talent for relating fascinating anecdotes concerning the moral character of ancient historical figures suited him perfectly for the individualistic and moralistic, but largely nonreligious, American romantics. For instance, Nathaniel Hawthorne read Plutarch with "great satisfaction."[51]

Plutarch was one of Ralph Waldo Emerson's favorite authors. Emerson wrote, "We cannot read Plutarch without a tingling of the blood," and called the biographer "the elixir of Greece and Rome." He thought of Plutarch's heroes when traveling in Sicily. He made certain that Plutarch's *Lives* was on the reading list of young Hillman Simpson, whose education Emerson financed and supervised following the death of Hillman's father. In 1837 Emerson wrote: "Plutarch I esteem a greater benefactor than Aristotle. To him we owe the Brasidases, the Dions, the Phocions & the other men." In an 1841 letter to his brother William, Emerson wrote: "Do you never read Plutarch? I can never have done with him. Only yesterday I read the life of Cleomenes & of the Gracchi & Demosthenes." He often quoted from Plutarch's life of Agesilaus the Spartan king's response to hearing the word "great" applied to the Persian king: "How is he greater than I if he be not more just?" He admired Plutarch's reverence for poetry: "The way in which Plutarch & the ancients usually quote the Poets is quite remarkable, as it indicates a deep & universal reverence for poetry, indicates a faith in

Inspiration. They quote Pindar much as a pious Christian does David or Paul. Where is that reverence now?" He also wrote: "Plutarch fits me better than [Robert] Southey or [Walter] Scott. . . . Plutarch is charming by the facility of his associations, so that it matters little where you open his book, you find yourself instantly at the Olympian tables. His memory is like the Olympic Games wherein all that was noble & excellent in all Greece was assembled." Regarding Plutarch, Emerson added: "I must think we are more deeply indebted to him than to all the ancient writers. . . . A wild courage, Stoicism not of the schools but of the blood, shines in every anecdote and has given that book its immense fame. . . . The opinion of the world is expressed in the innumerable cheap editions, which make it as accessible as a newspaper." In 1840 Emerson wrote, "There is hardly a life in Plutarch that does not infuse a new courage & prowess into the youth & make him gladder & bolder for his own work." The following year he added, "Plutarch's heroes are my friends and relatives."[52]

Henry David Thoreau admired Plutarch as well. He liked the courage portrayed in his *Parallel Lives*. He also agreed with Plutarch that historical events themselves were less important than what they revealed about character: "The value of human traits in Grecian history depends not so much on their importance in history, as [on] the readiness with which they accept a wide interpretation, and illustrate the poetry and ethics of mankind. When they announce no particular truth, they are yet central to all truth. They are like those examples by which we improve, but of which we never formally extract the moral."[53]

Plutarch contributed more than any other author, ancient or modern, to the "great-man theory," the belief that individual heroes were the primary determinant of the course of history, a theory prevalent during the antebellum period. It is no accident that when Emerson wrote history, he focused on important individuals and entitled the book *Representative Men*. Biographies of George Washington in imitation of Plutarch, ranging in authorship from John Marshall to Parson Weems, abounded, as did biographies of other "great men." Even the first great national historians of the United States, such as the classically educated George Bancroft, emphasized the role of key political leaders; the emphasis on socioeconomic factors and other impersonal forces lay in the future of historiography. William Ellery Channing claimed that children should read Plutarch's *Parallel Lives* to learn that the "causes of historical events are to be found in gifted, energetic persons."[54]

The most uncommon characteristic of Emerson's love of Plutarch was that it was based as much on Plutarch's *Moralia*, a collection of moral essays filled with anecdotes and epigrams that was little appreciated before

Emerson, as on Plutarch's highly acclaimed *Parallel Lives*. Emerson noted: "Plutarch's *Morals* is less known and seldom reprinted. Yet such a reader as I am writing to can as ill spare it as the *Lives*." Emerson claimed regarding the *Moralia*, "If the world's library were burning, I should as soon fly to rescue that as Shakespeare and Plato, or next afterwards." Emerson wrote: "I keep the 'Morals' always near me. They are admirable Prayer books." In 1837 he wrote in his journal, "After raffling all in Plutarch's *Morals* . . . or shall I say angling there for such fish as I might find, I sallied out this fine afternoon through the woods to Walden Water." The next day he wrote: "The charm of Plutarch & Plato & Thucydides for me, I believe, is that there I get ethics without cant. I am struck with the splendor of the sentences I meet in books, especially in Plutarch."[55]

Plutarch's contributions to Emerson included the moral essay, the preference for Greece over Rome, "Spartomania," and Emerson's conception of the hero as a moral exemplar. In Emerson's essay on Abraham Lincoln, delivered as a eulogy in Concord in 1865, he borrowed this line from James Russell Lowell's commencement ode at Harvard:

> Here was a type of the true elder race,
> And one of Plutarch's men talked with us face to face.

In 1870, in his introduction to William W. Goodwin's new edition of the *Moralia*, an edition that created widespread interest in the work for the first time, Emerson wrote that Plutarch had "a unique place in literature as an encyclopedia of Greek and Roman antiquity." Emerson claimed that Plutarch's enduring popularity was based on his humanity and on his delight in self-sacrifice, qualities that made his works "a bible for heroes." Emerson wrote:

> Though he never used verse, he had many qualities of the poet in the power of his imagination, the speed of his mental associations, and his sharp, objective eyes. But what specifically marks him, he is a chief example of the illumination of the intellect by the force of morals. . . . I do not know where to find a book—to borrow a phrase of Ben Jonson's—so rammed with life, and this in chapters chiefly ethical, which are so prone to be heavy and sentimental. No poet can illustrate his thought with more novel or striking similes or happier anecdotes. His style is realistic, picturesque, and varied. . . . His surprising merit is the general facility with which he deals with manifold topics. There is no trace of labor or pain. . . . He is ever manly, far from fawning, and would be welcome to the sages and warriors he reports. . . . I find him a better teacher of rhetoric than any modern. . . . He disowns any attempt to rival Thucydides, but I suppose he has a hundred readers where Thucydides finds one, and Thucydides must often thank Plutarch for that one.

Emerson concluded, "Plutarch will be perpetually rediscovered from time to time as long as books last."[56]

While the romantics' admiration for Plutarch and interest in classical philosophy united them with the founders' generation, their deep love for, and extensive use of, the emotional and mystical elements of classical mythology separated them from the founders. Their application of the ancient myths of Greece to the new realities of American life produced a vibrant national literature that served the aesthetic and emotional needs of antebellum Americans. They draped American clothing around the universal themes of classical mythology. In attempting to adopt the spirit rather than copy the artifacts of the ancients, the romantics, like the architects of the Greek Revival, believed that they were paying the greatest possible tribute to a race of nonconformists.

CHAPTER SIX

Christianity

During the Second Great Awakening most orthodox Christians shared the romantics' disapproval of the Enlightenment's emphasis on reason over intuition and matter over spirit. While it is true that the evangelical focus on an emotional attachment to Christ undermined some Christians' devotion to the classics, most antebellum Americans followed in the path of their ancestors, attempting to reconcile Christianity with the Greco-Roman classics.

The Traditional Partnership

Christians had always possessed a love-hate relationship with the classics. Even while inveighing against pagan religion and while suffering severe persecution at the hands of pagans, educated Christians like the apostle Paul referred to classical teachings on natural law and other subjects (Rom. 2:14–15; 1 Cor. 15:33). Indeed, the New Testament itself was written in Koine (Common) Greek, which had become the literary language of the eastern Mediterranean following Alexander the Great's conquest of the Persian Empire. Ambrose, one of the Church Fathers of the fourth century, used Cicero's *On Duties* as the model for an important manual on Christian ethics. Jerome, another of the Fathers, read so many of Cicero's works that he thought he heard God ask him once, "What art thou?" When Jerome replied, "A

Christian," God answered, "No, thou art not a Christian, but a Ciceronian." In remorse, Jerome swore never to read worldly books again. But both the style and the substance of Jerome's writings continued to show the imprint of Cicero. When taunted with this, Jerome replied that his promise had been for the future; it was impossible for him to forget what he had already learned. In the *Confessions* Augustine claimed that it was Cicero's *Hortensius* that had led him to love virtue. Plato also influenced Augustine greatly.[1]

If it were not for the Christian monks who preserved and copied classical texts after the fall of the Roman Empire, the classics would have been lost to the West. Instead, Latin became the universal language of the medieval West, and the classics dominated university curricula from the very beginning. While maintaining orthodox Catholicism as the engine of their theology, Thomas Aquinas and the Scholastics stripped Aristotle for spare parts.[2]

The Protestant Reformation did not alter this pattern of cautious reconciliation with the classics. Protestant ministers were as thoroughly trained in the classics as Catholic priests. Martin Luther called Cicero "a wise and industrious man, [who] suffered much and accomplished much." Luther added, "I hope our Lord God will be merciful to him and to those like him." The Puritans, who were thoroughgoing rationalists within the bounds of their theology, had seen nothing wrong with using those aspects of the classics that coincided with Christian teaching while ignoring or criticizing objectionable passages. The Puritan minister Charles Chauncy argued that "great moral truths may be found in Plato, Aristotle, Plutarch, Seneca, etc." Cotton Mather, a student of the great classics teacher Ezekiel Cheever, was an ardent classicist who loaded his eulogy for Cheever with allusions to the ancients. In fact, the Puritans were part of a seventeenth-century movement, centered at Cambridge University, to restore Christianity to Augustinian Platonism after its flirtation with Scholastic Aristotelianism.[3]

The Great Awakening not only inaugurated the phenomenon of religious revivals in America, but also produced a raft of new denominational colleges, including the College of New Jersey (Princeton, 1746), King's College (Columbia, 1754), the College of Rhode Island (Brown, 1764), Queen's College (Rutgers, 1766), and Dartmouth College (1769). These colleges taught the traditional classical curriculum from a Protestant perspective, thereby serving as a crucial incubator of the American Revolution. The combination of classical republicanism with a revival of the Puritan fear of the spiritual effects of "British corruption" and the Puritan hope of creating a "city upon a hill" proved a lethal combination for British rule in America. Many of the founders, including James Madison and Alexander Hamilton, were trained in the new colleges. Rightly called the "Father of the American Revolution" for his able leadership of the Boston Sons of Liberty, Samuel Adams was energized by the Great Awakening while a student at Harvard in the 1730s. His dream was to construct a "Christian Sparta," a nation that would combine Christian piety with republican frugality, courage, and patriotism. He claimed that some classical heroes had been as virtuous as any Christian.[4]

In the early nineteenth century, William Ellery Channing and the Unitarians of New England surpassed even their more orthodox Puritan ancestors in seeking to reconcile Christianity with Platonism. Harvard became a bastion of Unitarian Platonism. In this effort, the New England Unitarians differed from Thomas Jefferson, a materialist who despised Plato and derived his own Unitarianism from Epicurus.[5]

Criticism of Classical Morality

The antebellum evangelical emphasis on faith, defined as an emotional attachment to Christ, as the key to salvation was incompatible with the cold sense of duty commonly identified with classical virtue. For this reason, Charles Sumner considered classical morality incompatible with the Sermon on the Mount. When advising Henry Ware, a graduating senior at Harvard, about his Latin oration, Sumner wrote: "No Roman ever wrote from the elevation of the Second Commandment, 'Love thy neighbor as thyself.' [Even] the gentle nature of Virgil, formed for the reception of such a truth, was unconscious of it." In an 1846 oration to the Phi Beta Kappa Society of Harvard, Sumner explained:

> The classics possess a peculiar claim, as models, I might say masters, of composition and form. In the contemplation of these august teachers we are filled with conflicted emotions. They are the early voices of the world, better remembered and more cherished than any intermediate voice—as the language of childhood still haunts us, when the utterances of later years are effaced from the mind. But they show the rudeness of the world's childhood, before passion yielded to the sway of reason and the affections. They want purity, righteousness, and that highest charm which is found in love to God and man. Not in the frigid philosophy of the Porch and the Academy are we to seek these; not in the marvelous teachings of Socrates as they come mended by the mellifluous words of Plato; not in the resounding line of Homer, on whose inspiring tale of blood Alexander pillowed his head; not in the animated strain of Pindar, where virtue is pictured in the successful strife of an athlete at the Olympian games; not in the torrent of Demosthenes, dark with self-love and the spirit of vengeance; not in the fitful philosophy and boastful eloquence of Tully; not in the genial libertinism of Horace, or

the stately atheism of Lucretius. To these we give admiration; but they cannot be our highest teachers. In none of these is the way of life. For eighteen hundred years the spirit of these classics has been in constant contention with the Sermon on the Mount, and with those two sublime commandments on which "hang all the law and the prophets." The strife is still pending, and who shall say when it will end! Heathenism, which possessed itself of such Siren forms, is not yet exorcised. Even now it exerts a powerful sway, imbuing youth, coloring the thought of manhood, and haunting the meditation of age. Widening still in sphere, it embraces nations as well as individuals, until it seems to sit supreme.

Our own productions, though yielding to the ancient in arrangement, method, beauty of form, and freshness of illustration, are superior in truth, delicacy, and elevation of sentiment—above all, in the recognition of that peculiar revelation, the Brotherhood of Man. Vain are eloquence and poetry compared with the heaven-descended truth. Put in one scale that simple utterance, and in the other all the lore of antiquity, with its accumulating glosses and commentaries, and the latter will be light in the balance. Greek poetry has been likened to the song of the nightingale, as she sits in the rich, symmetrical crown of the palm-tree, trilling her thick-warbled notes; but these notes will not compare in sweetness with those teachings of charity which belong to our Christian inheritance.

These things cannot be forgotten by the scholar. From the Past he may draw all it can contribute to the great end of life, human progress, and happiness— progress, without which happiness is vain. But he must close his soul to the hardening influence of that spirit, which is more to be dreaded, as it is enshrined in compositions of such commanding authority.

Sumner then quoted William Cowper, the famous translator of Homer:

> Sunk in Homer's mine,
> I lose my precious years, now soon to fail,
> Handling his gold; which howsoe'er it shine,
> Proves dross, when balanced in the Christian scale.[6]

Like the early pagan converts to Christianity and like the American founders, Sumner preferred the warmth and positive benevolence of Christian ethics to the cold classical admonition to avoid injuring oneself and others. In his famous dialogue between his head and his heart, Thomas Jefferson's Christian heart had reminded his Epicurean head of the numerous times when the head had chosen safety over aiding those in need, concluding, "In short, my friend, as far as my recollection serves me, I do not know that I ever did a good thing on your suggestion, or a dirty one without it." Similarly, after expressing admiration for *The Golden Verses of Pythagoras*, with its maxims on the sanctity of oaths, the respect due to parents, affection for friends, and connection to humankind, John Adams had added, nevertheless: "How dark, mean, and meagre are these Golden Verses, however celebrated and really curious, in comparison with the Sermon on the Mount and the Psalms of David or the Decalogue!"[7]

Sumner also noted that the classical emphasis on fame and glory as the chief rewards of virtue conflicted with Christian humility and the Christian recognition of the insignificance of this life compared with the eternal afterlife. In a speech at Amherst College in 1847, Sumner noted that while most Greek city-states lavished praise on Olympic athletes and warriors, Athens honored orators, philosophers, historians, and artists, thereby winning greater glory. Sumner declared, "And yet this brilliant renown, admired through a long succession of ages, must fade and grow dull by the side of triumphs grander and holier than any achieved by force or intellect alone." The achievements of Christianity were greater than those of the classical heroes.[8]

According to Sumner, Rome had then relapsed into the glorification of warfare. Sumner declared: "Cato the Censor, that model Roman, hearing that the Athenian ambassadors had captivated the youth of Rome by the charms of philosophy, abruptly dismissed them, and, with the spirit of a Mohawk Indian, declared his reprehension of such corrupting influence on a people whose only profession was war. Even Cicero, in his work of beautiful but checkered morals, where heathenism blends with truth almost Christian, commends to youth the Glory of war." Cicero's obsession with fame and glory not only produced "the iterations of self-praise with which his productions abound" but even led him to recommend that his friend Lucceius exaggerate Cicero's own accomplishments when writing about Catiline's conspiracy.[9]

Sumner feared that the genius of classical authors like Cicero might delude American youth into placing an unwarrantable emphasis on the acquisition of fame. He declared:

> A character like Cicero, compact of so many virtues, resplendent with a genius so lofty, standing on one of the most commanding pinnacles of classical antiquity, still admired by the wide world, hardly less than by the living multitudes that once chafed about the rostrum like a raging sea and were stilled by the music of his voice—such a character cannot fail to exert a magical charm over the young, especially where his lessons harmonize with the weakness rather than with the sternness of our nature—with the instinctive promptings of selfishness rather than with that disinterestedness which places duty, without hope of reward, without fear or favor, above all human consideration. It is most true that he has kindled in many bosoms something of his own inextinguishable ardors; and the American youth—child of a continent beyond

the Atlantis of his imagination, and lifted by institutions he had never seen, even in his vision of a Republic—feels a glow of selfish ambition, as, in tasks of the school, he daily cons the writings of the great master.

But Sumner was confident that the love of glory diminished "with advancing years, with the growth of the moral and intellectual nature, with the development of Christian character, and in proportion as the great realities of existence here and hereafter engross the soul."[10]

Sumner's critique of Greco-Roman ethics was especially powerful coming from a man who had cherished the classics throughout his life. As a young boy, when his father had initially decided not to give him a classical education, Sumner had secretly bought a Latin grammar text, taught himself, and then recited passages for his astonished father. Changing his mind, his father had then enrolled him in Boston Latin School. There he had won third prize for a translation from Ovid and second prize for a Latin hexameter poem. At a junior exhibition at Harvard, he had played the part of an orator in a Greek dialogue. He had translated one of his lines: "Demosthenes and Pericles, examples of former days, will be like stars to point out the pathway to glory; and their glory will always be the object of my desire." One of his classmates recalled: "Many a time have I known him to rush down to my room and begin a speech in which he would introduce quotations from Virgil, Horace, and Juvenal. He had many parts of these authors at his tongue's end, and his quotations from them were always accurate; and if they were quoted by others, he would detect the least inaccuracy."[11]

In 1839 Sumner had raved about his tour of Italy. He had written regarding Pompeii:

> With all my ardent expectations, I never adequately conceived the thrilling influences shed by these ancient classical sites and things. You walk the well-adjusted pavement of Pompeii and distinctly discern the traces of wheels worn into its hard stone; and in the houses you see mosaics and frescoes and choice marbles that make you start. But reach the Forum and there you are in the midst of columns and arches and temples that would seem wonderful to us if found in a grand city, but are doubly so when disentombed in a humble town. What must Rome have been, whose porches and columns and arches excited the wonder of the ancient world, if this little place, of whose disastrous fate only we have heard an account, contained such treasures! I do not believe there is a single town of the size of ancient Pompeii in modern Europe where you will find so much public or private magnificence, where you will enter so many private dwellings enriched by the chisel and pencil, or stand in a public square like her Forum.

He had written on Rome and Tivoli: "What joys open to one in Rome! . . . Art in these noble galleries, and antiquities in these noble ruins, afford constant interest. . . . What a day I have passed at Tivoli! I was with French companions, one of whom lent me his pocket 'Horace.' The others strolled away to see some ruin or catch a near spray of the falling water. I lay on the grass with the *praeceps Anio* before me, in the very Tiburtine grove that Horace had celebrated, and there I read the first books of his odes, and on the spot saw and felt the felicity of his language." He had urged Henry Wadsworth Longfellow to persuade their former classics professor, Cornelius Felton, to come to Alba Longa, where Sumner was staying: "In our garden we will show him a tomb with the fasces still boldly visible, where reposes the dust of a consul of the Republic! How those ancient Romans did build! Not only for themselves nor for their children simply, but for generations. . . . [After I return] my soul will long for . . . some one who has seen the things that I have seen and who will join with me in reproducing them to our eager imaginations." He had visited Tusculum, Cicero's residence, and ridden down the road in which the gang leaders Milo and Clodius had encountered one another, an encounter fatal to the latter. Sumner had written of himself and his traveling companions: "Many an hour have we sat upon a broken column or a rich capital in the Via Sacra, or the Colosseum, and called to mind what has passed before them, weaving out the web of the story they might tell." Even as late as 1844, long since back in the United States, he recalled: "How pleasant is the memory of my Roman life!—the happiest days I have ever passed. . . . [I] mused in the Forum and, in the shadows of summer evenings, sat on the stones of the Colosseum. . . . Such another summer would make me forget much unhappiness." Sumner's critique of classical ethics was not the work of a philistine, suspicious of learning and oblivious to the seductive power of the classics, but the lament of one who knew only too well what it meant to love the classics deeply.[12]

Sumner was not the only American to become disenchanted with pagan morality under the influence of the Second Great Awakening. As a young man, Hugh Swinton Legaré was so enamored of the classics that his vision became blurred from reading them fifteen hours per day. To keep from becoming as blind as Homer, one of his favorite authors, Legaré had his sister read to him in Latin, which she did not always comprehend, until his vision recovered. Legaré wrote: "We have always been accustomed to think that if those [ancient] refined ages have left us anything in any department of knowledge of which the excellence is beyond all dispute it is (after Greek geometry perhaps) their moral philosophy. We presume it will not be considered as derogating from their merit in this particular that they did not by mere dint of reasoning, *a priori*, make themselves partakers of the Christian Revelation." Although Plato's *Republic* was dangerously impractical, his ethical writings were lofty and noble. Legaré wrote regarding Platonic philosophy, "It is delivered in a lofty and glowing strain and addresses itself to the imagination, which it inflames and elevates with visions of perfection and hopes of bliss." While Legaré admitted that the ancients had occasionally engaged in some "strange customs and heathenish practices," he was not particularly troubled by these lapses.[13]

But by the 1830s Legaré was emphasizing the superiority of Christian morality. He had come to believe that the fifth-century Christian emperor Justinian had humanized the Roman civil law he so admired—that Justinian should be regarded not as the last of the Romans but as the first of the medieval Christian adapters of Roman law who gave it its humanity. He now believed that the Law of the Twelve Tables (449 B.C.), the foundational document of Roman law, was "savage and strange." Legaré wrote: "[In the Twelve Tables] we see the rude forms of process, and the cruel modes of execution. We see the despotic authority of the father over the son, who stands to him in the relation of a chattel. . . . We find libels punished with death." By then Legaré was writing that the ancient world had been marked by a "deep and disgusting moral depravity," adding:

> There was scarcely a great man of Greece whose biography is free from some of those dark stains which no virtues would now be thought sufficient to compensate and no glory to conceal. Without citing the examples of Themistocles and Lysander, notoriously, and even for their own times, remarkably unprincipled, however gifted and celebrated men, Plutarch has scarcely a hero who would pass muster as a gentleman now. . . . The Athenians were a people steeped in profligacy to the very lips, and wholly without shame or sensibility on subjects of honor. This shocking contrast between the exquisite in art, the polite in diction, the sublime in thought, and occasionally the great and heroical in sentiment and a tone of manners and the topics of discourse often the most low, vicious, brutal, and cynical is one of the most striking peculiarities of the ancient Greek world. . . . Cruelty, rapacity, and violence were the characteristics of all forms of government in antiquity.

Furthermore, in stark contrast to the aristocratic qualities of Greco-Roman paganism, Christianity "enjoined and consecrated labor; it made honest poverty honorable; it exalted the humble and lowly."[14]

John Quincy Adams agreed that Christianity was superior to classical philosophy. He wrote: "Almost all the Greek philosophers reasoned and meditated upon the nature of the gods, but scarcely any of them ever reflected enough even to imagine that there was but one God, and not one of them ever conceived of him as the Creator of the world. Cicero has collected together all their opinions on the nature of the gods and pronounces that they are more like the dreams of madmen than the sober judgments of wise men." Ovid came closest to the truth when he wrote that one of the gods, whom he did not identify, had separated the elements of Chaos to form a world, but "thus far and no farther could human reason extend" in pagan Rome. By contrast, Adams wrote, "The first words of the Bible are, 'In the beginning God created the heaven and the earth.' This blessed and sublime God, the creator of the universe—the source of all human virtue and all human happiness, for which the sages and philosophers of Greece groped in darkness and never found, is revealed in the first verse of the Book of Genesis." The reason that Cicero had been unable to decide whether piety was essential to virtue was that Greco-Roman piety was based on "low, unsettled, and inconsistent notions." Adams concluded: "To such a God [as is found in the Bible] the heart of man must yield with cheerfulness the tribute of homage, which it never could pay to the bleating gods of Egypt, to the dissolute debauchees of the Grecian mythology, nor even to the more elevated, but no less fantastical, imaginations of the Grecian philosophers and sages."[15]

Adams was especially harsh in his estimation of the Epicureans, materialists who believed that death was nothingness and that the gods did not intervene in human affairs. He claimed: "There is an ardor partaking of passion in all Cicero's attacks upon Epicurus, but I believe it was well founded. The principles of that philosophy may properly be called the philosophy of corruption, and it has always prevailed in company with the greatest licentiousness of morals and the most infamous vices." Adams added, "Horace, who avows himself a very swine from the sty of Epicurus, whenever he inculcates virtue, resorts to the Stoic fountain." Adams noted regarding Horace, "A remarkable difference between his Odes to the Gods and the Psalms of David is that his devotion never dwells upon any moral attribute of his deities." After praising some aspects of Horace's work, Adams added, "Many of his amatory odes, however, are grossly indelicate."[16]

Adams argued that the Greeks, while certainly interesting and important, were less intriguing than the Hebrews and that the Greeks' religious and philosophical works were less compelling than the Bible. He wrote: "I believe that the respect and veneration of any person for the Bible will increase in proportion to the intimacy of his acquaintance with its contents." Regarding Plutarch's "On the Delay of Divine Justice," the historian-philosopher's attempt to explain why injustice often seemed to prevail in life, Adams wrote: "Plutarch reasons well, but leaves much of the mysterious veil over his subject which nothing but Christian doctrine can remove. If the existence of man was limited to this life, it would be impossible for me to believe the universe under any moral government. . . . It is not the affliction of the righteous, but the prosperity of the wicked, which would contribute most to stagger my faith in Divine Justice." Like Thomas Jefferson, John Quincy Adams reasoned that an afterlife of rewards and punishments was crucial to divine justice, since outcomes in this life were often clearly unfair. He considered the Roman emperor Hadrian's attempt to laugh off his impending death—a feeble effort made out of deference to the "heathen philosophers'" doctrine "that death was to be met with indifference"—pathetic, especially in light of the common view that Hades was a world of "darkness and gloom."[17]

Charles Francis Adams possessed the same acute sense of the fatal deficiencies of classical morality when measured against Christianity as his father. In 1831 he wrote in his diary: "The period of Cicero's Proconsulship is, on the whole, one of the most creditable portions of his career. He abstained from the Commission of any of the enormities so usual with Roman Provincial Governors. Yet so little had he in his mind the principles of true morality, which directs human conduct in the path of virtue, by motives drawn from its innate value, that in all the letters to Atticus, it is plain [that] he regards fame, the reputation of the world, as the great object to be gained. Perhaps even this is a great deal, apart from the knowledge given us through the religion of Christ." A Christian like his father, Charles Francis did not realize that his criticism of the classical quest for fame as an impure motive for virtue could also serve as a criticism of his own grandfather, John Adams. Far less orthodox in religion, John, like his hero Cicero, had always viewed fame as the greatest reward of virtue. In fact, John had once inscribed this line from Tacitus in his own diary: "Contemptu Famae, contemni Virtutem," which he translated as "A Contempt of Fame generally begets or accompanies a Contempt of Virtue."[18]

Charles Francis was even more vocal in noting the ethical limitations of another revered Roman philosopher-statesman, the Stoic Seneca. Charles Francis wrote regarding Seneca: "The forgiveness of injuries is perhaps the greatest Pagan approximation to the doctrines of the Christian Religion. But he mixes it with advice which does not suit a Code of Ethics or a Moral Philosopher, however well it may turn out practically in life. Submission to the caprices of the powerful is a maxim of policy for a tyrant's Court, not a principle of morals." Regarding Seneca's flattery of Nero, Charles Francis contended: "It is not possible to suppose him [Nero] such an adept at dissimulation as to conceal his propensities. And Seneca must have known them if any body. He should therefore have spared his encomiums." (Ralph Waldo Emerson agreed, writing regarding Seneca, "His thoughts are excellent, if only he had the right to say them.") Furthermore, Charles Francis was hardly impressed with Seneca's fatalistic justifications for the suffering of good men, concluding, "It will not do. Nothing but the belief of a future state will satisfy the mind in considering that question." Regarding Seneca's defense of suicide, Charles Francis wrote: "With the doctrine of the Pagans, there is no reason to object to it. But it would seem as if any person having sense enough to believe in a Deity would see that the object of his creation is not to put his life in his own power." On the Stoic equation of happiness with the absence of pain, Charles Francis wrote, "The Stoics pursue the negative principle, but many a man feels at his heart, without any need of reasoning long over the matter, that the absence of suffering from any cause does not satisfy his aspirations."[19]

Even Louisa McCord, the author of *Caius Gracchus*, emphasized the superiority of Christian over classical ethics. When comparing the prospect of South Carolina's separate secession from the Union in 1851 with suicide, she could not help but add, "The ancient Roman was half a barbarian when he sought death as a cure for life's evils; a higher civilization—a nobler philosophy—teaches us to bear and conquer them." Suicide for the sake of honor was dishonorable. It is no accident that McCord's classical play contained a Christian conclusion: Gracchus, a Christlike figure, is killed in the Grove of the Furies, where he offers himself as a sacrifice to the vengeful goddesses to spare Rome from its rightful punishment. He is killed by Septimuleius, a Judas-like figure whose life Gaius had once saved but who sells him out for money. To sacrifice oneself for others, in imitation of Christ, was noble, but to kill oneself in order to avoid pain or dishonor was ignoble.[20]

The Reverend James Warley Miles, though a theological liberal, was even more critical of the ancients. He declared, "The notions with which the ancients invested their conceptions of the divine were gross, terrific, or Platonically undefined and shadowy." He added that "the lofty conceptions of morality and duty, before which every page of ancient literature must blush," came from Christianity, as did "the religious life of purity, holiness, charity, faith, and hope," which "the best of the ancients had only faintly and confusedly dreamed." Christianity arrived "at a period when the world had sunk to such a point of demoralization and scepticism as almost to justify the speculation of Plato that there are cycles in which the world reaches such a condition of intense moral disharmony as imperatively to call for the rectifying interposition of Deity, lest the whole frame of society should go to utter wreck in the wild deluge of corruption."[21]

Some evangelical preachers complained that the traditional system of instruction for ministers emphasized a cold knowledge of dead languages over an emotional attachment to Jesus Christ. When a fellow citizen of Illinois asked the minister Peter Cartwright why the prairies possessed so few doctors of divinity, he replied, "Because our divinity is not sick, ma'am, and doesn't need doctoring." He once ridiculed a college-bred

Presbyterian who was quoting Greek by tossing out a sentence in southern Illinois German.[22]

Though some orthodox Christians criticized the coldness of classical philosophy, they were even more alarmed by the horrendous vices showcased in Greco-Roman mythology. As early as 1769 John Wilson had resigned as Latin master at the Friends' Latin School in Philadelphia, partly on moral grounds. His resignation letter contained this tirade:

> Is it not surprizing? Is it not monstrous? That Christian Children intended to believe and relish the Truths of the Gospel should have their early and most retentive years imbued with the shocking Legends and abominable Romances of the worst of Heathens and should be obliged to be the Pimps of the detestable Lusts of Jupiter & Mars, attend the thefts & Villainy of Mercury, or follow Aeneas on his Murdering Progress, while the Actions and Sufferings of the great and worthy Propagators of our Holy Religion that Succeeded the Apostles are totally hid from their Eyes? Is Bacchus preferable to Ignatius, Apollo to Origen or will Helena and Clytemnestra yield an affecting Instruction or warm our Hearts with the Love of Virtue like the Virgin Martyrs & Heroines of Christian Story?

John Wesley, the founder of Methodism, had written to his brother Samuel, who was headmaster of Tiverton School, regarding immoral literature: "But of this sort are most of the classics usually read in the great schools: many of them tending to inflame the lusts of the flesh, and more to feed the lust of the eye and the pride of life. I beseech you, therefore, by the mercies of God ... that you banish all such poison from your school." Similarly, the Christian romantic poet William Blake had written: "The stolen and perverted writings of Homer and Ovid, which all men ought to contemn, are set up by artifice against the sublime of the Bible.... We do not want either Greek or Roman models if we are but just and true to our imaginations, those Worlds of Eternity in which we shall live for ever in Jesus Our Lord.... The Greek and Roman Classics is the Anti-Christ."[23]

Although he was as apt to quote classical authors as anyone, Benjamin Rush had charged classical mythology with the promotion of vice, paganism, and militarism. In 1789 he wrote: "The study of some of the Latin and Greek classics is unfavorable to morals and religion. Indelicate amours and shocking vices of gods and men fill many parts of them. Hence, [they impart] an early and dangerous acquaintance with vice; and, hence, from an association of ideas, a diminished respect for the unity and perfections of the true God." He wrote to John Adams: "I shall class them hereafter with Negro slavery and spiritous liquors and consider them as, though in a less degree, unfriendly to the progress of morals, knowledge, and religion in the United States." He explained: "If the years spent teaching boys the Greek and Roman mythology were spent in teaching them Jewish antiquities and the connection between the types and prophecies of the Old Testament with the events of the New, don't you think we should have less infidelity and, of course, less immorality and bad government in the world? . . . Men love royalty, titles, and the Latin and Greek languages. They make wars, enslave their fellow creatures, distill and drink rum, all because they are not formed by Reason."[24]

These sharp attacks on pagan mythology continued in the antebellum period. Thomas Grimké, the most severe of all the critics of the Greek and Latin requirement in the schools, made such criticism the centerpiece of his *Oration on the Comparative Elements and Dutys of Grecian and American Eloquence* (1834), a comprehensive assault on classical civilization and its influence in America. Claiming that "the virtues of Jesus Christ [are] . . . the very reverse of what are called the heroic virtues of classical antiquity," Grimké denounced the militarism, paganism, and immorality inherent in the classics. Grimké argued that Americans should study their own past instead. He promoted "the cause of Christian American eloquence." While claiming that Athenian politics had been "stamped by fraud and violence, by rapin, ambition, and injustice" and that Athenian democracy was "unprincipled, degrading, and violent; equally marked by insolence, tyranny, and ingratitude," Grimké saved most of his venom for Greek religion. Pagan mythology was "a mass of the absurd and the immoral, of folly and indecency"—"a scheme as complete as ever was devis'd to brutalize the heart, darken the conscience, and degrade the mind." Greek poetry was "awkward," "preposterous," and filled with such characters as "the insolent and brutal Achilles" and "the mean and treacherous Aeneas." Grimké added, "I am strangely mistaken if there be not more power, fidelity, and beauty in Walter Scott than in a dozen Homers and Virgils." He bewailed "the degrading, polluting, deforming influence of the classics over modern poetry." He confessed concerning the classics, "It has been my misfortune to have spent so much time upon them that my stock deriv'd from other sources is comparatively small."[25]

Grimké conceded that he had once been seduced by what he had then perceived as the nobility and beauty of the classics, until, coming to maturity as a Christian and as an American, he had begun to recognize how perniciously un-Christian and un-American they really were. Grimké demanded that the schools be cleansed of this "foreign and pagan influence." He repudiated "the narrow-minded, narrow-hearted, and therefore selfish, eloquence of Greece and Rome." He was outraged that "a clergyman, the head of a college," had declared Cicero's *On Duties* essential to a moral education. In reality, the New Testament, which possessed "a perfect code of morality," far surpassed the works of Cicero, Epictetus, and Marcus Aurelius, works that had no more value in moral education than Ptolemy in astronomy. God had ordained that a purely secular literature like the classics "must be inferior to a literature descended from Heaven." Paradoxically, Grimké concluded that if the United States held fast to biblical principles, it would be "the Greece of the Modern World, unrivalled by the Literature of three thousand years."[26]

Grimké found the morality of Homer and Virgil particularly disturbing. He asked, "As for their morals, who would be willing to have a son or brother like . . . the mean and treacherous Aeneas, the hero of the *Aeneid,* if indeed it has a hero?" Grimké noted that Aeneas acted with ingratitude and perfidy in abandoning Dido and with violence in killing Turnus. Grimké added: "The beauties of Shakespeare are worth all the beauties of Homer and Virgil. . . . I do not doubt that *Paradise Lost* is worth the *Iliad, Odyssey,* and the *Aeneid* all together; there is more sublime, rich, and beautiful poetry in Childe Harold than half a dozen Georgics." Grimké believed that students should read the Gospels, the early Church Fathers, and the Protestant reformers in place of the classics for moral instruction.[27]

Grimké was not alone in his condemnation of pagan mythology. While a student at Harvard, George Bancroft referred to Greek mythology as "a pool of pollution." Agamemnon had committed a beastly crime by sacrificing his virgin daughter Iphigenia to propitiate the goddess Artemis, whose altar then "smoked with human gore." (Bancroft failed to note that the Greeks of the classical period who repeated this myth were as horrified by the idea of human sacrifice, which they portrayed as an ancient form of barbarism, as Bancroft himself. It was for this heinous crime that Agamemnon himself was butchered by his wife and her lover.) Bancroft believed that mythology corrupted the heart, "vitiated the imagination," and sanctified vile deeds. Thomas Cooper, who had served as president of South Carolina College, objected to the "numerous absurdities, the silly fictions, the coarse descriptions, and plentiful obscenities" of classical literature. He observed nothing "like good taste in the naked and over strained sculptures" of antiquity and regarded the "inexorable banditti who inhabited the soil of Greece and Rome" as mere "ruffians." Instead, Cooper urged the study of science as the vehicle of progress. While president in 1825, John Quincy Adams rejected a depiction of Hercules for the pediment of the U.S. Capitol as "too much of the heathen mythology for my taste," substituting instead "a figure of Hope with an anchor—a Scriptural image, indicating that this Hope relies upon a Supreme Disposer of events, which hope we have as an anchor to the soul, sure and steadfast."[28]

George Frederick Holmes contended that the modern world was superior to the ancient, partly because Christianity promoted humility and caution, which fostered science. As a result, modern historical writing was more philosophical, modern poetry more emotional, modern understanding of human nature more complete, and modern people more pragmatic and less speculative. Concerning the Greeks he wrote: "The degrading practice of pederasty was universal and sanctioned by law. The whole literature of Greece, and particularly the vaunted dialogues of Plato, are filled with allusions to it, or illustrations drawn from it. And the familiarity with which it is habitually mentioned proves the shamelessness with which it was regularly regarded." Greek religion was sensual in nature, characterized by sexual immorality, lying, corruption, vanity, and greed. The Romans were no better, subordinating religion to the state, thereby giving it a sterility that led to its replacement by Christianity. Roman religion was "an anomalous monster of state machinery . . . wholly devoid of any irradiation, any enthusiasm from above."[29]

Even as unorthodox a Christian and as great a lover of classical mythology as Ralph Waldo Emerson noted the thuggish nature of some of the Greek gods. Emerson wrote regarding "unprincipled bandits": "In Greece, such a person was a hero in the second generation, a giant in the third & a god in the fourth." He also wrote regarding Athens, "The progress of debased manners is sufficiently marked by the successive character of the comedy from its primal innocence at its institution to the grossness which disgraces the dramas of Aristophanes." Though Emerson favored making the classics available to women, he drew the line at those works imbued with "defective morality." Emerson placed the poems of Ovid in the latter category, but not those of Homer and Virgil.[30]

Because of concerns about the deleterious influence of the classics, students at Oberlin College, an evangelical Protestant institution, petitioned for the elimination of Latin in 1836. Some students even burned classical texts. One speaker alleged that "the heathen classics" were unnecessary because "the poetry of God's inspired prophets is better for the heart, and at least as good for the head as that of the Pagans." This was all the more remarkable considering that just two years earlier an observer at the college had recorded nonchalantly: "The exercises of that first commencement afforded Greek and Latin orations [and] a colloquy in which the vexed question of the study of the 'dead languages' was settled upon an orthodox basis." By "orthodox" the observer meant the obvious conclusion that the classical languages should continue to be studied.[31]

Many evangelicals opposed the nude statues of classical sculptors and their modern imitators as ardently as the lascivious poetry of antiquity. According to John Quincy Adams, the sculptor Luigi Persico "at first contemplated giving more nudity [in the pediment of the U.S. Capitol], but he was warned that the public sentiment in this country would not admit of it." When Horatio Greenough's colossal statue of George Washington in the pose of Phidias' *Zeus* was delivered to the Rotunda of the U.S. Capitol in 1847, some were offended by its partial nudity. Philip Hose sniffed, "Washington was too careful of his health to expose himself thus in a climate so uncertain as ours." Regarding Jacques-Louis David's painting of Themistocles, Frederick Porcher wrote, "To the civilization formed under the influence of Christianity, nakedness is revolting and humiliating." Similarly, Porcher remarked concerning Hiram Powers's *Greek Slave*, "A naked woman in chains is not a very pleasing subject of contemplation." Porcher accused the defenders of classical nudity of hypocrisy: "We question whether the most enthusiastic classicist in America would be pleased that his wife, his sister, or his daughter should appear in marble, as either the Psyche or Persephone of Powers." In 1850 the board of trustees at Bowdoin College approved the sale of the college's copy of Titian's *Danae and the Golden Shower* and another artist's *Nymphs Bathing* in order to protect students from "contamination from spectacles thought among us to be in bad taste." Indeed, most college art galleries adorned their classical sculptures with fig leaves. Some suggested that if naked forms were exhibited, the genders should view them separately.[32]

The Defense of Classical Morality

Other antebellum Americans defended the nudity in Greek, Roman, and neoclassical art. In 1821 the *Charleston Courier* raved concerning John Vanderlyn's *Ariadne Asleep on the Island of Naxos*, which depicted Theseus' lover nude and peacefully asleep, oblivious to his betrayal: "No man of taste and sensibility, no student of love and beauty, no connoisseur of graceful form should fail to gladden his eyes, to charm his fancy, and refresh his imagination with [the] exquisite performance of Mr. Van Derlyn where the sleeping and unconscious Ariadne is sweetly reclining." Many families seem to have shared the *Courier*'s comfort level with nudity in classical art, if their own household paintings are any indication. For instance, an 1848 painting of the Richard K. Haight family of New York depicts a rather staid, though colorfully dressed, Victorian family in the foreground—while featuring prominently in the center background the family's nude sculpture group of the Three Graces embracing one another. A greater contrast between art and its owners is scarcely possible, yet the family seems serenely oblivious to it.[33]

The *New York Mirror*'s art critic even turned the moral argument about, claiming to be offended by the fig leaf on H. K. Brown's statue of Adam (1846). The critic wrote: "We were very sorry to see that Mr. Brown had insulted the moral taste of the New York public, to say nothing of the outrage on their aesthetic perceptions, by putting a fig leaf upon the figure. It could only have been the suggestion of a prurient mind, and we trust that he will have the good sense to remove it. The naked figure is a legitimate object of representation in art, and we believe that the public of New York are too refined to endure patiently so squeamish an imputation on their taste and morals as is evidenced by this fig leaf." The critic evidently recognized what the sculptor of the *Venus de Medici* understood: that to single out genitalia for coverage was to draw the viewer's attention to that part of the body.[34]

American artists defended their own works, of course. In an essay entitled "Do Not Be Afraid of Grace and Beauty!" (1846) Horatio Greenough wrote, "To me there is a devotional feeling attached to such appreciation of our own bodies." He loved to behold "the marvelous capacities of this noble frame." While "the senses have their full share in this pleasure," it was as innocent as one's gratitude for "sun in winter." His disgust at "the gymnastics of the brothel" would not cause him to deny "the charm I find in the poetry of motion." It was "the full power of womanhood revealing itself to man—strongly, for it is the origin of all strength—gracefully, for it is natural—innocently, because it is what God has made it." It was "humanity not ashamed of itself." The Greeks "took the world as they found it" and "did not flinch from fact." Hiram Powers wrote, "The body of man is always innocent, for it only operates [at] the command of his will."[35]

Ralph Waldo Emerson applauded the partial nudity of his friend Greenough's statue of Washington. Having been treated by the sculptor to a dramatic showing of the statue by torchlight, along with John C. Calhoun, Emerson enthused, "I was afraid it would be feeble but it is not." Noting the statue's similarity to Phidias' *Zeus*, Emerson added, "The statue is simple & grand, nobly draped below & nobler nude above." Emerson considered the neoclassical statue's initial place in the Rotunda of the neoclassical Capitol especially apt, the grandeur of each enhancing that of the other. Emerson once formed a distinction between nonclassical and classical nudity: "Now the adult figure is ugly & we are thankful it is clothed to save our eyes from offence. But Phidias's men are as lovely & majestic in their nakedness as is the child."[36]

Nathaniel Hawthorne had similarly mixed feelings about nudity in art, believing that the propriety of a nude sculpture depended on the historical epoch of the artist and the subject and the attitude conveyed by the statue.

He recorded in a notebook in 1858, "Man is no longer a naked animal; his clothes are as natural to him as his skin, and sculptors have no more right to undress him than to flay him." For this reason he was impatient with his friend Hiram Powers's fondness for nudity. After hearing the sculptor complain about having to clothe George Washington in a statue commissioned by the Louisiana legislature, Hawthorne wrote: "What the devil would the man do with Washington, the most decorous and respectable personage that ever went ceremoniously through the realities of life!? Did anybody ever see Washington naked!? It is inconceivable. He had no nakedness, but, I imagine, was born with his clothes on, and his hair powdered, and made a stately bow on his first appearance in the world. His costume, at all events, was a part of his character, and must be dealt with by whatever sculptor undertakes to represent him." Yet Hawthorne admired the semi-nude statue of Pompey he saw in Rome, considering it austere and majestic and claiming that it was worth the whole sculpture gallery of the Vatican because of its moral dignity. He was even more captivated by the completely nude *Venus de Medici*, which portrays the goddess discovered while bathing and covering herself in response. The difference between this exquisite work and Titian's *Venus de Urbino* (1538) was the modest attitude of the former, which rendered her lovely, in sharp contrast to the "lustful" pose of the latter on a couch. Hawthorne wrote regarding the *Venus de Medici*: "Her modest attitude—which, before I saw her, I had not liked, deeming that it might be an artificial shame—is partly what unmakes her as the heathen goddess and softens her into woman. . . . I am glad to have seen this Venus, and to have found her so tender and so chaste."[37]

In *The Marble Faun* Hawthorne, speaking through Miriam, seems to assault all modern nudes, even those based on classical themes. He declares: "Every young sculptor seems to think that he must give the world some specimen of indecorous womanhood and call it Eve, Venus, a Nymph, or any name that may apologize for a lack of decent clothing. . . . An artist, therefore, as you must candidly confess, cannot sculpture nudity with a pure heart, if only because he is compelled to steal guilty glimpses at hired models. The marble inevitably loses its chastity under such circumstances." This was especially true if the modern sculptor "robbed the marble of its chastity by giving it an artificial warmth of hue," so that his goddesses "stood forth to the eyes of the profane in the guise of naked women." Miriam adds speciously: "An old Greek sculptor, no doubt, found his models in the open sunshine, and among pure and princely maidens, and thus the nude statues of antiquity are modest as violets, and sufficiently draped in their own beauty." Apparently, what was good for the Greeks was not good for modern ganderers.[38]

As Hawthorne's experience shows, some affluent Americans became at least partially acclimated to the nudity of classical and neoclassical art by spending extended time in Europe, where artistic nudity was more common. As the historian William Douglas Smyth put it: "No matter how upsetting nudity may have been, South Carolinians [touring Europe] could hardly escape from it. In almost every drawing room, pastry shop, or public park, naked figures were displayed. This repeated exposure tended to blunt the beholder's delicacy. Visitors were also amazed at how matter-of-factly Europeans accepted naked representations. Men and women mingled together while viewing these works. Even in the presence of gentlemen, a group of ladies would surround a Venus or Apollo and discuss the merits of the statue. South Carolinians gradually became acclimated." Like Hawthorne's Miriam, some rationalized their love of classical sculpture by arguing that the cold, white marble, so different from the warmth and color of human skin, cooled the passions rather than excited them. After praising Antonio Canova's *Venus*, South Carolinian Alicia Middleton wrote from Florence in 1835, "[We] go to the different galleries, looking at beautiful pictures and statues which would have horrified us at home."[39]

The defense of classical morality went well beyond the defense of nudity in art. Lyman Beecher, one of the most famous revival preachers of the age, declared that the very future of the nation depended on training men in philosophy, logic, Greek, Latin, and the Bible. George Fitzhugh went so far as to deny that modern Christendom was morally superior to the ancient pagan world, though this was largely because commercialism had undermined Christianity:

> We flatter ourselves that we are more enlightened as well as more moral than the ancients, yet we imitate them in all else save the mechanic arts. Our hearts, we think, are not as hard and callous as theirs, for they delighted in gladiatorial combats which would fill us with horror. But we are as much pleased to hear of victories won by our countrymen as they, and our pleasure mounts the higher as we hear of more of the enemy killed in battle. Our nerves are too delicate to witness the pangs of the dying, but we rejoice to hear they are dead. Now, our moral code is one of the purest selfishness. The ancients were divided between Stoicism and Epicur[ean]ism—the philosophy of the Sadducees and that of the Pharisees. Neither the Epicurean nor the Sadducee professed as low, selfish and groveling a morality as that which our prevalent political economy inculcates. Divest us of our Christian morality, and leave us to our moral philosophy, and we might dread the comparison with any era of the past. We have but one moral code, and that the selfish one; the ancients always had two, one of which was elevated, self-denying and unselfish. In truth, a material and infidel philosophy has prevailed for a century, and seemed to threaten the overthrow of Christianity. But man is a religious animal. His mind may

become distempered and distressed for a time, and he may cavil and doubt as to Deity, immortality and accountability—but "conscience that makes cowards of us all" soon forces upon him the conviction that he is living in the presence of a God.... The Bible fortunately is a more common book than Adam Smith.

Fitzhugh considered the Bible and the classics complementary and equally necessary. In this he was much like the Presbyterians of the frontier, of whom the historian Louis B. Wright wrote: "They were as convinced of the civilizing value of Greek and Latin as they were [of] the truth of Holy Writ and when they combined the classics and the Bible in their educational efforts, they were certain that they had found the way to cultural and spiritual salvation."[40]

Even Horace Mann, who emphasized the scientific and technological superiority of the modern world, viewed some of the ancients as ethical models and championed the use of classical stories to teach morality. In 1840 Mann wrote: "By nature, there were boiling seas of passion in the breasts of Socrates and of Washington; but godlike sentiments of justice and duty and benevolence kept down their rage.... When subordinated to conscience and the will of God, these propensities give ardor to our zeal and strength to our exertions." In urging the establishment and enlargement of school libraries Mann wrote: "Let a child read and understand such stories as the friendship of Damon and Pythias, the integrity of Aristides, the fidelity of Regulus, the purity of Washington, the invincible perseverance of Franklin, and he will think differently and act differently all the days of his remaining life."[41]

Others contended that classical philosophy was not as distant from Christianity as was often assumed. For instance, some classical philosophers had believed in the immortality of the soul. William H. McGuffey, a Presbyterian minister, included in one of his readers a passage from Addison's *Cato* in which Cato engages in a Platonic reflection on the immortality of the soul before committing suicide to avoid capture by Caesar. After noting that Caesar had digressed into an attack on the doctrine of the immortality of the soul when opposing the execution of Catiline's accomplices before the Senate, George Fitzhugh wrote: "Cicero, on the contrary, invoked the sword of the law and the thunderbolts of the gods against the traitors. Leonidas, at Thermopylae, supping with his companions in arms, the moment before executing the most heroic design that human virtue ever conceived, invited them for the next day to another banquet in a new life." Fitzhugh wrote regarding the Stoics: "Brutus and the illustrious conspirators who shared his danger and his glory, belonged also to that sublime sect of Stoics, which had such lofty ideas of the dignity of man, which carried the enthusiasm of virtue to such a height, and which was extravagant in heroism only. Stoicism saved the honor of human nature, degraded by the vices of the successors of Caesar, and still more by the patience of the people." Cornelius Felton believed that the Athenian tragedians had come close to Christianity in some of their writings: "In point of morality, they reach the highest point of heathen purity.... In moments of poetical enthusiasm, the kindling soul, even of the heathen bard, seems to render asunder the veil of ignorance, weakness, and doubt, and to have a sudden comprehension of those truths, dimly shadowed out by tradition, but set in broad sunlight by the Christian revelation." James Henley Thornwell, a professor at South Carolina College, wrote, "There is a tenfold nearer approximation to the teachings of the Bible in Aristotle than there is in [William] Paley; more affinity with the Gospel in Cicero than in the whole tribe of utilitarians," for the ancients understood that "all virtue is a species of truth." Thornwell added, "Aristotle, among the ancients, was unquestionably in advance of every age which preceded the introduction of Christianity and is still in advance of many who call themselves Christians, in his clear and steady perception of the indissoluble connection betwixt the cogitative and practical departments of man's nature in reference to duty."[42]

Ralph Waldo Emerson often emphasized the similarities between classical philosophy and Christianity. Indeed, he went well beyond most Christians when he wrote: "An exemplary Christian of today, and even a Minister, is content to be just such a man as was a good Roman in the days of Cicero or of the imperial Antonines. Contentment with the moderate standard of pagan virtue implies that there was no very urgent necessity for Heaven's last revelation; for the laws of morality were written distinctly enough before, and philosophy had pretty lively dreams of the immortality of the soul. After Plato's dialogue & Cicero's declamations upon the subject, it must have been no uncommon matter of belief. And indeed it is very hard to conceive how sensible men should have passed their lives without it, whilst life itself was an abstruse enigma as long as it wanted this ready & simple explanation." In fact, though Emerson once argued that Christianity was superior to Stoicism in its emphasis on humility and love, on a different occasion he claimed that he preferred classical philosophy because the philosophers' ethics came without any organized church or threat of divine sanction. Emerson credited ancient Greek intellectuals not only with monotheism but also with a Unitarianism similar to his own: "It is an opinion as old as Theism, tho' not as universal, that God is One. Apart from sacred history, the oldest records in the world of human opinions conspire in this tradition.... Plato and Aristotle are not only Unitarians themselves but affirm the antiquity of their faith." Emerson quoted Aristotle: "God, being one, has thus received many names according to the variety of effects of which he is the cause." Emerson wrote regarding Anaxagoras: "He first announced that the phenomena of the universe are strictly connected—that they form one whole, that one order reigns, that its Unity supposes one mind which ordains it."[43]

Emerson argued that some Greek philosophers shared with Christians the belief in a creator. He quoted Plato regarding the creation: "Let us declare the cause which led the Supreme Ordainer to produce and compose the universe. He was good; and he who is good has no kind of envy. Exempt from envy, he wished that all things should be as much as possible like himself. Whoever, taught by wise men, shall admit this as the prime cause of the origin and foundation of the world, will be in the truth." Emerson also quoted the Greek physician Galen on the hand and foot: "In explaining these things, I esteem myself as composing a solemn hymn to the great architect of our bodily frame, in which I think there is more true piety than in sacrificing hecatombs of oxen or burning the most costly perfumes, for I first endeavor from his works to know him myself & afterwards by the same means to show him to others, to inform them how great his Wisdom, his goodness, his Power."[44]

Emerson's favorite author, Plutarch, believed in the immortality of the soul, divine Providence, and divine justice. In fact, Emerson quoted Plutarch's criticism of the traditional stories of the gods that depicted them as immoral: "I had rather a great deal that men should say, 'There was no such man as Plutarch' than they should say that there was one Plutarch that would eat up his children as soon as they were born, as the poets speak of Saturn. . . . When you are persuaded in your mind that you cannot either offer or perform anything more agreeable to the gods than entertaining a right notion of them, you will then avoid superstition as no less evil than atheism." Emerson claimed that Plutarch's *Moralia* contained "a more sweet and reassuring argument on the immortality [of the soul] than in the *Phaedo* of Plato, for Plutarch always addresses the question on the human side and not on the metaphysical." Recognizing Plutarch's closeness to Christianity, Emerson wrote: "All his judgments are noble. He thought, with Epicurus, that it is more delightful to do than to receive a kindness."[45]

Such were the similarities of Christianity and classical philosophy that Emerson even repeated the popular Christian notion that God may have used classical philosophy to prepare the world for Christianity. On several occasions he wrote, "The Stoic was the forerunner of the Christian." Emerson concluded passionately:

> Rather let me be "a pagan in creed outworn" than cowardly deny or conceal one particle of my debt to Greek art or poetry or virtue. Certainly I would my debt were more, but it is my own fault, not theirs, if 'tis little. But how pitiful if a mind enriched & infused with the spirit of their severe yet human Beauty

modulating the words they spake, the acts they did, the forms they sculptured, every gesture, every fold of the robe, especially animating the biography of their men with a wild wisdom and an elegance as wild & handsome as the sunshine; the brave anecdotes of Agesilaus, Phocion & Epaminondas; the death of Socrates, that holy martyr, a death like that of Christ; the purple light of Plato which shines yet into all ages & is a test of the sublimest intellects—to receive the influences, however partial, of all this & to speak of it as if it were nothing.[46]

Though more orthodox in his Christianity, John Quincy Adams agreed with Emerson on the compatibility of much of classical philosophy and Christianity. Adams wrote regarding Plato, "His argument upon the existence and nature of the gods, upon the immortality of the soul, and upon future rewards and punishments is inferior to nothing but Christianity." Adams particularly appreciated Plato's "ingenious" argument "that spirit is a simple and not a compound essence, and therefore not liable to decomposition." Adams considered Plato's second *Alcibiades* "an admirable treatise upon the duty and objects of prayer," though he added, "And Jesus himself has comprised in the short prayer which he prescribed to his disciples all that man can need to ask of Heaven." Similarly, Cicero had proved the immortality of the soul, "as far as it can be shown by the light of nature." In 1813 Adams wrote: "Nothing can stand in comparison with the genuine doctrines of Christianity in their application to the pursuit of happiness; but, setting them aside, the Socratic and Ciceronian moral philosophy is the most exalted system of human conduct that ever was presented to the world. Its tenets are beyond the ordinary level of human infirmity, and so are those of Christianity. It made the essence of virtue to consist in self-subjugation, and so does Christianity. It gave out a theory of perfection to [be] the aim of man, and made the endeavor to attain it his duty. So does Christianity. The perfect example indeed was not given, as by Christ; not even by Socrates. Yet he, and Cicero, and many of the sectaries of this philosophy, did attain an eminence of practical virtue highly laudable." Unlike Epicureanism, Platonism was praiseworthy, though still inferior to Christianity in many ways, such as in its dubious arguments for "the existence of the soul before the body" and in its coldness. (Adams was particularly disturbed by Socrates' "coldness which he shows at parting from his wife and children" before drinking the hemlock.) Significantly, what Adams found most noteworthy in Plato's *Phaedo* was Simmias' observation, hardly emphasized by Plato, "that to establish firmly the soul's immortality a special revelation from Heaven is necessary." Forgetting his own reservations about Greco-Roman mythology, Adams claimed that the classics harmonized so well with Christianity that he "invariably found that a light estimate of the study of Greek and Latin and an irreverent estimate of the Bible are inseparable companions."[47]

Thomas Dew also argued for the compatibility of classical philosophy and Christianity, especially with regard to the unity of the divinity. Dew noted: "Cicero speaks of one law and one God governing the universe, as the human soul governs the body which it animates. Seneca tells us that the different names given to the deities were only descriptive of the different characters in which the God of nature appears to us in his works. Plutarch expresses himself to the same effect—as [the] sun is common to all the world, though called by different names in different places, so there is but one supreme mind that governs the world, though worshipped under different names, and has inferior powers for his ministers." Even some of the earlier Greeks, such as Socrates and Anaxagoras, were also "supposed to have been impressed with the unity of divinity." Dew concluded, "Thus, we clearly see how philosophy is the ally of true religion, while ignorance leads on to idolatry and superstition. Ignorance scatters the divine nature into countless multitudes of gods, whilst philosophy and reason concentrate it into one eternal, sublime, supreme God, such as the Christian adores."[48]

Elizabeth Peabody and her friend Margaret Fuller sought to synthesize elements of Greek thought with Christianity. Peabody called for just such a synthesis in her periodical *Aesthetic Papers* in 1849. She wrote, "The Greeks dared to look the prime difficulty, the great mystery of life, in the face, and reverently to bow before it." Peabody recorded an exchange between Fuller and Eliza Quincy, wife of Josiah Quincy, the president of Harvard, that captured Fuller's view of Greek mythology:

> Mrs. Quincy expressed a doubt of these fables ever having been of serious import to the minds of the enlightened Greeks & a feeling that they were gross & harmful superstitions of the vulgar. . . . [She] expressed wonder & some horror at the thought of Christians enjoying Heathen Greeks. . . . Miss Fuller explained that she spoke with qualification. She had no desire to go back. She believed that we had the elements of a deeper & higher cultivation than any preceding the Christian cultivation, but the Christian cultivation was in its infancy, the Greek in its maturity. She could not look upon the expression of a great nation's intellect as a series of idle fancies. These fables & forms of Gods were the reverence for & idealization of the universal sentiments of religion—aspiration—intellectual action of a people whose political & aesthetic life had become immortal. We should approach it then with respect & distrust our own contempt of it.

However, it should be noted that Fuller was not typical of the orthodox Christian majority of her day. At one point she referred to the Old Testament and Greek mythology interchangeably as "the fables—the Hebrew & the Greek."[49]

In his popular historical novel *Zenobia* William Ware insisted that the synthesis between Christian and Roman virtue had already occurred and had been beneficial to Western civilization. While Roman cruelty and devotion to the state had required an opposing influence to moderate it, so had Christian otherworldliness. Ware depicted Roman virtue as masculine, Christian ethics as feminine. Thus Western civilization had benefited from the mixture, which was courage and tenderness joined. Ware wrote: "The Roman element is purified, while the Christian inherits the stoic strength and worldly realism of the Romans. The synthesis is opposed both to sensual debauchery and to ascetic fanaticism."[50]

Like many Americans of his day, James Fenimore Cooper was able to countenance classical paganism by interpreting the gods as mere representations of the different attributes of the one God rather than, as many early Christians had interpreted them, as very real demons who pretended divinity in order to mislead humans. Like many other antebellum Americans, Cooper saw in the Pantheon not a house to honor demons, but a universal expression of the divine. The "noble vault" and circular opening of the structure sent one's thoughts soaring to another realm: "Here is, at once, a suitable physical accompaniment to the mind, and the aid of one of the most far-reaching of our senses is enlisted on the side of omnipotence, infinite majesty and perfect beauty. Illimitable space is the best prototype of eternity." Cooper noted that despite the name of the temple (Pantheon is Greek for "all the gods"), the number of niches in the wall was insufficient for all the pagan gods, so that the temple was really dedicated to the one God in whom all of "the divine attributes are assembled." After all, "the gods themselves, it is fair to presume, represented merely so many different attributes of infinite power and excellence." Cooper had just published *The Prairie*, in which the frontiersman Natty Bumppo expresses the same conception of the divine as he gazes at the dome of the sky. Cooper considered the Pantheon the next best thing to nature in inspiring devotion to the divine.[51]

The Continuation of the Partnership

Like their forebears, most antebellum American Christians were acutely aware of the ethical flaws of the classics when viewed from a Christian perspective, but did not allow this awareness to stop them from admiring the ancients, from reading and appreciating the classics, from making classical allusions, and from advocating classical education as essential to the survival of the new republic. Despite his belief in the moral superiority of Christianity, John Quincy Adams urged even ministers to study the classics. He considered them essential to a Protestant minister's composition of good sermons:

> To qualify him for the performance of this duty is no useless lumber. It is so no unprofitable study to him, that which enables him to read the Scriptures in their original languages, which acquaints him with the writings of the fathers, which makes him familiar with the philosophers, the poets, the historians, [and] the orators of Greece and Rome. If the teachers of religion can use the language in which Christ spoke [Jesus actually spoke Aramaic, not Greek] and his apostles wrote, to no better purpose than to compose a dissertation upon the Greek particle; if the teachers of morals can draw no available funds from the language of Pythagoras and Plato; if the Christian orator can draw no shaft from the quivers of Aristotle and Quinctilian, or of Demosthenes and Cicero, the fault is surely not in his studies. If his lamp affords no light, it is not for lack of oil, but because he hides it under a bushel.

Adams practiced what he preached. A typical day found him translating the fifteenth psalm from the original Hebrew into his own verse and then translating Ovid's letter from Phyllis to Demophon.[52]

Most Americans believed that a republic must combine Christian piety with classical republicanism. If their vision was no longer that of Samuel Adams's "Christian Sparta," it was now that of a Christian Athens. When laying the cornerstone of Wofford College in Spartanburg, South Carolina, the Reverend William Wightman declared concerning the neoclassical structure: "We make this beautiful grove classic ground. . . . The building will be constructed in the Italian style of architecture—a style peculiarly adapted to our climate. When completed it will constitute one of the noblest specimens of architecture among the public buildings in the State, attracting the eye of the visitor to this flourishing town, and forming the most notable object in its vicinity." But he added:

> Republican forms of government are adapted only to a wise and virtuous people! Antiquity boasts of Republicans—in their way, many of them models to our own time. But where are they today? Had they not their civilization? Were they not polished and refined? Did not letters, oratory, and the arts rain selective influences over their people? Are not the literary productions of those times, confessedly, the purest models of style? . . . Why then have the nations perished and their governments crumbled into ruins? The answer is that brilliant as was the intellect of those ancient Republics, it was not irradiated with the lights of true religion. The popular heart was not imbued with the vital influence of those fundamental, everlasting, and indispensable moral principles which underlie all social and national life and prosperity among a

people possessing free institutions. Prosperity produced luxury, and luxury led to a general corruption of manners, in the absence of the corrective restraints found in a true religion popularly and extensively embraced. And so they fell.

The lesson was clear: for a republic to last, it must combine republican principles with Christian faith.[53]

Daniel Webster agreed with most of his contemporaries that classical republicanism must be combined with Christianity if the United States was to avoid the fate of its republican ancestors. In his final speech in 1852 Webster declared:

> Let me say, gentlemen, that if we and our posterity shall be true to the Christian religion, if we and they shall live always in the fear of God and shall respect His commandments, if we and they shall maintain moral sentiments and such conscientious convictions of duty as shall control the heart and life, we may have the highest hopes of the future fortunes of our country; and if we maintain those institutions of government and that political union, exceeding all praise as much as it exceeds all former examples of political associations, we may be sure of one thing, that while our country furnishes materials for a thousand masters of the historic art, it will afford no topic for a Gibbon. It will have no decline and fall. It will go on prospering and to prosper. But if we and our posterity reject religious instruction and authority, violate the rules of eternal justice, trifle with the injunctions of morality, and recklessly destroy the political constitution which holds us together, no man can tell how sudden a catastrophe may overwhelm us that shall bury all our glory in profound obscurity.

Webster's reference to Edward Gibbon was ironic in light of Gibbon's controversial conclusion that the rise of Christianity had been one of the chief causes of the fall of the Roman Empire.[54]

Most Americans thought that the solution to classical lapses in morality was not to ban the classics but to bowdlerize them. After noting that it was unfair to judge the ancients who lived before the rise of Christianity for failing to meet the religion's high ethical standards, Cornelius Felton added that while Greek writers were "singularly free from the charge of indecency," Roman poetry was "the growth of a dissolute and ribald age." He concluded, "To the scholar we would say, then, expurgate your Horaces and your Ovids, till not an obscene thought shall stain their pages; and you may be sure that nothing will be lost in your inquiries respecting the classic religion." Victorian editors did just that; they excised the more lascivious passages of Ovid from school texts, passages that the supposedly "puritanical" Puritans had left undisturbed. Even relatively benign passages were altered. For instance, in Ovid's *Metamorphoses* Proserpine tucks flowers into her bosom; in Thomas Bulfinch's version she tucks them into her apron. Bulfinch assured the readers of his compendium of classical mythology: "Such stories or parts of stories as are offensive to pure taste and good morals are not given. But such omissions are not often referred to, and if they occasionally should be, the English reader need feel no mortification in confessing his ignorance of them." A typical Christian classicist, Bulfinch had published *Hebrew Lyrical History,* an attempt to put the Psalms into their historical context for Sunday school teachers and students, two years earlier.[55]

Nathaniel Hawthorne assured the publisher of his own *Wonder Book* collection of myths, "Of course, I shall purge out all the old heathen wickedness, and put in a moral wherever practicable." Hawthorne saw nothing wrong with this practice since the very universality of the myths made them legitimate objects of revision by each generation: "No epoch of time can claim a copyright in these immortal fables. They seem never to have been made; and certainly, so long as man exists, they can never perish; but, by their indestructibility itself, they are legitimate objects of every age to clothe with its own garniture of manners and sentiment, and to imbue with its own morality." Hawthorne's *Tanglewood Tales* narrator Eustace Bright claims that these tales from the childhood of the human race were distorted in the corrupt age of Ovid and that all he is doing is restoring them to their original childlike innocence for the children of his own time. Hawthorne writes: "The objectionable characteristics seem to be a parasitical growth, having no essential connection with the original fable. . . . Thus the stories (not by any strained effort of the narrator's, but in harmony with their inherent germ) transform themselves and re-assume the shapes which they might be supposed to possess in the pure childhood of the world." Hawthorne's version of the myth of Proserpine presents her as a little girl whom Pluto kidnaps not for amorous reasons but simply because he wants to hear the pitter-patter of little feet on his subterranean stairs.[56]

When editors failed to properly censor classical works, school officials were apt to intervene. In defense of the classics the Catholic bishop John English noted that all sensible schools expurgated Greek and Latin works to weed out pernicious influences.[57]

As in all previous ages, the classics easily survived their Christian critics during the antebellum period. Even at Oberlin the classical curriculum was restored in the 1850s, so that by 1858 the Phi Delta Society there was debating such questions as "whether the revival of the athletic sports of the ancient Greeks would be beneficial to the mental and moral condition of the present age" and "whether the times of ancient Greece and Rome were more favorable to the production of poetry than the present." Like the Puritans before them, antebellum ministers quoted Aristotle as well as Paul. Greek Revival architecture continued to be as popular in the Burned-Over District, that hotbed of evangelical fervor in western New York, as elsewhere in the country.[58]

For almost two millennia the cart of Western civilization had been pulled by two horses, the classical and Christian traditions. Though they might occasionally pull in different directions, both generally trod the path of reason and virtue together. Even as John and John Quincy Adams quarreled about the divinity of Jesus (the father taking the deistic view, the son the orthodox), they could agree on the high ideals of the Sermon on the Mount and on the beauty and enduring value of the Greek and Roman classics.[59]

CHAPTER SEVEN

Slavery

JUST AS ANTEBELLUM southerners referred to the Bible in defense of slavery, they also appealed to the other seminal texts of the Western canon, the Greek and Roman classics. The growth of democracy in antebellum America was not the only factor that caused a shift in the southern perception of Athens from that of the founding generation, who had perceived the polis as too democratic and unstable. Another factor was Athens' usefulness in support of the southern argument that slavery was a positive good. Ironically, when Athens finally achieved the popularity it had been denied for over two millennia because of its political egalitarianism, that popularity, at least in the South, was based partly on its social inequalities. Most abolitionists responded by arguing that slavery had been the greatest flaw of Athens and the other classical republics and by invoking the classical theory of natural law, the theory from which modern republicans like the founders had derived the theory of natural rights.

Slavery as a Positive Good

As the Industrial Revolution intensified in Great Britain, France, and the northeastern United States, the demand for cotton transformed the crop into white gold, just as Eli Whitney's cotton gin greatly increased the efficiency of its extraction. At the same time, an increasingly vocal and radical abolitionist movement in the North heightened southern defensiveness. As a result of such defensiveness, far fewer antebellum southerners claimed, as had George Washington, Thomas Jefferson, James Madison, James Monroe, George Mason, and the other southern founders, that slavery was at best a necessary evil until African Americans could be recolonized in Africa. These founders gave way to statesmen and social critics who believed that the best way to defend slavery was to go on the offensive. George Fitzhugh summarized the new sentiment: "Slavery is now treated as a positive good, not a necessary evil."[1]

Slavery and the Classical Republics

The advocates of slavery viewed Athens as an ideal society, in which the labor of slaves made political equality among the citizens possible. As Senator Robert Toombs of Georgia put it in 1853, "Public liberty and domestic slavery were cradled together." Like Athens, Sparta possessed a strict division between citizens and forced labor (though the helots, who received half the crop, were technically serfs, not slaves), allowing for a rough economic equality among the citizens. Indeed, after praising Lycurgus for prohibiting Spartan citizens from engaging in manual labor, thereby restricting it to the helots, Thomas Dew wrote, "We want no legislation in the south to secure this effect—it flows spontaneously from our social system." But Athens' democratic political system, free-market economy, and individual freedom among citizens made it preferable to Sparta as a model for the antebellum South. The Spartan system featured state distribution of land to the citizenry and state indoctrination of citizens from birth to death, a system abhorrent to American libertarians. It was much better to imitate the Athenians, whose equality had been political, not economic, and who had valued the integrity of the family and freedom of expression. Dew sounded like Aristotle when he criticized Sparta for subordinating happiness, which was "the great object of our exertions in the world," so completely to patriotism: "We should be patriotic because it conduces to our happiness. Lycurgus's system sacrificed the happiness of individuals to make them patriotic and hardy—converting the means into the end." Dew added that the Spartan practices of infanticide and institutionalized adultery were immoral and that the Spartan character was "untempered by benevolence, amiability, or mercy."[2]

A hierarchy of argumentation can be discerned in proslavery appeals to classical history. At the simplest level, some references merely alluded to the universality of slavery, implying that anything universal must be natural and, therefore, good. Others slightly higher up the scale emphasized slavery's venerable antiquity, implying that anything old and lasting must be natural and, therefore, good. Others still more advanced involved the claim that since the Greeks and Romans, whom most Americans considered to have been admirable peoples, owned slaves, slavery must be good. In its highest development, the argument put forward the dazzling cultural achievements of Greece and Rome and the liberty and political equality singularly associated with the classical republics as evidence of the positive good of slavery. This use of the classical republics conferred enormous psychological benefits on proslavery southerners. As the historian Joseph Berrigan put it: "By becoming another Athens the South came into a rich inheritance of political and cultural responsibility. She ennobled her experience and dignified her action[s]. . . . Her defense of her way of life now seemed the battle against barbarians or against those who did not respect the values of Athens-South. . . . Men like [abolitionist William Lloyd] Garrison seemed all the madder and more dangerous in the light of the naturalness of slavery. They were not trifling with mere statistics or produce, they were tampering with nature itself."[3]

Southern advocates of slavery attributed to it the love of liberty, equality among citizens, stability, and intellectual and artistic achievements of the classical republics. George Fitzhugh wrote:

[Slavery] elevates those [poor] whites; for it makes them not the bottom of society, as at the North—not the menials, the hired day laborers, the work scavengers and scullions—but privileged citizens, like Greek and Roman citizens, with a numerous class far beneath them. In slave society, one white man does not lord it over another; for all are equal in privilege, if not in wealth. . . . Whilst we hold that all government is a matter of force, we yet think the governing class should be numerous enough to understand, and so situated as to represent fairly, all interests. The Greek and Roman masters were thus situated, so were the old Barons of England, and so are the white citizens of the South. If not all masters, like Greek and Roman citizens they all belong to the master race, have exclusive rights and privileges of citizenship, and an interest not to see this right of citizenship extended, disturbed, and rendered worthless and contemptible.

Fitzhugh also wrote: "We need never have white slaves in the South, because we have black ones. Our citizens, like those of Rome and Athens, are a privileged class. We should train and educate them to deserve the privileges and to perform the duties which society confers on them. . . . It is a distinction to be a Southerner, as it was once to be a Roman citizen." He added: "The abolitionists say that it is one of the necessary consequences of slavery that the poor are neglected. It was not so in Athens, and in Rome, and should not be so in the South. . . . We should furnish honorable occupation to all our citizens, whilst we cultivate and improve their minds by requiring them all to take part in the administration of justice and of government. We should thus make poverty as honorable as it was in Greece and Rome; for to be a Virginian would be a higher distinction than wealth or title could bestow." Thomas Dew wrote: "It has been contended that slavery is unfavorable to a republican spirit; but the whole history of the world proves that this is far from being the case. In the ancient republics of Greece and Rome, where the spirit of liberty glowed with the most intensity, the slaves were more numerous than the freemen. Aristotle and the great men of antiquity believed slavery necessary to keep alive the spirit of freedom."[4]

Rare was the southerner who disputed this analysis. In the *Southern Review* Hugh Swinton Legaré dared to conclude that the omnipresence of slavery at Rome reduced poor freemen into "the ready instruments and accomplices of unprincipled demagogues." Legaré added, "The same effect upon the labouring classes is noticed by Tacitus at Rome, and it was mainly to remedy this very evil—which seems inseparable from the institution of domestic servitude, under certain circumstances—that the Gracchi undertook their 'reforms.'" Perhaps Legaré believed that the phrase "under certain circumstances" provided him with sufficient cover. Similarly, Louisa McCord has Gaius Gracchus say:

> From the depopulated country fly
> The shepherd and the husbandman, to make
> Room for the rich man's slave.[5]

But neither Legaré nor McCord was an abolitionist. They merely sought to emphasize that the success of a slaveholding republic depended on a broad base of landowners. Poor freemen must have access to land and the protection from aristocratic oppression it afforded, else they would rise up, overthrow both slavery and republican government, and turn to the dictatorship of a Caesar. For this reason, most southerners, despite having misgivings about some of the "demagogic" methods employed by the Gracchi, applauded their ill-fated effort to restore the yeoman class of the Roman republic through land redistribution. George Frederick Holmes astutely noted that the Gracchi had never intended to undermine slavery. The antebellum South must avoid the fatal mistake of the Roman republic in resting itself on too narrow an economic base.[6]

Most southerners also maintained that slavery, in addition to creating a sense of equality and comradeship among the citizenry, also contributed a beneficial conservatism and stability to the ancient republics. Fitzhugh contended regarding these societies, "They were afraid of change, because insurrection was dangerous." He added, "Moses, Lycurgus, Solon, and Numa built their institutions to last, enjoined it on the people never to change them, and threw around them the sanctity of religion to ward off the sacrilegious hand of future innovation." Similarly, William J. Rivers, professor of Greek literature at South Carolina College, noted that the Athenians prohibited political proposals that conflicted with existing laws. Rivers claimed that if the United States adopted this model instead of paying heed to abolitionists, so as to protect "slavery and its effect in elevating the national character," the nation would have peace and prosperity. If not, there would be "instability in the Republic," which would lead to tyranny. Political stability, combined with "a love of liberty" grounded in "state pride," was crucial to the success of the republic. Rivers declared, "With respect to these characteristics, nowhere can we find a people more resembling the Greek than our own people."[7]

Best of all, southern advocates of slavery contended, slavery produced intellectual genius and artistic achievement. Fitzhugh claimed regarding slavery:

> To it Greece and Rome, Egypt and Judea, and all the other distinguished States of antiquity, were indebted for their great prosperity and high civilization, a prosperity and a civilization which appears almost miraculous, when we look to their ignorance of the physical sciences. . . . This high civilization and domestic slavery did not merely coexist, they were cause and effect. Every scholar whose mind is at all imbued with ancient history and literature sees that Greece and Rome were indebted to this institution alone for the taste, the leisure, and the means to cultivate their heads and their hearts; had they been tied down to Yankee notions of thrift, they might have produced a Franklin, with his "penny saved is a penny gained"; they might have had utilitarian philosophers and invented the spinning jenny, but they never would have produced a poet, an orator, a sculptor, or an architect; they would never have uttered a lofty sentiment, achieved a glorious feat in war, or created a single work of art. . . . The lonely and time-defying relics of Roman and Grecian art, the Doric column and the Gothic spire, alike attest the taste, the genius and the energy of society where slavery existed. . . . Scipio and Aristides, Calhoun and Washington, are the noble results of domestic slavery.

He added: "It is a common remark that the grand and lasting architectural structures of antiquity were the results of slavery. The mighty and continued association of labor requisite to their construction, when mechanic art was so little advanced, and labor-saving processes unknown, could only have been brought about by a despotic authority, like that of a master over his slaves." (Evidently, Fitzhugh did not know that the temples of the

Athenian Acropolis were constructed by free labor.) Fitzhugh implied that Athenian education was predicated on slavery: "We ought, like the Athenians, to be the best educated people in the world. When we employ all our whites in the mechanic arts, in commerce, in professions, &c., and confine the negroes to farmwork and coarse mechanical operations, we shall be in a fair way to attain this result."[8]

Other southerners agreed with Fitzhugh's analysis of the effects of slavery. Thomas Dew noted that the slaveholding societies of the ancient world had produced Lycurgus, Demosthenes, and Cicero "without for one moment loosing the ties between master and slave." Similarly, George Frederick Holmes noted that slave societies had produced Pindar, Thucydides, Plato, and Aristotle. Roman slaveholders had "conquered the world, legislated for all successive ages, and laid the foundations of modern civilization and modern institutions." Holmes added that the ancient states had declined because of corruption, not slavery.[9]

Louisa McCord connected the South with ancient Rome through paternalism, the belief that masters should serve as fathers to their childlike slaves. In *Caius Gracchus* she has Gaius say:

> Man has, in every station, rights his due.
> Our slaves look to their masters for support.
> The very claims we hold upon their labor
> Make us a rule to tender them again
> What comforts we can furnish to their lot.
> If placed by circumstance, necessity,
> Beneath our rule, protection thence we owe:
> And he evading basely these, degrades
> Himself below the defrauded slave.

This sense of obligation and affection between master and slave worked both ways. McCord made certain to note that Philocrates, Gaius' slave, died defending him rather than flee. Furthermore, McCord considered the maternalism of a plantation mistress as essential as the paternalism of a male master. She envisioned herself as a Cornelia, a mother figure, to her slaves; when asked why she wore no jewelry, she said, "A woman with two hundred children could hardly afford diamonds." This was a clear reference to the famous tale of Cornelia presenting her two sons as her jewels.[10]

Some southerners further tied the South to Greece and Rome by distinguishing northern civilizations from southern. J. D. B. De Bow alleged, "The civilization of the world has come from the South, as all history shows." He referred to the "Southern slave states of Greece and Rome [that] had given to the world all the civilization, arts, literature, laws, and government which antiquity offered." By the 1850s De Bow, forgetting his earlier assault on classical education, was attempting to persuade southern families to send their young men to southern colleges that were teaching the classics and the Scriptures rather than to their northern counterparts, who, he claimed, were preaching abolitionism instead. De Bow wrote, "Grave and Reverend professors leave the pulpit and the desk to sign and circulate incendiary political addresses, substituting rifles for Euclid or the Bible, and finding in Kansas fields more classic and consecrated ground than were ever before furnished to them by Attica or Palestine." By 1861 Fitzhugh was even going to the absurd extent of attempting to trace those colonists who had originally settled in what was now the southern United States to the ancient Romans, their Yankee counterparts to Anglo-Saxon serfs. Yet some southerners noted with anxiety that both Greece and Rome had been conquered by northern enemies (the Macedonians and the Germanic tribes, respectively) with inferior civilizations. As a writer in the *Daily South Carolinian* put it in 1855: "If there is one portion of Greek history more important than any other—one which addresses itself with resistless force to us of the South—it is that which records the gradual destruction of Grecian liberty by Northern foes—a work commenced by Philip of Macedon and completed by Alexander. . . . As Greece stood, so stand the Southern states of this Confederacy. We, too, are menaced with danger from the North; we, too, have a name and a heritage of liberty to defend."[11]

Aristotle, the Southern Spokesman

If Athens was the social model of most southern advocates of slavery, Aristotle was their favored spokesman. In the *Politics* (1.2) Aristotle had argued that some men were born to lead and others to follow: "The element which is able, by virtue of its intelligence, to exercise forethought is naturally a ruling and master element; the element which is able, by virtue of its bodily power, to do the physical work, is a ruled element, which is naturally in a state of slavery." Just as the mind should rule the body, so those with better minds should rule those with better bodies. Aristotle connected slavery with the universal rule of humans over animals, adults over children, and males over females, power relationships he considered equally natural (though he claimed that the rule of male over female should more closely resemble that of a statesman over fellow citizens than that of a monarch over subjects). Slavery was both natural and beneficial to the slave (1.5): "Those whose function is to use the body and from whom physical labor is the most that can be expected are by nature slaves, and it is best for them, as it is for all inferior things I have already mentioned, to be ruled." The master was distinguished from his slave not only by his greater intelligence (though Aristotle conceded that in actual practice the slave was sometimes more intelligent than his master) but also by his greater love of liberty. At one point Aristotle implied that anyone who would allow himself to be enslaved, rather than taking his own life, did not possess the passion for liberty requisite for a citizen in a republic: "For he is by nature a slave who is capable of belonging to another and therefore does belong to another." Aristotle sometimes seemed to suggest, as had Plato (*Republic* 5.469–470), that while it was wrong to enslave fellow Greeks, it was appropriate to enslave at least some barbarians—a doctrine useful to Aristotle's pupil, Alexander the Great, in his conquest of the Persian Empire. For centuries slaveholders throughout the Americas wielded Aristotle's defense of slavery as a powerful weapon.[12]

Antebellum southerners were no exception. In 1840 John C. Calhoun had advised a young man to study ancient history "and to read the best elementary treatises on Government, including Aristotle's, which I regard as among the best." (By contrast, Calhoun could only partially endorse *The Federalist* essays. He liked their support for mixed government but disliked their advocacy of a strong central government.) George Fitzhugh was shocked, upon reading Aristotle's *Politics* in 1855, to discover that he had been plagiarizing Aristotle for years without realizing it. Fitzhugh wrote to George Frederick Holmes: "I find that I have not only adopted his theories, his arguments, and his illustrations, but his very words. Society is a work of nature and grows. Men are social like bees; an isolated man is like a bird of prey. Men and society are coeval. . . . I used to think I was a little paradoxical. I now find I am a mere retailer of truisms and common places." Fitzhugh added, "With the world at large our authority was merely repulsive, whilst the same doctrine, coming from Aristotle, had, besides his name, two thousand years of human approval and concurrence in its favor." Fitzhugh called Aristotle "the wisest philosopher of ancient times." Fitzhugh's only disagreement with Aristotle concerned the philosopher's characterization of humans as inherently rational beings; conversely, Fitzhugh believed that humans' fundamental irrationality necessitated the stabilizing power of religion and tradition. He concluded: "The Bible (independent of its authority) is (by far) man's best guide, even in this world. Next to it, we would place Aristotle."[13]

Calhoun and Fitzhugh were not the only antebellum southerners to use Aristotle. George Frederick Holmes wrote: "The more I study Aristotle the less necessity do I discover for any other philosophy than modernized and

Christianized Peripateticism. Aristotle is still, as in the thirteenth century, 'Il maestro di che chi sanno' [the master of those who know]." Holmes liked Aristotle's emphasis on empiricism over ideological system building and admired his ability to explore the full range and methods of human reasoning in order to create the science of logic. Thomas Dew wrote that Aristotle, unlike the aristocratic Plato, "was exempt from all passion or prejudice for or against democratic institutions" and did not express an "extravagant admiration of Spartan institutions." Dew added regarding Aristotle: "He writes always in the true spirit of philosophy. . . . He is a true and impartial witness who reports after the most ample experience on both sides." William J. Grayson wrote in *De Bow's Review*:

> The maxim of Mr. Calhoun is that a democratic government cannot exist unless the laboring class be slaves. . . . It is not a new thing, but is two thousand years old. So far from being "first enumerated" by Mr. Calhoun, it is as ancient as Aristotle. In his "Politics"—which should be a textbook in all Southern colleges—in words as clear and emphatic as language can furnish, he lays down the maxim that a complete household or community is composed of freemen and slaves. He was writing to democracies. He maintains also that slaves should be barbarians, not Greeks, as Mr. Calhoun now holds it to be an advantage that the slaves of the South are negroes, a barbarian race sufficiently strong and docile for labor. The whole proposition, both to slavery itself and the race of the slave, is distinctly stated by the Greek philosopher.

Grayson failed to note that however prejudiced against "barbarians" (non-Greeks) Aristotle may have been, his distinction between the Greek and the barbarian had been cultural, not racial.[14]

Nevertheless, Aristotle's concept of the "natural slave" was ideally suited to southern advocates of slavery, who had only to racialize it to suit their purposes. In his *Disquisition on Government* Calhoun sounded much like Aristotle:

> Liberty, then, when forced on a people unfit for it, would, instead of a blessing, be a curse, as it would in its reaction lead directly to anarchy—the greatest of all curses. No people, indeed, can long enjoy more liberty than that to which their situation and advanced intelligence and morals fairly entitle them. . . . It is a great and dangerous error to suppose that all people are equally entitled to liberty. It is a reward to be earned, not a blessing to be gratuitously lavished on all alike—a reward reserved for the intelligent, the patriotic, the virtuous, and deserving, and not a boon to be bestowed on a people too ignorant, degraded, and vicious to be capable either of appreciating or of enjoying it. . . . Every effort to elevate a people in the scale of liberty above the point to which they are entitled must ever prove abortive and end in disappointment. The progress of a people rising from a lower to a higher point in the scale of liberty is necessarily slow.

Through this implicit denigration of the intellectual and moral capacities of African Americans, Calhoun converted them into Aristotle's "natural slaves," thereby denying them the same right of resistance to "majority tyranny" he recognized in southern whites. Elsewhere, Calhoun wrote regarding the Jeffersonian principle that all men were created equal and its influence upon the abolitionists, "We now begin to experience the danger of admitting so great an error to have a place in the Declaration of our Independence. For a long time it lay dormant; but in the process of time it began to germinate and produce its poisonous fruits."[15]

Fitzhugh agreed that African Americans were natural slaves. He claimed: "It is clear that Athenian democracy would not suit a negro nation, nor will the government of mere law suffice for the individual negro. He is but a grown up child, and must be governed as a child." When Fitzhugh was not referring to African Americans as children, he was referring to them as savages, another category of people unfit for self-government. He wrote: "The Greeks and Romans were very lavish of the term barbarian, but we doubt whether they ever saw a savage. Herodotus treats of men without heads and with eyes in their breasts, but says not a word of men with black skins and woolly heads." (As we shall see, Herodotus did indeed refer to Ethiopians, a people he admired.) In fact, Fitzhugh intimated that Africans were the *real* "natural slaves" in a way that Greek and Roman slaves had not been: "There is one strong argument in favor of negro slavery over all other slavery: that he, being unfitted for the mechanic arts, for trade, and all skillful pursuits, leaves those pursuits to be carried on by the whites, and does not bring all industry into disrepute, as in Greece and Rome, where the slaves were not only the artists and mechanics, but also the merchants."[16]

While the northern Transcendentalists embraced Plato, antebellum southerners preferred Aristotle, who had considered the family unit coextensive with civilized humanity, to his mentor, whose *Republic* had championed socialism and the removal of children from their parents (at least among the elite). Fitzhugh compared abolitionists with utopians like Plato, whom the realistic Aristotle had far surpassed in wisdom. Fitzhugh wrote facetiously, "Modern Abolitionists, wiser than Moses and Aristotle, have discovered that all men should be free." He also noted: "The Socialists derive the idea of dispensing with or restricting the use of money from Sparta and other ancient States; and to the same sources may be traced almost all their schemes for social improvement. Plato, in his philosophy, borrowed from those sources, and subsequent Socialists have borrowed from him." But while the socialists were right to oppose unrestricted capitalism, their solutions were impractical. Fitzhugh also preferred Aristotle's views on the genders to Plato's (which allowed gifted women into the ruling elite), blaming Plato for the burgeoning women's rights movement as well. In Fitzhugh's eyes, nature itself was under assault from modern Platonists in the form of the socialist, feminist, and abolitionist movements. Regarding Aristophanes' *Assembly-women* (392 B.C.), a farce in which the Athenians turn the government over to women, who then institute socialism, Fitzhugh wrote: "It is in the main a faithful picture of the isms of the North and of Western Europe, except that our modern socialists exceed somewhat in absurdity and profanity the Black Republicans and strongminded women of Athens." Nevertheless, Fitzhugh wondered, "May not Athenian corruption and effeminacy have grown out of the Greeleyite isms inculcated by Plato, and may not the sound and natural philosophy of Aristotle have formed the character of Alexander and his invincible Macedonians?" (Here Fitzhugh reversed the common formulation of the South as Athens, the North as Macedon.) While Plato had proposed "to throw husbands, wives and children into a sort of common public stock," Aristotle had seen it as the first duty of the polis to preserve the family.[17]

Other antebellum southerners expressed the same preference for Aristotle over Plato. "Southron" stated southern opinion aptly in 1838 when he wrote in the *Southern Literary Messenger:* "To Aristotle, one of the most profound philosophers of antiquity, we confidently appeal, and with the more confidence, because in this iron age of utilitarianism, his material philosophy . . . has been preferred to the spiritual sublimity of the divine Plato. Aristotle has expressly declared that 'in the natural state of man, from the origin of things, a portion of the human family must command and the remainder obey' and that this distinction which exists between master and servant is a distinction at once natural and indispensable, and when we find it existing among freemen and slaves, it is not man, but nature herself, which has ordained the distinction." A decade later another contributor to the journal wrote regarding Plato and Aristotle: "The former delighted more to revel in the pure and lofty regions of imagination and sometimes lost himself in the mazes of his renowned and subtle speculations. The latter, with far more judgment and far more success, devoted his gigantic powers to the elucidation and unfolding subjects of much more use to his fellow men than metaphysical abstractions." Dr. D. McCauley, a contributor to *De Bow's Review*, agreed, calling Aristotle "one of the greatest intelligences that ever appeared in the world . . . whose philosophy maintained such an unlimited sway over the human mind for centuries."[18]

The advocates of slavery sided with Aristotle not only against utopian Platonists but also against what they regarded as the other source of abolitionism, the hypothesis of Thomas Hobbes and John Locke that a "state of nature," in which autonomous individuals had enjoyed complete freedom and equality, had preceded society and government. John C. Calhoun blamed this erroneous hypothesis for Jefferson's equally erroneous doctrine that "all men are created equal" and "are endowed by their Creator with certain unalienable rights." Adopting Aristotle's organic conception of society, Calhoun wrote concerning Locke's "state of nature," "It never did nor can exist, as it is inconsistent with the preservation and perpetuation of the [human] race." Humans were social and political animals, as Aristotle had alleged. Society preceded the individual, both historically and in order of importance. Far from being born free and equal, humans were "subject not only to parental authority, but to the laws and institutions of the country where they are born and under whose protection they draw their first breath." Nevertheless, Calhoun was too American to deny completely the importance of individual liberty. On the contrary, although he denied that individuals possessed any unalienable rights, he insisted that each society should grant them the maximum amount of liberty consistent with their intellectual and moral capacities and consistent with the degree of danger posed by that society's external enemies. Calhoun defined the role of government in both negative (Lockean) and positive (Aristotelian) terms. The proper objects of government were both to "guard the community against injustice, violence, and anarchy within, and against attacks from without" and "to develop the faculties, intellectual, and moral, with which man is bestowed." In this sense Calhoun was partly a modern republican and partly a classical republican.[19]

George Fitzhugh shared Calhoun's preference for Aristotle's organic conception of society over Hobbes's and Locke's concept of the state of nature. Fitzhugh wrote: "Man is naturally a social and gregarious animal, subject, not by contract or agreement, as Locke and his followers assume, but by birth and nature, to those restrictions of liberty which are expedient or necessary to secure the good of the human hive, to which he may belong. . . . Such is the theory of Aristotle, promulgated more than two thousand years ago, generally considered true for two thousand years, and destined, we hope, soon again to be accepted as the only true theory of government and society." Fitzhugh continued:

> Aristotle understood this subject thoroughly; and it seems to have been generally so well comprehended in his day that he takes little trouble to explain and expound it. He commences his treatise on Politics and Economics with the family, and discourses first of the slave as a part of the family. He assumes that social life is as natural to man as to bees and herds, and that the family, including husband, wife, children, and slaves, is the first and most natural development of that social nature. As States are composed of families, and as a sound and healthy whole cannot be formed of rotten parts, he devotes much

of his treatise to family education and government. Would that modern statesmen, philosophers, and politicians would become practical like Aristotle, and not attempt to build social and political edifices, until they were sure of the soundness of the materials of which they would construct them."[20]

According to Fitzhugh, classical virtue was based on this understanding. Fitzhugh claimed: "The loftiest patrician in those days valued himself not on selfish, cold individuality, but on being the most devoted servant of society and his country. In ancient times, the individual was considered nothing, the State every thing. And yet, under this system, the noblest individuality was evolved that the world has ever seen. . . . The doctrines of individuality, of the social contract, and of laissez-faire had not then arisen."[21]

Fitzhugh claimed that the modern United States was blessed with sound institutions and practices (republican government and slavery) but cursed with unsound political theory (Lockean nonsense). Fitzhugh declared: "Never were people blessed with such wise and noble Institutions as we, for they combine most that was good in those of Rome and Greece, of Judea, and of Medieval England. But the mischievous absurdity of our political axioms and principles quite equals the wisdom and conservatism of our political practices."[22]

Fitzhugh contended that the industrialism of Britain and the northern United States was merely a new and harsher form of slavery. He argued: "Liberty in England, as in Rome and Greece, has been, and is now, the privilege of the few—not the right of the many. But in Rome, Greece, and the Southern States of America, the many have gained in protection what they lost in liberty. In England, the masses have neither liberty nor protection." While it was true that factory workers, unlike slaves, could move from place to place, they merely moved from one hopeless situation to another. Fitzhugh added sarcastically, "So much for locomotion." His analysis ignored the fact that southern plantations, far from being idyllic, pastoral havens from the commercialism he condemned, were large commercial enterprises whose chief customers were the very textile factories he despised. Fitzhugh also contended that modern socialism was akin to slavery, in that both sought to remedy the failure of laissez-faire capitalism by establishing communalism and social stability.[23]

The Abolitionists and the Classical Republics

Most abolitionists responded that slavery was Athens' greatest flaw. The historian David Brion Davis has written, "Assuming that cultural achievement could never depend on moral evil, most historians and classicists tended to ignore ancient slavery or to relegate it as a deplorable defect unrelated to the glories of Greece and Rome." The Frenchman Henri Wallon, who published the first comprehensive study of ancient slavery in 1847, wrote of the Greek and Roman civilizations, "The bad points were the direct results of slavery, the good ones of freedom." On the basis of such a view, William Lloyd Garrison adopted the pseudonym "Aristides" for an essay because he considered the Athenian a model of justice, and quoted Demosthenes. Frederick Douglass, who had learned to read by studying the neoclassical speeches of Edward Everett contained in the 1832 edition of *The Columbian Orator*, proudly called Boston "the Athens of America," though he also argued that slavery had been the downfall of the first Athens. Douglass contended: "Greece has vanished, her life disappeared as it were, in a trance of artistic beauty and architectural splendor.... The lesson taught by the history of nations is that the preservation or destruction of communities does not depend on external prosperity.... They are not saved by art, but by honesty." Similarly, the luxury made possible by slavery had corrupted the Roman Empire: "The lap of pleasure, the pursuit of ease and luxury, are death to manly courage, will, and enterprise!" The notion that luxury produced effeminacy, which, in turn, caused the downfall of civilizations, was itself a classical idea. During the Civil War, when advocating the Union army's deployment of black troops in a speech entitled "Fighting the Rebels with One Hand," Douglass declared: "Egypt, Palestine, Greece, and Rome all had their warnings. They disregarded them, and they perished." Prejudice had deprived these states of the full use of all their citizens.[24]

Douglass also used the Egyptian influence on Greece to disprove the theory that light-skinned people were intellectually superior to dark-skinned people. He claimed: "Greece and Rome—and through them Europe and America—have received their civilization from the ancient Egyptians.... The ancient Egyptians were not white people but were, undoubtedly, just about as dark in complexion as many in this country who are considered genuine negroes.... The Egyptians were once superior to the Greeks, and the Greeks to the Romans, and the Romans were superior to the Normans, and the Normans superior to the Saxons, and now the Anglo-Saxon is boasting his superiority to the negro and to the Irishman."[25]

Douglass was not the first to use the Egyptian influence on Greece in this fashion. In 1833 Lydia Maria Child had written: "It is well known that Egypt was the great school of knowledge in the ancient world. It was the birth-place of Astronomy.... Herodotus, the earliest of the Greek historians, informs us that the Egyptians were Negroes. This fact has been much debated and often contradicted. But Herodotus certainly had the best means of knowing the truth on this subject, for he traveled in Egypt and obtained his knowledge of the country by personal observation." This was a reference to the line in Herodotus' *Histories* (2.104) in which he referred to the Egyptians as "black skinned" and as having "woolly hair." Child added, "Even the proud Grecians evinced respect for Ethiopia almost amounting to reverence and derived thence the sublimest portions of their mythology." She noted that modern whites' disapproval of the physical appearance of African Americans was cultural, a result of black people's lowly status as slaves. She quoted Herodotus (3.11): "The Ethiopians surpass all other men in longevity, stature, and personal beauty."[26]

Nor was the belief that the Egyptians were a black race confined to abolitionists. Nathaniel Hawthorne even went so far as to ascribe an African physiognomy to Cleopatra, the Macedonian queen of Egypt. In *The Marble Faun* (1860) he congratulates his fictional sculptor Kenyon for the accurate depiction of Cleopatra: "The sculptor had not shunned to give the full Nubian lips and other characteristics of the Egyptian physiognomy. His courage and integrity had been rewarded; for Cleopatra's beauty shone out richer, warmer, more triumphantly, beyond comparison than if, shrinking timidly from the truth, he had chosen the tame Grecian type." Hawthorne's description of the fictional statue was based on a real one by William W. Story.[27]

The historian David S. Wiesen has noted the power of the Christian and classical traditions over the abolitionists. Wiesen wrote: "The most ardent enemies of slavery always used as a touchstone to prove the natural gift of Negroes for civilization, first their readiness to be Christianized and then their association with the classical tradition, either in historical fact or in their ability to absorb the best classical education." Indeed, the abolitionist propensity to highlight the classical knowledge of some African Americans as proof of the intellectual capacity of the whole race tended to encourage such learning wherever possible. During the Reconstruction period Booker T. Washington marveled at the "craze for Greek and Latin learning" among the new freedmen, a craze he attributed to the widespread belief "that a knowledge, however little, of the Greek and Latin languages would make one a very superior human being, something bordering almost on the supernatural."[28]

There was even a sustained effort by antebellum abolitionists to portray runaway slaves as classical heroes. In 1837 the *Anti-slavery Record* compared the act of escape by runaway slaves to the retreat of the Greeks under Xenophon from the heart of the Persian Empire in 401 B.C., explaining: "To escape from a powerful enemy often requires as much courage and generalship as to conquer." When a runaway slave named Margaret Garner, on the verge of being captured by a posse of armed men in 1856, killed her own children rather than see them reenslaved, Ellen Wilkins Harper published a poem comparing her to Roman heroes. Harper added:

> Even Rome had altars 'neath whose shade
> Might crouch the wan and weary slave.

This was a reference to the Roman practice of allowing abused slaves to seek refuge at sanctuaries. Other abolitionists compared Garner to Virginius, who had killed his daughter Virginia rather than see her enslaved.[29]

Even Charles Sumner, who was more critical of Greco-Roman civilization than most, could not help fixating on a few obscure critics of slavery among the ancients. Sumner conceded that Euripides, Plato, and Aristotle all endorsed slavery and even added that Greek civilization, "though brilliant to the external view as the immortal sculptures of the Parthenon, was, like that stately temple, dark and cheerless within." Yet he was quick to assert: "We learn from Aristotle himself that there were persons in his day—pestilent Abolitionists of ancient Athens—who did not hesitate to maintain that liberty was the great law of Nature, and to deny any difference between master and slave—declaring at the same time that slavery was founded upon violence, and not upon right, that the authority of the master was unnatural and unjust. 'God sent forth all persons free; Nature has made no man a slave' was the protest of one of these agitating Athenians against this great wrong." Sumner identified the latter Athenian as Alcidamas, a disciple of the Sophist Gorgias of Leontini. Sumner added that the antislavery statements of these Athenians were identical to those asserted at modern abolitionist meetings. He even suggested, more than a little improbably, that Homer was an enemy of slavery because the poet had written (in Alexander Pope's translation), "Jove fixed it certain that whatever day makes man a slave takes half his worth away."[30]

While rebuking Roman civilization for its slavery, Sumner praised its recognition of higher principles. He claimed: "The spirit of freedom which animated the [Roman] Republic was of that selfish and intolerant character which accumulated privileges upon the Roman citizen while it heeded little the rights of others. But, unlike the Greeks, the Romans admitted in theory that all men are originally free by the Law of Nature; and they ascribed the power of masters over slaves, not to any alleged diversities in the races of men, but to the will of society. The constant triumphs of their arms were signalized by reducing to servitude large bodies of subjugated people." Indeed, Sumner seemed to attribute Roman cruelty to Roman slavery rather than the reverse. After noting that "Terence and Phaedrus, Roman slaves, teach us that genius is not always quenched even by degrading bondage," Sumner added, "The writings of Cato the Censor, one of the most virtuous slave-masters in history, show the hardening influence of a system which treats human beings as cattle." Thus even Charles Sumner, a leading critic of classical ethics, felt the need to portray the Romans more as victims, albeit as self-victims, than as victimizers.[31]

In a similar vein Ralph Waldo Emerson blamed his mentor Edward Everett's support for the Fugitive Slave Law of 1850 on a diminution of classical influence over him. Emerson wrote, "His old Scholars cannot but ask him whether there was no sincerity in all those apostrophes to freedom & adjurations of the dying Demosthenes: was it all claptrap?" But Emerson rejected insincerity as the cause of Everett's apostasy and that of other northern statesmen and settled on a different explanation: "Their reading of Cicero & of Plato & of Tacitus has been drowned under . . . the bad company they have kept. . . . [They] are as obsequious to Mr. [Daniel] Webster as he is to the gentlemen of Richmond & Charleston." Years of political involvement and compromise with southern slaveholders had corrupted northern politicians. Note that neither of Emerson's theories, the hypothesis of insincerity and that of the corrupting influence of politics, placed any blame on Demosthenes, Cicero, Plato, or Tacitus, all of whom had penned the encomiums to liberty that northern statesmen loved to quote while living in slaveholding societies. It was emotionally easier for Emerson and the other abolitionists to charge their own politicians with hypocrisy than to charge the revered ancients with the same vice, for to do so, given their own abolitionist ideology, might have led to the conclusion that the whole classical tradition of liberty in which they had been socialized had been a sham from the start.[32]

Only rarely did the abolitionist attack on classical civilization go beyond the assault on ancient slavery to imply a deeper cruelty. In her "Appeal to the Christian Women of the South" in the 1830s, Angelina Grimké wrote that southern women must be prepared to suffer like the Christian apostles had suffered at the hands of the Romans in order to oppose the moral evil of slavery. Grimké wrote concerning the martyrs: "At Rome, proud mistress of the world, they thundered out the terrors of the law upon that idolatrous, war-making, slaveholding community. Why were the martyrs stretched upon the rack, gibbeted, and burnt, the scorn and diversion of a Nero, while their tarred and burning bodies sent up a light which illuminated the Roman capital? . . . Because they dared to speak the truth, to break the unrighteous laws of their country, and chose rather to suffer affliction with the people of God." A woman's gender did not excuse her from the obligation of speaking Christian truth to this new

Roman power, the antebellum South: "Roman *women* were burned at the stake, their delicate limbs were torn joint from joint by the ferocious beasts of the Amphitheatre, and tossed by the wild bull in his fury, for the diversion of that idolatrous, warlike, slaveholding people. Yes, *women* suffered the ten persecutions of heathen Rome with the most unshrinking constancy and fortitude; not all the entreaties of friends, nor the claims of new born infancy, nor the cruel threats of enemies could make *them* sprinkle one grain of incense upon the altars of Roman idols" (emphases in original). Likewise, in William Ware's *Zenobia,* Piso, who owns 500 slaves himself, says that slavery makes him "hate my country and my nature and long for some power to reveal itself . . . capable to reform a state of society rotten as this is to its very core." This was a clear reference to Christianity, though the rise of Christianity had not ended slavery. In the sequel *Probus,* Ware has Piso attack Roman civilization even more forcefully: "Rome never was a republic. It was simply a faction of land and slave holders who blinded and befooled the ignorant populace by parading before them some of the forms of liberty, but kept the power in their own hands. . . . And among the people there can be no liberty where slavery exists. . . . He who holds slaves cannot in the nature of things be a republican." Slavery destroyed the virtue of both the slave and the slaveholder, and republics were based on virtue.[33]

David Walker's *Appeal to the Coloured Citizens of the World* (1829) portrayed Greco-Roman civilization as the evil start of an evil race. Walker contended: "The whites have always been an unjust, jealous, unmerciful, avaricious and blood-thirsty set of beings, always seeking after power and authority. We view them all over the confederacy of Greece, where they were first known to be any thing (in consequence of education), we see them there, cutting each other's throats—trying to subject each other to wretchedness and misery—to effect which, they used all kinds of deceitful, unfair, and unmerciful means. We view them next in Rome, where the spirit of tyranny and deceit raged still higher." Yet even Roman slavery was milder than the American brand, despite the statements of Thomas Jefferson to the contrary: "Every body who has read history knows that as soon as a slave among the Romans obtained his freedom, he could arise to the greatest eminence in the State, and there was no law instituted to hinder a slave from buying his freedom. Have not the Americans instituted laws to prohibit a man of colour from obtaining and holding any office whatever under the government of the United States of America? Now, Mr. Jefferson tells us that our condition is not so hard as the slaves were under the Romans!" Walker portrayed Hannibal as "a mighty son of Africa" who would have prevailed over Rome if the Carthaginians had been united, just "as the coloured people are now [disunited] in the United States of America, the reason our natural enemies are enabled to keep their feet on our throats." He prophesied that God would raise up another Hannibal to destroy the new Rome and pleaded for black support for him when he arose.[34]

The Debate Concerning Natural Law

Abolitionists championed the classical theory of natural law, the belief in a universal code of ethics inherent in nature, but interpreted it in a different manner from the ancients themselves, to invalidate slavery. Whereas Plato, Aristotle, and other classical philosophers, as members of highly communal societies faced with the constant threat of war, had interpreted the theory narrowly to recognize few individual rights, modern republicans had placed a new emphasis on the natural rights to life, liberty, and property. This emphasis had culminated in the Glorious and American revolutions and in the English and U.S. bills of rights.[35]

Antebellum opponents of slavery often invoked the theory of natural law. In an 1851 speech to his fellow citizens of Concord concerning the Fugitive Slave Law of 1850, Emerson cited Cicero on the principle that "an immoral law could not be valid," a truth the Roman had considered "the foundation of States." Emerson then noted the doctrine of the Greek playwrights that divine justice inevitably overtook those who violated natural law. The same year, when Horace Greeley visited Rome, he could not help but make an implicit comparison between the Roman violation of natural law in the case of gladiatorial combat and the Fugitive Slave Law's compulsion of northern citizens to aid in the return of runaway slaves. Although Greeley was so impressed with the classical art he saw in Rome that he was tempted to say that "if mankind were compelled to choose between the destruction of what is in Rome or that of all the rest of the world, the former should be saved at the expense of the latter," and although he was genuinely awed by the Colosseum, he wrote: "It is among the traditions of Rome that a great number of the early Christians were compelled by their heathen persecutors to fight and die here as gladiators, as a punishment for their contumacious, treasonable resistance to the 'lower law' then in the ascendant, which the high priests and circuit judges of that day were wont in their sermons and charges to demonstrate that everyone was bound as a law-abiding citizen to obey, no matter what his private, personal convictions with regard to it."[36]

In an 1852 speech proposing the repeal of the Fugitive Slave Law, Charles Sumner cited Cicero on natural law. He related: "After assailing indignantly that completest folly which would find the rule of justice in human institutions and laws, and then asking if the laws of tyrants are just simply because [they are] laws, Cicero declares that, if edicts of popular assemblies, decrees of princes, and decisions of judges constitute right, then there may be a right to rob, a right to commit adultery, a right to set up forged wills; whereas he does not hesitate to say that pernicious and pestilent statutes can be no more entitled to the name of law than robber codes; and he concludes, in words as strong as those of St. Augustine, that an unjust law is null." (Sumner neglected to mention that Cicero, like nearly all aristocratic Romans, owned slaves.) Likewise, in a debate in Philadelphia in 1858, Abram Pryne, a Congregational minister and abolitionist editor of the *Central Reformer,* cited Cicero on the idea that laws must be just to be worthy of obedience. It was no accident that Sophocles' *Antigone,* a play about a woman who violates the edict of a ruler on behalf of a higher law, became popular in the 1840s and 1850s, the very decades when the dispute over slavery reached its height.[37]

In 1860 Charles Sumner used natural law to combat what he considered the illegitimate use of another venerable Greek theory, the theory of popular sovereignty. This theory, which held that the people had the right to choose their own form of government, had proved as crucial to the American Revolution and to the U.S. Constitution as the theory of natural law. In 1854 the Kansas-Nebraska Act had nullified the prohibition of slavery in Kansas and Nebraska that had been instituted by the Missouri Compromise (1820), replacing it with the right of settlers in these territories to determine for themselves whether to permit slavery. Sumner declared at the Massachusetts Republican Convention: "The sacred name of Popular Sovereignty is prostituted to cover the claim of a master over his slave.... To protect this 'villainy,' as John Wesley would call it, the right of the people to govern themselves is invoked—forgetful that this divine right can give no authority to enslave others, that even the people are not omnipotent, and that never do they rise so high as when, recognizing the everlasting laws of Right, they bend to the behests of Justice." William Seward made a similar appeal to the classical theory of natural law that year, declaring that there was a "higher law" than the U.S. Constitution, which condoned slavery, a declaration that probably cost him the Republican nomination and the presidency.[38]

In response some southerners rejected the theory of natural law itself, while others denied that it mandated equality, since nature herself produced inequality. These southerners defined freedom in the same fashion as their fellow disciples of Aristotle, the medieval Scholastics, as the right to occupy one's proper place in society.[39]

Northerners who disliked slavery but valued the Union above all and feared that radical abolitionists were undermining it emphasized the pragmatic, nationalist side of Cicero over his idealistic, universalist side. Senator Rufus Choate of Massachusetts, a lifelong fan of Cicero and a renowned orator who translated Latin into English every day to increase his verbal acuity, protested against the abolitionists' use of Cicero's rhetoric concerning natural law. Choate had learned from Cicero that there was a hierarchy of duties and virtues, at the top of which stood those that contributed most to the maintenance of one's society and nation, without which all other goods, including the moral life itself, were impossible. He loved to repeat Cicero's dictum that the building of states was the most acceptable of human acts to God. Therefore, sympathy for the slave, however good in itself, must not be allowed to destroy the Union. Choate claimed that philanthropy must be "arrested and rebuked by a higher law." He added, "In this competition of affections, Country—'omnes omnium charitates complectens,' the expression, the sum total of all things most dearly loved, surely holds the first place." In referring to the preservation of the Union as "a higher law" Choate was clearly challenging the abolitionist claim that Ciceronian natural law favored the abolition of slavery, no matter the cost. For this reason, Choate admired the sacrifice of his colleague, Daniel Webster, whose speeches on behalf of the Compromise of 1850, including the Fugitive Slave Law, secured its passage but also earned him the vilification of many northerners. After Webster's death in 1852, Choate declared in a speech that Webster had had the misfortune of living in a "quiet, civil age." Choate explained, "Assisted by that unequalled organ of speech, the Greek language of Demosthenes, might he not have rolled an equal thunder and darted an equal flame?" This was too much for Horace Greeley's abolitionist newspaper, the *New York Tribune,* which retorted: "Why should we suppose that Webster 'would have rolled an equal thunder and flashed an equal flame' with Demosthenes over the threatened liberties of fifty thousand Greeks, when he rolled no thunder and flashed no flame over the threatened liberties of thirteen million Americans [the actual slave population was about 3.5 million]? . . . Would he 'have breathed virtue into decaying Greece' when he had very little to breathe into our decaying Democracy?"[40]

The Emotional Hold of the Classics

In *Life on the Mississippi* (1883) Mark Twain claimed, with complete and rare seriousness, that Sir Walter Scott was "in great measure responsible" for the U.S. Civil War. One of the reasons for Twain's lifelong determination to eviscerate romanticism with his sharp, satirical wit was his sincere belief that the catastrophic Civil War had been caused by southern planters who had read too many novels by Scott, novels that had glorified feudalism. Steeped in such nonsense, the planters had convinced themselves of their own moral rectitude in retaining and expanding slavery.[41]

It is indicative of the romantic hold of the classics on even hard-boiled skeptics like Twain that when searching desperately for the cause of the tremendous catastrophe that had befallen his region and nation, he should make Scott and his fictitious barons the villains rather than Aristotle and the very real ancients. While Twain was ridiculing the "sham castle" Louisiana had constructed for its capitol—not only for its fraudulence but also for the feudal values it presumably represented—it did not occur to him that it was one of only two state capitols in the entire nation constructed in the Gothic style (the other was Georgia's capitol). Nearly every other state capitol in the country, North and South, was constructed in the neoclassical style. And while Scott had merely written a few novels romanticizing the Middle Ages, Aristotle had written a serious treatise—one of the most influential in history—in which he had directly defended the practice of slavery. Although Twain wrote a series of novels skewering the Middle Ages—such classics as *A Connecticut Yankee in King Arthur's Court*—he devoted not a single short story to overturning the far more prominent romanticism of Athens and Rome. Even his brief satirical reference to Roman gladiatorial contests in *Innocents Abroad* (1869) was largely an excuse to spoof American drama critics.[42]

Perhaps it was precisely because the roots of Gothic romanticism were so shallow in the United States—virtually nonexistent in the North and of exaggerated depth even in the South—and the roots of classicism so deep throughout the nation that Twain did not even consider assaulting the classics. Northerners, along with antislavery southerners like Twain, could regard slavery as the greatest flaw of the democratic civilization of Athens, just as it had, until recently, been the greatest flaw of the democratic civilization of the United States. These Americans considered Greco-Roman slavery a painful embarrassment to be ignored, whenever possible, much as the adoring son of an alcoholic father might wish to dismiss his father's bouts of drunkenness as an aberration. While Twain and others considered the glorification of feudalism an unforgivable act of betrayal against the nation's foundational principles—after all, had not the American Revolution been a struggle against the remnants of feudalism?—classical civilization, on the other hand, had supplied the founders with the intellectual resources necessary to defend republicanism against feudalism. Therefore, not even the staunchest abolitionist could feel entirely comfortable assaulting the fountainhead of republicanism for what he perceived to be its greatest impurity.[43]

But slavery was an important element of classical civilization, not an aberration, a universally accepted practice, not a passing evil, and Greco-Roman slavery exerted a profound influence on the antebellum South. While the classics provided vital inspiration to the forces of republicanism and democracy in the United States during the American Revolution, the Constitutional Convention, and the age of Jacksonian democracy, they also provided equally essential support to the proslavery forces of the Old South. While they helped build the modern Athens, they also helped cleave it asunder.

Epilogue

LOOKING BACK FROM the early twentieth century, Henry Adams's chief complaint about his Harvard education in the 1850s was that its classical emphasis had left him unprepared for life in the modern world. Writing about himself in the third person, he claimed:

> At any other moment in human history, this education, including its political and literary bias, would have been not only good, but quite the best. Society had always welcomed and flattered men so endowed. Henry Adams had every reason to be well pleased with it, and not ill pleased with himself. He had all he wanted. He saw no reason for thinking that anyone else had more.... Only on looking back, fifty years later, at his own figure in 1854, and pondering on the needs of the twentieth century, he wondered whether, on the whole, the boy of 1854 stood nearer to the thought of 1904, or to that of the year 1.... The education he had received bore little relation to the education he needed. Speaking as an American of 1900, he had as yet no education at all. He knew not even where or how to begin.

Charles Francis Adams Jr. shared his brother's perception of the classics as outmoded. In a Phi Beta Kappa address at Harvard in 1883, Charles Francis Jr. assaulted the traditional classical curriculum as irrelevant and useless, labeling it "A College Fetich." Greek and Latin, he declared, "are much more remote from the world of to-day than they were from the world of thirty years ago." He attributed this transformation to the swift progress of science: "The human mind, outside of the cloisters, is occupied with a class of thoughts—scientific thoughts—which do not find their nutriment in the remote past."[1]

While Henry Adams's numerous admirers might question the notion that his education served him poorly, John Adams would certainly have been appalled by both of his great-grandsons' assaults on the classics. Having bequeathed land for the creation of a Greek and Latin academy at Quincy, the second president wrote in his will: "If any descendant of mine should ever presume to call it in question, I hereby pronounce him unworthy of me, and I hereby petition all future Legislators of the Commonwealth to pass a special law to defeat his impious intentions."[2]

This fundamental difference of opinion concerning classical education between the generation of John Adams and that of his great-grandsons epitomizes the vast change that had occurred between the eighteenth and twentieth centuries. To be more precise, by Henry's own testimony, the bulk of this change must have occurred between his graduation from Harvard in the 1850s and the start of the twentieth century. No Adams before Henry and Charles Francis Jr.—certainly not their direct ancestors, John, John Quincy, and Charles Francis—had ever questioned the utility of the classics. On the contrary, each of them had argued passionately, against a vocal minority of critics, that the classics were indispensable to what mattered most: the teaching of virtue and republicanism. Even Henry was content with his own classical training for a long period of time, until "looking back, fifty years later."

As with so much else, the Civil War was the great turning point in the history of the classics in America. The war laid to rest the issue of slavery and produced new controversies, nearly all of them economic. The Second Industrial Revolution, which received much of its initial capital in the United States from the Union government's massive wartime spending, transformed American life, creating, for the first time, a large European-style proletariat. The agricultural lifestyle experienced a dramatic decline, not since reversed; put out of work by the global glut of grain that resulted from European peace and the farmers' own productivity, many farmers migrated to the cities to hold factory jobs. The classics could not address the prevailing issues of the protective tariff, the gold standard, and the regulation of corporations. Neither could the classics offer much in the dispute over Charles Darwin's theory of natural selection, though the ancient Greek philosopher Anaximander had been the first to allude to the possibility of evolution. Economics, engineering, and the sciences were viewed as the proper subjects of study in an industrial age; indeed, the federal government subsidized the study of engineering and agriculture under the Morrill Act of 1862. Most of the leading industrialists, the era's greatest role models, were self-made men with little formal education who scoffed at the classics. Andrew Carnegie wrote in the *New York Tribune* in 1890: "The prizetakers [in American business] have too many years the start of the [college] graduates; they have entered the race invariably in their teens—in the most valuable of all the years for learning anything—from fourteen to twenty, while the college student has been learning a little about the petty squabbles of a far-distant past, or trying to master languages which are dead, such knowledge as seems adapted for life on another planet." Meanwhile, the growth of international trade placed a premium on the knowledge of modern languages, and science so captivated public adulation that even the study of humanity was reconceived under the rubric of "social science," as though humans were as predictable as atoms.[3]

The Civil War, a catastrophe that caused the death of one out of every fifty Americans, generated a great crisis for both Christian theism and classical humanism, which shared an emphasis on the existence of a universal moral order. One can see this in the transformation of leading intellectuals like the influential jurist and Supreme Court justice Oliver Wendell Holmes, who lost faith in the moral platitudes of both the Bible and classical literature. Having served in a regiment that fought in some of the bloodiest battles of the Civil War, Holmes had been wounded three times and had seen numerous friends killed. He had come to blame the unprecedented carnage of the war on the unbending moral certitude of both the abolitionists and the defenders of slavery—on their blind devotion to shadowy and unreal concepts that hardly justified the horrific deaths of so many flesh-and-blood men. He wrote, "It is well that some of us don't know that we know anything." The Civil War had stripped Holmes of his belief in strongly held belief, whether in God or in human reason. While there were still a few things for which he was willing to fight, he noted, "Instead of saying that they ought to be I merely say they are part of the kind of world that I like." Such subjective moral preference "hardly warrants our talking much about absolute truth." As late as the 1930s, shortly before his death, Holmes dissolved in tears when attempting to read a poem about the Civil War. Looking back so many years later, what grieved Holmes deeply was not so much the loss of his close friends as the loss of the innocent, idealistic antebellum world, a world that had bled to death on Civil War battlefields and was now irretrievable. According to a friend, "He told me that after the Civil War the world never seemed quite right again." In a series of influential books and essays Holmes assaulted the classical doctrine of natural law, claiming that both moral and statutory law were ever-changing products of experience, not universal rules inherent in nature and accessible by human reason.[4]

The Civil War itself seemed a monumental refutation of the Aristotelian notion that humans were rational creatures capable of discerning and applying universal moral laws. In this respect, as the first modern war, the Civil War played much the same role within the American intelligentsia that World War I, the first modern war in Europe, played among European intellectuals. It was no coincidence that Oxford and Cambridge abolished the Greek entrance requirement after World War I.[5]

Both the Bible, which was also under assault from "higher critics" who called into question its reliability, and the works of classical antiquity began to seem to many American intellectuals like outdated relics of a primitive past. Because of its emphases on faith and original sin, the Bible was better able to endure the onslaught of the skeptics than the classics, with their emphases on reason and the possibility of human improvement.

Finally, another reason that the aristocratic intellectual class, the historic defenders of the classics, might have abandoned their traditional post of defense against all "barbarians" who would dare to abolish the classical languages requirement in the schools is that by democratizing the classics, the antebellum period had drastically reduced their utility as aristocratic markers. By the Gilded Age, the very time when the classics seemed to be losing their intellectual utility, the American elite had lost their age-old monopoly on them, so that they no longer served as a reliable badge of social status. In short, a perfect storm of rising skepticism and moral relativism, materialism spawned by the Industrial Revolution, the increasing glorification of science, and the changing self-interest of the American elite finally granted the utilitarians the victory that had so often eluded them in the past. Of course, these are all hypotheses that must be tested by further research, since they lie outside the central focus of this study, the antebellum period.

At any rate, although the Civil War seems to have been crucial in inaugurating the decline of the classics, that decline was a gradual process. Overturning the pedagogical traditions of nearly two millennia was no easy task. The utilitarians had to spend several decades after the Civil War laying the groundwork before they were finally able to reap the victory. In 1886 Harvard eliminated its Greek entrance requirement. Other older universities like Yale, as well as new universities like Cornell, Johns Hopkins, and the University of Chicago, followed suit in the ensuing decade, as universities moved toward curricula that allowed greater specialization in business, science, and other "majors." There were thirty-nine different degrees by 1900, and graduate programs arose. By that time only one-third of Harvard students elected to take Latin, only one-sixth Greek. A 1912 study of 155 colleges found that two-thirds required neither Greek nor Latin. Like other college teachers, classics professors became specialized and insular, rarely writing for the general public. Students abandoned the old classical societies for sports and for thoroughly unclassical fraternities and sororities, ironically identified by Greek letters. Greek and Latin were subsumed into the "humanities," a category that also included modern history, literature, philosophy, and music. As Caroline Winterer has noted, "At the same time that colleges began to liquidate Greek and Latin requirements, the humanities quietly wrapped themselves in the mantle of culture previously worn by the classical languages alone." As the percentage of educated Americans studying the classics decreased, the role of classical knowledge in the political culture declined.[6]

The classics continued to influence Americans surreptitiously, of course. Just as Henry Adams assaulted the classics with a sharpness of mind that had been produced, at least partly, by years of classical study, so the classically educated Emma Lazarus seemed to repudiate classical models even in a poem written for one of the most famous neoclassical icons of the modern world, the Statue of Liberty. For the gigantic lady with the classical robes and the strikingly classical features, who was clearly based on the colossi of the ancient Mediterranean, Lazarus wrote a poem called, what else, "The New Colossus." The first two lines of the poem declare:

> Not like the brazen giant of Greek fame,
> With conquering limbs astride from land to land.

This was a clear reference to the Colossus of Rhodes, one of the famed Seven Wonders of the Ancient World, which was long mistakenly believed to have straddled its harbor, an impossibly unstable position. Lest Lazarus's opening seem like a mundane reference to an alleged difference in statuary posture, seven lines later the poet, like a modern Pygmalion, gives life to the statue and has her speak to the very race of Pygmalion, albeit in the manner of a ventriloquist:

> "Keep, ancient lands, your storied pomp!" cries she
> With silent lips. "Give me your tired, your poor."

Lazarus's implication is that the United States will far outshine the ancient republics through its mercy to the world's poor and downtrodden. Yet, like the numerous claims of American superiority to the Greeks and Romans in the antebellum period, the poem's intense concern with antiquity belies its own pretense to originality and superiority, even if one leaves aside its dedication to a neoclassical icon. Like her predecessors, the poet doth protest too much.[7]

Nevertheless, reinforced by the ever-decreasing role of the classics in the American educational system, the belief that the classics were an outdated relic of a preindustrial order became so pervasive that by the mid-twentieth century even highly educated historians began to deny that the classics had ever played a large role in the American past. After all, if the classics were so irrelevant to modern concerns, how could they have contributed to the ideas of sober men like the founders of the United States? In 1967 Bernard Bailyn claimed that the founders had employed the classics as mere "window dressing." In an otherwise excellent chapter of his *History of the American Revolution* (1969) entitled "Britain in the Year 1763," John R. Alden wrote regarding eighteenth-century British education: "It was ancient rather than modern, classical rather than liberal, narrow rather than broad." This was an odd statement, since, in the eighteenth century at least, a "liberal education" was synonymous with a classical education, and since most critics of classical education accused it of being too broad and unspecialized, not too narrow. Alden then proceeded, in a mystified tone: "Even so, talent and genius bloomed, within and without the universities, and the annals of Britain in the first decades of the reign of George III are studded with the names of brilliant poets, orators, dramatists, novelists, and artists. Interspersed among them are a few gifted politicians." Alden seemed perplexed that so many Britons had managed to prevail over the handicap of a classical education and produce so many works of genius.[8]

This is not to say that non–classics majors ceased all study of Greece and Rome. Beginning in World War I, Western civilization courses that portrayed Greece and Rome as the founders of that civilization arose, quickly becoming a core requirement at most universities. Furthermore, Latin continued to be popular in high schools until the 1940s. As late as 1900, one-half of all public high-school students, and an even larger percentage of parochial-school students, were studying Latin.[9]

Nor did the popular culture cease to express interest in the ancient world. The "sword and sandals" movies of the 1950s and early 1960s (e.g., *Spartacus* and *Antony and Cleopatra*) were successful at the box office. Journalists continued to allude to the classics. The most popular analogy in 1940–1941 was the comparison of Adolf Hitler with Philip of Macedon. Both Hitler and Philip had used many of the same tactics to lull rival nations to sleep in order to render them incapable of armed resistance. But once the United States entered World War II, Nazi Germany became Sparta, the United States Athens: the one harsh, anti-intellectual, totalitarian, and militaristic, the other mild, intellectual, democratic, and peaceful. Mars M. Westinghouse even contended, with some evidence, that Hitler had consciously modeled Nazi Germany on ancient Sparta. During the Cold War the Soviet Union easily assumed Germany's position in the minds of journalists as the modern Sparta. NATO was compared to the Athenian (Delian) League, the Warsaw Pact to the Spartan (Peloponnesian) League. The analogy was especially chilling since Sparta had won the Peloponnesian War, a fact not lost on some journalists, who compared both the Korean and Vietnam wars to Athens' fatal invasion of Sicily. Their critique of the Peloponnesian War was quintessentially twentieth-century American. They blamed the war itself and Athens' defeat on Athenian imperialism—in other words, on Athens' unwillingness to extend the blessings of its egalitarianism beyond the home front. By contrast, Thucydides and Plutarch had seemed to fault the mob hysteria that they considered endemic to democracy for these tragedies. The ancient historians had blamed the volatile democracy's mistreatment of its leaders for Nicias' fatal vacillation and had perceived the catastrophic Sicilian expedition as the triumph of the mobs' arrogance and ignorance over calculation and prudence. What the ancients and early moderns viewed as a defeat produced by excessive democracy, twentieth-century journalists perceived as a failure caused by an insufficiency of democracy. To these journalists, Athens was like one of its own tragic characters, a nearly perfect entity possessing a single, fatal flaw. The lesson for the United States was to apply its own democratic principles to its foreign policy, not to abandon them.[10]

Not until the 1960s did Americans begin to question Athens' claim to the now-crucial title—one claimed even by Communist nations and other authoritarian regimes—of "democracy." Feminists pointed to Athens' disfranchisement and harsh treatment of women, along with its institution of slavery, to challenge its credentials as a democracy. It was ironic that these critics should assault Athens for its lack of egalitarianism, since the founders had criticized the polis for its excessive egalitarianism. This difference in perception reveals an ambiguity in the word "democracy," the Greek term for "rule by the people." Those who argued, as did the founders, that democracy entailed direct legislation by the citizenry, however narrowly constituted, considered it a purely ancient phenomenon. By contrast, those who argue that democracy entails the potential political participation, however indirect, of all adults, consider it a purely modern phenomenon.[11]

American perceptions of the ancients have undergone a dramatic transformation since the days of the founders, a transformation that mirrors tremendous changes in American society. The founders viewed Rome and Sparta as partial republican models, while considering Athens an antimodel because of the alleged instability and violence of its direct democracy. By contrast, antebellum Americans considered Athens a model precisely because of its democracy, to which many attributed the polis's staggering intellectual and artistic achievements. Southerners especially admired Athens because its egalitarianism within the ranks of adult male citizens was joined to the inegalitarian institution of slavery, as in the antebellum South. Most modern Americans who have any knowledge of classical history consider Athens a partial model, a city of democratic geniuses whose only unforgivable fault was the narrowness of its franchise, while detesting Sparta as the horrid breeder of totalitarianism and faulting republican Rome for its oligarchic government.

Although a decline in popular knowledge of the classics has reduced the number of classical analogies in recent years, the comparisons will probably never cease while humans still have the same fundamental problems and still have access to the classics. For the Greek and Roman classics, by portraying the human condition in all of its forms, lend themselves to universal application. The classics have provided a giant smorgasbord, from which various individuals and societies have concocted the feasts that have best suited their tastes. But classical works have not been mere reflectors of the personalities and cultures of the individuals and societies that have read them. They have also reinforced and helped give precise form to these often vague tendencies.

Notes

Preface

1. Books concerning the influence of the classics on the founders include Paul A. Rahe, *Republics, Ancient and Modern: Classical Republicanism and the American Revolution* (Chapel Hill: University of North Carolina Press, 1992); Susan Ford Wiltshire, *Greece, Rome, and the Bill of Rights* (Norman: University of Oklahoma Press, 1992); Carl J. Richard, *The Founders and the Classics: Greece, Rome, and the American Enlightenment* (Cambridge, Mass.: Harvard University Press, 1994); M. N. S. Sellers, *American Republicanism: Roman Ideology in the United States Constitution* (New York: New York University Press, 1994); and Gary L. Gregg, ed., *Vital Remnants: America's Founding and the Western Tradition* (Wilmington, Del.: ISI, 1999).
2. Meyer Reinhold, *Classica Americana: The Greek and Roman Heritage in the United States* (Detroit: Wayne State University Press, 1984); Caroline Winterer, *The Culture of Classicism: Ancient Greece and Rome in American Intellectual Life, 1780–1910* (Baltimore: Johns Hopkins University Press, 2002); Caroline Winterer, *The Mirror of Antiquity: American Women and the Classical Tradition, 1750–1900* (Ithaca: Cornell University Press, 2007), pp. 138–194.
3. Reinhold, *Classica Americana*, pp. 59–108, 125–136, 179.

1. Classical Conditioning: School, Home, and Society

1. Sheldon D. Cohen, *A History of Colonial Education, 1607–1776* (New York: John Wiley and Sons, 1974), pp. 11, 22–24; Robert Middlekauff, "A Persistent Tradition: The Classical Curriculum in Eighteenth-Century New England,"

William and Mary Quarterly, 3d ser., 18 (January 1961):56; Howard Mumford Jones, *Revolution and Romanticism* (Cambridge, Mass.: Harvard University Press, 1974), pp. 121–123, 343.

2. Meyer Reinhold, *Classica Americana: The Greek and Roman Heritage in the United States* (Detroit: Wayne State University Press, 1984), p. 183; Frederick Rudolph, *Curriculum: A History of the American Undergraduate Course of Study since 1636* (San Francisco: Jossey-Bass Publishers, 1977), p. 60; James McLachlan, *American Boarding Schools: A Historical Study* (New York: Scribner's Sons, 1970), p. 85.

3. Edward L. Pierce, ed., *Memoir and Letters of Charles Sumner* (London: Sampson Low, 1878), vol. 1, p. 37; Aida DiPace Donald et al., eds., *Diary of Charles Francis Adams* (Cambridge, Mass.: Harvard University Press, 1964–), June 20, 1824, vol. 1, p. 198.

4. Joseph R. Berrigan, "The Impact of the Classics upon the South," *Classical Journal* 64 (Winter 1968–1969):18–20; Robert Meriwether et al., eds., *The Papers of John C. Calhoun* (Columbia: University of South Carolina Press, 1959–), Robert M. T. Hunter, "The Life of John C. Calhoun," 1843, vol. 17, pp. 8–9; John C. Calhoun, *A Disquisition on Government and Selections from the Discourse*, ed. Gordon Post (New York: Macmillan, 1953), p. viii; John Niven, *John C. Calhoun and the Price of Union: A Biography* (Baton Rouge: Louisiana State University Press, 1988), pp. 3–16; Charles M. Wiltse, *John C. Calhoun* (Indianapolis: Bobbs-Merrill, 1944–1951), vol. 1, p. 29; Edgar W. Knight, ed., *A Documentary History of Education in the South before 1860* (Chapel Hill: University of North Carolina Press, 1949–1953), A Description of the University of Georgia, 1849, vol. 3, pp. 344; Introduction, vol. 4, pp. 2–3.

5. Kim Tolley, "Science for Ladies, Classics for Gentlemen: A Comparative Analysis of Scientific Subjects in the Curricula of Boys' and Girls' Secondary Schools in the United States, 1794–1850," *History of Education Quarterly* 36 (Summer 1996):132n9, 143, 151; Christie Ann Farnham, *The Education of the Southern Belle: Higher Education and Student Socialization in the Antebellum South* (New York: New York University Press, 1994), p. 31. For reference to the exclusion of girls from Germany's famous classical schools (*gymnasia*) see Suzanne L. Marchand, *Down from Olympus: Archaeology and Philhellenism in Germany, 1750–1970* (Princeton: Princeton University Press, 1996), p. 5.

6. Mary Kelley, "Reading Women/Women Reading: The Making of Learned Women in Antebellum America," *Journal of American History* 83 (September 1996):404; Caroline Winterer, *The Mirror of Antiquity: American Women and the Classical Tradition, 1750–1900* (Ithaca: Cornell University Press, 2007), pp. 146–147.

7. Michael O'Brien, *Conjectures of Order: Intellectual Life and the American South, 1810–1860* (Chapel Hill: University of North Carolina Press, 2004), p. 592.

8. Winterer, *Mirror of Antiquity*, pp. 181–182, 187.

9. William H. McGuffey, ed., *McGuffey's Sixth Eclectic Reader* (New York: American Book Company, 1880), pp. 205–206, 234–238, 281–285, 390–392,

401–405; John H. Westerhoff III, *McGuffey and His Readers: Piety, Morality, and Education in Nineteenth-Century America* (Nashville: Abingdon, 1978), pp. 14, 136, 150.

10. Richard M. Gummere, *The American Colonial Mind and the Classical Tradition: Essays in Comparative Culture* (Cambridge, Mass.: Harvard University Press, 1963), pp. 56–57.

11. George P. Schmidt, "Intellectual Crosscurrents in American Colleges, 1825–1855," *American Historical Review* 42 (October 1936):46; Knight, *Documentary History*, Extracts from the Ordinances for the Government of the University of Alabama, vol. 3, p. 244; William D. Williamson of Maine Visits and Comments on the University of North Carolina, 1843, vol. 3, p. 297; Minutes of the Board of Trustees of Davidson College, North Carolina, 1836–1854, vol. 4, pp. 308–309; Announcement of Sharon College, Mississippi, 1842, vol. 4, p. 331; Michael O'Brien, *A Character of Hugh Legaré* (Knoxville: University of Tennessee Press, 1985), p. 14.

12. Charles Coleman Sellers, *Dickinson College: A History* (Middletown, Conn.: Wesleyan University Press, 1973), p. 221; Rudolph, *Curriculum*, pp. 54, 64–66; Niven, *John C. Calhoun and the Price of Union*, p. 17.

13. Walter R. Agard, "Classics on the Midwest Frontier," *Classical Journal* 51 (1955):106–110; Rudolph, *Curriculum*, p. 60; Schmidt, "Intellectual Crosscurrents in American Colleges," p. 62; Reinhold, *Classica Americana*, p. 330.

14. Rudolph, *Curriculum*, p. 79; Knight, *Documentary History*, William D. Williamson of Maine Visits and Comments on the University of North Carolina, 1843, vol. 3, pp. 297–298; Schedule of Classes, South Carolina College, 1854, vol. 3, p. 375; Classification of Students in the University of Virginia by Subjects Studied, 1857, vol. 3, p. 424; An Act to Establish the University of Texas, 1858, vol. 3, p. 442; Minutes of the Board of Trustees of Davidson College, North Carolina, 1836–1854, vol. 4, p. 309; Laws of Wake Forest College, North Carolina, 1839, vol. 4, p. 324; Announcement of Sharon College, Mississippi, 1842, vol. 4, pp. 331–333; O'Brien, *Conjectures of Order*, p. 1007; Richard Beale Davis, *Intellectual Life in Jefferson's Virginia* (Chapel Hill: University of North Carolina Press, 1973), pp. 55–57, 69; Schmidt, "Intellectual Crosscurrents in American Colleges," pp. 62, 66; O'Brien, *Character of Hugh Legaré*, p. 14.

15. Knight, *Documentary History*, Robert Edward Lee Is Endorsed to Secretary of War John C. Calhoun for Appointment to the United States Military Academy, 1824, vol. 4, p. 150; Board of Visitors of Virginia Military Institute Memorializes the General Assembly, 1845, vol. 4, p. 174; Comments on James H. Thornwell's Letter to Governor Manning on Military Schools in South Carolina, 1854, vol. 4, p. 192; Editorial on the Opening of the Military Academy of Louisiana, 1860, vol. 4, pp. 229; Regulations Prepared by Sherman for the Military Academy of Louisiana, 1860, vol. 4, p. 230; Elizabeth Fox-Genovese and Eugene D. Genovese, *The Mind of the Master Class: History and Faith in the Southern Slaveholders' Worldview* (Cambridge: Cambridge University Press, 2005), p. 254; Meriwether et al., *Papers of John C. Calhoun*, James H. Rion to Calhoun, November 18, 1843, vol. 17, p. 551.

16. Tolley, "Science for Ladies, Classics for Gentlemen," p. 135; Winterer, *Mirror of Antiquity*, pp. 150, 154; Louis B. Wright, *Culture on the Moving Frontier* (Bloomington: Indiana University Press, 1955), pp. 104, 152; Farnham, *Education of the Southern Belle*, p. 32.
17. Knight, *Documentary History*, Educational Activities of the Baptists in Mississippi, 1852, vol. 4, pp. 399; Report on the Inauguration of Spartanburg Female College, South Carolina, 1855, vol. 4, pp. 441–442; A Syllabus of a Course of Vacation Reading Is Provided for the Students at South Carolina Female Collegiate Institute, 1836, vol. 5, pp. 413–416; Sharon Female College Is Established in Madison County, Mississippi, 1843, vol. 5, p. 421; Suggestions for Placing a Daughter at School Are Made, 1853, vol. 5, p. 435; The Purposes of Spartanburg Female College, South Carolina, Are Given, 1855, vol. 5, p. 440; Farnham, *Education of the Southern Belle*, pp. 15, 17–18, 20, 22, 24–25, 27; Fox-Genovese and Genovese, *Mind of the Master Class*, p. 257; Barbara Solomon, *In the Company of Educated Women: A History of Women and Higher Education in America* (New Haven: Yale University Press, 1985), p. 23; O'Brien, *Conjectures of Order*, p. 260.
18. Susan Phinney Conrad, *Perish the Thought: Intellectual Women in Romantic America, 1830–1860* (Oxford: Oxford University Press, 1976), pp. 196–198, 208.
19. Caroline Winterer, *The Culture of Classicism: Ancient Greece and Rome in American Intellectual Life, 1780–1910* (Baltimore: Johns Hopkins University Press, 2002), pp. 32–33, 56–57; Reinhold, *Classica Americana*, pp. 185–186; Richard Hofstadter and Wilson Smith, eds., *American Higher Education: A Documentary History* (Chicago: University of Chicago Press, 1961), Robert Finley on National Uniformity in Textbooks, 1815, vol. 1, pp. 220–221.
20. James McLachlan, "Classical Names, American Identities," in John W. Eadie, ed., *Classical Traditions in Early America* (Ann Arbor: Center for the Coordination of Ancient and Modern Studies, 1976), pp. 87–91; James McLachlan, "The Choice of Hercules," in Lawrence Stone, ed., *The University in Society* (Princeton: Princeton University Press, 1974), vol. 2, pp. 474, 478; Reinhold, *Classica Americana*, p. 154; Rudolph, *Curriculum*, pp. 95–96.
21. Knight, *Documentary History*, Hampden-Sydney College Holds Commencement Exercises, 1825, vol. 4, p. 287; Spartanburg, South Carolina, and Its Colleges Are Praised, 1857, vol. 4, p. 481; Commencement Exercises at Normal College, North Carolina, Are Reported, 1857, vol. 5, p. 256; Wayne K. Durill, "The Power of Ancient Words: Classical Teaching and Social Change at South Carolina College," *Journal of Southern History* 65 (August 1999):478.
22. Paul Revere Frothingham, *Edward Everett: Orator and Statesman* (Boston: Houghton Mifflin, 1925; reprint, Port Washington, N.Y.: Kennikat Press, 1971), pp. 58–59; Reinhold, *Classica Americana*, pp. 184–185, 205; Winterer, *Culture of Classicism*, p. 52; William H. Gilman et al., eds., *The Journals and Miscellaneous Notebooks of Ralph Waldo Emerson* (Cambridge, Mass.: Harvard University Press, 1960–1982), April 4, 1820, vol. 1, p. 13; Donald et al., *Diary of Charles Francis Adams*, September 27, 1824, vol. 1, p. 340; October 7, 1824, vol. 1, p. 366.

Notes to Pages 12–18 — 217

23. Winterer, *Culture of Classicism*, pp. 59–61, 76, 95.
24. Donald et al., *Diary of Charles Francis Adams*, December 26, 1831, vol. 4, p. 205; Gilman et al., *Journals of Ralph Waldo Emerson*, February 11, 1855, vol. 13, p. 401.
25. Michael O'Brien, "Politics, Romanticism, and Hugh Legaré: The Fondness of Disappointed Love," and Richard Lounsbury, "Ludibria Rerum Mortalium: Charlestonian Intellectuals and Their Classics," in David Moltke-Hansen and Michael O'Brien, eds., *Intellectual Life in Antebellum Charleston* (Knoxville: University of Tennessee Press, 1986), pp. 142, 339, 347–348, 354, 357, 359; O'Brien, *Character of Hugh Legaré*, pp. 81, 95, 97, 104.
26. George Fitzhugh, *Cannibals All: Slaves without Masters* (Richmond: A. Morris, 1857; reprint, Cambridge, Mass.: Harvard University Press, 1960), p. 58; George Fitzhugh, *Sociology for the South, or The Failure of Free Society* (Richmond: A. Morris, 1854; reprint, New York: Burt Franklin, 1965), p. 159.
27. Winterer, *Culture of Classicism*, pp. 92, 150; Charles M. Wiltse, ed., *The Papers of Daniel Webster: Correspondence* (Hanover, N.H.: University Press of New England, 1974–), Daniel Fletcher Webster to Webster, December 24, 1830, vol. 3, pp. 92; Durill, "Power of Ancient Words," pp. 483, 489; Reinhold, *Classica Americana*, p. 333; Charles Minnigerode, "The Greek Dramatists," *Southern Literary Messenger* 8 (1842):606–611, 793–798; 9 (1843):96–104.
28. Durill, "Power of Ancient Words," p. 495; Michael O'Brien, ed., *All Clever Men, Who Make Their Way: Critical Discourse in the Old South* (Athens: University of Georgia Press, 1992), George Frederick Holmes, "Hegel's Philosophy of History," 1843, p. 222; Neal Gillespie, *The Collapse of Orthodoxy: The Intellectual Ordeal of George Frederick Holmes* (Charlottesville: University Press of Virginia, 1972), pp. 10, 72, 89–90.
29. Reinhold, *Classica Americana*, pp. 204–208, 211; Ward W. Briggs Jr., "Basil L. Gildersleeve at the University of Virginia," in Herbert W. Benario and Ward W. Briggs Jr., eds., *Basil Lanneau Gildersleeve: An American Classicist* (Baltimore: Johns Hopkins University Press, 1986), p. 9; Durill, "Power of Ancient Words," pp. 471, 487; Frank Friedel, *Francis Lieber: Nineteenth-Century Liberal* (Baton Rouge: Louisiana State University Press, 1947), pp. 39, 138, 184.
30. Winterer, *Culture of Classicism*, pp. 59–60, 79–80; Briggs, "Basil L. Gildersleeve at the University of Virginia," pp. 12–13; George A. Kennedy, "Gildersleeve, the Journal, and Philology in America," in Benario and Briggs, *Basil Lanneau Gildersleeve*, pp. 42, 44.
31. Richard Beale Davis, *Literature and Society in Early Virginia, 1608–1840* (Baton Rouge: Louisiana State University Press, 1973), p. 301.
32. Winterer, *Culture of Classicism*, pp. 125–129.
33. George H. Callcott, *History in the United States, 1800–1860* (Baltimore: Johns Hopkins Press, 1970), pp. 58, 92–94.
34. Winterer, *Culture of Classicism*, pp. 34, 36; Durill, "Power of Ancient Words," pp. 469–470; Lounsbury, "Ludibria Rerum Mortalium," p. 365.
35. Wiltse, *Papers of Daniel Webster*, Autobiography, 1829, vol. 1, pp. 9–10, 13; John Adams to Webster, December 23, 1821, vol. 1, p. 298; Daniel Fletcher Webster to Webster, December 24, 1830, vol. 3, p. 92.

36. Stephen Botein, "Cicero as Role Model for Early American Lawyers," *Classical Journal* 73 (April–May 1978):318–320; Lounsbury, "Ludibria Rerum Mortalium," p. 338; O'Brien, *Character of Hugh Legaré*, p. 19; Davis, *Literature and Society in Early Virginia*, p. 302.
37. O'Brien, *Character of Hugh Legaré*, pp. 106, 109; Fox-Genovese and Genovese, *Mind of the Master Class*, p. 277; Arthur H. Shaffer, "David Ramsay and the Limits of Revolutionary Nationalism," in Moltke-Hansen and O'Brien, *Intellectual Life in Antebellum Charleston*, p. 48.
38. Reinhold, *Classica Americana*, pp. 268–272; William Charvat et al., eds., *The Works of Nathaniel Hawthorne* (Columbus: Ohio State University Press, 1962–1988), French and Italian Notebooks, March 23, 1858, vol. 14, p. 138; April 12, 1858, vol. 14, p. 166; June 2, 1858, vol. 14, p. 267; June 11, 1858, vol. 14, pp. 307–308; William Vance, *America's Rome* (New Haven: Yale University Press, 1989), vol. 1, pp. 294, 363–364; Pierce, *Memoir and Letters of Charles Sumner*, Sumner to George S. Hilliard, May 19, 1839, vol. 2, p. 99; July 13, 1839, vol. 2, p. 103; David B. Tyack, *George Ticknor and the Boston Brahmins* (Cambridge, Mass.: Harvard University Press, 1967), p. 70.
39. O'Brien, *Conjectures of Order*, p. 153.
40. Peter Stein, "The Attraction of the Civil Law in Post-Revolutionary America," *Virginia Law Review* 52 (1966):404–411, 419–420; Peter Shaw, *The Character of John Adams* (Chapel Hill: University of North Carolina Press, 1976), p. 31; Joseph Towne Wheeler, "Reading Interests of the Professional Classes in Colonial Maryland, 1700–1776," *Maryland Historical Magazine* 36 (September 1941):283; Richard J. Hoffman, "Classics in the Courts of the United States, 1790–1800," *American Journal of Legal History* 22 (January 1978):57, 62, 68–69, 71–73; M. H. Hoeflich, *Roman and Civil Law and the Development of Anglo-American Jurisprudence in the Nineteenth Century* (Athens: University of Georgia Press, 1997), pp. 44, 135, 139.
41. Hoeflich, *Roman and Civil Law*, pp. 27–28, 42, 52, 57–64, 68.
42. Ibid., pp. 2, 7, 51, 72, 134, 138.
43. Vance, *America's Rome*, vol. 1, pp. 17–18; Winterer, *Mirror of Antiquity*, p. 216n26.
44. Gilbert Chinard, *Honest John Adams* (Boston: Little, Brown, 1933), pp. 11–12; Adrienne Koch and William Peden, eds., *The Selected Writings of John and John Quincy Adams* (New York: Alfred A. Knopf, 1946), John Adams to Benjamin Waterhouse, April 24, 1785, p. 72; Charles Francis Adams, ed., *Memoirs of John Quincy Adams, Comprising Portions of His Diary from 1795 to 1848* (Philadelphia, 1874–1877; reprint, New York: AMS Press, 1970), June 6, 1795, vol. 1, pp. 168–169; Douglas Adair and John A. Schutz, *The Spur of Fame: Dialogues of John Adams and Benjamin Rush, 1805–1813* (San Marino, Calif.: Huntington Library, 1966), John Adams to Benjamin Rush, July 23, 1806, p. 59.
45. Reinhold, *Classica Americana*, pp. 239, 259; Adams, *Memoirs of John Quincy Adams*, August 13, 1809, vol. 2, p. 5; August 14, 1809, vol. 2, p. 6; December 7, 1809, vol. 2, p. 76; October 9, 1811, vol. 2, p. 315; October 13, 1811, vol. 2, pp. 316–317; February 12, 1812, vol. 2, p. 342; April 5, 1813, vol. 2, p. 456; May 10, 1819, vol. 4, p. 361.

46. Adams, *Memoirs of John Quincy Adams*, June 30, 1825, vol. 7, p. 30; October 15, 1826, vol. 7, p. 151; November 18, 1827, vol. 7, p. 356; November 30, 1827, vol. 7, p. 365; June 29, 1828, vol. 7, p. 415; February 4, 1828, vol. 7, p. 421; March 16, 1828, vol. 7, p. 475; March 17, 1828, vol. 7, pp. 475–476; Donald et al., *Diary of Charles Francis Adams*, Introduction, vol. 4, p. vii.
47. Adams, *Memoirs of John Quincy Adams*, March 16, 1829, vol. 8, p. 114; March 17, 1829, vol. 8, p. 114; March 20, 1829, vol. 8, p. 117; April 3, 1829, vol. 8, pp. 127–128; April 10, 1829, vol. 8, p. 135; October 24, 1830, vol. 8, p. 243; November 8, 1830, vol. 8, p. 248; Donald et al., *Diary of Charles Francis Adams*, February 18, 1830, vol. 3, p. 166n1; Jack Shepherd, *Cannibals of the Heart: A Personal Biography of Louisa Catherine and John Quincy Adams* (New York: McGraw-Hill, 1980), p. 6.
48. John Quincy Adams, *Lectures on Rhetoric and Oratory* (Cambridge, Mass: Hilliard and Metcalf, 1810; reprint, New York: Russell and Russell, 1962), vol. 2, pp. 396–397; Gilman et al., *Journals of Ralph Waldo Emerson*, 1861, vol. 6, pp. 330–331.
49. Adams, *Memoirs of John Quincy Adams*, April 24, 1829, vol. 8, p. 143; April 30, 1829, vol. 8, pp. 148–149; April 6, 1835, vol. 9, p. 231; October 17, 1837, vol. 9, p. 415; March 14–18, 1839, vol. 10, pp. 119–122.
50. Ibid., September 3, 1838, vol. 10, pp. 32–35; May 22, 1839, vol. 10, p. 123.
51. Samuel Flagg Bemis, *John Quincy Adams and the Union* (New York: Alfred A. Knopf, 1956), p. 210; William Lee Miller, *Arguing about Slavery: The Great Battle in the United States Congress* (New York: Alfred A. Knopf, 1996), pp. 179, 465; Anthony Everett, *Cicero: The Life and Times of Rome's Greatest Politician* (New York: Random House, 2003), pp. 79, 83.
52. Shepherd, *Cannibals of the Heart*, pp. 165, 274; Donald et al., *Diary of Charles Francis Adams*, May 1, 1824, vol. 1, p. 106; February 4, 1828, vol. 2, p. 171n2; February 10, 1828, vol. 2, p. 171n2; November 15, 1832, vol. 4, p. 399n1; Bemis, *John Quincy Adams and the Union*, p. 204.
53. Reinhold, *Classica Americana*, pp. 149, 151, 233; Shaw, *Character of John Adams*, p. 317; Koch and Peden, *Selected Writings of John and John Quincy Adams*, John Quincy Adams to John Adams, October 29, 1816, p. 291; Adams, *Memoirs of John Quincy Adams*, June 11, 1819, vol. 4, pp. 391–392.
54. Donald et al., *Diary of Charles Francis Adams*, January 4, 1820, vol. 1, p. 2; January 8, 1820, vol. 1, p. 4; January 20, 1820, vol. 1, p. 5; December 18, 1823, vol. 1, p. 10; March 8, 1824, vol. 1, p. 101; May 4, 1824, vol. 1, p. 115; May 10, 1824, vol. 1, p. 129; May 13, 1824, vol. 1, p. 136; May 18, 1824, vol. 1, p. 147; June 9, 1824, vol. 1, p. 177; June 23, 1824, vol. 2, p. 203; September 12–November 12, 1825, vol. 2, pp. 11–19; April 25, 1827, vol. 2, p. 124; July 31, 1827, vol. 2, p. 146; November 25, 1827, vol. 2, p. 172n2; February 10, 1828, vol. 2, p. 172n2; December 13, 1827, vol. 2, p. 192; January 4, 1828, vol. 2, p. 202; February 3–4, 1828, vol. 2, p. 210; July 14–15, 1828, vol. 2, pp. 256–257.
55. Ibid., August 20, 1836, vol. 7, p. 74; April 10, 1837, vol. 7, p. 221; May 22, 1837, vol. 7, p. 248; February 2, 1839, vol. 8, pp. 183. For some of Charles Francis's interesting comments about specific classics see October 11, 1829, vol. 3,

p. 42; November 20, 1829, vol. 3, p. 81; November 27, 1829, vol. 3, p. 88; February 5, 1830, vol. 3, p. 155; February 11, 1830, vol. 3, p. 159; February 18, 1830, vol. 3, pp. 165–166; March 2, 1830, vol. 3, p. 177; March 9, 1830, vol. 3, p. 182; March 23, 1830, vol. 3, p. 194; March 27, 1830, vol. 3, p. 198; October 16, 1830, vol. 3, pp. 340–341; November 12–13, 1830, vol. 3, p. 361; December 13–15, 1830, vol. 3, pp. 381–382; February 8, 1831, vol. 3, p. 418; June 20, 1831, vol. 4, p. 71; June 25, 1831, vol. 4, p. 75; July 8, 1831, vol. 4, p. 85; August 1, 1831, vol. 4, p. 102; August 12, 1831, vol. 4, p. 110; September 7, 1831, vol. 4, pp. 130–131; September 22, 1831, vol. 4, p. 143; November 24, 1831, vol. 4, p. 184; December 23, 1831, vol. 4, p. 203; January 10, 1832, vol. 4, p. 218; January 25, 1832, vol. 4, p. 228; February 25, 1832, vol. 4, p. 247; March 2–3, 1832, vol. 4, pp. 252–253; March 6–7, 1832, vol. 4, pp. 254–255; April 15, 1832, vol. 4, p. 279; June 11, 1832, vol. 4, p. 312; July 13, 1832, vol. 4, p. 328; September 12, 1836, vol. 7, p. 92; February 10, 1837, vol. 7, p. 182; July 10, 1837, vol. 7, p. 276; September 1, 1837, vol. 7, pp. 306–307; December 3, 1837, vol. 7, p. 353; February 13, 1838, vol. 7, p. 399; March 17, 1838, vol. 8, p. 8; September 21, 1838, vol. 8, p. 113; September 27, 1838, vol. 8, p. 116; December 8, 1838, vol. 8, p. 152; December 27, 1838, vol. 8, p. 161; February 7, 1839, vol. 8, p. 185; May 8, 1839, vol. 8, p. 230; June 28, 1839, vol. 8, p. 256; July 22–24, 1839, vol. 8, pp. 268–269; August 1, 1839, vol. 8, p. 273; October 9–10, 1839, vol. 8, p. 306; December 11, 1839, vol. 8, p. 340; January 31, 1840, vol. 8, p. 368; February 27, 1840, vol. 8, p. 379.

56. Charles Francis Adams, ed., *The Life and Works of John Adams* (Boston: Little, Brown, 1850–1856), vol. 1, p. 637.

57. Meriwether et al., *Papers of John C. Calhoun,* Calhoun to Thomas J. Johnson, March 20, 1836, vol. 13, p. 117; Calhoun to James Edward Calhoun Jr., November 3, 1847, vol. 24, p. 642; Calhoun to Anna Maria Calhoun Clemson, December 26, 1847, vol. 25, p. 40; Calhoun to James Edward Calhoun Jr., January 22, 1848, vol. 25, p. 142; Fox-Genovese and Genovese, *Mind of the Master Class,* p. 126.

58. Gilman et al., *Journals of Ralph Waldo Emerson,* March 18, 1836, vol. 5, p. 159; April 3, 1836, vol. 5, p. 159; 1850, vol. 11, p. 303; Ralph L. Rusk, ed., *The Letters of Ralph Waldo Emerson* (New York: Columbia University Press, 1939), Emerson to William Emerson, November 30, 1850, vol. 4, p. 236n230; Emerson to Ellen Emerson, December 18, 1852, vol. 4, p. 333; January 23, 1854, vol. 4, p. 422; Emerson to Lidian Emerson, January 7, 1853, vol. 4, p. 341.

59. Bernard Mayo, *Henry Clay: Spokesman of the New West* (Boston: Houghton Mifflin, 1937), vol. 1, pp. 26–27; Glyndon G. Van Deusen, *The Life of Henry Clay* (Boston: Little, Brown, 1937), pp. 11, 14.

60. Agard, "Classics on the Midwest Frontier," pp. 103–105. For references to Boston, Charleston, and the North Carolinian see Edwin A. Miles, "The Old South and the Classical World," *North Carolina Historical Review* 48 (1971):271. For references to Ovid, New York, and the Athenaeums see Talbot Hamlin, *Greek Revival Architecture in America* (Oxford: Oxford University Press, 1944), pp. 98, 266. For reference to Lexington see Wright, *Culture on the Moving Frontier,* p. 94. For reference to Syracuse see George R. Stewart,

Notes to Pages 32–35 — 221

Names on the Land: A Historical Account of Place-Naming in the United States (New York: Random House, 1945), p. 239. For reference to the ship names see Adams, *Memoirs of John Quincy Adams,* April 24, 1811, vol. 2, p. 256; June 22, 1811, vol. 2, p. 276; August 6, 1811, vol. 2, p. 289; September 29, 1820, vol. 5, p. 181. For references to Philippi and the *Leonidas* see Roy Basler, ed., *The Collected Works of Abraham Lincoln* (New Brunswick, N.J.: Rutgers University Press, 1953), Lincoln to Simon Cameron, July 18, 1861, vol. 4, p. 451n1; Lincoln to the House of Representatives, December 23, 1861, vol. 5, p. 79n1. For reference to Neptune see Francis H. Allen and Bradford Torrey, eds., *The Journal of Henry David Thoreau* (Salt Lake City: Gibbs M. Smith, 1984), September 12, 1853, vol. 5, p. 427n2. For references to Roman Nose and slave names see Sam B. Smith et al., eds., *The Papers of Andrew Jackson* (Knoxville: University of Tennessee Press, 1980), Eastern Cherokees to Jackson, July 2, 1817, vol. 4, p. 122; James Jackson Hanna to Jackson, January 30, 1820, vol. 4, p. 35; Drew Gilpin Faust, *James Henry Hammond and the Old South: A Design for Mastery* (Baton Rouge: Louisiana State University Press, 1982), pp. 84, 88; O'Brien, *Character of Hugh Legaré,* p. 5.

61. Hamlin, *Greek Revival Architecture in America,* p. 98; Rusk, *Letters of Ralph Waldo Emerson,* Emerson to John Boynton Hill, July 3, 1822, vol. 1, pp. 119–120; Winterer, *Mirror of Antiquity,* p. 157.
62. Wright, *Culture on the Moving Frontier,* pp. 230–231, 234.
63. Callcott, *History in the United States,* p. 93.
64. Marie Sally Cleary, *The Bulfinch Solution: Teaching the Ancient Classics in American Schools* (Salem, N.H.: Ayer, 1989), pp. 1, 20, 40–41, 48, 52, 74, 76; Burton Feldman and Robert D. Richardson, eds., *The Rise of Modern Mythology, 1680–1860* (Bloomington: Indiana University Press, 1972), pp. 509–510.
65. Knight, *Documentary History,* Extracts from the Speech of John Tyler in the General Assembly of Virginia on the Proposal to Move the College of William and Mary to Richmond, 1825, vol. 4, p. 267; Gene Waddell, "The Introduction of Greek Revival Architecture to Charleston," in David Moltke-Hansen, ed., *Art in the Lives of South Carolinians: Nineteenth-Century Chapters* (Charleston: Carolina Art Association, 1979), pp. Gwa-1–Gwa-2, Gwa-6; Reinhold, *Classica Americana,* pp. 218–219; Garry Wills, *Lincoln at Gettysburg: The Words That Remade America* (New York: Simon and Schuster, 1992), p. 43; Agard, "Classics on the Midwestern Frontier," p. 104.
66. Winterer, *Culture of Classicism,* p. 65; Hamlin, *Greek Revival Architecture in America,* pp. 70, 81, 86–87; Robert E. Riegel, *Young America, 1830–1840* (Norman: University of Oklahoma Press, 1949; reprint ed., Westport, Conn.: Greenwood Press, 1973), p. 10; Wendy A. Cooper, *Classical Taste in America, 1800–1840* (New York: Abbeville Press and Baltimore Museum of Art, 1993), pp. 78–79.
67. Hamlin, *Greek Revival Architecture in America,* pp. 97, 326; Kenneth W. Severens, "Architectural Taste in Ante-bellum Charleston," and Herbert A. Johnson, "Courthouse Design, Financing, and Maintenance in Antebellum South Carolina," in Moltke-Hansen, *Art in the Lives of South Carolinians,* pp. KS-4, HJ-2; Riegel, *Young America,* p. 365.

68. Cooper, *Classical Taste in America*, pp. 14, 32–33, 40, 46–50, 97, 142, 144, 146, 153, 165–168, 201–203, 208–209; Winterer, *Culture of Classicism*, pp. 144–145; Agard, "Classics on the Midwestern Frontier," p. 104.
69. Cooper, *Classical Taste in America*, pp. 238–239.
70. Ibid., pp. 15, 261–263; Miles, "Old South and the Classical World," p. 259; Vance, *America's Rome*, vol. 1, pp. 204, 226–228, 232–233, 248–249, 260, 320, 346; Caroline Winterer, "Venus on the Sofa: Women, Neoclassicism, and the Early American Republic," *Modern Intellectual History* 2 (Spring 2005):10.
71. R. A. McNeal, "Athens and Nineteenth-Century Panoramic Art," *International Journal of the Classical Tradition* 1 (Winter 1995):81–84; Winterer, *Culture of Classicism*, pp. 66–67; Cooper, *Classical Taste in America*, pp. 88–91.
72. Vance, *America's Rome*, vol. 1, pp. 4–5, 51, 77, 92–94.
73. Wayne Craven, "Horatio Greenough's Statue of Washington and Phidias' Zeus," *Art Quarterly* 26 (Winter 1963):429–430; Garry Wills, *Cincinnatus: George Washington and the Enlightenment* (Garden City, N.Y.: Doubleday, 1984), pp. 12–13, 70, 118; Callcott, *History in the United States*, p. 29; Cooper, *Classical Taste in America*, pp. 19–20, 65, 73, 165–166, 247–248.
74. Winterer, *Culture of Classicism*, p. 53.
75. Wills, *Lincoln at Gettysburg*, pp. 63–64; Cooper, *Classical Taste in America*, p. 21.
76. Meriwether et al., *Papers of John C. Calhoun*, vol. 10, p. 248; vol. 13, p. 67; vol. 14, p. 17; vol. 15, p. 7; vol. 17, p. 158; vol. 20, p. 185; vol. 22, p. 565. For reference to the use of "Gracchus" see Eugene D. Genovese, "The Gracchi and Their Mother in the Mind of American Slaveholders," *Journal of the Historical Society* 2 (Summer/Fall 2002):455. For reference to the Minerva Club see Wright, *Culture on the Moving Frontier*, p. 228. For reference to Cimon see Donald et al., *Diary of Charles Francis Adams*, May 2, 1831, vol. 4, p. 39.
77. Gillespie, *Collapse of Orthodoxy*, pp. 8, 10, 67–72, 90; Reinhold, *Classica Americana*, p. 331; O'Brien, *Character of Hugh Legaré*, pp. 60–61, 75, 247; Cooper, *Classical Taste in America*, pp. 191–192; Fox-Genovese and Genovese, *Mind of the Master Class*, p. 258.
78. Davis, *Literature and Society in Early Virginia*, pp. 278–279, 281, 284–285; Davis, *Intellectual Life in Jefferson's Virginia*, p. 114.
79. Margaret Malamud, *Ancient Rome and Modern America* (London: Wiley-Blackwell, forthcoming, 2009), p. 46; Wright, *Culture on the Moving Frontier*, p. 116.
80. Davis, *Intellectual Life in Jefferson's Virginia*, pp. 162, 372; Davis, *Literature and Society in Early Virginia*, pp. 280–281.

2. Democracy

1. Richard Hofstadter and Wilson Smith, eds., *American Higher Education: A Documentary History* (Chicago: University of Chicago Press, 1961), Daniel Webster Argues the Dartmouth Case, 1819, vol. 1, pp. 212–213; Charles

M. Wiltse, ed., *The Papers of Daniel Webster: Correspondence* (Hanover, N.H.: University Press of New England, 1974–), Autobiography, 1829, vol. 1, p. 13; William H. Gilman et al., eds., *The Journals and Miscellaneous Notebooks of Ralph Waldo Emerson* (Cambridge, Mass.: Harvard University Press, 1960–1982), May 1, 1845, vol. 9, pp. 379–381; Marcus Cunliffe, *George Washington: Man and Monument* (Boston: Little, Brown, 1958), p. 192; Kenneth E. Shewmaker, ed., *Daniel Webster: "The Completest Man"* (Hanover, N.H.: University Press of New England, 1990), The Dignity and Importance of History, 1852, pp. 131–132; Edwin A. Miles, "The Young American Nation and the Classical World," *Journal of the History of Ideas* 35 (April–June 1974):267; Freeman Cleaves, *Old Tippecanoe: William Henry Harrison and His Time* (New York: Scribner's Sons, 1939), pp. 6, 10.
2. Douglas L. Wilson, "What Jefferson and Lincoln Read," *Atlantic* 267 (January 1991):54–57, 60.
3. William Herndon, *Herndon's Life of Lincoln* (Cleveland: World Publishing Company, 1942; reprint, New York: Da Capo Press, 1983), p. 248; Garry Wills, *Lincoln at Gettysburg: The Words That Remade America* (New York: Simon and Schuster, 1992), p. 174.
4. Wills, *Lincoln at Gettysburg*, pp. 41, 52–59, 249–254.
5. Susan Ford Wiltshire, "Sam Houston and the *Iliad*," *Tennessee Historical Quarterly* 32 (Fall 1973):249–254.
6. Miles, "Young American Nation and the Classical World," p. 265; Talbot Hamlin, *Greek Revival Architecture in America* (Oxford: Oxford University Press, 1944), pp. 46, 238–239; Caroline Winterer, *The Mirror of Antiquity: American Women and the Classical Tradition, 1750–1900* (Ithaca: Cornell University Press, 2007), p. 38; Elizabeth Fox-Genovese and Eugene D. Genovese, *The Mind of the Master Class: History and Faith in the Southern Slaveholders' Worldview* (Cambridge: Cambridge University Press, 2005), p. 254; Wendy A. Cooper, *Classical Taste in America, 1800–1840* (New York: Abbeville Press and Baltimore Museum of Art, 1993), p. 73.
7. Miles, "Young American Nation and the Classical World," p. 267n34.
8. Edwin A. Miles, "The Old South and the Classical World," *North Carolina Historical Review* 48 (1971):258; Richard Beale Davis, *Intellectual Life in Jefferson's Virginia* (Chapel Hill: University of North Carolina Press, 1973), pp. 111, 380; Fox-Genovese and Genovese, *Mind of the Master Class*, p. 250.
9. Jennifer Tolbert Roberts, *Athens on Trial: The Antidemocratic Tradition in Western Thought* (Princeton: Princeton University Press, 1994), pp. 236–237, 240, 247–248.
10. Caroline Winterer, "Classical Oratory and Fears of Demagoguery in the Antebellum Era," in Michael Meckler, ed., *Classical Antiquity and the Politics of America: From George Washington to George W. Bush* (Waco, Tex.: Baylor University Press, 2006), p. 50; Wills, *Lincoln at Gettysburg*, p. 46; Caroline Winterer, "Victorian Antigone: Classicism and Women's Education in America, 1840–1890," *American Quarterly* 53 (March 2001):76; Thomas R. Dew, *A Digest of the Laws, Customs, Manners, and Institutions of the Ancient and Modern Nations*, 2d ed. (New York: D. Appleton, 1870), pp. 84, 207–208;

Gilman et al., *Journals of Ralph Waldo Emerson*, July 23, 1848, vol. 10, p. 345; Ralph Waldo Emerson, *The Complete Works of Ralph Waldo Emerson* (Boston: Houghton Mifflin, 1903–1904; reprint, New York: AMS Press, 1968), *Society and Solitude*, vol. 7, pp. 201–202.

11. Caroline Winterer, *The Culture of Classicism: Ancient Greece and Rome in American Intellectual Life, 1780–1910* (Baltimore: Johns Hopkins University Press, 2002), p. 72; Dew, *Digest*, pp. 153, 159; Charles Francis Adams, ed., *Memoirs of John Quincy Adams, Comprising Portions of His Diary from 1795 to 1848* (Philadelphia, 1874–1877; reprint, New York: AMS Press, 1970), December 21, 1811, vol. 2, p. 331; "Ancient and Modern Eloquence," *Southern Literary Messenger* 8 (1842):169, 179–180, 185.
12. Wills, *Lincoln at Gettysburg*, pp. 215, 247.
13. Daniel Walker Howe, "Classical Education and Political Culture in Nineteenth-Century America," *Intellectual History Newsletter* 5 (Spring 1983):12.
14. Robert Meriwether et al., eds., *The Papers of John C. Calhoun* (Columbia: University of South Carolina Press, 1959–), Speech in Reply to Daniel Webster on the Force Bill, February 26, 1833, vol. 2, p. 120; Dew, *Digest*, pp. 206, 210–211; Michael O'Brien, ed., *All Clever Men, Who Make Their Way: Critical Discourse in the Old South* (Athens: University of Georgia Press, 1992), Thomas Roderick Dew, "Republicanism and Literature," 1836, pp. 156–157; Miles, "Old South and the Classical World," pp. 270–271.
15. Aida DiPace Donald et al., *Diary of Charles Francis Adams* (Cambridge, Mass.: Harvard University Press, 1964–), June 14, 1824, vol. 1, pp. 185–186; June 17, 1824, vol. 1, p. 192; June 18, 1824, vol. 1, pp. 193–194; June 21, 1824, vol. 1, p. 200; June 23, 1824, vol. 1, p. 203; July 9, 1824, vol. 1, p. 230; July 15, 1824, vol. 1, p. 241; July 16, 1824, vol. 1, p. 244; July 18, 1824, vol. 1, p. 246.
16. Ibid., October 27, 1829, vol. 3, p. 58; November 24, 1829, vol. 3, p. 85; December 25, 1829, vol. 3, p. 115; January 25, 1830, vol. 3, pp. 142–143; June 1, 1830, vol. 3, p. 251; June 8–9, 1830, vol. 3, pp. 256–257; June 3, 1831, vol. 4, p. 61; July 31, 1832, vol. 4, p. 338.
17. Susan Pendergast Schoelwer, *Alamo Images: Changing Perceptions of a Texas Experience* (Dallas: De Golyer Library and Southern Methodist University Press, 1985), pp. 3, 5.
18. Wiltse, *Papers of Daniel Webster*, vol. 1, p. 332; Webster to Edward Everett, December 2, 1823, vol. 1, pp. 339–340; Jeremiah Mason to Webster, February 1, 1824, vol. 1, p. 351; Webster to Jeremiah Mason, February 15, 1824, vol. 1, p. 354; Daniel Webster, *The Great Speeches of Daniel Webster* (Boston: Little, Brown, 1919), "The Revolution in Greece," January 19, 1824, pp. 57–58; Donald et al., *Diary of Charles Francis Adams*, January 22, 1824, vol. 1, p. 58; January 23, 1824, vol. 1, p. 61. For reference to Webster's statue of Demosthenes see John Stephens Crawford, "The Classical Orator in Nineteenth-Century American Sculpture," *American Art Journal* 6 (November 1974):56.
19. Wiltse, *Papers of Daniel Webster*, January 2, 1824, vol. 1, p. 345n2.
20. Adams, *Memoirs of John Quincy Adams*, December 21, 1811, vol. 2, pp. 330–331; August 15, 1823, vol. 6, p. 173; March 5, 1828, vol. 7, p. 463.

21. Neal Gillespie, *The Collapse of Orthodoxy: The Intellectual Ordeal of George Frederick Holmes* (Charlottesville: University Press of Virginia, 1972), p. 73; Michael O'Brien, *A Character of Hugh Legaré* (Knoxville: University of Tennessee Press, 1985), pp. 98, 107; Edgar W. Knight, ed., *A Documentary History of Education in the South before 1860* (Chapel Hill: University of North Carolina Press, 1949–1953), Charles Fenton Mercer's Discourse on Popular Education, 1826, vol. 2, pp. 315–318; William Vance, *America's Rome* (New Haven: Yale University Press, 1989), vol. 1, p. 14.
22. Adrienne Koch and William Peden, eds., *The Selected Writings of John and John Quincy Adams* (New York: Alfred A. Knopf, 1946), John Quincy Adams to Abigail Adams, December 31, 1812, p. 284; Cleaves, *Old Tippecanoe*, pp. 183, 212–213, 239, 296–297.
23. Meriwether et al., *Papers of John C. Calhoun*, vol. 11, p. 594; Fitzwilliam Byrdsall to Calhoun, June 29, 1846, vol. 23, p. 245; Miles, "Old South and the Classical World," p. 268.
24. William Y. Robinson, *Robert Toombs of Georgia* (Baton Rouge: Louisiana State University Press, 1966), p. 65.
25. O'Brien, *All Clever Men*, Henry Augustine Washington, "The Social System of Virginia," 1848, p. 253; Winterer, *Mirror of Antiquity*, pp. 134, 140, 158; Knight, *Documentary History*, C. G. Memminger Gives Address at the Opening of the Female High and Normal School in Charleston, South Carolina, 1859, vol. 5, p. 271; Meriwether et.al., *Papers of John C. Calhoun*, "A Visit to Fort Hill," by "A Traveller," *New York Herald*, July 26, 1849. vol. 26, p. 527.
26. Richard Lounsbury, "Ludibria Rerum Mortalium: Charlestonian Intellectuals and Their Classics," in David Moltke-Hansen and Michael O'Brien, eds., *Intellectual Life in Antebellum Charleston* (Knoxville: University of Tennessee Press, 1986), pp. 332–336; Richard C. Lounsbury, ed., *Louisa S. McCord: Poems, Drama, Biography, Letters* (Charlottesville: University Press of Virginia, 1996), *Caius Gracchus*, pp. 170–171, 173, 220, 228; McCord to William Porcher Miles, June 12, 1848, p. 274.
27. Lounsbury, "Ludibria Rerum Mortalium," pp. 325, 328; Lounsbury, *Louisa S. McCord*, Afterword, pp. 414–415, 418.
28. Susan Smythe Bennett, "The Cheves Family of South Carolina," *South Carolina Historical and Genealogical Magazine* 35 (July 1934):90–91.
29. Lounsbury, *Louisa S. McCord, Caius Gracchus*, pp. 183, 200–201; Margaret Farrand Thorp, *Female Persuasion: Six Strong-Minded Women* (New Haven: Yale University Press, 1949), pp. 182, 200.
30. Frederick M. Litto, "Addison's *Cato* in the Colonies," *William and Mary Quarterly*, 3d ser., 23 (July 1966):431, 448; Gillespie, *Collapse of Orthodoxy*, p. 73; Winterer, "Victorian Antigone," p. 80; George Fitzhugh, *Sociology for the South, or The Failure of Free Society* (Richmond: A. Morris, 1854; reprint, New York: Burt Franklin, 1965), p. 218.
31. Elizabeth Ann Bartlett, ed., *Sarah Grimké: Letters on the Equality of the Sexes and Other Essays* (New Haven: Yale University Press, 1988), "Letters on the Equality of the Sexes," pp. 52, 63, 65.
32. Ibid., p. 51; *The Education of Women*, p. 112.

33. Michael O'Brien, *Conjectures of Order: Intellectual Life and the American South, 1810–1860* (Chapel Hill: University of North Carolina Press, 2004), pp. 254, 274.
34. Caroline Winterer, "Venus on the Sofa: Women, Neoclassicism, and the Early American Republic," *Modern Intellectual History* 2 (Spring 2005):30.
35. Dew, *Digest*, pp. 162, 164–165.
36. Winterer, *Culture of Classicism*, p. 65.
37. Koch and Peden, *Selected Writings of John and John Quincy Adams*, John Quincy Adams to William Plumer, August 16, 1809, p. 269; Meriwether et al., *Papers of John C. Calhoun*, "Patrick Henry" to the Editor of the *National Journal*, June 7, 1826, vol. 10, p. 126; Dickson D. Bruce, "The Conservative Use of History in Early National Virginia," *Southern Studies* 19 (Summer 1980):135.
38. Kimberly C. Shankman, *Compromise and the Constitution: The Political Thought of Henry Clay* (Lanham, Md.: Lexington Books, 1999), p. 39; Edwin A. Miles, "The Whig Party and the Menace of Caesar," *Tennessee Historical Quarterly* 27 (Winter 1968):362–364; Stephen Botein, "Cicero as Role Model for Early American Lawyers," *Classical Journal* 73 (April–May 1978): 319–320.
39. Miles, "Whig Party and the Menace of Caesar," pp. 361, 367.
40. Ibid., p. 370; Meriwether et al., *Papers of John C. Calhoun*, Speech on the Removal of the Deposits, January 13, 1834, vol. 12, p. 221.
41. Meriwether et al., *Papers of John C. Calhoun*, Remarks on an Article in *The [Washington] Globe*, February 2, 1835, vol. 12, p. 410; John Rhodehamel and Louise Taper, eds., *"Right or Wrong, God Judge Me": The Writings of John Wilkes Booth* (Urbana: University of Illinois Press, 1997), pp. 4, 16, 35; Louis J. Weichmann, *A True History of the Assassination of Abraham Lincoln and the Conspiracy of 1865* (New York: Alfred A. Knopf, 1975), p. 41. For reference to Lawrence see Robert V. Remini, *Andrew Jackson and the Course of American Democracy, 1833–1845* (New York: Harper and Row, 1977), p. 229.
42. Meriwether et al., *Papers of John C. Calhoun*, Andrew Jackson to John C. Calhoun, May 30, 1830, vol. 11, p. 193.
43. Botein, "Cicero as Role Model for Early American Lawyers," p. 319; Miles, "Whig Party and the Menace of Caesar," pp. 368–369.
44. Miles, "Whig Party and the Menace of Caesar," p. 373.
45. Ibid., pp. 371–373; Meriwether et al., *Papers of John C. Calhoun*, Speech on the Force Bill, February 15–16, 1833, vol. 12, p. 72; Remarks on the Executive Patronage Report in Exchange with Thomas H. Benton, February 13, 1835, vol. 12, p. 464; Remarks on Expunging the Senate Journal, March 3, 1835, vol. 12, p. 514; Remarks on the Motion to Expunge the Senate's Censure of Andrew Jackson, January 13, 1837, vol. 13, p. 363.
46. Ralph Ketcham, *Presidents above Party: The First American Presidency, 1789–1829* (Chapel Hill: University of North Carolina Press, 1984), pp. vii, x, 3–4, 92, 121–124, 140; Gordon S. Wood, *The Radicalism of the American Revolution* (New York: Alfred A. Knopf, 1992), pp. 298–303; Daniel Walker

Howe, *The Political Culture of the American Whigs* (Chicago: University of Chicago Press, 1979), p. 8.
47. Miles, "Whig Party and the Menace of Caesar," pp. 364–365, 374–376. For Henry's Stamp Act Speech and an editor's endorsement of its genuineness see Robert Douthat Meade, ed., *Patrick Henry* (Philadelphia: J. B. Lippincott, 1957–1969), vol. 1, pp. 31, 173–178.
48. Wiltshire, "Sam Houston," p. 254; Miles, "Whig Party and the Menace of Caesar," p. 376.
49. Miles, "Whig Party and the Menace of Caesar," p. 374.
50. Ibid., p. 379; Meriwether et al., *Papers of John C. Calhoun*, Franklin Smith to Calhoun, December 22, 1847, vol. 25, pp. 35–37; James Gadsden to Calhoun, December 28, 1847, vol. 25, p. 46; Sylvester Graham to Calhoun, August 17, 1848, vol. 26, p. 12; Lounsbury, "Ludibria Rerum Mortalium," p. 360.
51. William Charvat et al., eds., *The Works of Nathaniel Hawthorne* (Columbus: Ohio State University Press, 1962–1988), Letters, Hawthorne to Franklin Pierce, July 5, 1852, vol. 16, p. 562.
52. Meriwether et al., *Papers of John C. Calhoun*, Speech on the Revenue Bill, January 31, 1816, vol. 1, p. 326; Miles, "Old South and the Classical World," pp. 269, 275. De Bow may have gotten the analogy of the North and the Germanic invaders who toppled the Roman Empire from George Frederick Holmes. See Drew Gilpin Faust, *A Sacred Circle: The Dilemma of the Intellectual in the Old South, 1840–1860* (Baltimore: Johns Hopkins University Press, 1977), p. 76.
53. Meriwether et al., *Papers of John C. Calhoun*, William Henry Harrison to John C. Calhoun, April 30, 1832, vol. 11, pp. 575–576, 578.
54. Miles, "Old South and the Classical World," p. 274; Winterer, *Culture of Classicism*, p. 93; O'Brien, *All Clever Men*, Thomas Roderick Dew, "Republicanism and Literature," 1836, pp. 157–158, 175; Fitzhugh, *Sociology for the South*, p. 202.
55. Knight, *Documentary History*, Charles Fenton Mercer's Discourse on Popular Education, 1826, vol. 2, p. 322; Meriwether et al., *Papers of John C. Calhoun*, Speech on the Dangers of Factious Opposition, January 5, 1814, vol. 1, p. 196.
56. Bruce, "Conservative Use of History in Early National Virginia," p. 133; Fitzhugh, *Sociology for the South*, p. 295; Miles, "Whig Party and the Menace of Caesar," p. 376.
57. Paul K. Conkin, *Self-Evident Truths* (Bloomington: Indiana University Press, 1974), p. 146; John Calvin, *Institutes of the Christian Religion*, trans. Henry Beveridge (Grand Rapids: William B. Eerdman, 1970), vol. 2, pp. 656–657; Niccolò Machiavelli, *The Discourses of Niccolò Machiavelli*, trans. Leslie J. Walker (New Haven: Yale University Press, 1950), vol. 1, pp. 212–215; vol. 2, pp. 7–12, 271–315; Francesco Guicciardini, *Maxims and Reflections of a Renaissance Statesman*, trans. Mario Domandi (New York: Harper and Row, 1965), p. 13; Algernon Sidney, *Discourses concerning Government* (1751; reprint, London: Gregg International Publishers, 1968), pp. 130, 139–140, 434.
58. J. G. A. Pocock, ed., *The Political Works of James Harrington* (Cambridge: Cambridge University Press, 1977), pp. 459, 607.

59. Gordon S. Wood, *Creation of the American Republic, 1776–1787* (Chapel Hill: University of North Carolina Press, 1969), pp. 201–203, 208, 211, 213–214, 232–233.
60. Ibid., pp. 410, 473, 554, 557–559; Max Farrand, ed., *The Records of the Federal Convention of 1787*, 3d ed. (New Haven: Yale University Press, 1966), vol. 1, pp. 299–300, 308, 402, 422–424, 431–432; vol. 2, p. 299; Alexander Hamilton, John Jay, and James Madison, *The Federalist: A Commentary on the Constitution of the United States* (New York: Random House, 1941), nos. 47 and 63, pp. 313, 410–411, 415; John Adams, *A Defence of the Constitutions of Government of the United States of America* (1787–1788; reprint, New York: Da Capo Press, 1971); Paul Leicester Ford, ed., *Pamphlets on the Constitution of the United States: Published during Its Discussion by the People* (1888; reprint,, New York: Burt Franklin, 1971), pp. 34–43, 57–58, 65, 189–190; Herbert J. Storing, ed., *The Complete Antifederalist* (Chicago: University of Chicago Press, 1981), vol. 2, pp. 138–139; Jonathan Elliot, ed., *Debates in the Several State Conventions on the Adoption of the Federal Constitution* (1888; reprint, New York: Burt Franklin, 1968), vol. 3, p. 218; vol. 4, pp. 326–329.
61. Hamilton, Jay, and Madison, *Federalist*, no. 10, pp. 58–59. Madison makes a similar argument in no. 51 as well. For reference to democratic reforms and to the rise of political parties see Conkin, *Self-Evident Truths*, pp. 184, 187, 193.
62. For reference to a famous attack on northern economic policies by the South's chief economist, John Taylor of Caroline, see Paul K. Conkin, *Prophets of Prosperity: America's First Political Economists* (Bloomington: Indiana University Press, 1980), pp. 57, 59, 61–78. For reference to the dispute over the expansion of slavery see David M. Potter, *Division and the Stresses of Reunion, 1845–1876* (Glenview, Ill.: Scott, Foresman, and Co., 1973), p. 24.
63. John C. Calhoun, *Disquisition on Government and Selections from the Discourse*, ed. C. Gordon Post (New York: Macmillan, 1953), pp. 20, 28, 37–38, 50–51.
64. Ibid., pp. 23, 26–28, 35–36, 51; John M. Anderson, ed., *Calhoun: Basic Documents* (State College, Penn.: Bald Eagle Press, 1952), On the Revenue Collection Bill, February 15–16, 1833, p. 181.
65. Calhoun, *Disquisition on Government*, pp. 56, 71–73.
66. Ibid., p. 49; Selections from "A Discourse on the Constitution and Government of the United States," p. 102; Meriwether et al., *Papers of John C. Calhoun*, Exposition Reported by the Special Committee, December 19, 1828, vol. 10, pp. 492–494, 514; William W. Freeling, *Prelude to Civil War: The Nullification Controversy in South Carolina, 1816–1836* (New York: Harper and Row, 1966), pp. 265, 296–297.
67. Calhoun, *Disquisition on Government*, p. 53; Adams, *Defence*, vol. 3, p. 505; Eugene D. Genovese, "The Gracchi and Their Mother in the Mind of American Slaveholders," *Journal of the Historical Society* 2 (Summer/Fall 2002):469.
68. Meriwether et al., *Papers of John C. Calhoun*, Calhoun to A. D. Wallace, December 17, 1840, vol. 15, p. 389.

69. David M. Potter, *The Impending Crisis, 1848–1861* (New York: Harper and Row, 1976), pp. 281–284, 419; Potter, *Division and the Stresses of Reunion*, p. 142.
70. John Niven, *John C. Calhoun and the Price of Union: A Biography* (Baton Rouge: Louisiana State University Press, 1988), p. 1; Potter, *Impending Crisis*, p. 446.
71. Potter, *Division and the Stresses of Reunion*, pp. 142, 214–215.

3. Pastoralism and Utilitarianism

1. David B. Tyack, *George Ticknor and the Boston Brahmins* (Cambridge, Mass.: Harvard University Press, 1967), p. 128; Ralph Waldo Emerson, *The Complete Works of Ralph Waldo Emerson* (Boston: Houghton Mifflin, 1903–1904; reprint, New York: AMS Press, 1968), "Thoughts on Modern Literature," vol. 12, p. 311; Richard L. Bushman, introduction to Wendy A. Cooper, *Classical Taste in America, 1800–1840* (New York: Abbeville Press and Baltimore Museum of Art, 1993), p. 22.
2. William H. Gilman et al., eds., *The Journals and Miscellaneous Notebooks of Ralph Waldo Emerson* (Cambridge, Mass.: Harvard University Press, 1960–1982), Date Unknown, vol. 6, p. 175.
3. Dorothea Wender, ed. and trans., *Roman Poetry from the Republic to the Silver Age* (Carbondale: Southern Illinois University Press, 1980), pp. 59–60.
4. Paul A. Rahe, *Republics, Ancient and Modern: Classical Republicanism and the American Revolution* (Chapel Hill: University of North Carolina Press, 1992), p. 414.
5. A. Whitney Griswold, "Jefferson's Agrarian Democracy," in Henry C. Dethloff, ed., *Thomas Jefferson and American Democracy* (Lexington, Mass.: D. C. Heath, 1971), pp. 40–42, 46–50; Richard K. Matthews, *The Radical Politics of Thomas Jefferson: A Revisionist View* (Lawrence: University Press of Kansas, 1984), pp. 43, 109–110. For a full discussion of classical economics, both in Europe and in America, see Paul K. Conkin, *Prophets of Prosperity: America's First Political Economists* (Bloomington: Indiana University Press, 1980).
6. Rowland Bertoff, "Independence and Attachment, Virtue and Interest: From Republican Citizen to Free Enterpriser, 1787–1837," in Richard L. Bushman, ed., *Uprooted Americans: Essays to Honor Oscar Handlin* (Boston: Little, Brown, 1979), p. 109; John William Ward, *Andrew Jackson: Symbol for an Age* (Oxford: Oxford University Press, 1955), pp. 229–230; William Vance, *America's Rome* (New Haven: Yale University Press, 1989), vol. 1, pp. 89, 96–97.
7. Francis H. Allen and Bradford Torrey, eds., *The Journal of Henry David Thoreau* (Salt Lake City: Gibbs M. Smith, 1984), February 16, 1838, vol. 1, p. 29.
8. Ibid., September 2, 1851, vol. 2, pp. 444–445; September 3, 1851, vol. 2, p. 450; December 22, 1855, vol. 8, p. 56; March 26, 1856, vol. 8, p. 229; December 13, 1859, vol. 13, pp. 26–27; March 15, 1860, vol. 13, p. 195; Ethel

Seybold, *Thoreau: The Quest and the Classics* (New Haven: Yale University Press, 1951), pp. 17, 70–71.

9. For a full discussion of the educational proposals of Franklin, Rush, and Paine and their own uses of the classics see Carl J. Richard, *The Founders and the Classics: Greece, Rome, and the American Enlightenment* (Cambridge, Mass.: Harvard University Press, 1994), pp. 196–223.

10. Wayne K. Durill, "The Power of Ancient Words: Classical Teaching and Social Change at South Carolina College," *Journal of Southern History* 65 (August 1999):478–479.

11. Ibid., pp. 479–480; Tyack, *George Ticknor and the Boston Brahmins*, pp. 69–72, 112; Melvin I. Urofsky, "Reforms and Response: The Yale Report of 1828," *History of Education Quarterly* 5 (March 1965):54–57; Elizabeth Fox-Genovese and Eugene D. Genovese, *The Mind of the Master Class: History and Faith in the Southern Slaveholders' Worldview* (Cambridge: Cambridge University Press, 2005), p. 261; George P. Schmidt, "Intellectual Crosscurrents in American Colleges, 1825–1855," *American Historical Review* 42 (October 1936):52–53, 57–58.

12. Richard Hofstadter and Wilson Smith, eds., *American Higher Education: A Documentary History* (Chicago: University of Chicago Press, 1961), Henry Vethake Proposes Curricular and Teaching Changes, 1830, vol. 1, pp. 293–294, 296.

13. Caroline Winterer, "Classical Oratory and Fears of Demagoguery in the Antebellum Era," in Michael Meckler, ed., *Classical Antiquity and the Politics of America: From George Washington to George W. Bush* (Waco, Tex.: Baylor University Press, 2006), p. 43.

14. Robert A. McCaughey, *Josiah Quincy, 1772–1864: The Last Federalist* (Cambridge, Mass.: Harvard University Press, 1974), p. 166.

15. "Modern Ideas Concerning Education," *Southern Literary Messenger* 8 (1842):627.

16. Harvey Wish, "Aristotle, Plato, and the Mason-Dixon Line," *Journal of the History of Ideas* 10 (April 1949):265; Fox-Genovese and Genovese, *Mind of the Master Class*, p. 281.

17. Schmidt, "Intellectual Crosscurrents in American Colleges," pp. 59–60.

18. Edgar W. Knight, ed., *A Documentary History of Education in the South before 1860* (Chapel Hill: University of North Carolina Press, 1949–1953), Henry Harrisse of the University of North Carolina on Collegiate Education, 1854, vol. 3, p. 382; A Senator in the Legislature of Texas Opposes the Bill for a University, 1856, vol. 3, p. 412; President James H. Thornwell of South Carolina College Writes to Governor Manning on Public Education in South Carolina, 1853, vol. 5, p. 153; Robert Meriwether et al., eds., *The Papers of John C. Calhoun* (Columbia: University of South Carolina Press, 1959–), Anna Maria Calhoun Clemson to John C. Calhoun, December 5, 1844, vol. 20, p. 466.

19. Daniel Walker Howe, *Making the American Self: Jonathan Edwards to Abraham Lincoln* (Cambridge, Mass.: Harvard University Press, 1997), p. 162; Louis Filler, ed., *Horace Mann on the Crisis in Education* (Yellow Springs, Ohio: Antioch Press, 1965), pp. 23, 128, 221. For reference to the contribu-

Notes to Pages 94–99 — 231

tions of Aristarchus and the other Greek scientists see Carl J. Richard, *Twelve Greeks and Romans Who Changed the World* (Lanham, Md.: Rowman and Littlefield, 2003), pp. 17–27.

20. Louis B. Wright, *Culture on the Moving Frontier* (Bloomington: Indiana University Press, 1955), p. 165.

21. Jurgen Herbst, "The Yale Report of 1828," *International Journal of the Classical Tradition* 11 (Fall 2004):228; Caroline Winterer, *The Culture of Classicism: Ancient Greece and Rome in American Intellectual Life, 1780–1910* (Baltimore: Johns Hopkins University Press, 2002), p. 49; Frederick Rudolph, *Curriculum: A History of the American Undergraduate Course of Study since 1636* (San Francisco: Jossey-Bass Publishers, 1977), p. 66; Hofstadter and Smith, *American Higher Education*, The Yale Report of 1828, vol. 1, pp. 282–283, 287.

22. Hofstadter and Smith, *American Higher Education*, The Yale Report of 1828, vol. 1, pp. 288; Meyer Reinhold, *Classica Americana: The Greek and Roman Heritage in the United States* (Detroit: Wayne State University Press, 1984), pp. 193–194.

23. Hofstadter and Smith, *American Higher Education*, The Yale Report of 1828, vol. 1, pp. 290–291.

24. Rudolph, *Curriculum*, pp. 67, 72; Herbst, "Yale Report of 1828," p. 227.

25. Reinhold, *Classica Americana*, p. 194; Herbst, "Yale Report of 1828," pp. 213, 221; Schmidt, "Intellectual Crosscurrents in American Colleges," pp. 53, 57–58, 65; Winterer, "Classical Oratory and Fears of Demagoguery in the Antebellum Era," p. 43; McCaughey, *Josiah Quincy*, pp. 147–148, 167–168; Ronald Story, "Harvard Students, the Boston Elite, and the New England Preparatory System, 1800–1870," *History of Education Quarterly* 15 (Fall 1975):285; Rudolph, *Curriculum*, p. 73; Urofsky, "Reforms and Response," pp. 55, 62–63.

26. Schmidt, "Intellectual Crosscurrents in American Colleges," p. 62; Winterer, *Culture of Classicism*, pp. 68–69; Siobhan Moroney, "Latin, Greek, and the American Schoolboy: Ancient Languages and Classical Determinism in the Early Republic," *Classical Journal* 96 (February–March 2001):301; McCaughey, *Josiah Quincy*, p. 168.

27. Richard Lounsbury, "Ludibria Rerum Mortalium: Charleston Intellectuals and Their Classics," in David Moltke-Hansen and Michael O' Brien, eds., *Intellectual life in Antebellum Charleston* (Knoxville: University of Tennessee Press, 1986), pp. 361, 365–366; Michael O'Brien, *A Character of Hugh Legaré* (Knoxville: University of Tennessee Press, 1985), pp. 92–93.

28. O'Brien, *Character of Hugh Legaré*, pp. 73, 92, 100; Lounsbury, "Ludibria Rerum Mortalium," p. 366.

29. Fox-Genovese and Genovese, *Mind of the Master Class*, p. 262; Michael O'Brien, *Conjectures of Order: Intellectual Life and the American South, 1810–1860* (Chapel Hill: University of North Carolina Press, 2004), pp. 1090–1091.

30. Charles Fraser, "On the Condition and Prospects of the Art of Painting in the United States," in David Moltke-Hansen, ed., *Art in the Lives of South*

Carolinians: Nineteenth-Century Chapters (Charleston: Carolina Art Association, 1979), pp. CF-2, CF-10.
31. Henry David Thoreau, *Walden and Other Writings* (New York: Random House, 1981), p. 91; Seybold, *Thoreau*, pp. 57–58.
32. Gilman et al., *Journals of Ralph Waldo Emerson*, June 27, 1846, vol. 9, p. 440; 1850–1851, vol. 11, p. 324.
33. Edwin A. Miles, "The Old South and the Classical World," *North Carolina Historical Review* 48 (1971):260.
34. Knight, *Documentary History*, Extracts from President Basil Manly's Report on Collegiate Education to the Trustees of the University of Alabama, 1852, vol. 3, pp. 354–356.
35. Ibid., A Committee of the Faculty of the University of Alabama Opposes the Elective System of the University of Virginia, 1854, vol. 3, pp. 401–403.
36. Ibid., Criticisms of the Colleges, 1852, vol. 4, p. 379.
37. Vance, *America's Rome*, vol. 1, p. 364.
38. George Fitzhugh, *Cannibals All: Slaves without Masters* (Richmond: A. Morris, 1857; reprint, Cambridge, Mass.: Harvard University Press, 1960), p. 193.
39. George Fitzhugh, *Sociology for the South, or The Failure of Free Society* (Richmond: A. Morris, 1854; reprint, New York: Burt Franklin, 1965), pp. 159, 242; Harvey Wish, *George Fitzhugh: Propagandist of the Old South* (Baton Rouge: Louisiana State University Press, 1943), p. 263.
40. Fitzhugh, *Sociology for the South*, pp. 155–156.
41. Drew Gilpin Faust, *James Henry Hammond and the Old South: A Design for Mastery* (Baton Rouge: Louisiana State University Press, 1982), pp. 266, 273–274.
42. Cooper, *Classical Taste in America*, p. 210.

4. Nationalism

1. Richard M. Gummere, *Seven Wise Men of Colonial America* (Cambridge, Mass.: Harvard University Press, 1967), p. 86; William van der Wyde, ed., *The Life and Works of Thomas Paine* (New Rochelle, N.Y.: Thomas Paine National Historical Association, 1925–1927), "The American Crisis," 1776, vol. 3, pp. 34–35; A. Owen Aldridge, "Thomas Paine and the Classics," *Eighteenth Century Studies* 1 (Summer 1968):376.
2. Robert Green McCloskey, ed., *The Papers of James Wilson* (Cambridge, Mass.: Harvard University Press, 1967), Miscellaneous Papers, Oration Delivered on the Fourth of July, 1788, vol. 2, pp. 773–774; "On the Study of Law," 1790, vol. 1, pp. 69–71.
3. Garry Wills, *Lincoln at Gettysburg: The Words That Remade America* (New York: Simon and Schuster, 1992), p. 48; George Fitzhugh, *Cannibals All: Slaves without Masters* (Richmond: A. Morris, 1857; reprint, Cambridge, Mass.: Harvard University Press, 1960), p. 64; Edwin A. Miles, "The Young American Nation and the Classical World," *Journal of the History of Ideas* 13 (April–June 1974):270.

4. William H. Gilman et al., eds., *The Journals and Miscellaneous Notebooks of Ralph Waldo Emerson* (Cambridge, Mass.: Harvard University Press, 1960–1982), July 11, 1822, vol. 2, p. 4; December 21, 1822, vol. 2, p. 73; February 1, 1823, vol. 2, p. 95; Letter to Plato, May 2, 1824, vol. 2, p. 246.
5. Miles, "Young American Nation and the Classical World," pp. 269, 274; Wendy A. Cooper, *Classical Taste in America, 1800–1840* (New York: Abbeville Press and Baltimore Museum of Art, 1993), p. 65.
6. Michael O'Brien, ed., *All Clever Men, Who Make Their Way: Critical Discourse in the Old South* (Athens: University of Georgia Press, 1992), Frederick Adolphus Porcher, "Modern Art," 1852, pp. 332, 334–336. For Washington's statement see John S. Crawford, "The Classical Tradition in American Sculpture: Structure and Surface," *American Art Journal* 11 (April 1979):41.
7. O'Brien, *All Clever Men*, Porcher, "Modern Art," p. 321; Richard Lounsbury, "Ludibria Rerum Mortalium: Charleston Intellectuals and Their Classics," in David Moltke-Hansen and Michael O'Brien, eds., *Intellectual Life in Antebellum Charleston* (Knoxville: University of Tennessee Press, 1986), pp. 350–351.
8. Talbot Hamlin, *Greek Revival Architecture in America* (Oxford: Oxford University Press, 1944), p. 56; Crawford, "Classical Tradition in American Sculpture," pp. 41–42.
9. Hamlin, *Greek Revival Architecture in America*, p. 60; Michael O'Brien, *Conjectures of Order: Intellectual Life and the American South, 1810–1860* (Chapel Hill: University of North Carolina Press, 2004), p. 595; O'Brien, *All Clever Men*, Henry Augustine Washington, "The Social System of Virginia," 1848, p. 231.
10. Garry Wills, *Cincinnatus: George Washington and the Enlightenment* (Garden City, N.Y.: Doubleday, 1984), pp. 35, 51.
11. Daniel Webster, *The Great Speeches of Daniel Webster* (Boston: Little, Brown, 1919), First Settlement of New England, December 22, 1820, pp. 28–29.
12. Ibid., The Character of Washington, February 22, 1832, p. 346.
13. Ibid., The Addition to the Capitol, July 4, 1851, pp. 641–642; Kenneth E. Shewmaker, ed., *Daniel Webster: "The Completest Man"* (Hanover, N.H.: University Press of New England, 1990), The Dignity and Importance of History, 1852, p. 136.
14. Michael O'Brien, *A Character of Hugh Legaré* (Knoxville: University of Tennessee Press, 1985), pp. 42–44.
15. Richard Beale Davis, *Intellectual Life in Jefferson's Virginia, 1790–1830* (Chapel Hill: University of North Carolina Press, 1973), pp. 372–373.
16. O'Brien, *All Clever Men*, Thomas Roderick Dew, "Republicanism and Literature," 1836, p. 139.
17. Robert Meriwether et al., eds., *The Papers of John C. Calhoun* (Columbia: University of South Carolina Press, 1959–), Speech on the Loan Bill, February 25, 1814, vol. 1, p. 211; Elizabeth Fox-Genovese and Eugene D. Genovese, *The Mind of the Master Class: History and Faith in the Southern Slaveholders' Worldview* (Cambridge: Cambridge University Press, 2005), p. 278.
18. Frederick M. Litto, "Addison's *Cato* in the Colonies," *William and Mary Quarterly*, 3d ser., 23 (July 1966):448.

19. Charles Sumner, *The Works of Charles Sumner* (Boston: Lee and Shepard, 1874–1883), "The True Grandeur of Nations," July 4, 1845, vol. 1, pp. 67–69.
20. William Vance, *America's Rome* (New Haven: Yale University Press, 1989), vol. 1, pp. 21, 32.
21. William H. Pierson Jr., *American Buildings and Their Architects: Technology and the Picturesque; The Corporate and the Early Gothic Styles* (Garden City, N.Y.: Anchor Books, 1978), p. 6; Hamlin, *Greek Revival Architecture in America*, pp. 3, 24, 35.
22. Hamlin, *Greek Revival Architecture in America*, pp. 8, 37, 80, 148, 347; Egon Verheyen, "'Unenlightened by a Single Ray of Antiquity': John Quincy Adams and the Design of the Pediment for the United States Capitol," *International Journal of the Classical Tradition* 3 (Fall 1996):229.
23. Hamlin, *Greek Revival Architecture in America*, pp. 148, 223–225, 346.
24. Ibid., pp. 61–62.
25. John Stephens Crawford, "The Classical Orator in Nineteenth-Century American Sculpture," *American Art Journal* 6 (November 1974):59–61, 67–69; Crawford, "Classical Tradition in American Sculpture," pp. 40, 43–47.
26. Ralph L. Rusk, ed., *The Letters of Ralph Waldo Emerson* (New York: Columbia University Press, 1939), Emerson to John Boynton Hill, July 3, 1822, vol. 1, p. 121; Gilman et al., *Journals of Ralph Waldo Emerson*, August 9, 1840, vol. 7, p. 390.
27. Francis H. Allen and Bradford Torrey, eds., *The Journal of Henry David Thoreau* (Salt Lake City: Gibbs M. Smith, 1984), February 9, 1851, vol. 2, p. 151; Elzbieta Foeller-Pituch, "Ambiguous Heritage: Classical Myths in the Works of Nineteenth-Century American Writers," *International Journal of the Classical Tradition* 1 (Winter 1995):98; Thomas R. Dew, *A Digest of the Laws, Customs, Manners, and Institutions of the Ancient and Modern Nations*, 2d ed. (New York: D. Appleton, 1870), p. 160.
28. Caroline Winterer, "Victorian Antigone: Classicism and Women's Education in America, 1840–1900," *American Quarterly* 53 (March 2001):76; Dew, *Digest*, p. 210.
29. George A. Kennedy, "Gildersleeve, the Journal, and Philology in America," in Herbert W. Benario and Ward W. Briggs Jr., eds., *Basil Lanneau Gildersleeve: An American Classicist* (Baltimore: Johns Hopkins University Press, 1986), p. 45.
30. Miles, "Young American Nation and the Classical World," p. 263.

5. Romanticism

1. Michael O'Brien, ed., *All Clever Men, Who Make Their Way: Critical Discourse in the Old South* (Athens: University of Georgia Press, 1992), Thomas Roderick Dew, "Republicanism and Literature," 1836, p. 130.
2. Ibid., pp. 131–132, 138.
3. Ibid., p. 139.
4. Meyer Reinhold, *Classica Americana: The Greek and Roman Heritage in the United States* (Detroit: Wayne State University Press, 1984), p. 329; Gay Wilson

Allen and Sculley Bradley, eds., *The Collected Writings of Walt Whitman: Notebooks and Unpublished Prose Manuscripts* (New York: New York University Press, 1984), Notebooks, 1850s, vol. 5, p. 1770; John Carl Miller, ed., *Edgar Allan Poe: Marginalia* (Charlottesville: University Press of Virginia, 1981), *Democratic Review*, July 1846, p. 118.

5. Arlin Turner, *Nathaniel Hawthorne: A Biography* (Oxford: Oxford University Press, 1980), p. 328; William Charvat et al., eds., *The Works of Nathaniel Hawthorne* (Columbus: Ohio State University Press, 1962–1988), Explanatory Notes, December 7, 1857, vol. 14, p. 725; Ralph Waldo Emerson, *Selected Essays* (New York: Penguin Books, 1982), "Self-Reliance," pp. 176, 183, 199–200; Ralph Waldo Emerson, *Essays: First and Second Series* (Mount Vernon: Peter Pauper Press, 1946), "History," p. 25; William H. Gilman et al., *The Journals and Miscellaneous Notebooks of Ralph Waldo Emerson* (Cambridge, Mass.: Harvard University Press, 1960–1982), August 19, 1832, vol. 4, p. 38; Carl Bode and Walter Harding, eds., *The Correspondence of Henry David Thoreau* (New York: New York University Press, 1958), Thoreau to H. G. O. Blake, July 21, 1852, p. 286.

6. L. H. Butterfield, ed., *The Adams Family Correspondence* (Cambridge, Mass.: Harvard University Press, 1963–1973), John Adams to John Quincy Adams, February 12, 1781, vol. 4, p. 80; George Fitzhugh, *Cannibals All: Slaves without Masters* (Richmond: A. Morris, 1857; reprint, Cambridge, Mass.: Harvard University Press, 1960), pp. 61–64. For reference to the adherence of eighteenth-century authors like Alexander Pope to the so-called classical laws of literature see Patrick Critwell, "The Eighteenth Century: A Classical Age?" *Arion* 7 (Spring 1968):120.

7. Gilman et al., *Journals of Ralph Waldo Emerson*, 1820, vol. 1, p. 228; May 31, 1840, vol. 7, p. 363; 1852, vol. 13, p. 59.

8. Ibid., March 26, 1839, vol. 7, p. 181; June 19, 1840, vol. 7, p. 505; Date Unknown, vol. 12, p. 233; Ralph Waldo Emerson, *The Complete Works of Ralph Waldo Emerson* (Boston: Houghton Mifflin, 1903–1904; reprint, New York: AMS Press, 1968), "Art and Criticism," vol. 12, pp. 304–305; "Thoughts on Modern Literature," vol. 12, pp. 309–310.

9. Emerson, *Selected Essays*, "History," pp. 163–164, 166; "Self-Reliance," pp. 199–200; Emerson, *Complete Works of Ralph Waldo Emerson*, "History," vol. 2, pp. 26, 30; Gilman et al., *Journals of Ralph Waldo Emerson*, March 27, 1826, vol. 3, p. 16; October 30, 1835, vol. 5, p. 105; May 4, 1836, vol. 5, p. 150; July 2, 1836, vol. 5, p. 185; September 20, 1836, vol. 5, pp. 198–199; January 7, 1837, vol. 5, p. 279; Date Unknown, vol. 6, p. 221; 1859, vol. 14, p. 268.

10. Allen and Bradley, *Collected Writings of Walt Whitman*, Notebooks, 1856, vol. 5, pp. 1752–1753; Miller, *Edgar Allan Poe, Graham's Magazine*, November 1846, p. 132; December 1846, p. 141; *Southern Literary Messenger*, April 1849, p. 169; Francis H. Allen and Bradford Torrey, eds., *The Journal of Henry David Thoreau* (Salt Lake City: Gibbs M. Smith, 1984), January 2, 1840, vol. 1, p. 117.

11. Perry Miller, *The New England Mind* (New York: Macmillan, 1939), vol. 1, p. 278; Howard Mumford Jones, *Revolution and Romanticism* (Cambridge,

Mass.: Harvard University Press, 1974), p. 128; Harvey Wish, "Aristotle, Plato, and the Mason-Dixon Line," *Journal of the History of Ideas* 10 (April 1949):255; Daniel Walker Howe, *Making the American Self: Jonathan Edwards to Abraham Lincoln* (Cambridge, Mass.: Harvard University Press, 1997), p. 204.

12. Gilman et al., *Journals of Ralph Waldo Emerson*, "The Character of Socrates," 1820, vol. 1, pp. 207, 234, 257; Journal, February 14, 1828, vol. 3, pp. 106–107; September 27, 1830, vol. 3, p. 199; 1845–1848, vol. 10, p. 474.

13. Ibid., Letter to Plato, May 2, 1824, vol. 2, p. 246; Journal, 1824, vol. 2, p. 374; June 25, 1831, vol. 3, pp. 260–261; 1840, vol. 7, p. 335; 1844–1845, vol. 9, pp. 179, 215–216; April 19, 1845, vol. 9, p. 245; 1845–1848, vol. 10, p. 483; Ralph L. Rusk, ed., *The Letters of Ralph Waldo Emerson* (New York: Columbia University Press, 1939), Introduction, vol. 1, pp. liv–lv; Emerson to Elizabeth Hoar, July 18, 1841, vol. 2, pp. 429–430; May 7, 1842, vol. 3, p. 50; Emerson to Mary Moody Emerson, September 21, 1841, vol. 2, p. 451; Emerson to James Elliot Cabot, August 19, 1846, vol. 3, p. 343; Emerson to Samuel Gray Ward, March 25, 1847, vol. 3, p. 387.

14. Gilman et al., *Journals of Ralph Waldo Emerson*, August 25, 1845, vol. 9, p. 248; 1845, vol. 9, p. 325; 1847, vol. 10, pp. 42–43; July 25, 1847, vol. 10, p. 115; 1845–1848, vol. 10, p. 478; Rusk, *Letters of Ralph Waldo Emerson*, Emerson to William Emerson, April 21, 1833, vol. 1, p. 380; October 2, 1845, vol. 3, pp. 305–306; July 27, 1849, vol. 4, p. 155; Emerson to John F. Heath, August 4, 1842, vol. 3, p. 77; Emerson, *Complete Works of Ralph Waldo Emerson, Representative Men*, vol. 4, pp. 40–41.

15. Emerson, *Complete Works of Ralph Waldo Emerson, Representative Men*, vol. 4, pp. 37, 39, 44, 57, 78, 87; *Society and Solitude*, vol. 7, pp. 191, 198–200.

16. Ethel Seybold, *Thoreau: The Quest and the Classics* (New Haven: Yale University Press, 1951), pp. 62, 73, 83; Howe, *Making the American Self*, pp. 217, 221–222, 230–231.

17. Vincent Buranelli, *Edgar Allan Poe* (New York: Twayne Publishers, 1961), pp. 36, 89, 111, 113.

18. Arthur Cushman McGiffert, ed., *Young Emerson Speaks: Unpublished Discourses on Many Subjects* (Boston: Houghton, Mifflin, 1938; reprint, Port Washington, N.Y.: Kennikat Press, 1968), pp. 133, 244; Emerson, *Selected Essays*, "Self-Reliance," p. 195; Gilman et al., *Journals of Ralph Waldo Emerson*, February 22, 1821, vol. 1, p. 203; 1830, vol. 3, pp. 365, 367.

19. Allen and Torrey, *Journal of Henry David Thoreau*, February 7, 1838, vol. 1, pp. 26–27; Allen and Bradley, *Collected Writings of Walt Whitman*, "Epictetus," 1870, vol. 2, p. 886; Buranelli, *Edgar Allan Poe*, p. 52.

20. Charles Capper and David A. Hollinger, eds., *The American Intellectual Tradition*, 3d ed. (Oxford: Oxford University Press, 1993), Ralph Waldo Emerson, "The Divinity School Address," 1838, vol. 1, p. 279; Taylor Stoehr, *Nay-Saying in Concord: Emerson, Alcott, and Thoreau* (Hamden, Conn.: Archon, 1979), p. 129; Emerson, *Complete Works of Ralph Waldo Emerson*, "Self-Reliance," vol. 2, p. 85.

21. Seybold, *Thoreau*, p. 17; Howe, *Making the American Self*, p. 245; Martin Luther King Jr., "Pilgrimage to Nonviolence," 1958, in Richard N. Current et al., eds., *Words That Made American History* (Boston: Little, Brown, 1978), vol. 2, p. 519. For Dickinson's quotation from *Antigone* see Richard M. Gummere, *The American Colonial Mind and the Classical Tradition: Essays in Comparative Culture* (Cambridge, Mass.: Harvard University Press, 1963), p. 115.
22. Stoehr, *Nay-Saying in Concord*, p. 129; Paul K. Conkin, *Puritans and Pragmatists: Eight Eminent American Thinkers* (Bloomington: Indiana University Press, 1968), pp. 163–165; Paul F. Boller Jr., *American Transcendentalism, 1830–1860: An Intellectual Inquiry* (New York: Putnam, 1974), p. 145; Gilman et al., *Journals of Ralph Waldo Emerson*, Date Unknown, vol. 6, p. 178.
23. Burton Feldman and Robert D. Richardson, eds., *The Rise of Modern Mythology* (Bloomington: Indiana University Press, 1972), pp. 517–518; Gilman et al., *Journals of Ralph Waldo Emerson*, October 1822, vol. 2, p. 23; 1853, vol. 13, pp. 133–134, 240–241; Emerson, *Complete Works of Ralph Waldo Emerson, Society and Solitude*, vol. 7, p. 197; "Solution," vol. 9, p. 221.
24. Seybold, *Thoreau*, pp. 30, 51–52, 76; Allen and Torrey, *Journal of Henry David Thoreau*, September 5, 1841, vol. 1, p. 284; January 8, 1842, vol. 1, p. 317; December 6, 1845, vol. 1, pp. 391, 393.
25. Seybold, *Thoreau*, pp. 29, 31–32, 52, 56–57; Allen and Torrey, *Journal of Henry David Thoreau*, November 20, 1837, vol. 1, p. 12; March 3, 1838, vol. 1, p. 31.
26. Seybold, *Thoreau*, pp. 10–12, 31; Feldman and Richardson, *Rise of Modern Mythology*, p. 527; Allen and Torrey, *Journal of Henry David Thoreau*, January 29, 1840, vol. 1, p. 116; January 10, 1851, vol. 2, p. 145.
27. Seybold, *Thoreau*, pp. 50–51; Allen and Torrey, *Journal of Henry David Thoreau*, July 14, 1845, vol. 1, p. 371. For reference to the theft of Thoreau's copy of the *Iliad* from his cabin see E. Christian Kopff, *The Devil Knows Latin: Why America Needs the Classical Tradition* (Wilmington, Del.: ISI, 1999), p. 99.
28. Seybold, *Thoreau*, pp. 16, 18, 35; Kevin P. Van Anglen, "The Sources of Thoreau's Greek Translations," in Joel Meyerson, ed., *Studies in the American Renaissance* (Boston: Twayne, 1980), pp. 293–294; Allen and Torrey, *Journal of Henry David Thoreau*, December 15, 1838, vol. 1, pp. 66–67; December 23, 1838, vol. 1, pp. 69–70; November 5, 1839, vol. 1, p. 93; November 8, 1839, vol. 1, p. 94; January 2, 1840, vol. 1, pp. 116–117.
29. Howe, *Making the American Self*, p. 214; Bell Gale Chavigny, ed., *The Woman and the Myth: Margaret Fuller's Life and Writings* (New York: Feminist Press, 1976), Memoirs, 1840, pp. 35, 38–41; Marie Cleary, "Freeing 'Incarcerated Souls': Margaret Fuller, Women, and Classical Mythology," *New England Classical Journal* 27 (Summer 2000):65; Susan Phinney Conrad, *Perish the Thought: Intellectual Women in Romantic America, 1830–1860* (Oxford: Oxford University Press, 1976), pp. 52, 54; Kopff, *Devil Knows Latin*, pp. 147–148; Talbot Hamlin, *Greek Revival Architecture in America* (Oxford: Oxford University Press, 1944), pp. 97, 315–316.

30. Cleary, "Freeing 'Incarcerated Souls,'" pp. 62–65; Nancy Craig Simmons, "Margaret Fuller's Boston Conversations," in Joel Meyerson, ed., *Studies in the American Renaissance* (Charlottesville: University Press of Virginia, 1994), p. 204; Conrad, *Perish the Thought*, p. 53; Kopff, *Devil Knows Latin*, p. 148; Feldman and Richardson, *Rise of Modern Mythology*, p. 520; Howe, *Making the American Self*, p. 223.
31. Mason Wade, ed., *The Writings of Margaret Fuller* (New York: Viking, 1941), pp. 176–178, 180, 199, 216; Cleary, "Freeing 'Incarcerated Souls,'" p. 66; William Vance, *America's Rome* (New Haven: Yale University Press, 1989), vol. 1, pp. 176–178.
32. Kopff, *Devil Knows Latin*, p. 157; Conrad, *Perish the Thought*, p. 48. For an interesting discussion of the role of the Hellenic movement, especially Greek drama and mythology, in strengthening nineteenth-century women's connection to the classics see Caroline Winterer, "Victorian Antigone: Classicism and Women's Education in America, 1840–1890," *American Quarterly* 53 (March 2001):70–93.
33. Gregory A. Staley, "Washington Irving's *Sketch Book*: American *Odyssey*," unpublished manuscript, pp. 19–20.
34. Feldman and Richardson, *Rise of Modern Mythology*, p. 506; Gerard M. Sweeney, *Melville's Use of Classical Mythology* (Amsterdam: Rodopi N.V., 1975), pp. 32–33; Charvat, *Works of Nathaniel Hawthorne, The Wonder Book*, vol. 7, pp. 10–171; *Tanglewood Tales*, vol. 7, pp. 183–368; Letters, Hawthorne to Robert Carter, March 19, 1853, vol. 16, pp. 652–653.
35. Feldman and Richardson, *Rise of Modern Mythology*, p. 514; Charvat, *Works of Nathaniel Hawthorne, The Marble Faun*, vol. 4, pp. 168, 173, 255, 457, 461; French and Italian Notebooks, May 1, 1858, vol. 14, p. 198.
36. Charvat, *Works of Nathaniel Hawthorne, The Marble Faun*, vol. 4, pp. 8–11; French and Italian Notebooks, April 18, 1858, vol. 14, pp. 173–174; April 22, 1858, vol. 14, p. 178; April 30, 1858, vol. 14, p. 192; Hubert H. Hoeltje, *Inward Sky: The Mind and Heart of Nathaniel Hawthorne* (Durham, N.C.: Duke University Press, 1962), p. 503.
37. Hoeltje, *Inward Sky*, pp. 500–501; Charvat, *Works of Nathaniel Hawthorne, The Marble Faun*, vol. 4, p. 3.
38. Sweeney, *Melville's Use of Classical Mythology*, pp. 18, 21, 23–25, 28.
39. Ibid., pp. 29–30, 40–41, 55, 64, 153; Herman Melville, *Moby-Dick, or The Whale* (Evanston, Ill.: Northwestern University Press, 1988), p. 164.
40. Sweeney, *Melville's Use of Classical Mythology*, pp. 38, 42–45, 47–49, 67.
41. Ibid., pp. 51–52, 53, 55, 64.
42. Ibid., pp. 73–74, 77–78, 82.
43. Ibid., pp. 84–87, 91.
44. Ibid., p. 97.
45. Ibid., pp. 103–108, 111–112.
46. Ibid., pp. 113–115.
47. Ibid., pp. 116–117, 124–126, 129.
48. Ibid., pp. 23–24.
49. Ibid., p. 139.

50. Thomas Ollive Mabbott, ed., *Collected Works of Edgar Allan Poe* (Cambridge, Mass.: Harvard University Press, 1969–1978), "To Helen," 1831, vol. 1, p. 166; "The Raven," 1845, vol. 1, pp. 366, 368, 372–374; Darlene Harbour Unrue, "Edgar Allan Poe: The Romantic as Classicist," *International Journal of the Classical Tradition* 1 (Spring 1995):116–119; Buranelli, *Edgar Allan Poe*, p. 100.

51. Charvat, *Works of Nathaniel Hawthorne*, Hawthorne to Francis Benoch, November 29, 1859, vol. 18, p. 204.

52. Rusk, *Letters of Ralph Waldo Emerson*, Introduction, vol. 1, pp. xxxi–xxxii; Emerson to Lidian Emerson, April 19, 1836, vol. 2, p. 9; Emerson to William Emerson, September 4, 1841, vol. 2, p. 444; Gilman et al., *Journals of Ralph Waldo Emerson*, October 14, 1832, vol. 4, pp. 50–51; November 14, 1835, vol. 5, p. 109; August 3, 1837, vol. 5, p. 351; October 11, 1839, vol. 7, p. 269; November 14, 1839, vol. 7, p. 303; May 10, 1840, vol. 7, p. 496; October 9, 1841, vol. 8, p. 108; Emerson, *Complete Works of Ralph Waldo Emerson*, "Heroism," vol. 2, p. 248; *Society and Solitude*, vol. 7, pp. 73, 199–200.

53. Allen and Torrey, *Journal of Henry David Thoreau*, July 9, 1840, vol. 1, p. 165.

54. Dixon Wecter, *The Hero in America: A Chronicle of Hero-Worship* (Ann Arbor: University of Michigan Press, 1966), pp. 5, 489; Conrad, *Perish the Thought*, p. 208.

55. Emerson, *Complete Works of Ralph Waldo Emerson*, Society and Solitude, vol. 7, p. 200; Reinhold, *Classica Americana*, p. 260; Rusk, *Letters of Ralph Waldo Emerson*, Introduction, vol. 1, p. xxxii; Gilman et al., *Journals of Ralph Waldo Emerson*, August 4, 1837, vol. 5, p. 352; August 5, 1837, vol. 5, p. 353.

56. Reinhold, *Classica Americana*, pp. 259–260; Rusk, *Letters of Ralph Waldo Emerson*, Emerson to James Elliot Cabot, April 13, 1857, vol. 5, p. 71; Emerson, *Complete Works of Ralph Waldo Emerson*, Introduction to 1871 edition of Plutarch's *Morals*, vol. 10, p. 297–298, 300–302, 318, 322.

6. Christianity

1. John C. Rolfe, *Cicero and His Influence* (Boston: M. Jones, 1925), pp. 115–118.

2. For reference to the medieval origins of the English and American colonial educational systems see Sheldon D. Cohen, *A History of Colonial Education, 1607–1776* (New York: John Wiley and Sons, 1974), pp. 11, 22–24.

3. Robert Middlekauff, "A Persistent Tradition: The Classical Curriculum in Eighteenth-Century New England," *William and Mary Quarterly*, 3d ser., 18 (January 1961):56; Rolfe, *Cicero and His Influence*, p. 146; Wilson Smith, ed., *Theories of Education in Early America, 1655–1819* (Indianapolis: Bobbs-Merrill, 1973), Charles Chauncy on Liberal Learning, 1655, p. 5; Cotton Mather, "An Essay on the Memory of My Venerable Master: Ezekiel Cheever," 1708, pp. 32–38. For reference to the influence of the Cambridge Platonists, see Daniel Walker Howe, *The Unitarian Conscience: Harvard*

Moral Philosophy, 1805–1861 (Cambridge, Mass.: Harvard University Press, 1970), p. 43.

4. Lawrence A. Cremin, *American Education: The Colonial Experience, 1607–1783* (New York: Harper and Row, 1970), pp. 175, 321; Cohen, *History of Colonial Education*, pp. 98, 166; Paul K. Conkin, *The Uneasy Center: Reformed Christianity in Antebellum America* (Chapel Hill: University of North Carolina Press, 1995), p. 57; Merrill D. Peterson, *James Madison: A Biography in His Own Words* (New York: Harper and Row, 1974), pp. 16, 18; James Thomas Flexner, *The Young Hamilton: A Biography* (Boston: Little, Brown, 1978), p. 47; John C. Miller, *Sam Adams: Pioneer in Propaganda* (Stanford: Stanford University Press, 1936), pp. 6, 85, 228–229; Richard M. Gummere, *The American Colonial Mind and the Classical Tradition: Essays in Comparative Culture* (Cambridge, Mass.: Harvard University Press, 1963), p. 115; Meyer Reinhold, *Classica Americana: The Greek and Roman Heritage in the United States* (Detroit: Wayne State University Press, 1984), p. 157.

5. Howe, *Unitarian Conscience*, pp. 43, 190–191; Albert Ellery Bergh and Walter A. Lipscomb, eds., *The Writings of Thomas Jefferson* (Washington, D.C.: Thomas Jefferson Memorial Association, 1903), Jefferson to William Short, October 31, 1819, vol. 15, pp. 219, 223–224; Jefferson to Benjamin Waterhouse, June 26, 1822, vol. 15, p. 385; Lester J. Cappon, ed., *The Adams-Jefferson Letters: The Complete Correspondence between Thomas Jefferson and Abigail and John Adams* (Chapel Hill: University of North Carolina Press, 1959), Jefferson to John Adams, July 5, 1814, vol. 2, pp. 432–433. For a fuller discussion of Jefferson's philosophical views, see Carl J. Richard, *The Founders and the Classics: Greece, Rome, and the American Enlightenment* (Cambridge, Mass.: Harvard University Press, 1994), pp. 187–194.

6. Edward L. Pierce, ed., *Memoir and Letters of Charles Sumner* (London: Sampson Low, 1878), Sumner to Henry Ware, August 22, 1843, vol. 2, pp. 266–267; Charles Sumner, *The Works of Charles Sumner* (Boston: Lee and Shepard, 1874–1883), The Scholar, the Jurist, the Artist, the Philanthropist, August 27, 1846, vol. 1, pp. 253–255.

7. Julian P. Boyd, ed., *The Papers of Thomas Jefferson* (Princeton: Princeton University Press, 1950), Jefferson to Maria Cosway, October 12, 1786, vol. 10, p. 451; Zoltán Haraszti, *John Adams and the Prophets of Progress* (Cambridge, Mass.: Harvard University Press, 1952), p. 302.

8. Sumner, *Works of Charles Sumner*, Fame and Glory, August 11, 1847, vol. 2, p. 12.

9. Ibid., vol. 2, pp. 13, 21–22.

10. Ibid., vol. 2, pp. 22–23.

11. Pierce, *Memoir and Letters of Charles Sumner*, Memoir, vol. 1, pp. 36–37, 53, 59.

12. Ibid., Letters, Sumner to George S. Hilliard, May 19, 1839, vol. 2, pp. 99–100; July 13, 1839, vol. 2, pp. 103–104; September 29, 1839, vol. 2, p. 115; Sumner to Henry Wadsworth Longfellow, July 26, 1839, vol. 2, p. 107; Sumner to Simon Greenleaf, July 27, 1839, vol. 2, p. 108; Sumner to Dr. Samuel G. Howe, May 31, 1844, vol. 2, p. 306.

13. Michael O'Brien, *A Character of Hugh Legaré* (Knoxville: University of Tennessee Press, 1985), pp. 19, 79–80, 102.
14. Ibid., pp. 253–254, 257–258.
15. Adrienne Koch and William Peden, eds., *The Selected Writings of John and John Quincy Adams* (New York: Alfred A. Knopf, 1946), John Quincy Adams to George Washington Adams, September 1, 1811, pp. 279–281.
16. Charles Francis Adams, ed., *Memoirs of John Quincy Adams, Comprising Portions of His Diary from 1795 to 1848* (Philadelphia, 1874–1877; reprint, New York: AMS Press, 1970), April 5, 1813, vol. 2, pp. 455–456; April 6, 1835, vol. 9, pp. 231–232; May 18, 1839, vol. 10, p. 122.
17. Ibid., August 16, 1811, vol. 2, p. 297; January 12, 1812, vol. 2, pp. 333–334; October 13, 1822, vol. 6, pp. 78–79. For reference to Jefferson's belief in the necessity of an afterlife, see Bergh and Lipscomb, *Writings of Thomas Jefferson*, Jefferson to Benjamin Rush, April 21, 1803, vol. 10, p. 380; Jefferson to Benjamin Waterhouse, June 26, 1822, vol. 15, pp. 384–385; Jefferson to Augustus B. Woodward, March 24, 1824, vol. 16, p. 18.
18. Aida DiPace Donald et al., eds., *Diary of Charles Francis Adams* (Cambridge, Mass.: Harvard University Press, 1964–), September 17, 1831, vol. 4, pp. 138–139; Peter Shaw, *The Character of John Adams* (Chapel Hill: University of North Carolina Press, 1976), p. 35.
19. Donald et al., *Diary of Charles Francis Adams*, June 11, 1832, vol. 4, p. 312; July 7, 1832, vol. 4, p. 325; July 9, 1832, vol. 4, p. 326; July 23, 1832, vol. 4, p. 334; July 29, 1832, vol. 4, p. 337; Ralph Waldo Emerson, *The Complete Works of Ralph Waldo Emerson* (Boston: Houghton Mifflin, 1903–1904; reprint, New York: AMS Press, 1968), Introduction to 1871 Edition of Plutarch's *Morals*, vol. 10, p. 312.
20. Richard C. Lounsbury, ed., *Louisa S. McCord: Poems, Drama, Biography, Letters* (Charlottesville: University Press of Virginia, 1996), *Caius Gracchus*, p. 232; Afterword, p. 439.
21. Michael O'Brien, ed., *All Clever Men, Who Make Their Way: Critical Discourse in the Old South* (Athens: University of Georgia Press, 1992), James Warley Miles, "The Possibility and Nature of Theology," 1849, pp. 274–275.
22. Allan Nevins, *The State Universities and Democracy* (Urbana: University of Illinois Press, 1962), p. 40.
23. Jean S. Straub, "Teaching in the Friends' Latin School of Philadelphia in the Eighteenth Century," *Pennsylvania Magazine of History and Biography* 91 (October 1967):453; Patrick Critwell, "The Eighteenth Century: A Classical Age?" *Arion* 7 (Spring 1968):114–115.
24. Nathan G. Goodman, *Benjamin Rush: Physician and Citizen, 1746–1813* (Philadelphia: University of Pennsylvania Press, 1934), p. 316; Reinhold, *Classica Americana*, pp. 131, 158; L. H. Butterfield, ed., *The Letters of Benjamin Rush* (Princeton: Princeton University Press, 1951), Rush to John Adams, July 21, 1789, vol. 1, p. 525.
25. Edwin Miles, "The Old South and the Classical World," *North Carolina Historical Review* 48 (1971):261; Richard Lounsbury, "Ludibria Rerum Mortalium: Charleston Intellectuals and Their Classics," in David Moltke-Hansen

and Michael O'Brien, eds., *Intellectual Life in Antebellum Charleston* (Knoxville: University of Tennessee Press, 1986), pp. 345–346, 362, 367.
26. Lounsbury, "Ludibria Rerum Mortalium," pp. 362–363, 365, 367.
27. Reinhold, *Classica Americana*, p. 238; Caroline Winterer, *The Culture of Classicism: Ancient Greece and Rome in American Intellectual Life, 1780–1910* (Baltimore: Johns Hopkins University Press, 2002), p. 48.
28. Lilian Handlin, *George Bancroft: The Intellectual Democrat* (New York: Harper and Row, 1984), p. 42; Miles, "The Old South and the Classical World," p. 261; Egon Verheyen, "'Unenlightened by a Single Ray of Antiquity': John Quincy Adams and the Design of the Pediment for the United States Capitol," *International Journal of the Classical Tradition* 3 (Fall 1996):226.
29. Neal Gillespie, *The Collapse of Orthodoxy: The Intellectual Ordeal of George Frederick Holmes* (Charlottesville: University Press of Virginia, 1972), pp. 40, 73–74.
30. William H. Gilman et al., eds., *The Journals and Miscellaneous Notebooks of Ralph Waldo Emerson*, "The Character of Socrates," 1820, vol. 1, p. 211; Journal, December 21, 1823, vol. 2, p. 193; Marie Cleary, "'Vague Irregular Notions': American Women and Classical Mythology, 1780–1855," *New England Classical Journal* 29 (Winter 2002):229.
31. Walter R. Agard, "Classics on the Midwest Frontier," *Classical Journal* 51 (1955):105; Richard Hofstadter and Wilson Smith, eds., *American Higher Education: A Documentary History* (Chicago: University of Chicago Press, 1961), J. H. Fairchild on the Antislavery Commitment of Oberlin, 1833–1834, vol. 1, p. 422.
32. Verheyen, "'Unenlightened by a Single Ray of Antiquity,'" p. 228; Howard Mumford Jones, *O Strange New World: American Culture, the Formative Years* (New York: Viking Press, 1952), p. 265; O'Brien, *All Clever Men*, Frederick Adolphus Porcher, "Modern Art," 1852, pp. 324, 330–331; Lounsbury, "Ludibria Rerum Mortalium," p. 351; Frederick Rudolph, *Curriculum: A History of the American Undergraduate Course of Study since 1636* (San Francisco: Jossey-Bass Publishers, 1977), p. 141; Wendy A. Cooper, *Classical Taste in America, 1800–1840* (New York: Abbeville Press and Baltimore Museum of Art, 1993), p. 84.
33. Cooper, *Classical Taste in America*, pp. 88, 100–101.
34. Talbot Hamlin, *Greek Revival Architecture in America* (Oxford: Oxford University Press, 1944), p. 322.
35. William Vance, *America's Rome* (New Haven: Yale University Press, 1989), vol. 1, pp. 226–227, 241.
36. Ralph L. Rusk, ed., *The Letters of Ralph Waldo Emerson* (New York: Columbia University Press, 1939), Emerson to Lidian Emerson, January 12, 1843, vol. 3, pp. 120–121; Emerson to Margaret Fuller, January 13, 1843, vol. 3, pp. 121–122; Gilman et al., *Journals of Ralph Waldo Emerson*, August 17, 1837, vol. 5, p. 363.
37. Malcolm Cowley, ed., *The Portable Hawthorne* (New York: Penguin Books, 1976), p. 19; Hubert H. Hoeltje, *Inward Sky: The Mind and Heart of Nathaniel Hawthorne* (Durham, N.C.: Duke University Press, 1962), pp. 487,

490; William Charvat et al., eds., *The Works of Nathaniel Hawthorne* (Columbus: Ohio State University Press, 1962–1988), French and Italian Notebooks, June 4, 1858, vol. 14, pp. 281, 804; June 8, 1858, vol. 14, pp. 298–299.

38. Charvat et al., *Works of Nathaniel Hawthorne, The Marble Faun*, vol. 4, pp. 123, 134–135.

39. William Douglas Smyth, "The Artistic Experience of South Carolinians Abroad in the 1850s," and Gene Waddell, "Where Are Our Trumbulls?," in David Moltke-Hansen, ed., *Art in the Lives of South Carolinians: Nineteenth-Century Chapters* (Charleston: Carolina Art Association, 1979), pp. WS-3–WS-4, GWb-11.

40. Melvin I. Urofsky, "Reforms and Response: The Yale Report of 1828," *History of Education Quarterly* 5 (March 1965):61–62; George Fitzhugh, *Sociology for the South, or The Failure of Free Society* (Richmond: A. Morris, 1854; reprint, New York: Burt Franklin, 1965), pp. 115–116, 135; Louis B. Wright, *Culture on the Moving Frontier* (Bloomington: Indiana University Press, 1955), p. 172.

41. Horace Mann, *Lectures on Education* (Boston: Ide and Dutton, 1855; reprint, New York: Arno Press, 1969), pp. 168–169, 280.

42. William H. McGuffey, ed., *McGuffey's Sixth Eclectic Reader* (New York: American Books, 1880), pp. 438–439; Fitzhugh, *Sociology for the South*, pp. 111–112; Winterer, *Culture of Classicism*, p. 96; Michael O'Brien, *Conjectures of Order: Intellectual Life and the American South, 1810–1860* (Chapel Hill: University of North Carolina Press, 2004), p. 1143.

43. Rusk, *Letters of Ralph Waldo Emerson*, Emerson to John Boynton Hill, January 3, 1823, vol. 1, p. 128; Gilman et al., *Journals of Ralph Waldo Emerson*, 1825, vol. 2, pp. 413–415; 1830, vol. 3, p. 365; Emerson, *Complete Works of Ralph Waldo Emerson*, "Character," vol. 10, pp. 115–116; "The Sovereignty of Ethics," vol. 10, p. 209.

44. Emerson, *Complete Works of Ralph Waldo Emerson, Representative Men*, vol. 4, pp. 56–57; Gilman et al., *Journals of Ralph Waldo Emerson*, April 6, 1832, vol. 4, p. 11.

45. Emerson, *Complete Works of Ralph Waldo Emerson*, Introduction to 1871 Edition of Plutarch's *Morals*, vol. 10, pp. 305, 313–314, 316.

46. Albert von Frank et al., eds., *The Complete Sermons of Ralph Waldo Emerson* (Columbia: University of Missouri Press, 1989–1991), "We Should Live Soberly, Righteously, and Godly in This Present World," May 3, 1829, vol. 1, p. 275; "We Are of God," October 24, 1830, vol. 3, p. 21; Gilman et al., *Journals of Ralph Waldo Emerson*, December 28, 1834, vol. 4, p. 380.

47. Adams, *Memoirs of John Quincy Adams*, October 13, 1811, vol. 2, p. 317; November 10, 1811, vol. 2, p. 324; April 13, 1813, vol. 2, p. 461; April 17, 1813, vol. 2, p. 462; September 9, 1818, vol. 4, p. 129; December 16, 1827, vol. 7, p. 381.

48. Thomas R. Dew, *A Digest of the Laws, Customs, Manners, and Institutions of the Ancient and Modern Nations*, 2d ed. (New York: D. Appleton, 1870), p. 58.

49. Susan Phinney Conrad, *Perish the Thought: Intellectual Women in Romantic America, 1830–1860* (Oxford: Oxford University Press, 1976), p. 213; Nancy

Craig Simmons, "Margaret Fuller's Boston Conversations," in Joel Meyerson, ed., *Studies in the American Renaissance* (Charlottesville: University Press of Virginia, 1994), pp. 204, 207.

50. Vance, *America's Rome*, vol. 1, pp. 23, 25–26.
51. Ibid., pp. 164–165.
52. Adams, *Memoirs of John Quincy Adams*, April 1, 1829, vol. 8, p. 126; April 15, 1831, vol. 8, p. 354.
53. Edgar W. Knight, ed., *A Documentary History of Education in the South before 1860* (Chapel Hill: University of North Carolina Press, 1949–1953), Address of the Reverend William W. Wightman at the Laying of the Cornerstone of Wofford College, South Carolina, 1851, vol. 4, pp. 369–370, 374.
54. Kenneth E. Shewmaker, ed., *Daniel Webster: "The Completest Man"* (Hanover, N.H.: University Press of New England, 1990), The Dignity and Importance of History, 1852, p. 136.
55. Winterer, *Culture of Classicism*, pp. 80–81, 92; Mark Morford, "Early American School Editions of Ovid," *Classical Journal* 78 (Winter 1982–1983):152–153, 157; Marie Sally Cleary, *The Bulfinch Solution: Teaching the Ancient Classics in American Schools* (Salem, N.H.: Ayer, 1989), pp. 44–45, 49; Burton Feldman and Robert D. Richardson, eds., *The Rise of Modern Mythology, 1680–1860* (Bloomington: Indiana University Press, 1972), p. 513.
56. Feldman and Richardson, *Rise of Modern Mythology*, p. 506; Charvat et al., *The Works of Nathaniel Hawthorne*, *The Wonder Book*, vol. 7, p. 3; *Tanglewood Tales*, vol. 7, pp. 179, 301–302, 329.
57. Elizabeth Fox-Genovese and Eugene D. Genovese, *The Mind of the Master Class: History and Faith in the Southern Slaveholders' Worldview* (Cambridge: Cambridge University Press, 2005), p. 262.
58. Agard, "Classics on the Midwest Frontier," pp. 105, 107–108; Hamlin, *Greek Revival Architecture in America*, p. 369.
59. Koch and Peden, *Selected Writings of John and John Quincy Adams*, John Quincy Adams to John Adams, January 3, 1817, p. 292.

7. Slavery

1. William Peden, ed., *Notes on the State of Virginia* (Chapel Hill: University of North Carolina Press, 1955), pp. 138–143; P. J. Staudenraus, *The African Colonization Movement, 1816–1865* (New York: Columbia University Press, 1961), pp. 70, 107, 174, 183, 187, 245, 251; Kate M. Rowland, ed., *The Life and Correspondence of George Mason* (New York: G. P. Putnam's Sons; reprint, New York: Russell and Russell, 1964), Scheme for Replevying Goods under Distress for Rent, 1765, vol. 1, p. 378; Max Farrand, ed., *The Records of the Federal Convention of 1787*, 3d ed. (New Haven: Yale University Press, 1966), vol. 2, pp. 370–372; George Fitzhugh, *Cannibals All: Slaves without Masters* (Richmond: A. Morris, 1857; reprint, Cambridge, Mass.: Harvard University Press, 1960), p. 7.
2. William Sumner Jenkins, *Pro-slavery Thought in the Old South* (Chapel Hill: University of North Carolina Press, 1935), p. 291; Thomas R. Dew, *A Digest*

of the Laws, Customs, Manners, and Institutions of the Ancient and Modern Nations, 2d ed. (New York: D. Appleton, 1870), pp. 78–79; Michael O'Brien, ed., *All Clever Men, Who Make Their Way: Critical Discourse in the Old South* (Athens: University of Georgia Press, 1992), Thomas Roderick Dew, "Republicanism and Literature," 1836, p. 168; Eugene D. Genovese, "The Gracchi and Their Mother in the Mind of American Slaveholders," *Journal of the Historical Society* 2 (Summer/Fall 2002):466.

3. Joseph R. Berrigan, "The Impact of the Classics upon the South," *Classical Journal* 64 (Winter 1968–1969):19.
4. Fitzhugh, *Cannibals All*, pp. 220, 245–246; George Fitzhugh, *Sociology for the South, or The Failure of Free Society* (Richmond: A. Morris, 1854; reprint, New York: Burt Franklin, 1965), pp. 93, 256; Susan Ford Wiltshire, "Jefferson, Calhoun, and the Slavery Debate: The Classics and the Two Minds of the South," *Southern Humanities Review* 11 (1977):37.
5. Michael O'Brien, *A Character of Hugh Legaré* (Knoxville: University of Tennessee Press, 1985), p. 101; Richard C. Lounsbury, ed., *Louisa S. McCord: Poems, Drama, Biography, Letters* (Charlottesville: University Press of Virginia, 1996), *Caius Gracchus*, p. 189.
6. Genovese, "Gracchi and Their Mother in the Mind of American Slaveholders," pp. 458, 462–463, 465–466.
7. Fitzhugh, *Cannibals All*, pp. 133–134; Wayne K. Durill, "The Power of Ancient Words: Classical Teaching and Social Change at South Carolina College," *Journal of Southern History* 65 (August 1999):496.
8. Fitzhugh, *Sociology for the South*, pp. 89–90, 147, 241–244.
9. Jennifer Tolbert Roberts, *Athens on Trial: The Antidemocratic Tradition in Western Thought* (Princeton: Princeton University Press, 1994), p. 264; Drew Gilpin Faust, *A Sacred Circle: The Dilemma of the Intellectual in the Old South, 1840–1860* (Baltimore: Johns Hopkins University Press, 1977), p. 119.
10. Lounsbury, *Louisa S. McCord, Caius Gracchus*, pp. 188, 228, 232, 437. For reference to southern praise for Seneca's call for the humane treatment of slaves, a call southerners equated with paternalism, see Elizabeth Fox-Genovese and Eugene D. Genovese, *The Mind of the Master Class: History and Faith in the Southern Slaveholders' Worldview* (Cambridge: Cambridge University Press, 2005), p. 279.
11. Edwin A. Miles, "The Old South and the Classical World," *North Carolina Historical Review* 48 (1971):258, 263, 265; Edgar W. Knight, ed., *A Documentary History of Education in the South before 1860* (Chapel Hill: University of North Carolina Press, 1949–1953), A Southern Commercial Convention at Richmond Resolves on "Home Institutions," 1856, vol. 5, p. 301; Durill, "Power of Ancient Words," pp. 496–497.
12. Susan Ford Wiltshire, "Aristotle in America," *Humanities* 8 (January–February 1987):8–11.
13. Robert Meriwether et al., eds., *The Papers of John C. Calhoun* (Columbia: University of South Carolina Press, 1959–), Calhoun to A. D. Wallace, December 17, 1840, vol. 15, p. 389; Fitzhugh, *Cannibals All*, pp. x.xii–xxxiii, 12–13, 53; Fitzhugh, *Sociology for the South*, p. 253.

14. Neal Gillespie, *The Collapse of Orthodoxy: The Intellectual Ordeal of George Frederick Holmes* (Charlottesville: University Press of Virginia, 1972), pp. 102, 113, 135; Wiltshire, "Aristotle in America," pp. 10–11; Dew, *Digest*, p. 210; Harvey Wish, "Aristotle, Plato, and the Mason-Dixon Line," *Journal of the History of Ideas* 10 (April 1949):259–260.
15. John C. Calhoun, *A Disquisition on Government and Selections from the Discourse*, ed. C. Gordon Post (New York: Macmillan, 1953), pp. 42–44; Wiltshire, "Jefferson, Calhoun, and the Slavery Debate," p. 36.
16. Fitzhugh, *Sociology for the South*, pp. 83, 285; Fitzhugh, *Cannibals All*, p. 201.
17. Fitzhugh, *Cannibals All*, pp. 194, 207–208; Fitzhugh, *Sociology for the South*, p. 253; Roberts, *Athens on Trial*, p. 281; Harvey Wish, *George Fitzhugh: Propagandist of the Old South* (Baton Rouge: Louisiana State University Press, 1943), pp. 230–231.
18. Wish, "Aristotle, Plato, and the Mason-Dixon Line," p. 258; Paul F. Paskoff and Daniel J. Wilson, eds., *The Cause of the South: Selections from "De Bow's Review," 1846–1867* (Baton Rouge: Louisiana State University Press, 1982), Dr. D. McCauley, "Humbugiana," p. 142.
19. Calhoun, *Disquisition on Government*, pp. 40–41, 44–45.
20. Fitzhugh, *Cannibals All*, pp. 71, 193–194.
21. Fitzhugh, *Sociology for the South*, pp. 26–27, 70.
22. Fitzhugh, *Cannibals All*, p. 8.
23. Ibid., p. 78; Fitzhugh, *Sociology for the South*, p. 70.
24. David Brion Davis, *Slavery and Human Progress* (Oxford: Oxford University Press, 1984), pp. 24, 112; Walter M. Merrill et al., eds., *The Letters of William Lloyd Garrison* (Cambridge, Mass.: Harvard University Press, 1971–1981), To the Editor of the *Salem Gazette*, vol. 1, p. 20; Garrison to Henry E. Benson, November 4, 1836, vol. 2, p. 181; December 17, 1836, vol. 2, p. 192n; Daniel Walker Howe, *Making the American Self: Jonathan Edwards to Abraham Lincoln* (Cambridge, Mass.: Harvard University Press, 1997), p. 150; John W. Blassingame, ed., *The Frederick Douglass Papers* (New Haven: Yale University Press, 1979–), "The Significance of Emancipation in the West Indies," August 3, 1857, volume 3, p. 193; "Fighting the Rebels with One Hand," vol. 3, pp. 470, 474; Waldo E. Martin, *The Mind of Frederick Douglass* (Chapel Hill: University of North Carolina Press, 1984), p. 168.
25. Blassingame, *Frederick Douglass Papers*, "We Are in the Midst of a Moral Revolution," May 10, 1854, vol. 2, p. 488; "The Clans of the Negro Ethnologically Considered," July 12, 1854, vol. 2, p. 508.
26. David S. Wiesen, "Herodotus and the Modern Debate over Race and Slavery," *Ancient World* 3 (1980):3, 11.
27. William Charvat et al., eds., *The Works of Nathaniel Hawthorne* (Columbus: Ohio State University Press, 1962–1988), vol. 4, p. 126.
28. Wiesen, "Herodotus and the Modern Debate over Race and Slavery," p. 11; Elzbieta Foeller-Pituch, "Ambiguous Heritage: Classical Myths in the Works of Nineteenth-Century American Writers," *International Journal of the Classical Tradition* 1 (Winter 1995):101.

29. Caroline Winterer, *The Mirror of Antiquity: American Women and the Classical Tradition, 1750–1900* (Ithaca: Cornell University Press, 2007), pp. 185, 187.
30. Charles Sumner, *The Works of Charles Sumner* (Boston: Lee and Shepard, 1874–1883), "White Slavery in the Barbary States," February 17, 1847, vol. 1, pp. 396–398.
31. Ibid., vol. 1, pp. 398–399.
32. William H. Gilman et al., eds., *The Journals and Miscellaneous Notebooks of Ralph Waldo Emerson* (Cambridge, Mass.: Harvard University Press, 1960–1982), 1851, vol. 11, pp. 346, 353.
33. Larry Ceplair, ed., *The Public Years of Sarah and Angelina Grimké: Selected Writings, 1835–1839* (New York: Columbia University Press, 1989), Angelina Grimké, "Appeal to the Christian Women of the South," pp. 59–60, 62; William Vance, *America's Rome* (New Haven: Yale University Press, 1989), vol. 1, p. 32.
34. Sterling Stuckey, ed., *The Ideological Origins of Black Nationalism* (Boston: Beacon Press, 1972), David Walker, *Appeal to the Coloured Citizens of the World*, 1829, pp. 55–56; Margaret Malamud, *Ancient Rome and Modern America* (London: Wiley-Blackwell, forthcoming, 2009), pp. 70–71.
35. Paul A. Rahe, *Republics, Ancient and Modern: Classical Republicanism and the American Revolution* (Chapel Hill: University of North Carolina Press, 1992), pp. 71, 115, 509; Paul K. Conkin, *Self-Evident Truths* (Bloomington: Indiana University Press, 1974), pp. 92, 95, 100.
36. Ralph Waldo Emerson, *The Complete Works of Ralph Waldo Emerson* (Boston: Houghton Mifflin, 1903–1904; reprint, New York: AMS Press, 1968), The Fugitive Slave Law, May 3, 1851, vol. 11, pp. 226–227, 238–239; Lurton D. Ingersoll, *The Life of Horace Greeley* (New York: Beekman Publishers, 1974), pp. 250–251.
37. Sumner, *Works of Charles Sumner*, Freedom National, Slavery Sectional, August 26, 1852, vol. 3, pp. 192–193; Gordon F. Hostetler, "The Brownlow-Pryne Debate," in Jeffrey Auer, ed., *Antislavery and Disunion, 1858–1861: Studies in the Rhetoric of Compromise and Conflict* (New York: Harper and Row, 1963), p. 20; Caroline Winterer, "Victorian Antigone: Classicism and Women's Education in America, 1840–1900," *American Quarterly* 53 (March 2001):75.
38. Sumner, *Works of Charles Sumner*, Presidential Candidates and the Issues, August 29, 1860, vol. 5, pp. 252–253. For reference to the development of the Greek theory of popular sovereignty and its importance see Conkin, *Self-Evident Truths*, pp. 30, 50–51, 54, 59.
39. Wish, *George Fitzhugh*, pp. 98–99, 118; Faust, *Sacred Circle*, pp. 84, 120.
40. Jean V. Matthews, *Rufus Choate: The Law and Civic Virtue* (Philadelphia: Temple University Press, 1980), pp. 201–202, 228.
41. Mark Twain, *Life on the Mississippi* (New York: Bantam Books, 1981), pp. 219–220.
42. Ibid., p. 195; Talbot Hamlin, *Greek Revival Architecture in America* (Oxford: Oxford University Press, 1944), p. 266; Vance, *America's Rome*, vol. 1, p. 53.

43. For a discussion of the limited nature of the influence of Scott, who was actually against slavery, on the South, see Fox-Genovese and Genovese, *Mind of the Master Class*, pp. 135–136, 306–307, 328.

Epilogue

1. Henry Adams, *The Education of Henry Adams: An Autobiography* (Boston: Houghton Mifflin, 1918), vol. 1, pp. 52–53; Meyer Reinhold, "Survey of the Scholarship on Classical Traditions in Early America," in John W. Eadie, ed., *Classical Traditions in Early America* (Ann Arbor: Center for the Coordination of Ancient and Modern Studies, 1976), p. 4; Caroline Winterer, *The Culture of Classicism: Ancient Greece and Rome in American Intellectual Life, 1780–1910* (Baltimore: Johns Hopkins University Press, 2002), p. 139.
2. Zoltán Haraszti, *John Adams and the Prophets of Progress* (Cambridge, Mass.: Harvard University Press, 1952), p. 16.
3. Michael Meckler, "The Rise of Populism, the Decline of Classical Education, and the Seventeenth Amendment," in Michael Meckler, ed., *Classical Antiquity and the Politics of America: From George Washington to George W. Bush* (Waco, Tex.: Baylor University Press, 2006), pp. 69–71; A. R. Burn, *The Pelican History of Greece* (New York: Penguin Books, 1965), p. 130.
4. Louis Menand, *The Metaphysical Club* (New York: Farrar, Straus and Giroux, 2001), pp. 3–4, 35, 43, 46–47, 51, 55–56, 61–63, 68–69, 342–344; Oliver Wendell Holmes Jr., *The Common Law* (Cambridge, Mass.: Harvard University Press, 1963), p. 5; Oliver Wendell Holmes Jr., *The Path of the Law*, 1897, in Louis Menand, ed., *Pragmatism: A Reader* (New York: Vintage Books, 1997), pp. 146, 153–154; Oliver Wendell Holmes Jr., "Natural Law," 1918, in Charles Capper and David A. Hollinger, eds., *The American Intellectual Tradition*, 3d ed. (Oxford: Oxford University Press, 1997), vol. 2, pp. 128–129.
5. Frank M. Turner, *The Greek Heritage in Victorian Britain* (New Haven: Yale University Press, 1981), p. 5.
6. Winterer, *Culture of Classicism*, pp. 100–101, 107, 117–119, 142, 147–148; Robert A. McCaughey, "The Transformation of American Academic Life: Harvard University, 1821–1892," *Perspectives in American History* 8 (1974):242; Meyer Reinhold, *Classica Americana: The Greek and Roman Heritage in the United States* (Detroit: Wayne State University Press, 1984), p. 333.
7. For the complete text of the poem, see Caroline Winterer, *The Mirror of Antiquity: American Women and the Classical Tradition, 1750–1900* (Ithaca: Cornell University Press, 2007), p. 208.
8. Bernard Bailyn, *The Ideological Origins of the American Revolution*, 2d ed. (Cambridge, Mass.: Harvard University Press, 1992), pp. 23–27, 44; John R. Alden, *A History of the American Revolution* (New York: Alfred A. Knopf, 1969), p. 21.
9. Winterer, *Culture of Classicism*, pp. 102, 133–134; Daniel Walker Howe, "Classical Education and Political Culture in Nineteenth-Century America," *Intellectual History Newsletter* 5 (Spring 1983):13.

10. Frederick L. Schuman, "Final Warning to America: Excerpts from Demosthenes," trans. J. H. Vince, *Nation* 151 (August 17, 1940):132–134; Frederick H. Cramer, "Demosthenes Redivivus: A Page from the Record of Isolationism," *Foreign Affairs* 19 (April 1941):330–350; "Case Studies in Isolationism," *American Mercury* 53 (July 1941):49–55; Mars M. Westinghouse, "Nazi Germany and Ancient Sparta," *Education* 65 (November 1944):152–164; Robert Campbell, "How a Democracy Died: A Fateful War between Athens and Sparta Points to the Dangers to Freedom Today," *Life* 30 (January 1, 1951):88–90, 93–96; "Lessons of Athens," *New Republic* 124 (January 15, 1961):5–6; Buell G. Gallagher, "Hope and History," *Saturday Review* 36 (July 4, 1953):24–25; Gerald W. Johnson, "God Was Bored," *New Republic* 145 (September 11, 1961):10; Richard Ned Lebow, "Thucydides' Speech to the American Senate," *Bulletin of the Atomic Scientists* 35 (December 1979):7–8. For a fuller discussion of the post–Civil War influence of Rome on American novels, films, circuses, and casinos like Caesar's Palace, see Margaret Malamud, *Ancient Rome and Modern America* (London: Wiley-Blackwell, forthcoming, 2009), pp. 98–259.
11. For modern criticism of Athens' treatment of women, see Eva Keuls, *The Reign of Phallus: Sexual Politics in Ancient Athens* (New York: Harper and Row, 1985).

Index

Abolitionists, xii, 26, 38, 181–183, 185, 187, 190–191, 193–203
Achaean League, 49
Achilles, 118, 164
Adams, Abigail, 54
Adams, Charles Francis, 2, 11–12, 24, 27–29, 50–51, 53, 161–162, 205
Adams, Charles Francis Jr., 204–205
Adams, George Washington, 26–28
Adams, Henry, 14, 19, 204–205, 208
Adams, John, 18, 29, 112, 163; middle-class origins of, xiii; and Roman civil law, 21; and classical education, 22–23, 28, 124, 205; and antiparty sentiment, 67; and mixed government theory, 75, 79–80; and classical versus Christian ethics, 155–156, 161, 180
Adams, John Quincy, 37, 45, 47, 54; and classical education, 22–29, 124, 177, 205; and the Greek War of Independence, 53; and Julius Caesar, 62–63; and antiparty sentiment, 67; and the relationship between Christianity and the classics, 159–161, 174–175, 180; and neoclassical art, 165, 167
Adams, Louisa, 25, 28
Adams, Samuel, 154, 177
Addison, Joseph, 4, 25, 55, 59, 113, 171
Aeneas, 94, 99, 118, 141, 164–165

Aeschylus, 2, 6, 14, 29, 123, 127, 135, 137, 141–142
Aesop, 43
African Americans, xi, 1, 4, 40–41, 181–203
Agamemnon, 136, 144, 165
Agesilaus, 126, 148, 174
Ajax, 44
Alamo, battle of the, 44, 51–52
Alaric, 70
Alcott, Bronson, 88, 131
Alexander the Great, 5, 63, 72, 135, 152, 154, 187–188, 191
Ambrose, 152
American Philological Association, 16, 119
American Revolution, 29, 31, 43, 108; and classical education, 2; and classical history, 20, 112, 117; and antiparty sentiment, 67; and mixed government, 74; and the Great Awakening, 153–154; and natural law, 199; and popular sovereignty, 200; and feudalism, 202; classical inspiration for, 203
Amherst College, 89, 96, 156
Anacreon, 25, 36, 127, 137
Anaxagoras, 126, 132, 173, 175
Anaximander, 205
Anthon, Charles, 10, 17, 32
Antifederalists, 75

Antigone, 59, 133, 200
Antony, Mark (Marcus Antonius), 4, 24, 63, 66, 108, 209
Apollo, 4, 13, 20, 138–139, 145–147, 163, 170
Apollonius, 117
Aquinas, Thomas, 73–74, 153
Areopagus, 71
Ares (Mars), 138, 140, 163
Ariadne, 36, 167
Aristarchus, 93
Aristides the Just, 38, 107, 110, 171, 185, 194
Aristophanes, 14, 29, 51, 124, 166, 191
Aristotle, 32, 92, 98, 207; and slavery, xii, 80, 184, 186–193, 196, 202; in education, 7, 23, 29; and mixed government theory, 73, 77; and pastoralism, 85, 103; and science, 93; and the Transcendentalists, 127–128, 131, 148; and Christianity, 153, 172, 177, 180; and Sparta, 182; and natural law, 199–200
Artemis (Diana), 139, 165
Arthurian Legends, 134
Athena (Minerva), 11, 31, 38–39, 45, 138–140, 144, 147
Atlas, 31, 57, 140
Atreus, 144, 147
Attila, 70
Augustine, 125, 153, 200
Augustus (Octavian), 9, 24, 46, 62, 67, 84, 121
Aurelius, Marcus, 165

Bacon, Francis, 92
Bailyn, Bernard, 209
Bancroft, George, 2, 10, 15, 19–20, 46–47, 149, 165
Beecher, Catharine, 8
Beecher, Lyman, 170
Benjamin, Asher, 34
Benton, Thomas Hart, 68, 73, 87
Berrigan, Joseph, 3, 183
Bible, 34, 43, 73, 84, 177, 179, 207; and slavery, xii, 181; in education, 2–6, 170–171, 187; compared to the classics, 132, 135, 156, 160, 163–166, 172, 174–176, 188; and natural law, 152
Biddle, Nicholas, 24, 34, 44–45
Bird, Robert Montgomery, 22
Blake, William, 163
Bonaparte, Napoleon, 21, 54, 63
Booth, John Wilkes, 65
Boston Latin School, 2, 33, 157

Bowdoin College, 167
British Museum, 123
Brown University (College of Rhode Island), 5, 92, 96, 153
Brutus, Lucius Junius, 22, 65
Brutus, Marcus, 4, 24, 60, 65, 68, 121, 171–172
Buchanan, James, 68
Bulfinch, Thomas, 33, 179
Bulwer-Lytton, Edward, 32
Burke, Edmund, 25
Bushman, Richard L., 35, 84
Byron, George Gordon, Lord, 4, 11

Caesar, Julius, 124, 171–172; in education, 2, 5, 8, 18, 23, 99, 138; assassination of, 4, 42, 65; and the fear of conspiracies against liberty, 62–70, 184
Calhoun, Floride, 57
Calhoun, John C., 49, 57, 68, 113, 168; and classical education, 3, 8, 30, 93; sculpted as a Roman, 37, 108–109; and the Greek War of Independence, 53; compared to Roman heroes, 55; and Julius Caesar, 62, 64–66, 69; and Roman emperors, 66–67; and decentralized government, 70–71; and antiparty sentiment, 72; and mixed government theory, 73–82; and slavery, 80, 185, 188–190, 192
California Gold Rush, 94
Caligula, 66
Calvin, John, 73–74
Cambridge University, 128, 153, 207
Canova, Antonio, 36–37, 109, 170
Capitoline Museum, 140
Carlyle, Thomas, 139
Carnegie, Andrew, 206
Carthage, 31, 36; and the Punic Wars, 54–56, 68, 72, 198–199; and commercialism, 83, 85, 87, 92
Cass, Lewis, 55
Cassius, 4, 63
Catiline (Lucius Sergius Catalina), 5, 18, 28, 68, 156, 171
Cato the Elder, 84, 88, 103, 135, 156, 197
Cato the Younger, 28, 55, 59, 68–69, 110, 171
Catullus, 147
Chaeronea, battle of, 72
Channing, William Ellery, 10, 96, 149, 154
Charles I, king of England, 68
Chase, Samuel, 21
Chaucer, Geoffrey, 136
Cheever, Ezekiel, 153

Cheves, Langdon, 58–59
Child, Lydia Maria, 194–195
Choate, Rufus, 18, 201
Christianity, 111; and women, 60, 197; relationship to the classics, 104, 111, 114, 126–128, 133, 135, 152–180, 206–207; and slavery, 195, 198–199
Cicero, 60, 99, 147, 177; in education, 2, 4–9, 15, 97, 138; as an orator, 18–19, 40, 42, 47–48, 59, 72, 112, 116; and the Adams family, 23–29, 63; as a role model, 55, 64–65, 68–70, 107–109; and mixed government theory, 73, 78; and classical ethics, 114, 152–154, 156–158, 160–161, 164–165, 172, 174–175; and natural law, 133, 199–201; and the gods, 159–160, 171–172, 174–175; and slavery, 186, 197
Cincinnatus, 37–38, 54–55, 68–69, 85, 107, 110
Civil Law, Roman, 21–22, 102, 159
Civil War, U.S., x, 2, 22, 25, 43–44, 70, 83, 194; causes of, xii, 81, 201–202; and the decline of the classics, 96, 147, 205–207
Classical Education, ix, xi, 1–18, 22, 30, 40–41, 88–104, 153, 207–209
Classical Mythology, 33, 39; and Romanticism, xi–xii, 120, 134–148, 151; in education, 15; and Christianity, 160, 163–166, 175–176, 178–179
Clay, Henry, 31, 44, 53, 63–64, 66–69, 112
Clemson, Anna Calhoun, 30, 93
Cleopatra, 195, 209
Clytemnestra, 144–145, 163, 165
Cold War, 209–210
Cole, Thomas, 37, 87
College of William and Mary, 14, 47
Colosseum, 4, 20, 93, 111, 158, 199
Colossus of Rhodes, 208
Columbia University (King's College), 6, 10, 97
Columella, 88
Commodus, 122
Common Law, English, 21–22
Compromise of 1850, 44, 81, 201
Concurrent Majority, theory of, 77–82
Confederate States of America, 3, 56, 58, 62
Constantine, 121
Cooper, James Fenimore, 19–20, 34, 176
Cooper, Thomas, 165
Cooper, Wendy, 45
Copernicus, Nicolaus, 93
Cornelia, 32, 56–58, 60, 186
Cornelius Nepos, 2, 5

Cornell University, 207
Cowper, William, 39, 155
Crassus, 68
Crawford, Thomas, 36, 108, 115, 117
Crawford, William H., 2
Crockett, Davy, 109
Cromwell, Oliver, 62–63, 65, 68

Dartmouth College, 6, 42, 153
Darwin, Charles, 205
David, Jacques-Louis, 167
David, king, 149, 156, 160
Davidson College, 5, 7
Davis, David Brion, 193–194
Davis, Jefferson, 19
Day, Jeremiah, 6, 94–97
De Bow, J. D. B., 70, 92, 186–187
De Bow's Review, 58, 92, 189, 191
Decatur, Stephen, 114
Deism, 180
Delphi, oracle of, 145
Democracy, ix, xi, 38, 40–83, 120–122, 181, 210–211
Democratic-Republican Party, 67, 86
Demosthenes, 148, 194; in education, 7, 15, 97, 99; as an orator, 12–13, 18, 47–48, 59, 72, 177, 201; and the Adams family, 23–25, 27, 29; as a role model, 52–53, 55, 69, 111–112, 157, 197; and classical ethics, 154; and slavery, 186
Dew, Thomas Roderick, 71–72; and ancient Greek democracy, 47, 49–50, 118, 120; and ancient Greek women, 61–62; and nationalism, 112–113; and Augustan literature, 121–122; and Christianity, 175; and slavery, 182, 184, 186; and Aristotle, 189
Dickinson, John, 75, 133
Dido, 165
Dimock, Susan, 9
Diogenes the Cynic, 126
Dionysus (Bacchus), 138, 140, 163
Douglass, Frederick, 194
Dred Scott vs. Sandford, 81
Duane, William J., 64

Egypt, 54, 70, 72, 103, 160, 185, 194–195
Electra, 145–146
Elgin Marbles, 11, 123
Emerson, Ellen, 30, 32
Emerson, Ralph Waldo, 12, 25, 42, 110, 139; and classical education, 11, 30, 100; and classical and neoclassical art, 32, 168; and ancient Greek democracy,

47; and Plutarch, 84, 148–151; and nationalism, 107–108, 117; and nonconformity, 123–127; and Neoplatonism, 127–131; and Stoicism, 131–134, 161, 173; and classical mythology, 134–135, 138, 166; and the compatibility of the classics with Christianity, 172–174; and the Fugitive Slave Law of 1850, 197, 199

English, John, Roman Catholic bishop, 99, 179

English Bill of Rights, 199

Enlightenment, the, xii, 105, 120, 152

Epaminondas, 126, 174

Epictetus, 110, 132, 165

Epicureanism, 154–155, 160, 170, 173–174

Erechtheum, 34, 36

Eros (Cupid), 35, 38

Ethiopians, 190, 195

Euclid, 7–8, 31, 43, 130, 187

Euripides, 6, 12–14, 29–31, 124, 137, 141, 145–146, 196

Evangelicals, 154, 162, 166, 180

Evans, Augusta Jane, 62

Everett, Edward, 24, 52, 54; and classical education, 10–12, 14–15, 42; and neoclassical art, 36, 38; Ciceronian rhetoric of, 43, 48, 194; and ancient Greek democracy, 71; and nationalism, 107, 110; and the Fugitive Slave Law of 1850, 197

Fabius, 54, 107, 110

The Federalist, 75–76, 188

Federalist Party, 62, 66, 72, 113

Felton, Cornelius Conway, 12, 15, 39, 97, 158, 172, 178

Female Academies, 3, 56

Female Colleges, 8–9

Feudalism, 202

Fitzhugh, George, 13; and women, 59; and centralized government, 72; and human nature, 73; and commercialism and industrialization, 102–103, 193; and the slavish copying of classical models, 107, 110, 124–125; and classical ethics, 170–171; and the compatibility of the classics with Christianity, 171–172; and slavery, 182–188, 190; and Aristotle, 188, 190–193

Florence, Italy, 20, 100, 170

Forum, Roman, 18, 35, 37, 54, 57, 158

France, 22, 63, 76, 86, 115, 119, 124, 148, 181

Franklin, Benjamin, 43, 89, 98, 112, 171, 185

French, Daniel Chester, 117

French Revolution, 135

Frieze, Henry, 16

Fugitive Slave Law of 1850, 197, 199–201

Fuller, Margaret, 114, 131, 138–139, 175–176

Fuller, Timothy, 138

Furies, 145, 162

Gadsden, James, 69

Galen, 103, 173

Gallatin, Albert, 91, 96

Gandhi, Mohandas K., 133

Garfield, James, 6–7

Garner, Margaret, 195–196

Garrison, William Lloyd, 183, 194

George III, king of Great Britain, 67–68, 74, 86, 209

German Classicism, 2, 10, 14–15, 17, 21, 23, 46

Germanic Tribes, 70

Gettysburg, battle of, 48

Gettysburg Address, 43, 50

Gibbon, Edward, 30, 178

Gildersleeve, Basil Lanneau, 14–16, 119

Gilmer, Francis Walker, 40, 112

Gladiatorial Combat, 22, 36, 122, 126, 170, 199, 202

Glorious Revolution, 199

Goldsmith, Oliver, 17

Gorgias, 130, 196

Gothic Architecture, 125, 185, 202

Gracchus, Gaius, 22, 56–59, 87, 148, 162, 184, 186

Gracchus, Tiberius, 56–57, 80, 87, 148, 184

Great Awakening, 153–154

Great Britain, 2, 50, 129, 183; and the common law, 21; and ancient Greek democracy, 46; and mixed government theory, 74; and the Industrial Revolution, 76, 83, 181, 193; and pastoralism, 86–88; and imperialism, 113; and American neoclassical architecture, 115; and classical education, 209

Greek War of Independence, 11, 15, 52–53

Greeley, Horace, 191, 199, 201

Greenough, Horatio, 36–37, 108, 117, 167–168

Grimké, Angelina, 197–198

Grimké, Sarah, 60–61

Grimké, Thomas, 97–99, 164–165

Grote, George, 46

Hades, 147, 161
Hadrian, 117, 161
Hamilcar Barca, 56
Hamilton, Alexander, 21, 62, 75, 86, 153
Hamilton, Edith, 33
Hamlin, Talbot, 35, 116
Hammond, James Henry, 55, 103
Hannibal, 20, 32, 54, 56, 68, 110, 198–199
Harper's "Classical Library," 39, 141
Harrington, James, 74
Harrison, William Henry, 42, 54–55, 70–71
Harvard University, 36–37, 54, 128, 150, 157, 165; classical instruction at, 2, 11, 17; entrance requirements at, 5, 96; curriculum of, 6, 14, 18, 89, 91, 97, 204, 207; presidents of, 12, 28, 42, 83, 175; and the Adams family, 22–23, 28; and Neoplatonism, 154
Hawthorne, Nathaniel, 19–20, 69–70, 123, 140–141, 148, 168–170, 179, 195
Hayne, Robert Y., 56
Hector, 32, 39, 60
Helen, 147–148
Henry, Patrick, 62, 68, 112
Hera (Juno), 138, 144
Heracles (Hercules), 11, 23, 103, 139–140, 165
Herculaneum, 19–20
Hermes (Mercury), 138, 140, 163
Hermitage, 44–45
Herndon, William, 43
Herodotus, 12, 29, 31, 102, 135–136; in education, 6–7, 10, 15; and Africans, 190, 194–195
Hesiod, x, 84
Hippocrates, 103
Hobbes, Thomas, 191–192
Holmes, George Frederick, 14, 39, 54, 69, 100; and ancient Greek women, 59; on the superiority of Christian to classical ethics, 166; and slavery, 184, 186; and Aristotle, 188–189
Holmes, Oliver Wendell Jr., 206
Homer, 15–16, 31–33, 36, 39, 44, 102, 130, 134, 147, 158, 166; in education, 2, 6–8, 12, 17, 91–92, 97, 99; and the Adams family, 23–24, 27–29; and nonconformity, 124, 126–127; and Henry David Thoreau, 135–137; and Rip Van Winkle, 140; and Herman Melville, 141–142; and Christianity, 154–155, 163–165; and slavery, 196

Homestead Act, 87
Horace, 32, 89, 125, 147, 157–158; in education, 2–4, 6–7, 9, 18, 99, 138; and the Adams family, 23–29; and Augustus, 46, 122; and pastoralism, 84; and nationalism, 113; and nonconformity, 127; and Christianity, 154, 160, 178
Horatius, 55
Hortensia, 60
Hosmer, Harriet, 32, 36
Houdon, Jean-Antoine, 108–109
Houston, Sam, 42, 44, 53, 68, 137
Howe, Daniel Walker, 48–49, 128

Industrial Revolution, ix, 83, 89, 94, 181, 193, 205, 207
Irving, Washington, 5, 59, 139–140

Jackson, Andrew, 24, 37, 42, 44–45, 49, 63–70, 79
Jacksonian Democrats, 67–69
Jefferson, Thomas, 29, 31, 40, 75, 79; and Roman civil law, 21; and neoclassical architecture, 33–34; and classical rhetoric, 47; and Julius Caesar, 62; and pastoralism, 86–87; and nationalism, 105, 112, 115; and classical philosophy, 154–155, 161; and slavery, 182, 198; and the Declaration of Independence, 190, 192
Jerome, 152–153
Jesus, 126–127, 138, 152, 163–164, 174, 177, 180
Johns Hopkins University, 207
Jonson, Ben, 150
Jugurtha, 69
Justinian, 22, 102, 159
Juvenal, 2, 6–7, 9, 18, 157

Kansas-Nebraska Act, 200
Kant, Immanuel, 103
Keats, John, 123
King, Martin Luther Jr., 133
Kingsley, James Luce, 94–97
Kronos (Saturn), 138, 173

Ladies' Magazine, 56, 61
Landor, Walter Savage, 47
Laocoön, 19–20, 36, 99, 146
Latrobe, Benjamin, 33–34, 45, 115
Lawrence, Richard, 65
Lazarus, Emma, 208
Lee, Robert E., 8

Legaré, Hugh Swinton, 39, 54, 69; and Hellenism, 12–13; and classical education, 16–17, 97–99; and Cicero, 18–19; and Virgil, 19; and Roman civil law, 21–22; and nationalism, 113; on the superiority of Christian to classical ethics, 158–159; and slavery, 184
L'Enfant, Pierre, 115
Leonidas, 32, 51–52, 171
Lieber, Francis, 15, 21
Lincoln, Abraham, 34, 42–44, 50, 65, 81, 150
Lincoln Memorial, 117
Livy, 6–7, 9, 27, 29, 44, 78, 85, 89
Locke, John, 92, 131, 191–193
Long, Robert Cary, 116
Longfellow, Henry Wadsworth, 33, 158
Longinus, 23, 124
Louisiana Purchase, 86
Louisiana State University (Military Academy of Louisiana), 8
Lowell, James Russell, 150
Lucretius, 19, 27, 91, 155
Luther, Martin, 153
Lycurgus, 23, 38, 51, 106, 182, 185–186
Lysander, 159

Macaulay, Thomas, 46
Macedon, 47, 49, 53, 71–72, 112, 187, 191, 195, 209
Machiavelli, Niccolò, 73–74
Madison, James, 75–77, 79, 86, 153, 182
Maecenas, 84, 121
Manifest Destiny, 105, 112–114
Manly, Basil, 100–101
Mann, Horace, 5, 10, 26, 93–94, 171
Marathon, battle of, 46, 102, 107, 110–111
Marcellus, 55, 110
Marcia, 59
Marius, 36, 44, 62, 69
Marshall, John, 31, 149
Mason, George, 182
Mather, Cotton, 153
McCord, David, 57–58
McCord, Louisa S., 22, 57–61, 162, 184, 186
McGuffey, William H., 4–5, 59, 171
Medusa, 32, 140, 142
Melville, Herman, 19–20, 102, 141–147
Mercer, Charles Fenton, 54, 72
Methodists, 47, 163
Mexican War, 56, 69–70, 114
Middle Ages, 2, 74, 134, 153, 159, 193, 200, 202

Middleton, Conyers, 18, 28
Miles, Edwin A., 119
Mill, John Stuart, 46
Mills, Robert, 33–34, 44–45, 109–110
Miltiades, 68
Milton, John, 129, 165
Missouri Compromise, 200
Mitford, William, 28, 50–51
Mixed Government, theory of, 46, 73–82, 85
Monroe, James, 31, 52, 62–63, 182
Monroe Doctrine, 52–53
Montesquieu, Charles de Secondat, 61
Moral Relativism, 206–207
Morrill Act (1862), 205
Moses, 185, 190
Mount Olympus, 87, 137, 149
Munford, William, 39

Nationalism, ix–x, 105–122
Native Americans, 32, 39, 44, 79, 117, 124, 137, 156
Natural Aristocracy, concept of, 74, 77
Natural Law, theory of, xii, 21, 120, 133, 181, 196, 199–201, 206–207
Natural Slave, concept of, 80, 187–191
Neoclassical Architecture, x, 33–35, 38, 44–45, 115–116, 151, 177, 180, 202
Neoclassical Art, xi, 32, 35–38, 89, 108–109, 116–117, 166–170, 208
Neoplatonism, xii, 120, 126–132, 153–154, 173–174
Nero, 65–67, 122, 161
Nestor, 136
New Orleans, battle of, 68, 87
Newton, Isaac, 129
New York University, 91, 96
Nonconformity, doctrine of, 120, 123–127, 132
Nullification Crisis, 49, 66, 79
Numa, 106, 110, 185

Oberlin College, 166, 179–180
Odysseus (Ulysses), 32, 71, 94, 110, 137, 140
Oedipus, 143–144
Olympic Games, 149, 154, 156
Orestes, 142, 144–146
Original Sin, doctrine of, 207
Ottoman Empire, 11, 52–53
Ovid, 31, 33, 122, 125, 157; in education, 2, 5, 8, 10, 138; and John Quincy Adams, 23–25, 177; and Nathaniel Hawthorne, 140; and Edgar Allan Poe, 147; and Christianity, 160, 163, 166, 178–179
Oxford University, 207

Paine, Thomas, 89, 106
Paley, William, 172
Panic of 1837, 66–67
Pantheon, 140, 176
Parthenon, 13, 36, 39, 93, 99, 102, 196; as a model for the Second Bank of the United States, 34; and the Romantics, 117, 123, 126
Pastoralism, x, 84–88
Paternalism, 186
Paul, the apostle, 84, 149, 152, 180
Peabody, Elizabeth, 10, 175
Peale, Charles Willson, 37
Peloponnesian War, 43, 48, 51–52, 210
Pericles, 11, 43–44, 47–48, 50, 60, 68, 98–99, 157
Persephone (Proserpine), 36, 140, 167, 178–179
Perseus, the satirist, 6
Persian Wars, 9, 43, 49, 51–52, 55, 72, 107, 110–111
Persico, Luigi, 167
Phaedrus, 2, 37, 196
Pharsalus, battle of, 65
Phelps, Almira, 8
Phidias, 36, 109, 111, 117, 167–168
Philip II of Macedon, 47, 53, 71–72, 112, 187
Phocion, 38, 126–127, 148, 174
Phoenicians, 11, 72
Physiocrats, 86
Pickering, John, 10
Pierce, Franklin, 69–70
Pike, Albert, 22
Pilgrims, 18, 110–111
Pindar, 25, 137, 149, 154, 186
Plato, 4, 10, 18, 93, 98–99, 111; in education, 7, 15; and the Adams family, 23–24, 28–29; and democracy, 73, 189; and Ralph Waldo Emerson, 84, 107–108, 124, 126–131, 134–135, 150; and other Romantics, 131; and Christianity, 153–154, 158–159, 162, 166, 172–174, 177; and slavery, 186, 188, 196–197; versus Aristotle, 190–191; and natural law, 199
Pliny the Elder, 103, 147
Pliny the Younger, 27, 29, 89
Plotinus, 127–129
Plutarch, 31, 56–57, 64, 85; in education, 2; and the Adams family, 23–29; and Ralph Waldo Emerson, 30, 84, 107, 125–127, 135, 148–151; and the "great-man theory" of history, 120, 149; and

Christianity, 153, 159–160, 173, 175; and Athenian democracy, 210
Plymouth, Massachusetts, 6, 18, 25–26, 110–111
Poe, Edgar Allan, 123, 127, 131–132, 147–148
Polk, James Knox, 19, 45
Polybius, 56, 72–74, 76–79, 85
Polyclitus, 117
Pompeii, 19–20, 32, 157
Pompey (Gnaeus Pompeius), 37, 62–64, 66, 169
Pope, Alexander, 39, 44, 137, 196
Popular Sovereignty, theory of, 200
Porcher, Frederick, 108–109, 167
Portia, 60
Poseidon (Neptune), 31–32
Powers, Hiram, 36–37, 58, 108–109, 167–169
Praetorian Guard, 66–67
Praxiteles, 20, 117, 140
Presbyterians, 163, 171
Princeton University (College of New Jersey), 10, 34, 90, 153
Prometheus, 126–127, 137–138, 142–143
Protestant Reformation, 2, 91, 153
Psalms, 156, 160, 177, 179
Psyche, 138, 167
Ptolemy, Claudius, 165
Punic Wars, 54–56, 73, 85
Purdue University, 6
Puritans, 128, 133, 153–154, 178
Pygmalion, 208
Pythagoras, 27, 37, 93, 129, 132, 155–156, 177

Quincy, Eliza, 175
Quincy, Josiah, 91, 96–97, 175
Quintilian, 23, 29, 60, 116, 177

Ramsay, David, 19
Randolph, John, 45, 71
Randolph, Thomas Mann, 40
Regulus, 110, 171
Reinhold, Meyer, ix-x, 14, 96
Renaissance, xii, 74, 144
Resurrection, the, 132
Ricardo, David, 86
Rivers, William J., 14, 185
Rollin, Charles, 42
Roman Catholics, 2, 91, 99, 153, 179
Romanticism, ix, xi-xii, 120–152, 202
Romulus, 118
Round Hill School, 2

Rush, Benjamin, 89, 163–164
Russia, 23, 54
Rutgers University (Queen's College), 153
Rutledge, Harriot Horry, 4

Sallust, 2, 5–8, 18, 23, 38, 85
Sappho, 4, 28, 59, 147
Scholastics, medieval, 153, 200
Scientific Revolution, 93
Scipio Africanus, 54–56, 60, 110, 185
Scott, Walter, 149, 164, 201–202
Scott, Winfield, 69
Second Bank of the United States, 34, 64–66, 68
Second Great Awakening, ix, 152, 158
Sejanus, 66, 121–122
Seneca, 29, 31, 153, 161–162, 175
Seneca Falls Declaration, 131
Separation of Powers, theory of the, 78
Sermon on the Mount, 154–156, 180
Seward, William H., 200
Shakespeare, William, 107, 142, 150, 165; and *Julius Caesar*, 4, 65–66; and Greek drama, 30, 147; and nonconformity, 124, 127
Sherman, William T., 8
Sidney, Algernon, 74
Slavery, ix, 26, 38, 81, 163–164, 181–203; and Aristotle, xii, 80, 184, 186–193, 196, 202; and the founders, xii, 182; in Athens, 47, 210–211; in the western territories, 56, 70, 76–77; and the U.S. Civil War, 205–206
Smith, Adam, 86, 171
Smith, Margaret Bayard, 61
Socialism, 190–191, 193
Socrates, 93, 110–111, 128, 132, 171; in education, 7, 15; and John Quincy Adams, 23–24; and pastoralism, 86; and nonconformity, 120, 126; and Christianity, 154, 174–175
Solon, 23, 29, 72, 106, 185
Sophocles, 29, 31, 33, 98, 111, 134, 137, 141; in education, 2, 6, 14; and *Antigone*, 59, 133, 200; and nonconformity, 124, 133
Southern Literary Messenger, 14, 47–48, 91, 118–119, 191
Spartacus, 22, 32, 209
Spoils System, 66
Stanton, Elizabeth Cady, 8
State of Nature, concept of the, 191–193
Statue of Liberty, 208
Stephens, Alexander, 3

Stoicism, xii, 27, 120, 131–134, 149, 154, 160–162, 170–173, 176
Story, Joseph, 18, 21–22, 38, 65, 97
Story, William Wetmore, 36, 195
Stowe, Harriet Beecher, 8
Strabo, 136
Strickland, William, 34, 45, 115
Suetonius, 23, 29
Sulla, 62, 66
Sumner, Charles, 19–20, 114, 154–158, 196–197, 199–200
Syracuse, 31

Tacitus, 19, 122, 197; in education, 2, 6–8, 10, 18; and the Adams family, 23–24, 27–29, 161; and German women, 60; and slavery, 184
Tarquin, 65
Taylor, Zachary, 69–70
Telemachus, 45, 110
Terence, 6, 10, 28, 91, 196–197
Thebes, 32, 129
Themistocles, 50, 159, 167
Theocritus, 84
Thermopylae, battle of, 15, 44, 51–52, 107, 171
Theseus, 167
Thoreau, Henry David, 87–88, 99–100, 118, 120, 124, 127, 131–133, 135–138, 149
Thornwell, James Henley, 92, 172
Thucydides, 13, 31, 98, 106–107, 150; in education, 7; and the Adams family, 27, 29; and Pericles' Funeral Oration, 43, 60; and slavery, 186; and Athenian democracy, 210
Tiberius, the emperor, 62, 65–67, 121–122
Ticknor, George, 89, 97
Titans, 138
Toombs, Robert, 56, 182
Torso Belvedere, 20–21, 117
Trajan, 122
Transcendentalists, xi–xii, 120, 123, 127–139, 190
Troy, 31, 94, 118, 135, 140, 142
Trumbull, John, 37
Turner, Frederick Jackson, 7
Twain, Mark, 201–202
Tyler, John, 21, 33

Underground Railroad, 129
Unitarians, 17, 128, 139, 154, 172
University of Alabama, 5, 100–101
University of Chicago, 207

University of Georgia (Franklin College), 3
University of Göttingen, 14–15
University of Michigan, 6, 16
University of Mississippi, 100
University of North Carolina, 5, 19, 30, 92
University of South Carolina (South Carolina College), 165, 172, 185; entrance requirements at, 5; curriculum of, 7, 14–15, 89, 92; commencement exercises at, 11; classical instruction at, 17
University of Texas, 8
University of T?bingen, 12
University of Virginia, 7–8, 14–16, 33, 36, 39–40, 101
University of Wisconsin, 6
U.S. Capitol, 34, 37, 52, 109, 111, 115, 165, 167–168
U.S. Constitution, x, xii, 71, 75–76, 78, 106, 199–200, 203
U.S. Treasury Building, 34
Utilitarianism, x, 83, 88–105, 185, 191, 207

Van Buren, Martin, 66–67
Vanderlyn, John, 36, 167
Varro, 88, 103
Vatican Museum, 19–21, 146, 169
Venus, 20, 32, 36, 168–170
Venus de Medici, 20, 169
Venus de Milo, 36, 168
Virgil, 19, 31–33, 89, 112; in education, 2–9, 17–18, 30, 92, 97, 99; and the Adams family, 23–24, 29; and Augustus, 46, 122; and pastoralism, 84–88; and the Romantics, 135–136, 138, 141; and Christianity, 154, 157, 164–166
Virginia Constitutional Convention of 1830, 62, 72
Virginia and Kentucky Resolutions, 79
Virginia Military Institute, 8
Virginius, 196
Vulgate Bible, 91

Waddel, Moses, 2–3
Wake Forrest College, 7
Walker, David, 198–199
Wallon, Henri, 149
Walter, Thomas U., 34, 116
Ware, William, 114, 176, 198
War of 1812, 54, 113
Washington, Booker T., 195
Washington, George, 39, 43, 56, 68–70, 72–73, 111, 149; depicted in classical dress, 37–38, 108–109, 117, 167–169; compared to classical heroes, 54, 105, 107–108, 110, 112, 171; and antiparty sentiment, 67; and pastoralism, 86; and slavery, 182, 185
Washington College (Washington and Lee College), 7–8
Washington Monument, 34
Way, Caroline, 9
Wayland, Francis, 92, 96
Webster, Daniel, 26, 37–38, 55, 117, 124; and classical education, 14, 17–18; and classical rhetoric, 42, 49; and the Greek War of Independence, 52–53; and nationalism, 110–112; on the need to combine classical republicanism with Christianity, 178; and the Fugitive Slave Law of 1850, 197, 201
Webster, Noah, 59, 113
Weems, Parson, 110, 149
Wesley, John, 163, 200
West Point Academy, 8
Whig Party, 63–69
Whitman, Walt, 118, 123, 127, 132
Whitney, Eli, 181
Wills, Garry, 43
Wilmot Proviso, 70
Wilson, James, 21, 106
Winckelmann, Johann, 89
Winterer, Caroline, ix, xiii, 208
Winthrop, John, 5
Wise, Henry A., 66
Women, ix, 36, 131, 210; and classical education, xi, 1, 3–4, 8–10, 40–41; and classical mythology, xi, 138–139; in democratic society, 56–62; and slavery, 190–191, 197–198
World War I, 207, 209
World War II, 209
Wythe, George, 21, 31

Xenophon, 4–7, 11, 23, 99, 106–107, 132, 195
Xerxes, 72

Yale Report (1828), 94–97, 101
Yale University, 3, 6, 94–97, 101, 207
Young, Arthur, 86

Zama, battle of, 72
Zeno, 132
Zeus (Jupiter), 37, 116–117, 126–127, 138, 142, 163, 167–168, 196